Delgado, Sally J. 2019. *Ship English: Sailors' speech in the early colonial Caribbean* (Studies in Caribbean Languages 4). Berlin: Language Science Press.

Language Science Press
Unter den Linden 6
10099 Berlin, Germany
langsci-press.org

Storage and cataloguing done by FU Berlin

For Mervyn Alleyne 1933-2016

Contents

Contents

Contents

Acknowledgments

First and foremost, I would like to thank all the archivists, collections specialists, and librarians at the many libraries and archives I have visited, including the wonderfully helpful and kind staff of the National Archives in Kew, England; the knowledgeable and generous staff of the Merseyside Maritime Museum Archive and Library in Liverpool, England; and all of the volunteers and specialists who gave their time to guide me through the collections at the National Maritime Museum in Greenwich, England. I also thank the many volunteers and specialists at the Barbados Department of Archives, the Whim Archive in St. Croix, the Josefina del Toro Collection in Puerto Rico, and the National Archives of Trinidad and Tobago who are working tirelessly and often in difficult conditions with little funding to maintain and promote the documents located in collections around the Caribbean. I thank all of these wonderful individuals for their time and patience as they communicated with me on site and at distance about material that was critical to my understanding of this subject, regardless or not as to whether this information made it into the book.

I would like to acknowledge the many many hours of work that Ann Albuyeh, PhD, invested in her work as academic advisor to my doctoral dissertation that gave rise to this book. Her observations, suggestions, and guidance have been invaluable in helping me shape the final product. I am also hugely grateful for all the professional advice and insight she has given me throughout this process. I thank Nicholas Faraclas, PhD, another bedrock of my doctoral academic committee, whose work ethic, worldview and generosity have inspired so much more than my studies. I thank Mervyn Alleyne for guiding me in directions previously unknown to me and inspiring the confidence in myself to explore my hunches and find out where they led. I thank Michael Sharp, PhD, whose insightful comments and input as a reader were critical in enabling the completion of my doctoral degree after the devastating news of Mervyn Alleyne's passing in November of 2016. I thank the many professors and support staff at the University of Puerto Rico, Rio Piedras Campus for their motivation throughout my graduate studies and their continued support of my research and professional development. I owe specific thanks to the English Department and the Deanship of Graduate Studies and Research (DEGI by its Spanish acronym) for the financial support that their research assistant and teaching assistant positions, travel grants, and academic awards have given me throughout my time at the university.

I acknowledge the huge influence that Ian Hancock, PhD, has had on this book. His early work on creole genesis theory first suggested the idea and coined a phrase to describe "Ship English" a variety that was spoken by British sailors in the early colonial context (Hancock 1976: 33). Since I first contacted Ian Hancock with my ideas in 2011, he has given me valuable critical feedback, shared little-known resources, and offered valuable guidance in the development of my objectives and research plan. I have gained a great deal and continue to benefit from his mentorship and the many hours he has spent communicating with me about a subject that few people have an interest in beyond the acknowledgement of cultural stereotypes. I am very grateful to Ian for his time and particularly for his collaboration on a joint-presentation for the Society of Pidgin and Creole Linguistics that we gave in January of 2017, which also gave me the opportunity to explore his expansive personal library. I hope that this book might assume a humble place among that esteemed collection.

I thank all the artists, scholars, educators, and professionals who have created and permitted me to access, adapt and reproduce images for this book. Specifically, thank you to Gustavo D. Constantino for a clear representation of the mixed methodology research model used in the introductory chapter. Thank you, Mandy Barrow, for all the work you are doing on ProjectBritain.com that helped contextualize discussion in chapter 3. Thank you to all the professionals at Encyclopaedia Britannica, Inc. for your dedication and work on summarizing the patterns of Atlantic trading winds that helped me simplify trading patterns in chapter 4. Thank you to the curators of the image collections at the National Maritime Museum, Greenwich, London for access to George Cruikshank's artwork. And thank you to the, still unconfirmed, author of *A general history of robberies and murders of the most notorious pyrates* (published 1724, London) for your representation of a mock trial used in chapter 4. I also thank historian Marcus Rediker for bringing this image to my attention and for his inspirational work on maritime communities.

Last, but perhaps most important of all, I would like to thank my husband and rock, Jose Delgado, for the millions of ways, large and small, that he has supported my research and my writing. Without his emotional support and his tireless optimism that I could complete what I set out to do, none of this would have been possible. I also thank my mum, Kathleen Dobson, who instilled in me a work ethic and sense of dogged determinism that has been invaluable in the most challenging of weary dust-filled days during my time at the archives. Thanks to my brother, Nicholas Ruxton-Boyle for his encouragement and rent-free accommodation in London for some of my long-haul archive trips. I also thank my many friends, doctoral students, and faculty at the University of Puerto Rico, Rio Piedras Campus, and the University of Puerto Rico, Cayey Campus who have supported me with their feedback and encouragement. Finally, many thanks to my two wonderful boys, Luis Daniel and Patrick, who fill my life with love and meaning and have shared their mummy with this research for as long as they can remember.

Abbreviations

ADM   Admiralty Records
ASSI   Records of Justices of Assize
BL   British Library
CO   Colonial Office
HCA   High Court of Admiralty
SC   State Papers
TNA   The National Archives. Kew, England

1 Introduction

This introductory chapter is organized in three sections; the first section on background justification will provide selected context necessary to justify the need for research on maritime communities, including the prior claims in the literature that attest to "Ship's language" as a distinct variety. It also gives some of the reasons why this subject has been neglected in the scholarship of dialectology and contact linguistics. The second section, on the scope and purpose of the research, will provide the hypothesis, research aims and five research questions formulated to investigate characteristic features of sailors' speech in the early English colonial period. It will also give selected details on the ideological and academic context that has influenced my own thought process regarding the focus of this study. The last section presents the methodological framework of the study, with details on the research design and a description of the corpus with details on the three subsections of documentation used. This introduction ends with a brief outline of each of the subsequent chapter's contents.

1.1 Background justification

1.1.1 The need for research on maritime communities

We live in a world so interconnected by air travel, media and online networks that we rarely consider the importance of maritime travel or those who depended upon it in an age before we physically and digitally took to the skies. Yet maritime communities were profuse and critical to the development of the early European colonies during an age of expansion that set off dynamic and often unpredictable changes throughout the known world. Yet what we think we know about the culture and customs of the people who inhabited these communities owe more to popular stereotype than to scholarship.

At the center of diverse and multicultural maritime communities were a host of men, women and children who lived and worked predominantly at sea, yet who are all (inadequately) remembered through the stereotype of the able seaman in his mid-twenties who hauled ropes, drank grog, and served on a large naval ship of the line. Rarely do we consider the complexities of the real maritime communities that were composed of ranked strata in a three-tier class system. First in command, a small upper-class of commissioned and warrant officers included ranks such as admiral, captain, lieutenant, master, purser, surgeon, boatswain, gunner, and carpenter. Second in line, a moderate middle class of petty officers and militia included ranks such as armorer, cook, gunsmith, sailmaker, schoolmaster, master-at-arms, midshipmen, coxswain, quartermaster, gunners' mate, and soldier. Lastly, a majority of lower class workers included ranks such as able seaman, ordinary seaman, landsman, servant, and boy. And, in addition to these officially recognized crew, a range of largely undocumented transient passengers, workers, servants, wives, and slaves frequently accompanied the ship for short legs and entire voyages. Yet, these people were not wage-earners and so their presence is often hidden by the official records. Thus, what we think we know about the people who inhabited maritime worlds fails to incorporate the complex realities of these working and living spaces.

Further to our limited recognition of the people who made up the communities of large ships, we also fail to recognize the range of vessels that hosted different types of maritime communities. The shipping lanes of the seventeenth and early eighteenth centuries were replete not only with large naval and merchant vessels with the type of social hierarchy detailed above, including the caravel, carrack, galleass, galleon and hulk, but also a myriad of mid-to-small scale vessels. These smaller vessels ranged from the mid-sized barge, barque, brigandine, cromster, frigate and pinnacle, used for speed and maneuverability in long-range voyages, to the small-scale flute, flyboat, galley, hoy and shallop, used not only for support work such as supply and boarding enemy vessels, but also surprisingly long-range but small-scale trade operations designed to evade custom regulations and hence also documentation (Bicheno 2012). These smaller vessels were frequently employed in trade, but also made voyages of exploration, colonization, political expansion, passenger transit, salvage, supply and smuggling (Jarvis 2010). And these classifications of intention were not mutually exclusive, as a simplified historical glance has encouraged us to believe. Furthermore, all of the different vessel types likely had an on-board community that was unique to the size and requirements of the cargo space, rigging, defense system, and navigational capacities. By failing to recognize these vessels and their unique equipment, space and communities in our oversimplified historical representations, we cannot hope to understand the cultures of the people who worked and lived aboard them, and who were critical agents in the expansion of European colonial regimes.

1.1.2 Ship's language as a distinct variety

The linguistic focus of this research stems from the claim that there is a distinct "Ship English" that was spoken by British sailors in the early colonial context (the term coined by Hancock 1976: 33). However, long before the relevance of maritime language use was championed by Hancock in his theories on creole genesis (Hancock 1972; Hancock 1976; Hancock 1986; Hancock 1988) the idea that sailors used distinct language forms was attested to in a host of lexical compilations and user manuals. In 1627, Captain John Smith published *Smith's Sea Grammar*, in which he gives "expositions of all the most difficult words seldome used but amongst sea men" (Smith 1627 [1968], §Table of Contents) and offers explanations and translations for "the language both of ships and Seas" (Smith 1627 [1968], §In Authorem). This *Sea Grammar*, despite its name, was not so much a linguistic analysis as a handbook divided into content-specific chapters about how to manage oneself at sea, for which language skills were considered essential. The fact that this book was reprinted in 1627, 1636, 1641, 1653 and 1968 attests not only to the usefulness but also the popularity of its contents, a trend echoed by the subsequent publication of *The Sea-Man's Dictionary*, by Henry Manwayring (1644), reprinted in 1666, 1667, 1670 and 1675–82.

The concept of a "Sea Grammar" was not restricted to English. Not long after Smith's manual was published in English, publications about sailors' talk in French appear in the mid-seventeenth century such as Cleirac's *Explication des Termes de Marine [...]* (1639, reprinted 1647 and 1660) and the anonymous broadsheets *Déclaration des Noms Propres des Piàces de Bois et Autres Pièces Nécessaires Tant à la Construction des Navires de Guerre ...* (1657) and *Termes Desquels on Use sur Mer dans le Parler...* (1681 reprinted in 1693) followed by Desroches's *Dictionnaire des Termes Propres de Marine [...]* (1687). The late seventeenth century also saw the Dutch publication *W. à Winschootens Seeman...* (Winschooten 1681), the Spanish publication by Fernández de Gamboa *Vocabulario de los Nombres que Usan la Gente de Mar* (1698), and the anonymous publication *Vocabulario Marítimo y Explicacion de los Más Principales Vocablos* (1696, reprinted 1698). Hence, the concept of a distinct variety that was unique to maritime communities was not an isolated phenomenon around the trading routes of the British Isles but a common characteristic of maritime communities with enough salience to have grammars published as early as the seventeenth century in at least four European languages.

Since these early popular publications of the seventeenth century, a host of other manuscripts, pamphlets and books targeted readers with an occupational or personal interest in life and language at sea. These publications were invariably composed of lexical entries, as the titles reflect, e.g., Monke's *Vocabulary of Sea Phrases* (1799) and Neumann's *Marine Pocket-Dictionary* (1799). And this focus on sailors' lexicon has continued up until the more recent publication of works like Jeans's *Dictionary of Everyday Words and Phrases Derived from the Sea* (1993) and the web-based reference work *Seatalk, The Dictionary of English Nautical Language* (MacKenzie 2005). Although many of these lexicons are aimed at people with an occupational or historical interest in maritime studies, there are also a host of publications that cater to general interest and entertainment markets, such as *The Pirate Primer: Mastering the Language of Swashbucklers and Rogues* (Choundas 2007). Yet, despite the many publications that cater to different reader demographics, nearly all compose word-lists in the style of dictionary entries and perpetuate the belief that what made — and continues to make — maritime language different and interesting is its use of particular words or expressions common to the maritime profession and difficult for others to understand, suggesting that the variety is essentially a technical jargon.

1.1.3 A neglected subject in academia

Despite the rush of titles aimed at readers with an occupational interest in maritime use of language, very few academic papers have investigated the complexities of Ship English beyond its lexicon. The dearth of academic studies of maritime language use may reflect the fact that investigations would have be inter- and intra-disciplinary: the necessary archival research might be suited to a historian; the identification of correlating language forms in literary representations more suited to a literature specialist; the analysis of how maritime communities functioned more suited to an anthropologist or a researcher in maritime studies; and the understanding of inter-connectivity more appropriate for a researcher in Atlantic studies. Even within the discipline of linguistics, the suggestion that Ship English is a language variety alludes to theories of dialectology; the idea that it was formed by communication among multilingual communities necessarily involves theories of pidgin and creole studies; and the belief that the composition of the community directed language change involves theories of sociolinguistics. I do not suggest that the study of Ship English is unique in its complexities for the potential researcher, but these challenges, coupled with the fact that there is little groundwork on this subject upon which to base new studies, potentially impede investigations from being undertaken.

In addition to the theoretical complexities, a potential researcher is faced with a host of practical challenges. Even for the workers who left a record of their presence on the ships (and many didn't), they formed a transient and demographically complex group to determine (Adkins & Adkins 2008: 176–177; Fusaro 2015: 8). Particularly in the period of early colonial expansion, workers in the maritime world were often not required to provide any kind of information to officials such as their age, place of origin, social status or language abilities that a researcher could use to determine demographics (Litter 1999: 125, 191), nor were many of these workers obliged to remain in the same service vessel for a long period of time. It was entirely possible that they moved from vessel to vessel and port to port following the opportunities that appeared to be most beneficial at any given time. Sailors might remain working on one trade route and therefore spend time in its associated ports for years, or they might be regularly changing trade routes, locations, and port regions in addition to time potentially spent out of work in one place — whether that be a home port or a foreign location. Furthermore, studies indicate that as much as one third of shipping activity may have escaped the official records (Cook 2005: 15). It is therefore extremely difficult to determine probable regional influences on sailors' transient populations or to locate them in geographical models of dialect areas.

Practical difficulties for the researcher are compounded by the recognition that most seventeenth and eighteenth century seamen were illiterate (Kelly 2006: 167) and therefore were unlikely to have left any written evidence of the features common to their everyday speech. Even in cases where hand-written records existed, these records may not have made it into the public record, for example, sailors engaging in contraband trade, violence or theft at sea often burned, destroyed, or threw documentation overboard to evade the consequences that documentation of their actions might bring. The few records of authentic sailors' writing that we do have are often so formulaic and dry (e.g., logbook entries) so fraught with literary overtones (e.g., travel journals) or so affected by prescribed stylistic written forms (e.g., letters from the captain) that they are considered poor samples of actual speech. Furthermore, even if the researcher is lucky enough to find preserved writing samples reflective of authentic speech, the script is often extremely difficult to decipher as it was composed in Early Modern English prose in an age before consistent standardized spelling and punctuation, and very often written in nearly illegible handwriting owing to individual penmanship preferences, a moving vessel, or the unpracticed hand of its author. Yet even if the words *are* legible, the researcher also needs to recognize and interpret maritime abbreviations, acronyms and symbols before the meaning of a sentence can be analyzed for its syntax and grammatical structures. In short, designing an interdisciplinary research methodology that integrates the theories and practices of a range of linguistic sub-disciplines and mitigates the potential challenges of data collection and analysis with no tested model upon which to base a research strategy likely discourages even the most interested scholar.

Despite these significant methodological difficulties, a few scholars have attempted to break ground on the neglected subject of Ship English beyond its lexicon. Two notable studies are Matthews' (1935) monograph on sailors' pronunciation in the second half of the seventeenth century, based on phonetic spellings in ships' logbooks; and Bailey & Ross's (1988) article on the morphosyntactic features of Ship English that focuses on evidence of variation in tense marking and the copula, also based primarily on logbooks. Yet, to my knowledge, there have been no new studies of phonological, morphological, syntactic, or discourse-level features in Ship English since Bailey and Ross's last article in the late 1980s and no studies using a corpus that extends beyond logbooks and selected papers of the (English) Royal African Company. In response to the academic hesitation on this subject, this book has been conceptualized to continue the valuable earlier work of Matthews, Bailey and Ross and to motivate renewed academic interest in the subject based on empirical evidence rather than popular stereotype.

1.2 Scope and purpose of the research

1.2.1 Hypothesis, research aims and questions

This book presents evidence in support of the hypothesis that Ship English of the early Atlantic colonial period (determined roughly as the period between 1620 and 1750) was a distinct variety with characteristic features. Its two principal aims are firstly, to outline the socio-demographics of the maritime communities and examine how variant linguistic features may have developed and spread among these communities, and secondly, to generate baseline data on the characteristic features of Ship English. These aims will be addressed through five research questions that relate to establishing demographic data on sailors, collating sociolinguistic data that attest to how their speech communities functioned, and identifying characteristic features of their speech at the word, phrase, sentence, and discourse levels. The five research questions, each of which is discussed in a dedicated chapter, are as follows:

- Who were the English-speaking sailors of the early colonial Caribbean?

- How did sailors' speech communities function?

- What are the salient markers of sailors' speech in noun phrases?

- What are the salient markers of sailors' speech in verb phrases?

- What variation characterizes sailors' speech in syntax and discourse?

Anticipated findings will not only substantiate Bailey and Ross's claim that there is a distinct type of English that was spoken by sailors during the period of early English colonial expansion (1988: 194) but also provide baseline data that may serve as an entry point for scholars to integrate this language variety into the discourse on dialect variation and language contact in the early colonial period.

1.2.2 Ideological and academic context

It is perhaps important to explain that I came to the subject of Ship English through studies in Caribbean languages at the University of Puerto Rico, Rio Piedras campus. I formulated the research design and focus of the study as part of my doctoral degree in the literature and languages of the English-speaking Caribbean with a specialization in linguistics, and the final research on which this book is based formed the backbone of my doctoral dissertation. My academic preparation in Caribbean linguistics exposed me to theories of languages in contact and the formation of trade pidgins and new creole languages. I was intrigued by theories of universalism (e.g., Muysken & Smith 1986; McWhorter 2011) and scholarship on pan-Caribbean language forms (e.g., Allsopp 2003; Faraclas et al. 2012). I have been additionally motivated in my research endeavors by the late Mervyn Alleyne, whose work on sociolinguistics, creoles and dialects of the Caribbean has driven a whole generation of scholars fortunate enough to study under his tutelage. With an interest in creole universals and historical dialectology, I was fortunate enough to receive guidance from historical linguist Ann Albuyeh, creolist Nicholas Faraclas, and literature specialist Michael Sharp in the development of my research plans, all of whom composed the academic committee of my doctoral research, as did Mervyn Alleyne until his passing in November of 2016. Considering this academic context, it is perhaps no surprise that I came to the subject of Ship English through creole studies and I envision the intellectual merit of the findings in terms of how scholars may integrate this variety in future studies of languages in contact.

Yet, despite the creole focus in the academic context of this research, I would like to stress that I do not present these findings in support of any one theory of creole linguistics. Specifically, I do not propose that these findings promote either side of the polemic substrate–superstrate debate nor promote any specific theory of language transfer, dialect formation nor universalism, although I recognize the potential for the findings to be applied to such subjects. My intention differs from previous assertions that a potential type of language spoken on ships influenced creole development (e.g., Reinecke 1938; Hancock 1972) and instead aims to gather baseline data that substantiates the fundamental claim that Ship English of the early colonial period was a distinct variety. As an investigation into the characteristics of Ship English as a distinct variety, this study would therefore be more suited to dialect studies than creolistics. However, given the implications of the findings in light of creole theories, I will clarify my own position and highlight potential applications of the findings for different schools of thought in the last chapter containing conclusions and implications.

1.3 Methodological framework

1.3.1 Research design

A mixed methods triangulation design was employed in this research, selected to suit my intention "to directly compare and contrast quantitative statistical results with qualitative findings or to validate or expand quantitative results with qualitative data" (Creswell & Plano Clark 2007: 62). The specific triangulation model used was the traditional convergence model, in which a researcher collects and analyzes both qualitative and quantitative data concurrently and converges the data at the stage of comparison and contrast (see Figure 1.1 Based on Creswell & Plano Clark 2007).

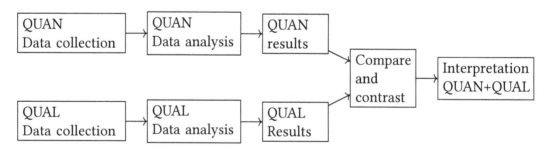

Figure 1.1: A mixed methods triangulation research design using the convergence model. , based on Creswell & Plano Clark 2007

The two main benefits of this triangulation convergence model are: firstly, its efficiency, in that data types are collected simultaneously during one phase of the research plan; and secondly, its potential to mitigate the weaknesses of the quantitative component (e.g., limited sample size and authenticity of written representations) with the strengths of the qualitative component (e.g., salience and data on perceptual dialectology). However, this model also has challenges, such as managing different sample sizes, comparing dissimilar data, and selecting differential evaluation methods for the data sets in a way that enables meaningful comparison and interpretation. An additional challenge of this model relates to the fact that none of the samples in the corpus were collected for the specific purpose of the research objectives; they are all archival documents. I therefore had to consider the original intention and audience of the material alongside the content and acknowledge potential bias in my analysis.

It is important to note that this triangulation convergence model was first pilot-tested and validated in a smaller study of sailors' phonology which I carried out in 2014. The pilot study focused on a linguistic cross-comparison of literary and historical data using standard statistical measures of correlation to determine general tendencies. Conclusions indicated significant points of comparison from which general phonological characteristics could be determined and findings were presented at the summer meeting of the Society for Pidgin and Creole Linguistics at the University of Graz, Austria, 7–9 July 2015 in a paper entitled 'The reconstructed phonology of seventeenth century sailors' speech.'

1.3.2 Description of the corpus

Data collection strategies were designed to target written representations of sailors' speech that were prepared or published between the dates 1620 and 1750, and which prioritized documents that were composed by working mariners. Both quantitative and qualitative data were sourced from archived originals or copies of documents maintained in one of the eight archives I visited, see Table 1.1 for details of archives, locations and dates of access.

The document corpus for this research is divided into three subsets of data classified as 1) depositions, 2) hand-written records, and 3) material for public consumption. The first subset, described more specifically as written records of witness depositions taken during the 1620–1750 period in admiralty court sessions, composes the majority of the corpus. Although the caveat remains that these are written accounts of spoken depositions, likely to have been written (and potentially interpreted) by a court clerk, they do nonetheless remain the closest account of sailors' spoken language available to a present-day researcher. Many of these depositions are also signed, initialed or somehow marked to show the speakers' corroboration of the material therein contained, after presumably having it read back to them or reading over the testimony themselves. The second substantial subset of hand-written records includes letters, receipts, log books and miscellaneous records attesting to personal grievances, vessel movements,

Table 1.1: Archival resources accessed for research

Archive	Location	Month/Year visited
Whim Archive	Frederiksted, St. Croix	May 2010
National Archives of Trinidad and Tobago	Port of Spain, Trinidad	July 2012
The Barbados Department of Archives	St. James, Barbados	July 2013
Barbados Museum and Historical Society	Bridgetown, Barbados	July 2013
Colección Josefina del Toro Fulladosa	San Juan, Puerto Rico	Jan, Feb 2014
The National Archives	Kew, London, England	June, July, Nov 2015
The Merseyside Maritime Museum	Liverpool, England	July 2015
The National Maritime Museum	London, England	November 2015

manning and/or trade activities during the 1620–1750 period in and around the Atlantic. These documents, although they were composed in the written mode, are potentially the most accurate reflection of idiomatic language use; however, they are necessarily reflective of only those crew members who were literate, and were also likely to have been composed following an accepted format or linguistic style customary or prescribed for the context of each document. The third and smallest subset of the corpus was written for public consumption and includes material such as broadsheets of sea-shanties, journals prepared for publication, and contemporary literary representations. It is important to note that whilst the maritime representations of speech contained in these documents remain valid, they are also the most likely to have been heavily revised, adapted, and stereotypically presented for entertainment purposes. However, these representations form an important part of the corpus as they potentially speak to perceptions of salience in sailors' speech that a popular audience might readily recognize.

The three subsets of data were collated and analyzed concurrently following the triangulation research design detailed above, and the findings of each data set were used to corroborate findings in the others, with the intention of motivating a comprehensive analysis in which the weakness of any one subset was mitigated by the strengths of the others. See Table 1.2 below for a summary of the characteristics of the corpus subsets.

Table 1.2: Characteristics of the corpus subsets

Corpus subset	Description	Strengths	Weaknesses
1) Depositions Est. 60% of corpus	Written records of witness depositions taken during admiralty court sessions	Composed in spoken mode, corroborated by speaker and includes potentially illiterate sailors	Likely to have been written (interpreted) by a court clerk
2) Hand-written records Est. 30% of corpus	Letters, receipts, log books and misc. documents of personal grievances, vessel movements, manning, trade	First-hand writing, reflects idiomatic language use	Reflective of literate crew only and potentially composed with a prescribed style
3) Material for public consumption Est. 10% of corpus	Published sea-shanties, journals, news items, literature, advertising	Shows perceptions of recognized salience in sailors' speech	Interpreted, revised, adapted, and possibly stereotypical

1.3.3 Outline of each chapter's contents

The first two chapters serve to orient the reader in terms of the aims, the research methodology and the chosen subject of focus. In this first introductory chapter, I have justified the need for the research, established its scope and purpose, and given details about the research design and corpus. Chapter 2: Review of the Literature will summarize the intentions and findings of the few scholars who have identified and studied Ship English in addition to presenting some theories of dialectology and methodological approaches in historical linguistics relevant to the research design.

The subsequent chapters 3 and 4 will have a socio-historical focus and respond to the first two of the research questions detailed above. Who were the English-speaking sailors of the early colonial Caribbean; and, how did sailors' speech communities function? Chapter 3: Sailors will present statistical and qualitative evidence attesting to demographic characteristics of sailors and will address the capacity of this population demographic to develop and sustain a distinct language variety. Chapter 4: Speech Communities will present socio-historical data on some defining characteristics of sailor's communities at sea and on land and will address how the social networks that bound these communities were likely to have impacted language transfer and change.

The next three chapters will be linguistic in focus and respond to the last three research questions detailed above, respectively: What are the salient markers of sailors' speech in noun phrases and verb phrases and what variation characterizes sailors' speech in syntax and discourse? Chapter 5: Noun Phrases will present features relating to the use of bare nouns, determiners, pronouns, and noun phrase modification. Chapter 6: Verb Phrases will present findings on syntactic verb usage, negation, and tense, aspect and modality in the verb phrase, with sections dedicated to the copula and the use of auxiliary verbs. Chapter 7: Clause, Sentence and Discourse Level Phenomena will address issues relating to syntax at the clause and sentence level and consider issues of subordination and coordination, in addition to presenting evidence and commentary on swearing as a recurrent discourse marker.

Chapter 8: Conclusions and Implications will clarify my own position on the distinctiveness, stability and typology of Ship English and consider how the newly presented baseline data might be integrated into theories and research in dialectology and contact linguistics.

2 Review of the literature

This chapter will begin with a summary of the work by the few scholars and enthusiasts who have recognized the importance of Ship English as a distinct and influential variety. This is followed by a more detailed presentation of studies on Ship English with a focus on the only two known published scholarly works with a focus on non-lexical characteristics of seventeenth century sailors' English, namely, Matthews' (1935) monograph on pronunciation and Bailey & Ross's (1988) article on morphosyntactic features. The second part of this chapter will present a selected theoretical framework that underpins my own ideological stance and contextualizes the research design. This framework is divided into a discussion of studies relating to dialect change and dialect formation, and an examination of some formative studies that have influenced my own thought process and the methodology for this research.

2.1 Ship English: The work already done

2.1.1 Recognizing the importance of Ship English

Since Captain John Smith published *Smith's Sea Grammar* in 1627, the unique nature of sailors' speech has been a popular subject of maritime training manuals and dictionaries for five centuries, as Bruzelius' lists of dictionaries of maritime and naval lexicon 17–19th century (Bruzelius 1996; 1999; 2006) and the entry on 'dictionaries' in the *Oxford Encyclopedia of Maritime History* (Hattendorf 2007) illustrate. And it is perhaps important to note that, in spite of the stereotyping present in fictional representations, there appears to be no stigma attached to learning this sea-language among occupational groups. Henry Manwayring states in the preface to his *Sea-Man's Dictionary* Manwayring (1672[1644]) "this book shall make a man understand what other men say, and *speak properly* himself" (emphasis added). Even those accustomed to more courtly circles took efforts to learn how to speak "properly" in maritime contexts. For example, Samuel Pepys, Clerk of the Acts and Secretary of the Navy Board, promoted later to secretary of the Admiralty, bought a copy of Manwayring's dictionary to learn the technical language of naval affairs. He notes in his diary (March 1661): "early up in the morning to read 'the Seaman's Grammar and Dictionary' I lately have got, which do please me exceedingly well" (The National Maritime Museum, Samuel Pepys: Plague, Fire, Revolution, exhibit PBE 6233). This was just as well, because, like many other naval officers and administrators, "he had little experience of the maritime world, and no real qualifications for the job" (Lincoln 2015: 144). Speaking "properly" was therefore perhaps conducive to Pepys maintaining his position and generally reflective of the potential need of a whole group of administrators elected to their positions as a result of nepotism rather than experience.

Administrators may have benefitted from manuals and dictionaries, but it was sailors themselves who learned though first-hand experience and were likely to have placed most value on the variety of speech native to their work and home environments, specifically, the use of a lexicon that constituted the professional jargon of the crew. In this respect, the fictional representation in Traven's *The Death Ship*, is likely accurate; the modern author describes how "each sailor picks up the words of his companions, until, after two months or so, all men aboard have acquired a working knowledge of about three hundred words common to all the crew" (Traven 1962: 237). And it is most likely that the majority of such words were related to equipment, navigational or military techniques and routine aboard ship. For this reliance on a distinctive vocabulary, Hancock (1986) describes Ship English as an "occupational dialect", and Bailey & Ross, recognize that "its lexical uniqueness is apparent" (1988: 207). Shopen and Williams note that sailors commonly spread new lexical features around the ports they visit. For this reason, they refer to the importance of trade centers and shipping explicitly as factors that explain the linguistic changes that took place in the British Isles around the Middle English period (1980: 49–52). Moreover, Hickey's (2004) edited volume *Legacies of Colonial English: Studies in Transported Dialects* additionally suggests that Ship English may have "incubated" new varieties of English that gave rise to dialects in places such as the United States, Australia and New Zealand (see Hickey 2004: 50). Hence, not only was the lexical uniqueness of sailors' speech critical to the successful operation of the vessel, it may have also been critical in the formation of dialect boundaries in the British Isles and potentially incubated overseas varieties.

Further to the impact that sailors potentially had in the formation of British dialects, Reinecke (1938) was the first to claim that "the seaman is a figure of the greatest importance in the creation of the more permanent makeshift tongues" (1938: 107). He goes on to explain how sailors may have been pivotal in what linguists now refer to as the pidgin–creole theory:

> Trade jargons may be regarded as the least developed forms of marginal language that have attained considerable fixity. Originally they arise out

of the casual intercourse of traders (generally seamen) with a fixed population, although later they may be extended to serve the intercourse between
the native population and resident foreigners. (Reinecke 1938: 110)

Subsequent scholars have echoed this claim, suggesting that maritime communities may have impacted the development of new languages derived from
contact situations. For example, Hancock draws attention to the logic of Ship English serving as a hypothetical protoform in creole genesis. He states, "Assuming
a common origin for these Creoles, now spoken over 12,000 sea-miles apart, then
the only possible historical link between them was the seamen and their speech"
(Hancock 1976: 33). Since this early assertion in his 1976 paper "Nautical Sources
of Krio Vocabulary", Hancock has continued his work to evidence the role of
mariners' language use in Krio, a creole of Sierra Leone. Similarly, Holm's extensive work on Nicaragua's Miskito Coast Creole identifies the importance of
sailors as the agents of language contact in his 1981 paper "Sociolinguistic History
and the Creolist". Both Hancock and Holm's work influenced how subsequent
scholars thought about the superstrate in creole genesis theory. In 1988 Bailey
and Ross made the claim that sailors' speech was the earliest form of English language contact in many coastal regions around the Atlantic and Caribbean. Ship
English therefore "seems to have been the earliest component of the superstrate"
in contexts of creole genesis (Bailey & Ross 1988: 194). They justify this statement
by explaining that "sailors were instrumental in founding and maintaining the
colonies where creole languages developed" (Bailey & Ross 1988: 195). Holm's
seminal text, *Pidgins and Creoles,* published the same year as Bailey and Ross's
paper, echoes this statement:

> Most Creoles arose in maritime colonies whose harbors docked slave ships,
> cargo ships, warships and countless smaller craft. Because of the mixture
> of dialects and even languages found among ships' crews, nautical speech
> has always constituted a distinctive sociolect. (Holm 1988: 78)

Holm's theory that a creole is an expanded pidgin (1988: 7) in addition to the
assertion that pidgins derive from language contact with sailor's sociolect in maritime colonies placed Ship English at the core of creole genesis in studies leading
up to the early 1980s. However, concurrently, there was a growing movement of
substrate theories prompted by the second International Conference on Creole
Languages, held at the University of the West Indies, Mona in April 1968 (Hymes
1971). In the decades following this seminal conference, scholars of creole studies
began to explore the importance of West African languages that had been, until
this point, all but ignored in creole genesis theory. The critical work of scholars such as Alleyne (1980), Alleyne (1996), Lefebvre (1986), Lefebvre (1998), and

Parkvall (2000) has led to a generally accepted idea that African substrates influenced creole phonology, syntax and semiotics whilst the superstrate European languages became synonymous with the term 'lexifier' and a general belief that they predominantly contributed lexical forms.

Given the explicit association with superstrate European languages and the term "lexifier" in creole studies, it is perhaps not surprising that evidence to support the claim that Ship English impacted new varieties is mostly lexical. Holm observes, there is "an enormous amount of lexicon common to both sailors and Creoles" (1978: 98) and reinforces this in the description of entries in the *Dictionary of Bahamian English* (Holm & Watt Schilling 1982). An example is the entry *sound* which means to examine a person and derives from the nautical method to investigate the depth of water with a line and lead. Similarly, Cassidy & Le Page's (2002) *Dictionary of Jamaican English* cites nautical etymology in a number of entries, e.g., the phrase *chock and belay*, which means tightly fastened and derives from a description of cargo that is perfectly and fully stowed. Allsopp's (2003) *Dictionary of Caribbean English Usage* lists 13 terms that are specifically traced to nautical origin and are used in regions from South-American Guyana, span the archipelago of the Caribbean, and reach as far as Central American Belize, e.g., *kellick* used in Tobago, the Cayman Islands and Belize, which means a heavy stone and derives from the sailor's word for a small anchor. Although few, there are also studies that suggest language transfer from maritime communities went beyond lexical items. For example, Lalla and D'Costa list 19 separate phonological features of maritime usage that are evident in eighteenth and nineteenth century Jamaican creole (1990: 100) and Sullivan's unpublished dissertation on pirate counterculture in the Caribbean, and specifically the use of songs, shanties and chants that typify synchronized speech and unified work efforts, suggest that language transfer was also happening at the discourse-level (2003: 458). In sum, evidence shows that Ship English contributed to lexicon in Atlantic and Caribbean littoral regions and potentially impacted language features at all levels from the smallest phonological unit to the shaping of speech events, yet studies on features beyond the lexicon are few, most probably as a result of trends in creole studies that associated European input with lexical influence.

2.1.2 Studies on Ship English

Only two publications on Ship English, both based on ships' logs, analyze features of the variety beyond its lexicon: Matthews's (1935) monograph on pronunciation and Bailey & Ross's (1988) article on morphosyntactic features. Yet neither of these papers make strong claims about Ship English as a comprehensive variety. Matthews states in his introductory notes that what he presents:

should be regarded as a cross-section in the history of pronunciation, an account of the various pronunciations in use among the tarpaulin seamen of the second half of the 17th century. It is not pretended that it describes the 'seaman's dialect' of the period. (1935: 196)

Bailey and Ross conclude that "it is not at all clear that *grammatically* Ship English is a unique sociolect, although its lexical uniqueness is apparent" (1988: 207, authors' italics). The only other paper on Ship English since these early publications is an unpublished Master's thesis (Schultz 2010) focusing on the sociolinguistic factors that caused the new variety to emerge, and, as a Master's thesis, it includes no original research into the characteristic features of the variety itself. Hence, despite the many claims in the field that Ship English existed and was important in shaping dialect boundaries in the British Isles and overseas, only two studies attempt an original analysis of non-lexical features that might have shaped language change around the colonies and trading posts, and neither make very strong assertions about these features as representative of a comprehensive variety.

Matthews' monograph on *Sailors' Pronunciation in the Second Half of the 17th Century* is an analysis of phonetic spelling in naval logbooks written between 1680 and 1700. The paper presents findings that describe "certain conventions of pronunciation for words used exclusively in the sea-trade" (1935: 13) and can thus be interpreted as indicative of general usage in wider maritime communities including aboard merchant and privateer vessels, and in port communities. Matthews presents evidence in support of 67 apparent deviations from contemporary standard phonology, which are summarized below in terms of the phonological tendencies they reflect relating to vowels and consonants.

Matthews' findings on sailors' pronunciation of vowels in the seventeenth century indicate a tendency to raise certain vowels, for instance, /e/ is raised to [i], particularly before a nasal consonant, e.g., *twinty* 'twenty', *frinds* 'friends' and *pinquins* 'penguins' (Matthews 1935: 200). Other vowels are lowered, for example the vowel /u/ was likely shifted to a pronunciation that suggests the use of [ʌ] as a free variant, e.g., *tuck* 'took', *stud* 'stood', and *luck* 'look' (p. 209).Matthews also notes that [i] was subject to lowering and variation with [e] illustrated in the words *wech* 'which', *seck* 'sick', and *wend* 'wind' (p. 199). Matthews records variants between orthographic 'a', 'e' and 'ea', suggesting that they were realized as [e] or [ɛ] e.g., *fedem* 'fathom', *Effreca* 'Africa', and *leattar* 'latter' (p. 201) and also notes a preference for unrounded variants in the realizations of the /ɔ/ phoneme. The two main variables that sailors appeared to use were [æ] e.g., *aspatall* 'hospital', *last* 'lost', and *shatt* 'shot', and [ʌ] e.g., *Hundoras* 'Honduras', *stupt* 'stopped', and *vulcano* 'volcano' (p. 204–205). Likewise, the realization of the lengthened /ɔː/ phoneme also had an unrounded variant which Matthews concludes was probably [aː] based on the orthographic use of 'a' 'aa' and 'ar', e.g., *sa* 'saw', *straa* 'straw', and *harse* 'hawse' (p. 206).

Matthews' findings on sailors' pronunciation of consonants in the seventeenth century shows a tendency towards free variation in pairs of interchangeable phonemes, e.g., the interchange of /w/ and /v/ in words such as *wery* 'very', *winegar* 'vinegar', *vayed* 'weighed', and *avay* 'away' (Matthews 1935: 235). Alveolar and bilabial nasals are also both commonly interchanged, e.g., *starm* 'astern', *hamsome* 'handsome', *inpressed* 'impressed, and *Novenber* 'November' (p. 239). Interchange of stops involving the phonemes /k/, /t/, /d/ and /g/ are also evident (p. 245), and this interchange seems to be more dependent on whether the consonant is voiced or voiceless rather than dependent on the place of articulation, e.g., voiceless /k/ for voiceless /t/ in *sleeke* 'sleet' and *Lord Bartley* 'Lord Berkeley', and voiced /d/ for voiced /g/ in *breidadeer* 'brigadier' (p. 245). Matthews observes that the phonemes /ŋ/, /θ/, /h/ and /w/ are commonly not pronounced in sailors' speech of the seventeenth century. The nasal /ŋ/ is often realized as [n], particularly affecting final '-ing' inflections as illustrated in the phonetic spellings of *bearin* 'bearing', and *lashens* 'lashings' (p. 239) and /h/ is omitted in initial position, e.g., *ospetall* 'hospital' and *Obson* 'Hobson' and medial position, e.g., *hogseds* 'hogsheads' and *likleood* 'likelyhood' (p. 230). Similar omission of /w/ in initial and medial positions is illustrated by the examples *ode* 'wood' and *Westerds* 'westwards' (p. 234). Yet, contrary to consonant omission, Matthews finds that other consonants are intrusive or metathesize, for instance, the addition of [b] that frequently occurs after nasals in words such as *Limbrick* 'Limerick' and *Rumbley* 'Romley' (p. 233) and the movement of [w] into word initial syllables, particularly after stops, e.g., *dwoune* 'down' and *twoer* 'tower' (p. 235).

Bailey and Ross's article "The Shape of the Superstrate: Morphosyntactic Features of Ship English" (1988) uses Matthews' work as a starting point and extends the date range of his corpus of naval logbooks from a twenty-year span between 1680–1700 to include all logs compiled up until 1725 and also the papers of the (British) Royal African Company. Their presentation of findings related to the morphosyntactic features of Ship English are qualified with the statement:

> Because the evidence from these sources is not easily quantifiable, our approach is necessarily inventorial, like that of creolists working with early historical records. We have attempted to document the presence of features that may have been influential in the evolution of Caribbean Creoles and BEV [Black English Vernacular] in the ships' logs and to establish the constraints on their occurrence whenever possible. (Bailey & Ross 1988: 198)

Thus, the work of Bailey and Ross was explicitly influenced by methodology common to creole studies. And their principal findings on verb tense variation, summarized below, were anticipated to have value in the scholarship of Caribbean creole studies and African American dialect studies of the United States.

Bailey and Ross's findings relate principally to variation and constraints of verb tense realization in the present and past preterit forms. They show that present tense marking is realized in three ways, specifically by Ø, -s, or -th inflections. Yet, although all of these three inflections are common to Standard Early Modern English, the distribution of the inflections in Ship English differs from contemporary standard usage.[1] The Ø inflection occurs with all verbs except second person, e.g., with the third person singular in "the Comondore [sic] who arrived here this Day and *seem* to be very well pleased" (Bailey & Ross 1988: 199; this and all quotations from same source show authors' italics). The -s inflection more commonly occurs on verbs other than the third person singular, e.g., with the first person singular in "I *takes* it to the all Dutch forgeries" (p. 199). The -th inflection almost exclusively occurs with verbs that are third person singular and is additionally constrained by the verb used, e.g., with the third person singular and the verb LYE [lie] in "my Cheif [sic] mate *Lyeth* desperately sick" (p. 200). Present tense realizations of the verb BE include *is, are* and *be*, with the *is* realization predominating as a plural form in the logbooks, e.g., "there *is* some Traders" (p. 201). However, Bailey and Ross note that variation occurs from log to log and also within passages written by single individuals.

Bailey and Ross observe that the very nature of the ships' logs as a record of events provides an abundance of past tense forms and conclude that "unmarked weak preterits (those without an <ed> or <t> suffix) are among the most common features of Ship English" e.g., "this day we *kill* a Deare" (1988: 202). They also recognize that strong verbs, typically called irregular verbs in Modern English, also commonly had unmarked preterits in the logbooks, e.g., "Capt masters in ye Diana *bring* a head" (p. 203). They additionally note that these unmarked strong preterits particularly occurred with certain verbs such as *run, come, see, bring*, and *got* (p. 204). However, strong verbs in the preterit form were also potentially regularized, e.g., "we *catched* at least 50" (p. 204) or used as past participle forms, e.g., "Captn Cooke *has broke* his instructions" (p. 204). The verb BE was realized most commonly in the logbooks as *was* in both first and third person subjects, singular and plural compared to the comparative rarity of the word *were* as a

---

[1]Note that the conjugations of verbs and the distributions of inflections were also variable across all English dialects.

past realization (p. 205). Overall, and despite the range of options available to them, Bailey and Ross conclude that "The high frequency of unmarked verbs, both strong and weak, suggests that past tense marking may have been optional for many speakers of Ship English" (p. 205).

In addition to the majority of their findings on variations on how tense is realized in verb phrases, Bailey and Ross mention potential realizations of aspect and modality. They note that periphrastic DO may be a manifestation of aspect, e.g., "in this bay vessels *doe* use to stop" (p. 206) and the use of 'like' to mean 'almost' may be a manifestation of modality, e.g., "we [...] had *like* to have taken" (p. 206). Yet these observations are limited to a few sentences supported by three examples and included in a miscellaneous section entitled "*Other* morpho-syntactic features of Ship English" (emphasis added); wording that attests to the relative value that the authors placed on the observations of aspect and modality in verb phrases. This miscellaneous section also includes lesser-observed features that affected noun phrases, such as unmarked plurals occurring with nouns of measure, e.g., "I see several *saile* to windward" (p. 205); relative pronoun omission when functioning as subject and object, e.g., "there was a vessel came out of Fadm bound for Swanzey" (p. 206); existential *it*, e.g., "*it* was very little wind" (p. 206); and determinative *them*, e.g., "ye Multitude of *Them* foules" (p. 206). Yet these observations are likewise brief and conclude with a statement alluding to the complexity of determining their frequency. However, Bailey and Ross nonetheless recognize that "their presence does suggest that Ship English is likely to have included a number of relevant features that we simply cannot document" (p. 206). This statement, coupled with the last comment in the conclusion, that "While the inventory presented here is hardly an exhaustive account even of the morphosyntax of Ship English, it provides *a place to begin*" (p. 209, emphasis added) suggests that the authors were pointing to potential directions for future studies. However, since the publication of this paper in 1988, there have been no other studies published.

2.2 Selected theoretical framework

2.2.1 Dialect change and new dialect formation

JohannesSchmidt's (1872) *Wellentheorie* proposed the metaphor of waves starting from a single point in a pond to explain dialect change. These waves could be of different strengths and concurrent with other waves that have different starting points, but the basic premise was that dialect features spread in a pattern that is based solely on geographic adjacency. Labov (2007) later adapted the wave model by proposing that these waves of change could move through social space in addition to geographical space, and thus expanded Schmidt's idea of adjacency to refer not only to geographical proximity, but also to social proximity (see Petyt 1980: 50 and Auer et al. 2005: 7–9). Nonetheless, the basic premise of the wave model and its geographical foci encourages assumptions about the obstruent nature of geographical features such as rivers and seas; yet according to Wakelin's discussion of factors relevant to how variant dialect forms emerge and are sustained:

> As far as dialectal divisions are concerned, political and administrative boundaries appear to be of greater significance than geographical ones... the Thames, the Severn, the Tees and Tamar rivers, for example, do not seem to be important dialect boundaries. Indeed, it is held that rivers (at least when navigable) act more often as a means of communication than as obstacles. (Wakelin 1977: 10)

Wakelin's statement foregrounds social rather than geographical divisions, yet social models of dialect change also use terms that perpetuate spatial associations and thus implicitly marginalize the potential influence of maritime communities. Many of these models integrate a concept of how linguistic innovations originate in "focal areas" that have cultural or political dominance, and which are also described as "places at the *social center* of a language or dialect" (Tagliamonte 2013: 15, emphasis added). Tagliamonte describes how language change spreads from these "centers" by diffusion across populations from core areas to peripheral locations (2013: 15). The very words used to conceptualize these theories, namely, *center, peripheral* and *focal* encourage us to visualize the theory in spatial (and hence geographical) terms regardless of the context of the discourse that foregrounds social, political, and cultural factors. Consequently, this encourages us to discount the importance of littoral regions, as they are necessarily not "central;" thus we also marginalize the agency of maritime workers in this paradigm. A brief overview of these traditional models serves to illustrate perhaps one of the reasons that maritime language communities have been excluded from consideration when investigating the factors that contribute to internal language change in the field of dialectology.

However, the role of sailors and maritime workers may have been pivotal to how dialect zones formed and were maintained in an age before technological and flight networks formed new methods of contact. Historical dialectology provides evidence that dialect boundaries cross bodies of water and that the presence of these bodies of water may indeed be the reason for the emergence of common features. For example, Tagliamonte's *Roots of English: Exploring the History of Dialects* (2013) explains how, around the start of the seventeenth century, south-west coastal Scotland and adjacent north-west coastal England had a common speech based on the Northumbrian dialect of Old English with many shared Scots features. Features of this pan-coastal dialect were then transported to coastal Northern Ireland by semi-transient maritime communities and were later reinforced by the speech varieties of settlers who moved from northern counties of England to the Ulster Plantations in Ireland at the beginning of the century. (Tagliamonte 2013: 17). Furthermore, Tagliamonte attests to a "pan-variety parallelism" across northern regions and across the Irish Sea in which "all communities share the same (variable) system in each case and it is only in the subtle weights and constraint of variation that the differences emerge" (2013: 192). This example suggests not only that water was no object to feature transfer, but also that maritime communities may have served as hubs in communication networks that facilitated the transported linguistic features and established supra-regional norms. Although there has been no substantial research on the role of sailors in British dialect zones, scholarship on the commonalities among coastal zones of the British Isles may provide key evidence for recognizing sailors as agents in the models and theories of language change and new dialect formation.

Further to their agency in the shaping of dialect zones in Britain, sailors may have also served a critical role in the development of overseas varieties. Thornton proposes that river and coastal trade routes, and hence also maritime speech communities, were a prime factor in shaping the seventeenth century Atlantic (2000: 56). Moreover, beyond the Atlantic, the role of sailors as agents of language change is recognized in Hickey's (2004) *Legacies of Colonial English: Studies in Transported Dialects*. Some theories presented in this edited collection have influenced how I conceptualize feature transfer and language change and, as such, are worth noting here. Wolfram and Schilling-Estes' paper on "Remnant Dialects in the Coastal United States" has been particularly influential in the preliminary stages of my thinking about how new dialects might be formed through not only linguistic factors but also sociolinguistic and sociohistorical factors (2004: 197). This paper provided my model for an earlier study on the viability of seventeenth century Pirate English as a distinct variety (Delgado 2013) and, as such, has been formative in my thinking about how Ship English may be considered as a distinct variety with characteristic features. Two other theories presented in Hickey's edited volume have also influenced my thinking: firstly, "colonial lag", also known as retention theory, in which variant features of modern day Englishes are directly attestable to differential input from the early contact situation (Hickey 2004: 8) and secondly, a contrasting theory that contact dialects in early colonial situations may have had a more restricted role, namely, that they were "largely embryonic, providing incentives, starting points for future [regional] developments" (Schneider 2004: 302).

Concurrent with the work by Schneider on "embryonic" language forms in the southern United States, Trudgill's (2004) book *New Dialect Formation: The Inevitability of Colonial Englishes*, published in the same year, develops his earlier theory of new dialect formation as a result of mixing, leveling, and simplification with a specific focus on Australian, New Zealand, and South African English varieties. Trudgill proposes that these new varieties of English were formed as a result of initial mixing among various regional British varieties in an isolated colonial territory that incubated the new form. The very fact that isolation is a factor in Trudgill's model negates the presence of the maritime communities in contact with settlers and thus ignores their potential influence, yet this model of new dialect formation has been influential in my own thinking and therefore deserves a closer examination. Trudgill describes the process of koineization in colonial territories in terms of its three stages: 1) *mixing* of features results from a contact situation between variant regional and social dialects; 2) *leveling* occurs when certain features are selected — or created from combining variants — and become the unmarked forms of the new speech community, whilst at the same time there is a reduction or attrition of marked variants, and 3) *simplification* happens with an increase in the morphophonemic, morphosyntactic and lexical regularity of the new standard forms (Trudgill 1986: 90–103). Although Trudgill's work on new dialect formation explicitly relates to colonial English in the southern hemisphere, I anticipate that what he says is equally applicable to a variety incubated in maritime communities. His comments on the linguistic spectrum of the input speakers seem equally applicable to maritime workers as they do to New Zealand settlers: "dialect mixture situations involving adults speaking many different dialects of the same language will eventually and inevitably lead to the production of a new, unitary dialect [...] eventual convergence of order out chaos, on a single unitary variety" (Trudgill 2004: 27). Furthermore, what Trudgill claims about linguistic leveling as a consequence of human desire for social conformity and group identification is equally applicable to sailors, and, as a result, his theory of mixing, leveling, and simplification has particularly influenced how I have conceptualized the development of Ship English as a distinct variety.[2]

---

[2] Although I argue here that Ship English was a distinct variety from other forms of speech, I also acknowledge the reality that all varieties of speech exist on a continuum and that nonstandard varieties particularly develop out of a situation of pluri-lectal variation.

If, indeed, sailors incubated a new variety of English in their own communities, then it is entirely possible that this form was the one transported to new locations. An overview, and synthesis, of some of the literature that supports this interpretation follows. The premise that Ship English was a distinct type of speech derives from Bailey and Ross's claim that it was "a changing and developing variety" (1988: 207), and Trudgill's theory suggests that this may have been formed by the leveling of other British regional and social dialects. Dobson's work on Early Modern Standard English recognizes the formation of "a mixed dialect, an amalgam of elements drawn from all parts of the country" (1955: 35) that formed through a process of admixture that happened in England concurrent with the emergence of a Standard English. And, although there is no published scholarship on Ship English as a leveled variety, Schultz's unpublished thesis claims that the development of Ship English by a process of dialect leveling was made possible by intensely consolidated and internally co-dependent maritime communities of practice, in which "linguistically, strong networks act as a norm enforcement mechanism" (2010: 7–8). Milroy's article on social networks and linguistic focusing (1986) supports this interpretation, by referring back to Le Page's theory that "the emergence of a closeknit group, a sense of solidarity and a feeling of shared territory are all conditions favouring [linguistic] focusing" (1986: 378). My own earlier work on Pirate English (Delgado 2013) showed how one specific sub-community of mariners developed and maintained a distinct dialectal variety as a direct result of their networks of communication and consequent linguistic focusing. This idea of the existence of a new variety that was then transported overseas appears to be an interpretation supported by certain scholars working on pidgin and creoles. For example, Linebaugh and Rediker claim that "nautical English" as a distinct variety was one of the four inputs to Atlantic Pidgins along with Cant, Sabir, and West African languages (2000: 153), and Hancock claims that "it was this kind of English, an English having no single regional source in Britain, which the Africans first heard on their shores" (1986: 86). Thus, although there is no single study attesting to the process of new dialect formation in maritime communities, selected theories and observations in historical dialectology support the premise.

2.2.2 Formative studies influencing methodology

Laing and Lass, in their article "Early Middle English Dialectology: Problems and Prospects", identify as the major challenge of historical dialect study the fact that "all of our informants are dead" (2006: 418). They claim that in this context, it is entirely feasible (and necessary) to base a research methodology on written sources, or what they describe as "text witnesses" of the contemporary dialects. These materials are then treated as if they were native speakers of the target dialect and consequently, "take the place of informants who can be questioned directly" (p. 418). Thus, much of the following discussion of early English dialectology is based on linguistic suppositions derived from non-linguistic sources such as: colonial records (Maynor 1988); reported speech, e.g., court records, depositions, executions, (Awbery 1988; Tagliamonte 2013); informal sources, e.g., letters, diaries (Tagliamonte 2013); literary representations, e.g., songs, drama (Russell 1883; Wright 1967) and retrospectively compiled word lists (Wright 1967; Smith 1627 [1968]). These studies support and justify my own historical comparative approach that makes use of written source material to derive linguistic hypotheses about Ship English.

Dublin's Trinity College and the 1641 Depositions Project (Trinity College Dublin, MSS 809–841) is just one example of how transcribed spoken sources might be used for research. The database generated by the project maintains transcribed witness testimonies and depositions relating to the first-hand experiences of the 1641 Irish rebellion and can be searched by county, potentially facilitating investigators who might be interested in the linguistic features of a specific area. This corpus of data and the observations of Laing and Lass on written sources serving linguistic research motivated my own focus on sailors' depositions and witness testimony, housed as part of the records of the Admiralty and Colonial State Papers at the National Archives, in Kew, London.

Despite the availability of depositions in collections such as these, however, the limitations of written sources in linguistic research have, of course, been acknowledged in the literature. For example, in his chapter entitled "Written Records of Spoken Language: How Reliable Are They?" Maynor stresses that "even in the best of circumstances it is difficult for [such] dialectal research to be completely accurate" (1988: 119). Given this caveat, the second aim of this research project, to generate baseline data, was formulated cautiously; I do not propose that my findings will form a comprehensive grammar of the dialect, nor are they anticipated to escape critical comments from those who find the corpus problematic. However, I believe that the aim of generating baseline data on the characteristic features of Ship English is reasonable and worthwhile given the limitations of the research design. Furthermore, scholars of historical dialectology who have chosen to investigate dialects of Old, Middle and Early-Modern English, or moribund and extinct varieties, have used written evidence to document features and thus validate the necessity and value of using such a methodology in this study.

Lipski's (2005) *A History of Afro-Hispanic Language* presents the findings of a study of reconstructed Afro-Hispanic speech over five centuries and spanning five continents. The aim of his extensive study is comparable to mine, in that Lipski investigates a marginalized speech variety that was often depicted with exaggeration and stereotype in the colonial period, yet, he theorizes, has had a significant influence throughout the Spanish-speaking world. He also recognizes that the agency of Africans in Spanish language change "is rarely considered on a par with more 'traditional' language contact situations" (Lipski 2005: 2). The speech of sailors has likewise been neglected in decades of scholarship on language contact and is often similarly depicted in exaggerated form with disdain or mockery when it is recognized as a distinct variety in non-academic and non-occupational writing. Similar to the varieties of Afro-Spanish that Lipski investigates, Ship English also has a limited and problematic corpus of documented usage in addition to literary representations, second-hand reports and fragments of rhymes. As a result, Lipski's comparative historical methodology served as an early model for my own preliminary studies. Specifically, his methodology influenced the research design of my own pilot study on seventeenth century sailors' phonological forms, presented at The Society for Pidgin and Creole Linguistics Summer Meeting, University of Graz, Austria, 7–9 July 2015 in a paper entitled "The Reconstructed Phonology of Seventeenth Century Sailors' Speech". My research design for this study compared Matthews's phonological features of seventeenth century sailors' speech to representations in two texts: Defoe's *Robinson Crusoe* (1998) and Johnson's *The Successful Pyrate* (Johnson 1713) and concluded that the literary representations were valid linguistic records based on significant concordance with the historical data that Matthews observed in ships' logs. This pilot study motivated the inclusion of shanties, fictional representations and third-party observations of sailor talk in documents such as travel journals in my corpus. Furthermore, in addition to the inclusion of literary documents and fragmentary data in his corpus, Lipski's ideological approach to linguistic analysis has also influenced my thinking. His analysis of linguistic data in conjunction with sociolinguistic data to present Afro-Hispanic language in human terms rather than a dispassionate list of features underpins the formation of my own research design that integrates demographic and socio-historical data on speech communities in research on linguistic features.

Shaw includes demographic and socio-historical data in her study on *Everyday Life in the Early English Caribbean: Irish, Africans, and the Construction of Difference* (Shaw 2013). Although Shaw's book is not linguistic in focus, she determines the characteristics of Irish and African community identity based on the implications in a range of data points cross-referenced with historical scholarship. Her research is comparable to mine in terms of the historical period of the populations in question and the geographical locations of their speech communities. It also analyses populations for whom we only have fragmentary and potentially biased documentation. Her findings are derived from "probing archival spaces and fissures" (p. 190) and informed reconstruction around the data points that she has access to, and thus provides a further model for my own approach to a corpus that includes fragmentary data.

Comparable to Shaw's book, Jarvis's (2010) *In the Eye of all Trade: Bermuda, Bermudians, and the Maritime Atlantic World 1680–1783* contributes to an increasing body of historical scholarship aiming to present the complex lives of "largely anonymous individuals [who] shaped colonial expansion" (p. 459), and his self-described maritime social history particularly succeeds in recognizing that maritime communities comprise more than the European-descended male figurehead that official documentation identifies. Jarvis explains that an extended kinship network was central to social cohesion and this has motivated my own efforts to include non-Europeans, women, children and various other undocumented workers aboard ships and living in extended maritime communities in the scope of my own research. Jarvis's introduction serves to highlight the importance of maritime movements to all interdisciplinary historical research:

> Motion was the defining characteristic of the Atlantic world. Connections and linkages across the space and central to all Atlantic histories. Whether the focus is people, plants, ideas, diseases, religious doctrines, texts, technologies, or commodities, crossing the water remains the assumed or explicit common denominator in most Atlantic studies. (Jarvis 2010: 9)

And although Jarvis does not include speech in his list of potential foci, linguistic studies around the Atlantic, and particularly at the time of early colonial expansion, also depend on crossing the water in order to contextualize the patterns of feature transfer, dialect leveling, and creole genesis in littoral communities. Thus, Atlantic studies round out the interdisciplinary framework of my own research, in addition to historical dialectology, socio-historical studies, and studies in pidgins and creoles that provide a comprehensive framework for my own investigation into Ship English of the early colonial period. The complexity and interconnected nature of this interdisciplinary review of the literature lends itself well to the complex socio-historical context of the communities who spoke Ship English, explored in detail in the following chapter on sailors.

3 Sailors

This is the first of two chapters that focus on socio-historical data about the sailors and their speech communities. This chapter specifically attempts to provide an overview on demographic data of English-speaking sailors of the early colonial Caribbean period by providing statistical (wherever possible) and qualitative data and in turn presenting the reasoning behind the capacity of this population to develop and sustain a distinct language variety. The chapter opens with a discussion of how sailors were recruited into maritime communities and subsequently presents sections that roughly correspond to census demographics: gender, age, health and mortality, family and marital status, social status, financial standing, place of origin, language abilities, literacy, and number of people residing in the ship community.

3.1 General considerations

Two problems characterize the misunderstanding about the people who worked and lived aboard sea-going vessels in the age of sail. The first problem arises from the uncertainty about the subjects discussed, while the second stems from the perpetuation of stereotypes in both popular culture and historical scholarship. The word 'sailor' carries with it a presumption of lower-class manual labor, and this most probably derives from the original association of the word 'sailor' with a seaman whose job it was to manage the sails (Adkins & Adkins 2008: xxvix). However, this definition is no longer what we mean when we use the word "sailor". In modern usage, this term is generically used to refer to any employed seaman and more specifically an experienced lower-class worker who is also explicitly an adult male, more appropriately correlating with the maritime rank "able seaman". This new definition, although more inclusive in scope than the original meaning, still does not include all the men, women, and children of different specializations, ranks, and experience who lived and worked aboard sea-going vessels. For example, the group denoted by the word does not typically include the maritime slave, the child apprentice, the captain's servant, the marine, the ship's doctor, the washerwoman, the carpenter, the landsman, and the admiral. Yet these people also lived at sea for significant periods if not the majority of their working lives. In contrast, the restricted group of lower-class experienced adult male workers who were free to enlist (i.e., the able seaman that people often think about when they use the word "sailor") represents only one section of the population in a large vessel of the seventeenth century. Thus, this chapter necessarily opens with a re-definition of the word to include all people, both male and female, young and old, experienced and novice, in all of the professions needed and preferred to navigate, defend, maintain, service, and populate the floating communities of large and small vessels in the early age of Atlantic colonial expansion. – The perpetuation of the sailor stereotype in both popular culture and historical scholarship is embodied by the term "Jack Tar", a term notably used by officers to describe enlisted men since the 1600s that derived from the ubiquitous application of tar as a waterproofing agent in wooden ships coupled with the epithet "Jack" referring to the common man (for more extensive discussion see the book *Jack Tar*, specifically pages, Adkins & Adkins 2008: xxviii–xxvix). Perhaps, in part, because of this stereotype motivated by our restricted interpretation of the word "sailor" we have typically failed to recognize the importance of real sea-going individuals in shaping our local and global histories. However, modern scholars such as Michael Jarvis are trying to recover the agency of individual sailors by recognizing that "[t]he decisions, innovations, adaptations, and self-organized enterprises of largely anonymous individuals shaped colonial expansion and Atlantic history as much as imperial bureaucracies, state navies, chartered trading companies and metropolitan merchants" (Jarvis 2010: 459). This chapter aims to promote the recognition of these "largely anonymous individuals" by recovering some of the demographic data that might help us understand who they were.

Demographic data is in part recoverable, but the record-keeping of the community itself does not make this an easy task. Difficulties are compounded by the fact that these communities were transient, with high levels of illiteracy, and many individuals were often not considered relevant enough to remark upon in official records. Other individuals may have purposely concealed their identity, for example, the witness who explains that he changed his name because "he thought himselfe in ill companie" [ASSI 45/4/1/135] and the deponent George Trivattin, who "After the pirating was committed [...] Changed his name to Edward Thomas" [HCA 1/14/154]. Others took false identities to evade or complicate the efforts of impressment officers and for this reason, many physical descriptions accompany the given name for newly enlisted men, for example, "Peter Fox abt 25 yeares old, of middle stature, slender body short fingers Reddish hair & short, wearing at present a flaxen perriwig, smooth faite, a blark quick nimble eye" [HCA 1/101/411]. Transient sailors were also a difficult entity to determine, often navigating the undocumented frontiers between the mercantile and naval worlds (Fusaro 2015) or the logging, turtling, and salt-raking labor of the Atlantic commons (Jarvis 2010). In short, in an effort to provide a comprehensive overview, the following sections on demography present data on sailors (redefined as all sea-going workers) that recognizes them as "highly complex *individuals* with recoverable life stories, shoreside ties, ambitions, and more self-determination than is usually allotted them" (Jarvis 2010: 465–466, author's italics) yet also acknowledges the limitations and complexities of the data from which my conclusions derive.

3.2 Recruitment

Sailors were typically recruited rather than born into their communities and the various methods of recruitment for manning sea-going vessels affected the resulting demographics of the community. While most commanding and many commissioned and warrant officers were professionals who sought placement and promotion at sea, many of the petty officers, militia, and operational crew would have been enlisted via methods involving some degree of coercion, manipulation, or outright force. Recruitment methods included voluntary enrollment, conscription, and the assignment of impressed, enslaved, or detained populations. Each of these methods is briefly discussed in the following paragraphs as a means to try and understand the common characteristics of the men they targeted.

The ideal method to cover the manning requirements of a vessel was by voluntary recruits, and this method was most successful for enlisting commissioned officers during the Anglo-Dutch wars of the seventeenth century. Privileged second and third sons of the landed gentry not eligible to inherit titles often sought commissions and favor from family members to help them advance in the navy whilst at the same time fulfilling their desires to travel and build reputation (Brown 2011: 53). In contrast, efforts to encourage volunteers for lower-ranked positions in the fleet was often less productive. The men needed for these positions would not enjoy the financial rewards and status associated with the ranks reserved for "gentlemen",[1] and their work was often hard and considered menial. Yet, popular broadsheet ballads commonly pandered to the working classes in order to motivate voluntary recruitment. Some songs glorified voyages, such as

---

[1]"Gentleman" in this context refers to landed gentry and the adult males of wealthy families of the period without the intention of suggesting any personal respectability or strength of character.

"The honour of Bristol", (cited in Palmer 1986: 24–26) that highlights the achievements of the ship *Angel Gabriel*, a Bristol Privateer that allegedly fought with three Spanish ships in the late 1620s, killing 500 men and gaining glory and riches for the crew. Other songs were much less factual, such as "Sailors for my Money" a self-conscious ditty that proposes to its readers, "Let's sail into the Indies where the golden grass doth grow" (cited in Palmer 1986: 29). Recruitment to the civilian fleets, including merchant and pirate vessels, offered more tangible incentives such as increased wages in times of high demand and shares in cargoes and captured goods; consequently, these fleets often enlisted more working-class volunteers than the navy.

Many working class sailors enlisted to escape poverty rather than to earn money. One volunteer states his reason, "not having any thing to Eat [...] I consented to goo" [HCA 1/98/44]. Another volunteer, hearing drums beat to announce recruitment, joined a group of would-be recruits that "desired the master to give them some victualls" [HCA 1/53/67]. Hugh Bicheno explains such motivation, in his 2012 study of *Elizabeth's Sea Dogs*:

> Only abject misery can explain how anyone would volunteer to crew the Queen's ships. Although in theory sailors serving in the Royal Navy in 1588 were paid 7s.6d. per month, in practice they were paid late or not at all and had little prospect of spoil. The only certain payment was in kind: accommodation on board was better than sleeping in the streets or in dosshouses, and while the food and drink was usually rank and sometimes poisonous, the alternative might be starvation. (Bicheno 2012: 182)

The need for bed and board may explain why some volunteers came directly from other ships without staying in port, as attested to in one logbook entry, "I brought along with me about 40 men out of the York who Voluntary offer'd their services" [ADM 51/4322/4] and a passenger account of how "The *English* [sailors] divided themselves, some aboard our ship, and some aboard the *Turk*" [445f.1/513]. Likewise, acute financial need characterises the testimony of another volunteer who "[w]as forced to hide himselfe and goe to sea for Debt" [HCA 1/11/110]. Indeed, poverty was likely the motivating factor for the majority of lower-ranked men on ships in addition to those workers whose voices are not recognized in official documentation such as female servants, child workers and indentured peoples.

Impressing sailors to man naval fleets in times of war was a common strategy that goes back to medieval times in Britain. The impress service (colloquially known as the press gang) predominantly targeted experienced sailors with offers of advanced pay and was conceived as a heavy-handed push to motivate volunteer recruits. Logbook entries attest to the extensive nature of such practices, for example, sailing in March 1691, "the *Mary* has presst all her men" [ADM 52/1/8] and The *Albemarle* receives "a Pressing having In 60 men" [ADM 52/2/5] on December 29 1691. Even on a smaller scale, the practice was routine, as attested to in the logbook of the *Antelope*, in a footnote that reads "to Day received 5 Prest men on board" [ADM 52/2/9] and an unnamed vessel that records how they "Came Downe here from London with 6 Prest men which ware putt onbord" [ADM 52/1/6]. Although the figure would have fluctuated in times of war and national need, the National Maritime Museum in London estimates that by 1790, some 16% of sailors were forced by press gangs. This routine procedure was also used to recruit some of the higher-ranking warrant officers, for example, in his study of sickness and health at sea, Kevin Brown observes that "the majority of sea-surgeons and surgeons' mates were pressed into service" (2011: 25) and the instructions for impressment in a letter from James City in Virginia, dated April 16 1700 specifies "Warrants for the impressing pylots, carpenters, or any other Workmen, as shall be necessary" [CO 5/1411/660].

The press was problematic however, and various documents attest to its inconsistent practices that coerced and exploited the poor. Although the press-gang was only meant to encourage seafaring volunteers, in practice they coerced landsmen, boys, vagrants, and convicts in addition to the forced conscription of seamen and port workers to complete crews of large naval warships in times of need. One letter dated March 1700 and signed by four representatives of the navy's supply services describes how port trade is affected because "by the impressing of some of their men others are frighted from their duty" [SP 42/6]. Yet, local governments recognized that the dregs of their societies could be put to work in this way and invariably supported impressment officers if complaints made it to trial. This situation created serious problems of corruption, extortion and abuse in the impressment service and led to practices such as seizing men indiscriminately before extorting money to let them go with the threat of forcing them into conscription if the sum was not paid. Adkins and Adkins explain that poor men who were unable to pay the press gangs off were forcibly removed from their families, often without any recourse to bid farewell or explain the situation (see Adkins & Adkins 2008: 43–58). In a contemporary diatribe of the practice, Lieutenant Haversham explains to Governor Vernon that the system is rife with corruption. He explains, "he that is prest may be represented by the press officer as coming voluntarily, especially when the press officer can find his own accts [rewards] in it, which I dont doubt but they may too often contrive to do" [SP 42/6]. As testimony to such coercion, the court records of a trial in 1722 describe a recruit who "had a trick put upon him there and was forced to make a sort of sale of himself to [an] officer for cleaning the Debt" [HCA 1/99/124]. As a result of such corrupt practices, the press-gangs were fiercely opposed and feared in equal measure and their appearance in port towns often led to rioting, murders and assaults committed on both sides.

Repeated testimony in court records between 1620 and 1750 refers to the profusion and violence of impressment. One deponent recalls how he was taken by press gangs at various times, and describes one of those experiences on land that occurred in 1660:

> I met four press-Masters, and I might have shunned them, but durst not; and when we met, they ask'd me, Whether I was a Master, or a Man; I denying to be a Master, they replied, you must go with us; not so, said I; then they took hold of me, two under my Arms, and another two under my Hams, and lifted me upon their Shoulders, and carry'd me about three hundred Yards [...] they heav'd me from their Shoulders, over the Wharf, cross the Boat-thaughts, which was about five Yards high; and had not Providence preserved me, they had killed, or else crippled me. [445f.1/26]

The same deponent relates a different experience with another press gang in 1662:

> No sooner we came to an Anchor, but a Press-Boat came on Board us [...] they ty'd a Rope about my Waste, and with a Tackle hoisted me; making a Noise, as if I had been some Monster; and lower'd me down upon the Main-Hatches. [445f.1/26–27]

Other deponents talk about being beaten with sticks, tied with ropes, grabbed in the night, and duped into going aboard (see series HCA 1/99/11). Yet most poor sailors had no choice but to accept the situation as normal. It was just another hard fact of life that some crewmates, like sailor David Creagh, were "kept in the Service by force and violence" [HCA 1/13/108].

Although press gangs focused their efforts on the port towns of the British Isles, colonial ports were not exempt from impressment. The records of the Colonial Office include various letters from administrators complaining about impressment activity around the Caribbean and on the coastal plantations of colonial North America. For example, one letter complains "against pressing seamen in the [Virginia] plantatons" [CO 5/1411/558] and another demands that "Captains shall not for the future be permitted to press" and urges impressment officers to make sure that pressed men "be good sailors [...] and not to carry off any Inhabitants from the sd [said] plantation" [CO 5/1411/624]. Hence, the press was likely to enlist a cross-section of lower-class workers in and around Britain's colonial holdings, regardless of profession, nationality, or native language who would disproportionately represent lower-class men of working age. These men were enlisted and kept in service by force, potentially subjected to confinement in the putrid darkness of a ship's hold, guarded by soldiers, and denied shore-leave for fear of desertion. Yet, these were the "volunteers" of the Royal Navy in Britain during the sixteenth and seventeenth century, and our recognition of their recruitment and experiences is an essential part of their demographic profile.

Men could also be pressed into service directly from another vessel. This type of ship-to-ship impressment was abhorred by merchant sailors with hopes of returning to their homes after an extended voyage yet was common practice in naval recruitment and commonly known as "turning over" the crew. Documentary evidence regularly refers to this practice, e.g., one sailor writes "Yesterday My Self with the Rest of the *Foresights* Company were turned over" [ADM 51/4170/2] and various logbook entries attest to large numbers of sailors coming from other vessels: "This morn Turned 20 men over Into the *Essex Prize*" [ADM 52/2/5]; "we have... this morn Sent 30 men on board the Dunkirk" [ADM 52/1/5]; "turned 50 men on board the Barwick" [ADM 52/2/3]; and more extensively, "Received on board out of the *Arendall* men that she brought out of the Downes from severall shipps Viz the *Colchester* 27 the *Sohampton* 12 the *English Begar* 11 the *Woolwitch* 43 & out of the *Brittainia* ketch 50 & out of the *St. Michael* Smaek 29. In all 172" [ADM 52/2/5]. Even individual court testimonies reflect the movement of sailors in this manner, e.g., the description of one deponent as "a Jersy Man forced out of the *Success* Sloop in the West Indies" [HCA 1/99/89]. Colonial administrators were complicit in this practice, issuing warrants like the one dated January 1699 from Francis Nicholson, governor of Virginia and Maryland, who granted captain John Aldred permission "to impress one able seaman out of any ship or vessel who hath fifteen seaman or upwards" [CO 5/1411/665]. Indeed, turning over a crew was such a successful practice for manning a vessel with experienced sailors that pirate crews adopted the custom. George Bougee's trial for piracy in October 1684 describes "30 and 40 men on board" captured from a taken vessel whose captain was on shore trading [HCA 1/12/1]. Yet, even in these non-negotiable transfers, captains attempted to coerce sailors to make declarations of compliance, e.g., in the September 9th trial records of Rhode Island and Providence Plantation 1725, one pirate captain is accused of forcing potential recruits to eat candles and to run a gauntlet of sticks wielded by the crew if they would not "volunteer" [HCA 1/99/5]. In the same trial, a witness testifies that the same "Capt Hunt... used him Barbarously threatening to cut of [off] one of his fingers for a ring he had on and Low beat out one of his Teeth & threatened to Pistol him if he would not sign their articles" [IICA 1/99/7]. Contemporary courts acknowledged this type of coercion, as evidenced by some surviving documents attesting to coerced impressment, to be used as certificates in case of capture, e.g., "Evan Jones Acknowledging of his forcing the Freeland to goe his surgeon" [HCA 1/98/181] dated October 29 1699. Also, in the trail of March 28 1722, court officials decided to try every one of the 88 accused pirates individually under the recognition that "many of the Prisoners found on Board were new entred men and forced thro fear to act the Part they did" [HCA 1/99/3/16]. Thus, not only naval fleets, but also pirate vessels were likely to have kept men for lengthy periods against their will and refused them any type of shore leave for fear of desertion.

Sailors who were turned over were not the only non-consenting crew members; indenture and slavery were also common routes to sea service. Piracy trials often concluded with a term of service for men found guilty, e.g., the men tried on 28 March 1722 were punished each with a seven-year term of indenture in the Royal African Company [HCA 1/99/174]. Boys and young men were also liable to be sold into indenture, e.g., one young man's description that "he was in a Storme at Sea in a Shipp belonging to Captain Thomas Shaft who was his Master, and with whom he hath lived 5 yeares, having bin bound to him for 7 yeares" [HCA 1/12/79]. Slaves were also used to complete crews, particularly in the privateer and pirate fleets that were not subject to the same compliance with Britain's 1651 Navigation Acts that required a crew to be at least three quarters British.[2] The use of slaves in addition to indentured workers including vagrants, prisoners, and the destitute meant that non-consenting sailors were a core component of crews in the early colonial period in addition to volunteers, conscripted men, and detained workers.

---

[2]The 1651 Navigation Acts specifically applied to the returning voyages of East India Company Ships and restricted the employment of non-English sailors to a quarter of the crew. However, their general aim to minimize foreign (and specifically Dutch) involvement in the colonial trade was legitimized by this legislation which was more widely applied that its originally specified scope.

3.3 Gender

As previously acknowledged in the discussion of the Jack Tar stereotype, we tend to presume that all sailors were male and women's presence on board was limited to the fleeting visits of prostitutes when stationed in port. Whilst it is no doubt true that the majority of sailors (i.e., all sea-going workers) were male, there was, nonetheless, a minority of women aboard. The presence of some of these women emerges in fleeting descriptions, such as the deposition of Anne Hoy in 1695, rather ambiguously described as "Liveing in Ship" [HCA 1/13/101]. It may have been that Anne Hoy was a personal servant, indeed, the most common role of these women who lived in the ships was in the guise of officers' servants performing the work of food preparation, cleaning, and general maid's duties, and potentially, even carrying gunpowder in times of conflict when enlisted men were operating the guns (as suggested in Brown 2011: 95). As these workers were employed independently, they do not appear on the ship's payroll and their work has consequently gone largely unrecognized. Yet, there is recoverable evidence of these women's presence and agency aboard sea-going communities, e.g., Anne Foster, described as a maid servant suffering abuse from her employer [HCA 1/101/426], "Marramitta (my Negore) Cook" serving on board the *Margarit* [HCA 1/98/100], and Rose Baldwin, Jane Alcocke, and Elizabeth Cammiothe who are described as servants aboard the *Elizabeth and Mary*. Interestingly, in this case, the deponent testifies that the three women "lay together in A Cabbin Standing neere the main mast between decks" [HCA 1/9/51] suggesting that there were allocated women's quarters onboard. Yet, this piece of information only comes to light because two of the women are deposed to give evidence in the murder trial of a man who was chained to the main mast near their cabin. In the same trial, William Dunston testifies that the light he saw "might be any of the men Servants, Mayd Servants or any of the Seamen" [HCA 1/9/51], suggesting the notable presence of both male and female servants aboard the naval vessel. Similarly attesting to a notable female presence on board a 250-man vessel, one journal writer describes how "the cries of the women terrify'd those that were most inured to those tempests" [445f.1/516]. Such fragmentary evidence recognizes women's work among sea-going communities despite the fact that they were unlikely to appear in any official ship's muster or payroll.

Women worked as maids and servants yet they also worked as enlisted crewmen in the navy. Adkins and Adkins explain the long, if somewhat covert, tradition of women serving at sea as evidenced by "documented instances of young women passing themselves off as boys on both merchant and naval ships" (Adkins & Adkins 2008: 182). These include, for example, Hannah Snell's publication of her experiences as a marine (published 1750) and Mary Lacy's experiences as a carpenter's servant and shipwright under the pseudonym William Chandler in the naval fleet, published in the compilation *The Lady Tars* (Snell et al. 2008: iv). Popular ballads, stories and songs also testify to the tradition of female crew, exemplified by titles such as "Susan's Adventures in a Man-of-War", "The "Female Tar", and "The Female Cabin Boy" (cited in Adkins & Adkins 2008: 181–182). In short, in spite of their own efforts to conceal their presence, recoverable evidence of their agency attests to their service in the navy.

Women were also active in pirate communities as evidenced in court records of trials. Aside from the more famous examples of pirates like Anne Bonny and Mary Read whose agency was recognized during their lifetimes (see Rediker 2004: 103–126), there were potentially many women who collaborated in piratical activity and served aboard pirate vessels, yet for whom we have either no record, or only fragmentary and circumstantial evidence. For instance, the witness testimony of a prisoner on a pirate ship explains how he and his men were "put down into the Cabbin and the Scuttle or hatch shut, and Mary Critchett sat down on it to keep the Deponent from opening it" [HCA 1/99 Williamsburg, Aug 14 1729]. Another document dated September 28 1638 includes witness testimony of Jane Handall and Margarett Pope, both charged with piracy. In her testimony, Pope accuses "Jane Handall being Damamed if she Did not Helpp her Husband about the tyme aforesaid" [HCA 1/101/252] suggesting that the husband and wife team worked in collaboration. Yet, despite these few documented references to the agency of women on board pirate ships, admiralty officials of the era rarely noted the presence or contributions of women on board any English pirate, naval, or merchant vessel. However, as Murphy explains in his 2015 conference paper on women in the navy, the English civil war in the seventeenth century forced many women to seek refuge on ships and these women likely worked in whatever capacity would gain them a berth on the ship. In short, we must accept that the demography of sailors' communities during this time necessarily included a minority of female crew and service providers beyond the caricature of the port prostitute.

3.4 Age

Determining the average ages of a population for whom documentary evidence is fragmentary and incomplete poses significant difficulties, yet, generally, we can assert that sailors were young. Peter Earle, a scholar who has done extensive work on age demographics of English sailors of the period under study, determines that the majority of sailors went to sea between the ages of 12 and 16 (see Figure 3.1 adapted from Earle 1993: 85). Additionally, the likelihood of children serving on vessels was increased by the practice of sending vagrant children to populate the English settlements in Virginia (shipments sent in 1619, 1620, and 1622) and also the custom of spiriting (i.e., kidnapping) children for work in the Americas, resulting in large numbers of children in the working Atlantic [Merseyside Maritime Museum, Information sheet 10: Child Emigration]. Testimonies of teenage sailors abound in court documentation, for example Stephen Bakes who went to sea as carpenter's mate at age 17 [HCA 1/13/97] and Thomas Francois de Fouret who served as a clerk in a man of war at age 16 [HCA 1/13/96]. Yet, even in their teen years, some sailors were considered too young for certain types of work; one sailor testified at the age of 17 that, despite his rank as yeoman of the stores, "being underAge he was never allowed to go on Board of Prizes" [HCA 1/99/148]. Other types of work were specifically designed for younger workers. Among officers, entry level was at 11 years for a volunteer first class or 13 years if not the son of a naval officer (Adkins & Adkins 2008: 64), yet rules were broken to permit younger recruits to acquire the 6 years' sea-service expected before making midshipmen level in the army. Among the lower-ranking sailors, the position of "Boy, Third Class" was created specifically for those under the age of 15, many of whom appear in the court records, for example, William Muller, servant to an officer at age 12 [HCA 1/52/176] and Peter Killing, a boatswain's boy at age 13 [HCA 1/48/102]. Among the list of 98 pirates captured in one court record, three are described as "boys" and one specifically listed as "10 ys old" [CO 5/1411/826–27] suggesting that very young sailors were potentially on board. The youngest recruit I found evidence of in the records was Francis Longley of Jamaica deposed at "about 12 years of age" who explains that he set out on a trading voyage about four and a half years ago, making him eight years old at most when he joined the crew [HCA 1/52/104]. Although Earle notes that such very young boys were by no means typical (Earle 1998: 20) there are repeated references to schoolteachers aboard naval vessels, for whom instructions were provided that indicate the young ages of their pupils: "When the hatchways are open, the youngsters should always be cautioned against playing inadvertently near them; and care should be taken at the same time to tighten a rope around them, to prevent accidents, if possible" (in a manual published 1801, cited in Adkins & Adkins 2008: 21). It is a sad fact that some of these boys may have been recruited for sexual exploitation, as discussed in Burg's (2007) *Boys at Sea* and in Fury's (2015) discussion of the abuses that happened on the voyages of the East

India Company. In sum, although the great majority of sailors were likely to have gone to sea between 12 and 16 (comparable to occupations on land), younger recruits were also employed, provided for, and used to service the needs of the crew.

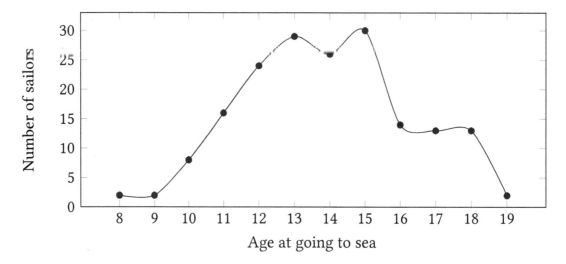

Figure 3.1: Age at which deposed sailors said they went to sea, adapted from the data presented in Earle 1998: 85 Table 6, source: PRO, HCA 13/75-86

The upper age of sailors, as suggested by the few academics who have worked on this subject and corroborated by depositions in court documentation of the 1620–1750 period, is around fifty years old. At the age of fifty, and particularly if he had been at sea most of his working life, a sailor would be considered old. In his journal, physician Gilbert Blane notes:

> [seamen] are generally short lived, and have their constitutions worn out ten years before the rest of the laborious part of mankind [manual workers]. A seaman at the age of forty-five... would be taken by his looks to be fifty-five, or even at the borders of sixty. (cited in Adkins & Adkins 2008: 88)

Archival records contain evidence of such professional seamen serving into their forties, e.g., the witness John Morphey, deposed at 46 years of age, who testifies that, since the age of ten, he "was bred up to the sea and hath ever since lived as a seaman" [HCA 1/53/9]. Yet, if sailors could avoid the natural hazards of a life at sea, then it was entirely possible for them to serve until a more advanced age. For example, the HCA 1/53 batch of depositions dated 1694–1710 include one mariner "George Burgis of Boston in New England mariner aged about 67 yeares"

[HCA 1/53/66] and another aged seventy [HCA 1/53/22]. The oldest deponent in the HCA 1/52 batch of court records dated 1683–1694 was seventy years of age, and the oldest deponent in the HCA 1/51 batch of court records dated 1674–1683 was a Waterman named Thomas Lowell, aged eighty-six [HCA 1/52/104]. Thus, although the average upper age of working sailors might be around forty-five, some survived to serve into more advanced years. It is also worth noting that there was an increase in the recruitment of very old and very young men on the merchant fleets in the wartime periods of heavy impressment (mostly between 1689–1713) because these individuals were excluded from the press and thus protected from being poached by naval vessels seeking men to turn over. For example, sixteen-year-old Edward Lindsfeild deposed in a court case of 1692 that they sailed "with two, three or four boyes, feareing to carry men last they should be imprest" and Edward Round, age 76, gave evidence in the same case (cited in Earle 1998: 200).

The average age of ships' crews is just over thirty-one, based on the of ages of sailors for whom ages are recorded in 1,101 depositions collected by the High Court of the Admiralty between 1601 and 1710 (see Table 3.1). Yet this number may be inflated by the fact that men called to give evidence in court were often deposed due to their long experience at sea.[3] Furthermore, many of the court records derive from trials of piracy, in which we might anticipate that many crew members were recruited directly from another vessel and hence spent time at sea already. If such a bias affects the data, then an adjusted average might be slightly lower, potentially in the late twenties.

The age composition of the crew would naturally reflect the age demographics of different ranks. For example, the average age of captains and officers was between thirty-five and forty-four (Earle 1998: 86); the average age of shipmasters was between twenty-five and thirty (Walsh 1994: 38–39); and the average age of common sailors was between twenty-five to twenty-nine (Earle 1998: 86) although this last category of "sailor" defined by Earle as "mariners, foremastmen, cooks, stewards, boys, apprentices, etc". (1998: 86) was likely to have the most variation as it included the youngest apprentice to the oldest cook, a role often given to a disabled or aging seaman and equitable to semi-retirement on the ship. In short, evidence suggests that the lowest ranks were in their late twenties, middle ranking officers might be in their early thirties and commanding officers might be around forty years old; however, it is important to remember that all

---

[3]This explanation accompanies Earle's data on median ages of sailors, officers and captains based on depositions in the collection HCA 13/75–86, a collection also included in my data (Earle 1993: 86–87).

of these data only reflect enlisted and documented sailors, typically of the navy, and fail to acknowledge the servants and slaves that were also likely to have composed the crews of naval, merchant, and independent vessels.

Table 3.1: The average age of seventeenth century ships' crews based on ages of witnesses deposed in court cases, sourced the records of the High Court of the Admiralty at The National Archives, Kew

Average age of deponents	Youngest deponent	Oldest deponent	Number of deponents	Nat. Arch. Collection (date range)
37.4	15	60	68	HCA 1/49 (1622–1633)
34.8	13	58	161	HCA 1/48 (1614–1620)
33.1	12	72	168	HCA 1/47 (1609–1612)
31.3	12	55	187	HCA 1/46 (1601–1607)
31.1	12	70	177	HCA 1/53 (1694–1710)
30.7	13	64	86	HCA 1/50 (1634–1653)
29.6	19	40	22	HCA 1/9 (1666–1674)
29.0	10	58	171	HCA 1/52 (1683–1694)
27.6	12	59	40	HCA 1/14 (1696–1700)
26.2	18	50	21	HCA 1/13 (1692–1696)
Avg.: 31.0	**Avg.: 13.6**	**Avg.: 58.6**	**Total: 1,101**	**Total: 10 collections (1601–1710)**

3.5 Health and mortality

Although generally, standards of personal health and hygiene were lower in the seventeenth century than we might expect today, maintaining personal hygiene aboard ship was particularly challenging in cramped and overcrowded conditions with restricted access to clean water. Despite this, the common sailor's lack of personal hygiene was often considered part of their low character; a sentiment echoed in modern scholarship, for example in Bicheno's observation that Queen Elizabeth's "Royal Navy was largely manned by the dregs of the population, pressed into service along with their dirt, parasites and diseases" (2012: 262). In response to health concerns, the Admiralty put measures in place to help sailors stay healthy in a challenging environment, such as the procedure of issuing seaman's clothes that came into effect in 1623 in an attempt to prevent the spread of disease (Brown 2011: 31). However, measures taken to address the health of common seamen were often underfunded and unsustainable, such as the commission appointed for the care of sick seamen, established in 1664 and discontinued in 1674 (Lincoln 2015: 145).

Personal hygiene might have been improved, but it was the limited access to a balanced and nutritious diet that caused more sickness and disease than any other factor at sea. Contemporary sea-songs such as "The Sailor's Complaint" reflected the impact of a poor diet and Palmer's collection of songs explains that "food was the subject of perennial complaint by seaman. Rotten meat, sour beer, smelly water, cheese hard as wood, biscuits full of weevils: the litany was long, and usually justified" (Palmer 1986: 72). Ships' logs and personal letters corroborate this situation, ranging from the mild complaint of "some bread decay'd" [ADM 106/300/16] to the more commonly recorded practice of condemning stores of food because of their poor condition, e.g., the description of bread, butter and cheese, "all rotten and stinking not fitt for men to eate" [ADM 52/2/5] and "two buts of beer Stinking...[and] 3 bushell of pease and on gall ould musty and roton" [ADM 52/2/3]. The end result of such provisioning meant that sailors often became, at best, "very Weak for want of Sustenance" [HCA 1/99] or, at worst, suffered from food-related disease and death. This may, indeed, explain the profusion of references to long, unspecified illness in contemporary accounts, for example the sailor who "with the sickness [...] Confined so 3 or 4 Months" [HCA 1/99/159] and another who "had been sick Seven or eight Months" [HCA 1/99/127]. Other accounts make specific reference to scurvy which became a pandemic among maritime communities when vessels began to make longer voyages and increase time spent at sea without access to fresh food. In such contexts of food scarcity, it was not unusual for the crew to resort to extreme measures. The curate passenger of a voyage across the Atlantic in 1666 describes the piteous situation that the crew found themselves in after seven months at sea, "after consuming all their provisions, to eat the cats, dogs, and rats that were in the ship... only five remained of four hundred men" [445f.1/486]. Yet, during a time of widespread starvation in the colonies and poverty among rural poor in Britain, the poor state of sailors' health in relation to food security was nothing exceptional.

Sailors' mortality rates are perhaps best introduced with the observation of a passenger on a transatlantic voyage in the late seventeenth century who comments, "tis a sort of miracle we should live amidst so many hardships" [445f.1/486] or the observation of one anonymous sixteenth-century sailor:

> mariners are but slaves to the rest, to moil and to toil day and night [...] and not suffered to sleep or harbour themselves under the decks. For in

fair or foul weather, in storms, sun, or rain, they must pass void of cover
or succour. (cited in Lavery 2009: 28)

Personal communications attest to the routine presence of death aboard ship,
for example one letter observing that "we make nothing of burying 3 men in a
day" [ADM 52/1/8] and another author's stoic comment "One Plamber is dead
and we want two more" [T 70/1/10]. Logbooks give similarly routine accounts of
death, for example, "by Accident one of our men was Drowned" [ADM 51/3797/1],
"faire weather and Little wind. dyed some of our Saylors. The wind varyable
from the SS Et" [ADM 52/3/7] and "got to St. Marys; where the men did mostly
die" [HCA 1/98/262]. Many records refer to the death of unnamed sailors for
unnamed reasons and so we can only assume that such high mortality was common. Bicheno supports this assumption, explaining that sixteenth century military victories were "marred by the death of hundreds of sailors from disease and
want" (Bicheno 2012: 259). Peter Earle provides a potential baseline for mortality
statistics among maritime workers, claiming that due to accident, disease and violence, "around five percent of Bristol's sailors were lost every year" (Earle 1998:
87). In comparison, Jarvis' work on smaller colonial communities with maritime
economies suggests that "between one-third and one-half of all Bermudian men
who went to sea died [at sea]" (Jarvis 2010: 261). Hence, based on the contemporary accounts of routine death and the concurrent opinions of scholars working
on different maritime populations, high mortality rates characterized maritime
communities.

The high mortality rates among sailors may have a link with issues of food
security and personal hygiene, but they also likely derive from military conflict,
the hardships of the work, environmental factors, and personal violence. Heavy
casualties and loss of life among lower classes characterizes the type of military
conflict of the era, and this was no different in the maritime communities that
formed the heart of Britain's fighting forces. Rival nations clamoring to claim
the New World perpetuated various human rights abuses on all sides, e.g., "the
killing of an English ship captain in Havana, merely for having requested water"
[deposition of Henry Wasey, CO 1/23 cited in Hatfield 2016: 12). The hardships of
work on a wooden sailing vessel also potentially increased mortality rates, particularly when, as illustrated by this logbook entry, "the ship was very old and
leaky" [HCA 1/52/76]. Examples of labour-related deaths include "a man putting
the main sheates out [...] drowned" [ADM 52/2/1] and "six men died at their
pumps with hard work" (cited in Adkins & Adkins 2008: 117). Yet the ship may
have been the safest place to be considering the range of environmental hazards
that sailors also had to contend with including storms, yellow fever, malaria,

smallpox, heat stroke and biting insects. The weather was also a major factor affecting mortality, e.g., "There hapned a very great storme [...] Ships bound from Barbadoes for England were all lost none of the said ships nor any of the Marrinrs on board them being ever heare off since to come alive to any place" [HCA 1/14/16]. Also, Gage's (1648) survey of the West Indies describes some of its environmental hazards: "the abundance of gnats is such, which maketh him to take no joy in his voiage, and the heat in some places so intolerable, that many doe die" (p.186). In other accounts, horrific pandemics are described dispassionately e.g., "the small pox still Amonst us" [T/70/1216/13]. Even attempts at leisure were replete with danger in the sailor's everyday life, for example one description of how "the Mariners fell to washing themselves and to swimming" until one was attacked by a shark which "made them suddenly leave off that sport" (Gage 1648: 20). Lastly, ubiquitous violence aboard sailing vessels, either in the guise of discipline, piratical activity, or personal grievance, increased the mortality rates of sailors as evidenced in "The Petition of a woman who prosecuted a master of a ship, for beating her son to Death" [HCA 1/101/225], and the pirate attack in which "his throat was cut and belly burst so that his bowells came out" [HCA 1/52/137]. High mortality was therefore not only an occupational hazard, but also a characteristic of sailors' communities that was exacerbated by cultural and environmental dangers.

Seamen lived in conditions that were physically very close and this promoted the spread of disease. The lowest ranking men in naval warships were assigned 14 inches width to hang a hammock, although the spaces were alternated by watch and so this effectively doubled to 28 inches if the adjacent space was free (Adkins & Adkins 2008: 188–189). In such confined spaces, illness often spread by contact, e.g., in the seventeenth century large-scale outbreaks and epidemics affected naval fleets, such as the typhus outbreaks of 1625 and 1627 (Brown 2011: 31). The idea of sick ships' crews was no new concept however, throughout the middle ages epidemics of the Black Death that were associated with ships and trading ports of the Mediterranean (Brown 2011: 2). In fact, the spread of infectious diseases could be interpreted as a somewhat pejorative metaphor of language contact and feature transmission among port communities as in both respects the physical proximity of mariners are key to the process of transmission. To explain further, the bubonic plague spread by the bite of the *Pullex irritans* flea which had been infected by the black rat *Yersinia pestis* (more widely known as "the ship rat") that infested merchant ships and often came ashore even when the mariners did not. Proximity was critical to the transmission in much the same way that language contact is crucial to feature transmission. The rat did not have to be in close or prolonged proximity to port workers in order for the flea to have an effect; and it is possible that language features could similarly have jumped ship even when mariners remained on-board. In another example, Yellow Fever, itself named for the yellow quarantine flag that would have been flown on an infected ship, after being first reported outside Africa in Barbados in the mid seventeenth century quickly spread around the trading ports of the Caribbean, to New York in 1668, Philadelphia and Charleston in 1690, and Boston in 1691 in addition to a southward spread to the trading ports of Colombia, Ecuador, and Peru (Brown 2011: 116). Just as infectious diseases proliferated among ships crews and spread outward to coastal communities and inland waterways before affecting land-locked areas, it is entirely possible that language features were making the same journey.

3.6 Family and marital status

Sailors were not always the single and free young men that stereotypes perpetuate; they had strong familial bonds and many worked hard to provide for their wives and children. Jarvis notes that, particularly in Bermuda, kinship defined the ownership and operation of the short-distance trade that made up the majority of the island's maritime activity (2010: 121). Evidence of strong family ties, mostly retrieved through personal letters, suggests the value and influence of kinship among sailors, e.g., a letter from Evan Jones to his father that states "I believe you shall not hear from me again this 5 years [...] but my Duty to you and Love to brothers and sisters and service to my Unkle" [HCA 1/98/183] and another that refers to the writer's "dutey to my father and mother and my Love to my sisters and brothers" [HCA 1/98/182]. The words "duty" and "service" in such personal letters suggests not only a respectful tone in comparison to the word "love" used when referring to siblings, but also potentially refers to the older generation's investment in the voyage. Such an interpretation is supported by Walsh's observation that sailors of the English colonies were often bred into service at sea and supported by a father or an uncle until they married in their mid-twenties (1994: 28–34). He further explains that, as a result, contact with and duty to the parental generation was paramount for many sailors, so much so that it was sometimes explicitly stated in ships accounts that wages should be paid to the sailor's father or widowed mother (Walsh 1994: 34). In this context, it is perhaps not surprising that, among miscellaneous documents of the Admiralty between 1620 and 1750, various letters addressed to fathers express duty and service alongside more traditional loving sentiments intended for sisters, brothers, cousins, nieces and nephews.

Sailors served at sea alongside family members. Jarvis (2010) gives various accounts of small Bermuda sloops that were manned by kinship groups, and this practice also extended to larger vessels. Evidence of what seems to be fathers and sons serving together shows up in ships' muster documents, for example "Robert Hartley (1st) and Robert Hartley (2nd)" [HCA 1/99/3/4–5] and in another vessel, "William Williamson" (1st) and "William Williamson" (2nd) [HCA 1/99/3/11–13]. Some court documentation also suggests the commonality of fathers and sons serving together, such as the decision of the court in one Williamsburg trial on 14 August 1729 when "they agreed to discharge the deponent and his servant, who had all along passed for his son" [HCA 1/99]. Brothers also served alongside each other, such as James and Henry Adams who testify in a piracy trial 23 October 1699 [HCA 1/14/166] and Valentine Roderigo who testifies in a court of Bahama Island 1722 that he was travelling to join his brother in Havana [HCA 1/99]. Not only immediate kin, but also the wives of mariners joined their husbands at sea. Brown explains, that many wives of common sailors were "smuggled aboard without the knowledge of the officers, [in addition to] [...] the wives of warrant officers, such as the gunner, carpenter, and purser" (Brown 2011: 95). The fact that the East India company forbade their officers from taking their wives to sea in the early voyages of the seventeenth century attests to the commonality of the practice as well (Fury 2015: 16). Court documentation also records the presence of wives at sea, for example: Martha Farley who accompanied her husband aboard a pirate ship and stands trial alongside him [HCA 1/99/8]; Elizabeth Trengove, described as a passenger of the *Onflow* accompanying her husband, Captain Trengove [HCA 1/99/79]; and the unnamed woman mentioned in the description of how one sailor "went down in a canoa with his wife" [HCA 1/99/7]. Additionally, the repeated use of the title "sea wife" in court appears to refer to women who accompanied their husbands to sea, for example: Anne Seayford [HCA 1/47/76], Alice Reeve and Anne Fladds [HCA 1/47/312], Elizabeth Leech [HCA 1/48/26], Ellen Rippingham [HCA 1/48/27], Margarett Weedes [HCA 1/48/29], and Dorothie Cooper [HCA 1/48/240], who are all referred to as "sea wife" in court records. In sum, sailors may have been accompanied to sea by a variety of family members, particularly in small sailing craft owned and operated by kinship groups, but even in large ships, sailors may have worked alongside fathers, uncles, brothers and wives.

Even when unaccompanied by their wives at sea, male sailors of age were likely to be married. Miscellaneous documentation of the Admiralty collection includes numerous letters that sailors wrote home to their wives expressing loving sentiments, such as this example sent in 1607 that not only elicits communication in return, but also expresses earnest desire to be reunited:

> My dere Love this is to satisfie you that I am on bord in gottenberg and came safe over [...] I am in very good health [...] and am thies day going with a small vessel for kopon hagen and hoping to get thither with five days and as soon as I kan get thether schall I write to my der Loving wife that my dearest may know how to send Letters to mee...[I am] thinking pon by dearest Love how god shi as to mee, and is me so alloen amongst a Compani of bad pipoll and when I doe soe Consider of it then it Cutts mee to the very hart [...] I am not at rest [...] for I can get a llatter from my dere Love [signed] your derest Loving husband. [HCA 1/101/527]

This type of letter is often accompanied in the archival records with a reply from the sailor's wife with similar sentiments, for example "Deare And Loving husband [...] with Dayly wishes for your Company" [HCA 1/98/116]; "Deare Jacob [to let you know] How it is with mee and your Children" [HCA 1/98/118]; and "[I] shall ever prey for your safe retorne & am your ever dutyfull & loving wife" [HCA 1/98/51–52]. Despite the stereotype of the profligate wanderer, it is clear that many sailors advocated for marriage, as expressed in the advice to a friend drafted on the back page of the *Pideaux*'s logbook "when you gett home that I would advise you to Mary with your old sweethart Elizabeth Raglis and not to lust after other women" [HCA 1/99/50]. Another married sailor describes a friend: "hi wants a vry god wife but hi is afraid [...] of thirty yers of age" [HCA 1/101/528] before he requests his own wife to find his friend a suitable match. Although the majority of letters that are recoverable reflect the sentiments of literate midshipmen and commanding officers, there is no reason to assume that less literate sailors on board did not also marry and cherish women in their lives. Indeed, evidence of lower-ranking married sailors is recoverable from Admiralty records, e.g., depositions such as Lewis Innes who refers to his wife [HCA 1/99] another anonymous sailor who testifies that "he hath lived at Dunkirk abt one year & a halfe and hath a wife & family living there" [HCA 1/52/100] and the simple testimony of another that "he had a family" [HCA 1/99/85]. Other documentation also corroborates the marital status of common sailors, for example, the letter that John Morris dictated on his deathbed after being savagely beaten by the ship's mate to his "Ever Loufing wief" entrusting her with the information and witness testimony to challenge the chief mate after his death and signed with the shaky initials of the barely literate [HCA 1/52/51]. Wills and inventories in Bermuda also list items that sailors gave to their wives (Jarvis 2010: 214) perhaps explaining the presence of a "a pair of women's shoes" among the contents of a sailor's chest itemized in court [HCA 1/99/8]. Additionally, Brown notes, it was common practice for a low-ranking sailor to have his clothes and other personal possessions returned to his wife in the event of death at sea (Brown 2011: 26). Hence, although fragmentary and incomplete, there is sufficient evidence to show that not only literate classes of sailors married but also that many lower-ranking workers on the ship were married men too.

The wives of these sailors may have formed a critical support network in port communities. Some wives managed a variety of caregiving responsibilities. For example, Admiralty records of a sailor's trial dated 17 December 1687 describe "a Woman coming into Court, and declaring that she had kept his Child and been at 20l. charge" [HCA 1/12/111]. Additionally, among the miscellaneous documents about the ship's business, Thomas Shaffer, master of the ship *Exchange*, kept a receipt from Anne Morrey, wife of (sailor) Richard Morrey for the tuition and care of his daughter [HCA 1/101/543]. This same wife also housed and cared for Thomas Shaffer and his companion Richard Isby for which they paid "at least twenty pounds for their maintenance" and she later petitions the Admiralty for money expended while Shaffer and Isby were both imprisoned [HCA 1/12/99–110]. In the same collection of court documents, money is claimed on behalf of the wife of (sailor) Mr Lowman for expenses incurred by one "Master Porter" during his imprisonment in the Marshalsea navy prison [HCA 1/12/110]. These petitions attest to the financial capacity of sailors' wives, many of whom managed their husbands' business and household affairs during their extended absences (Jarvis 2010: 115–116). And, in a time where women did not typically manage finances and estates, one letter of 1699 addressed to Mrs Whaley sends "youer husbondes will which so is left wholey to you and yr Child" [HCA 1/98/171]. Such references suggest that these women were not passive victims of their husbands' absence but that they potentially assumed important roles in the management of their husbands' affairs. In addition, sailors' wives were often well informed of their husbands' movements and so were routinely called to give evidence in court, e.g., the deposition of Elizabeth Shaw, wife of sailor Edward Shaw on 20 July 1699 [HCA 1/14/161]. Even when not called to testify, wives were enmeshed in the type of maritime activity that ended in court trials. Alexander Wyatt, accused of piracy, is arrested with four condemning letters in his possession written in his own handwriting, two of which are addressed to Mrs. Elizabeth Lesters and Mrs. Elizabeth Guott [HCA 1/99]. Thus, evidence shows many sailors were married to women whose contribution to the maritime world they lived in extended well beyond the imagined role of the passive and poverty-stricken wife.

Evidence that poor sailors not only married, but also had children, abounds in Admiralty records. Such records include the many petitions for wages made to the High Court of the Admiralty from widows of slain men. Examples of such cases include the 1683 petition of Mary Bush, a boatswain's widow, described as "a desolate and very poore Widow with five Small Children" whose husband was killed in a quarrel with a commanding officer [HCA 1/11/111] and the joint petition on behalf of eighteen widows and their children whose husbands died in the military action of the *Nightingale*, including Elizabeth Sydoy described as a "widdow having two small children in a miserable poore condition for the loss of William Sydoy her husband" [ADM 106/300/88]. Other records instigated by the sailors themselves refer to their children, e.g., wounded sailor James Kell's request for payment on behalf of "my wife and three children", [ADM 106/300/62] and that having failed, his request to return home "that I maybe inabled to maintaine my wife and family" [ADM 106/300/64]. Sailors who may not have been able to write requests or recruit others to do it for them have alternatively left us evidence of their marital status and children in court depositions e.g., "the Prisoner said he has a Wife and Family" [HCA 1/99/32], "talking pathetically of his Wife and Child" [HCA 1/99/61], "had a Wife and five Children" [HCA 1/99/92], "used to lament about a wife and children he had left at Bristol" [HCA 1/99/133], and "the prisoner replied he has a Wife and Child" [HCA 1/99/167]. Unfortunately, many of these depositions that provide evidence of sailors' children also suggest the dire poverty that they lived in.

Measures taken to mitigate the poverty and wants of destitute sailors' wives and children also attest to the fact that they existed. Thirty-eight alms houses at Deptford, established circa 1671 proposed "To house poor aged seamen, or their Widows" and naval regulations stipulated that "A percentage of prize money was to be appropriated for the relief of the sick and the aid of the dependents of the dead" (cited in Brown 2011: 41). Individual commanders also made pledges to the families of their enlisted men e.g., Admiral Henrick Fleming who promised that in the event that one of his sailors "received some incurable injury or has lost his life, I shall with the greatest energies (in so far as God spares me my life) help him, his wife and children" (cited in Brown 2011: 35). The number of orphaned children of sailors in Liverpool was so great that the city took measures to provide for the population (Litter 1999: 86) and, even when children were not recognized as sailors' progeny, the number of children with congenital (hereditary) syphilis appears to bear witness to the maritime professions of their fathers in places like Portsmouth and Plymouth (Brown 2011: 186). In short, recoverable evidence from court records, letters, petitions and miscellaneous documents debunks the popular stereotype of the single profligate sailor and corroborates the findings of scholars of maritime communities that sailors of all ranks commonly married and had children.

3.7 Social status

The social status of sailors was principally determined by their rank aboard the vessel. Although the size of a vessel and its purpose determined the size of the crew and also dictated the roles and therefore ranks of its enlisted men, the three-tier social strata established by the navy served as the customary hierarchy aboard most sea-going vessels of the early colonial Atlantic and Caribbean. This three-tier hierarchy composed of a small (2%) upper class, a moderate (34%) middle class, and a majority (64%) lower class, based on the National Maritime Museum's data on a typical English 100-gun ship of the line in the late seventeenth century.

The upper class generally mirrored class structure in British society at the time and included the highest-ranking commissioned officers, such as admiral, captain, lieutenants, and master who were eligible not by experience but by nepotism and the distinction of being "gentlemen". Adkins and Adkins note that "a career in the navy was particularly attractive to younger sons who were not in line to inherit landed estates and titles" (2008: 63) and thus many entered the profession with little-to-no experience or interest in maritime affairs. The incompetency of some of these commanding officers was sometimes evident to their enlisted men, e.g., one deponent testifies that he "verrily believeth that the capt after his late business at Legorne, was incapable of bearing Command, and was governed wholy by the Lieut" [HCA 1/9/155]. In recognition of the problems that incompetence perpetuated in the naval fleets, commissioned officers had to pass formal examinations stipulated in the Test Act of 1673. In addition to knowledge of maritime affairs and navigation, this act required an oath of allegiance with recognition of supremacy, and additionally specified that the applicant must receive sacrament by the Church of England (Adkins & Adkins 2008: 32), thus perpetuating a small commanding class with religious and political uniformity. Once among this officer class, advancement came not by achievement but in accordance with the mortality rate of more senior officers. The upper class also included a subordinate cohort of non-commissioned warrant-officers such as the boatswain, purser, surgeon, gunner and carpenter who were enlisted for a predetermined period according to their professional capacities.

The middle class formed an ideological and physical buffer between higher-ranking officers and common seamen. It typically included three distinct groups of workers: firstly, petty officers such as midshipmen, coxswain, quartermaster, and gunners' mates; secondly, tradesmen such as armorer, cook, gunsmith, and sailmaker; and lastly, combatants such as master-at-arms, soldiers and sentries, collectively restructured as the Royal Marines after 1802. The rank of Boy First Class (essentially an officer in training) also pertained to this middle-tier. The significant number of tradesmen aboard the ship reflected the period in which little was mechanized. One passenger on a transatlantic vessel in 1667 notes, "it was pleasant to see our ship, where every tradesman worked at his trade, as if he had been in his shop; there were gunsmiths, armorers, butchers, shoemakers, tailors, coopers, and cooks" [445f.1/510]. Combatant personnel were also a potentially large group, e.g., the logbook of the *St Andrew*, a ship of 96 guns with an estimated crew of between 500 and 600, records on May 4 1693, "last night two companys of soldiers came aboard from portsmouth containing 120 men" [ADM 52/2/3]. Significant numbers of tradesmen and military combatants in addition to the supervisory workers, meant that this middle tier was potentially a large group of professionals whose work on board was not primarily connected with sailing but rather the services that the ship, its cargo and crew required to function and a composite unit.

The lower class included workers such as able seamen, ordinary seamen, landsmen, servants, and second and third class boys (over and under 15 years of age, respectively). This group performed the majority of manual labor on board the vessel with respect to rigging and managing the sails, loading and unloading cargo and ballast, cleaning and keeping the vessel operational and watertight, rowing small craft, and climbing the masts to act as lookouts. The workers in this social strata were collectively referred to as "the men" or known by synecdoche that dehumanized them, e.g., "hands", or by locative phrases that prioritized the ship, e.g., "before the mast", "of the lower deck". Even among this group, the formal hierarchy was highly stratified, determined by experience and wages corresponding to each rank. Upward mobility, although possible within this lower-class tier as a result of gained experience, was minimal to impossible into the middle-class tier.

Some contemporary commanders, such as Francis Drake, encouraged a certain amount of empathy across social strata, for example in his requirement "I must have the gentlemen haul and draw with the mariners, and the mariner with the gentleman" (Drake, cited in Bicheno 2012: 141). And among communities of pirates, the common practice of granting shares to enrolled crewmembers, signing articles of compliance, and voting on major navigational decisions meant that the formal three-tier hierarchy was less rigid. One pirate encounter dated July 27 1699 shows the Captain's consideration of the crew before giving command, "one of the Quartermasters came and asked the Captain whether he would to sea, hi demanded what the Company were inclined to doe, who was answerd, they were willing" [CO 5/1411/639]. Even the notorious pirate Henry Every was voted into command, as illustrated in the testimony "they all chose Capt Every to be their Commandr" [HCA 1/53/10]. Yet, pirates often took crew members unwillingly and this likely created a sub-category in the social hierarchy that was equitable to indenture or slavery, for example, John Spake, aged 19 years and taken by a pirate ship, describes in his testimony dated 10 September 1696 how he was "a kind of a slave to wash their cloathes [...] and socks and light their pipes" [HCA 1/53/13]. This sub-category may have been equivalent to the group of unpaid workers (women, indentured laborers and slaves) aboard mercantile and navy ships who were largely occupied with individual food preparation, laundry, and menial chores. Earle explains that masters could recruit poor "apprentices" unpaid and bound for seven to nine years, and even when apprenticeships were sought and paid for by fathers keen to get their sons into the navy, "apprenticeship amounted to little more than several years of unpaid drudgery" (Earle 1998: 22). Thus, even in pirate ships, rank determined by type of recruitment and assigned wages established social status and ranged from the highest-ranking commissioned officer to the lowest unpaid workers in a rigid hierarchy that mirrored British society at the time.

3.8 Financial standing

In theory, enlisted sailors were either paid a monthly wage or assigned an amount per voyage corresponding to their rank (see Table 3.2). Higher ranking officers could also augment their wages by commissions and a share in freight. In addition, any sailor might augment his basic wages by selling personal items, a practice so common that a charter for the Royal African Company in 1675 includes a statement prohibiting it [CO/268–1/15].

Common sailors might seek inflated wartime pay on merchant vessels, but were more likely to suffer deductions in the guise of fines and purchases of clothes and drink. Earle notes "these deductions occasionally left a sailor with no pay at all, as could disasters as shipwreck or capture" (1998: 82). Furthermore, many of the common sailors who were enlisted and owed wages, if they had not already lost all their pay to fines, charges or disaster, were often paid intermittently, given insufficient money, or had their wages indefinitely withheld. Other sailors were not even on the pay-scale, such as newly-recruited boys gaining experience, women, indentured laborers and slaves.

Table 3.2: Wages of sailors in shillings per month according to rank in the 1680s. Shilling data sourced from Earle 1998: 84 and converted using The National Archives' Currency Converter tool
Currency converter tool available at http://www.nationalarchives.gov.uk/currency/results.asp#mid

Rank	sh/mth (1680)	£/mth (modern)	$/mth (modern)
Master	120	501.24	662.64
Mate (Petty Officer)	55–100	229.74 – 417.70	303.72 – 552.20
Quartermaster, Gunner's mate, Bosun's mate, Gunner, Bosun	30–40	125.31 – 167.08	165.66 – 220.88
Common Seaman	25	104.43	138.06

Maritime trading operations often suffered from a lack of solvency. Perpetual lack of money was one of the reasons that it became customary to defer sailors' wages; the other reason was that this practice, in theory, also deterred individuals from jumping ship or turning pirate. Wages owed was, therefore, often used as a case for the defense of sailors accused of piracy, e.g., the accused man who claims "He says he has served 16 or 17 years in the King's Service and [...] he has Money due from the Company" [HCA 1/99/129] and another who is acquitted based the fact that "he had 14 months Pay due [...] therefore unlikely to be a volunteer" [HCA 1/99/47]. Such testimony corroborates Fusaro's observation that "delays in payments were the norm" in the international naval and merchant fleets of the seventeenth century (2015: 21) and also suggests that the claim, "seamen were paid... at least six months in arrears" (Adkins & Adkins 2008: 169) might be a conservative estimate. Daniel Goodall explains that as late as 1801:

> The custom at the time prevalent in the navy was, that no person got any pay until he had been over six months in the service [and] [...] the first six months' was always retained until the ship was paid off [...] when a vessel of war was first commissioned her crew received no pay whatsoever until

they had been twelve months aboard of her. (cited in Adkins & Adkins 2008: 365)

In effect, the Admiralty's strategy was financially astute, hedging its losses in anticipation of high mortality rates, sailors abandoning ship or otherwise leaving service. However, in human terms, it meant that those enlisted sailors (and their dependents) who could not rely on family wealth or private commissions suffered abject poverty, and this was particularly felt upon demobilization when they could no longer depend on a hammock and ship's rations to sustain them. In such situations, captains often aided in petitioning the Admiralty on their behalf, e.g., Captain James Jenefer wrote a letter dated 3 June 1674 to higher-ranking naval officials on behalf of his crew to "beg your favor that their monneys may be payed them as soone as can be" [ADM 106/300/23]. In another example of the same year, Captain William Hennesy's letter to the Admiralty asks "about the pay of the ship [of which] I know not, having received none as yet from the clarke [...] although demanded of him before" [ADM 106/300/35]. A few days later, on 17 January, he writes another letter pleading on behalf of three specific men who are being withheld pay, one of whom apparently as a punishment for leaving the ship to seek provisions [ADM 106/300/37]. Other service-providers, such as ship's carpenter Moses Porter, seems to accept the futility of asking for pay and instead seeks redress in the form of goods; he testifies "they having not paid him some Fraight that was due to him" [HCA 1/12/111]. Sailors knew that delays in the payment of wages and prize money could last years and even when higher-ranking officials sympathized, their efforts were insufficient. For instance, Samuel Pepys, who petitioned for a range of reforms in the Admiralty in his position as Secretary to the Navy Board and later Secretary of the Admiralty, thought that it could "never be well with the navy till poor seaman can be paid *once a year* at furthest" (cited in Palmer 1986: 62, my italics) a conclusion he was forced to make presumably as a result of the petitions he encountered on a daily basis, such as the description of one "horrible Crowd and lamentable moan of the poor seaman that he starving in the streets for lack of money [...] a whole hundred of them fallowed us, some cursing, some swearing, and some praying to us" (cited in Lincoln 2015: 145). In short, although higher-ranking crew may have managed adequately, the financial status of the common sailor was likely to be either at poverty level or in destitution as a result of low wages that were perpetually in arrears if they were paid at all.

Incomplete and indefinitely deferred payments led to strike action, collective petitions, social unrest, and rioting both aboard ship and in port communities. Yet there was little to be done. The navy in the 1660s was in turmoil after rapid expansion as a result of the 1651 Navigation Acts and the 1652 Articles of War and, after years of neglect and amassing debt, the navy owed 1.25 million pounds and some ships in commission went unpaid for 4 years (Lincoln 2015: 144). In some situations pay was outright denied, such as detailed in a case regarding a pilot whose services were commissioned by the *Essex Prize* but, after the work, "major James Willson & Capt Samuel Bush will in no wise satisfy nor pay the petitioner for his services done" [CO 5/1411/650]. The financial fallout of the Admiralty's actions would impact sailors for more than a century, culminating in the mass mutinies of South England in the late 1700s. Yet even in times of peaceful service, tensions were anticipated in letters to the Admiralty from commanding officers, such as this one dated 12 March 1700 that warns, "there hath been but a small sume assigned them, and the course of payments being seaventeen months in arrear" [SP 42/6] and another's observation that "most men discourse for mony" [ADM 106/288/31]. Such discourse often led to threatened or actual strike action, evidence for which is based on data retrievable from court depositions, such as the cook who states, "if he did not pay his work before that he could not come at it" [HCA 1/52/46] and the crew who "would not suffer ought of the shippes Cargoe to be unladon to lighton her ere they had their wages" [E134/34Chas2/Mich36]. The aftermath of this strike action was often actual or perceived mutiny[4] and could end in imprisonment or capital punishment for the unpaid workers. One example of such a situation is described in a letter dated 10 December 1700 when a group of sailors claimed not only the wages due to them but also additional pay for being so heavily overworked on the journey:

> they all demanded their pay for the time being on board ships, as likewize short allowance money for the time they were six to four mens allowance... they [the Admiralty] could not give them more [...] at which they all made Genll mutiny [...] after 4 or 5 hours debate part of them surrendered themselves [...] the major part of them are in prisons (some of them being escaped) to morrow my lord intends to try them [...] they may come under the penalty of every tenth man to be hanged. [SP 42/6]

Certainly for the Admiralty, imprisoning men for social unrest and potentially even hanging them for mutiny was a more viable alternative to paying them. Admiralty records abound with petitions from sailors who have been imprisoned for indefinite periods of time, many without formal charges, who plead for charges

---

[4] "Mutiny" was defined loosely at the time as any collective action contrary to superior ranking officials.

to be brought and a trial date set before sickness and starvation resolve the Admiralty's problem by bringing about their early death, e.g., one petitioner is described as "in prison two months aboute, without any procedure made against him...[and] is reduced to such condition as he is ready to starve" [HCA 1/10/110]. Another petitioner asks "that you here would pledge either to put a speedy period to your poor petitioners confinemt by bringing on his tryall or to admitt him to Bayle or grant him to accustomed allowance" [HCA 1/14/164]. Such harsh reality perhaps renders more understandable the decisions of the multitude of sailors who turned to piracy towards the turn of the seventeenth century, such as the men who are described in one letter who "got away with the ship — for their wages" [HCA 1/53/12]. Indeed, if sailors wanted compensation for their work, the only guaranteed way to get it may have been to take it by force.

3.9 Place of origin

3.9.1 Difficulties in determining sailors' place of origin

Determining sailors' places of origin is seemingly critical to any study that attempts to determine the language forms they were most likely to use in their composite communities. However, the difficulty of obtaining this information is pronounced as there were no standard measures in place during the period in question to collect this data and there is a dearth of scholarship on the subject. Earle, one scholar who has attempted to investigate these communities, summarizes, "very little is known about the lives of these men. English historians have tended to neglect sailors...[and] little has been done on where the sailors came from" (1993: 75). Yet we do know that workers came to the ship through a variety of methods (discussed in §3.2) and although some of these may have included data on collection points, many did not. Furthermore, data collection was often inconsistent or lacking the type of uniformity that enables critical comparison. To illustrate, documented with the court records of a 1693 piracy trial, some of the deponents are described by nationality, e.g. "Thomas Jones, An Irishman", some by profession, e.g., Thomas Briant, "Gunner of the Charity of London", some by port of origin, e.g., "Tho. Howlis late come of the Deptford", and for others there is no data provided at all [HCA 1/13/11]. And even for the sailors who provided information on their origins, the data may not have been sufficient to determine what type of language forms they used, e.g., one sailor deposes that "his Father was a French man and his mother an Irish woman" yet gives no information about where he was raised [HCA 1/13/97] and another group of sailors are described whose origins and language use can only be guessed at based on the description of their recruitment that "they had been ship'd on board a portuguese vessel by an Irish Master at Lisbon who affirmed the sd vessel to be English" [HCA 1/99]. Yet sailors were a significant population group, estimated by Jarvis to have been at least 75,000 men for the British Atlantic alone by the end of the period under study (Jarvis 2010: 252); and this statistic does not include any women at sea nor is it likely to include a whole subordinate group of servants, slaves, indentured workers, and non-enlisted children whose work is not reflected in official ship's records. Although deriving the origins and thus asserting the type of language spoken when dealing with such a disparate and large-ranging group of workers will always be problematic, the following two sections present the archival evidence and scholarship that speak to their potential places of origin within and outside the British Isles.

3.9.2 Sailors born in the British Isles

Large numbers of sailors on British vessels were likely to have been born in the British Isles and considered "British" for the purposes of naval records. I accept that "British" is problematic word as it refers not only to a geographical space but also a political entity and an individual ideology that has changed over time. However, I use the term "British" in its geographical sense to refer to the British Isles, including the geographical islands of Great Britain (England, Scotland, Wales), Ireland, and all of the more than 1.000 smaller islands of the archipelago. Litter explains, "the British have a long tradition as a seafaring nation and it would be unusual for a family not to include at least one member who went to sea among its ranks" (1999: 125). To get an idea of the demographic profile of British-born sailors, we can look to census data for some idea of regional distribution. The census of 1582 recorded the numbers of sailors in every parish in England (Bicheno 2012: 246) and another in 1792 recorded the same data. Notable trends are that the Northeast (Northumberland, Durham, Yorkshire and Lincolnshire) and the Southwest (Dorset, Devon, Cornwall, Somerset, and Gloucester) had consistently supplied large numbers of sailors; the Northwest (Cheshire, Lancashire and Cumberland) and London saw a significant increase in the number of sailors in 1792, potentially owing to the activity around the Thames and Liverpool; and East Anglia (shown as East of England on the map, including Suffolk, Norfolk, and Cambridgeshire) and the Southeast (Essex and Kent) saw a significant drop in the number of sailors between the two dates, see Table 3.3 and accompanying map in Figure 3.2. Thus, although this data is highly generalized, it does suggest that in the early colonial period under study, there would have been a large number of sailors from the Northeast and Southwest of England who may have come from generations of seafarers involved in the coal trade and colonial trade with Ireland, respectively, and a significant and increasing number of new recruits from regions around the busy port cities of Liverpool and London. This assertion is corroborated by the data from over 1,500 depositions of individuals for whom place of origin is recorded and who gave testimony between the dates of 1620 and 1750 in the High Courts of the Admiralty. Over 70% of these depositions name port and river-trade towns of the Northeast e.g., York, Newcastle upon Tyne and Whitby; the Southwest, e.g., Dartmouth, Plymouth, and Bristol; and parishes of London, e.g., Deptford, Aldgate, Wapping, Shadwell, Greenwich, Whitechapel, East Smithfield and St. James' (based on Earle's (1998) data using collections HCA 1/9–14, HCA 1/46–53). Moreover, Earle claims that based on data in the court records collection HCA 13/75–86, three quarters of sailors were born within sight of the sea (1993: 82) thus narrowing down the scope of probable places of origin to large coastal and river-trade towns of the regions indicated in the census data.

Table 3.3: Regional distribution of British-born sailors based on census data, adapted from Earle (1998: 76)

Region	1582 sailors	1582 percent	1792 sailors	1792 percent
Northeast	2,180	14	18,197	21
East Anglia	2,952	18	4,820	6
Southeast	1,888	12	4,347	5
London	1,325	8	30,200	34
South	983	6	2,414	3
Southwest	5,461	34	11,658	13
Wales	790	5	3,296	4
Northwest	536	3	12,637	14
Total	16,115	100	87,568	100

Although maritime laborers came from ports all over the British Isles, London was the capital of the expanding Royal Navy, with Liverpool and Bristol serving as second-tier ports and Greenock, Hull, Plymouth, Southampton, and Portsmouth playing vital roles in shipbuilding, merchant shipping and slave trading supported by an emerging inter-colonial trade with bases in Leith, Dublin, Waterford, Cork, and Ballyhack (Jarvis 2010: 259). As a result of London's cen-

Figure 3.2: Regions of Britain corresponding to the regional distribution data in Table 3.3. CC-BY-SA https://commons.wikimedia.org/wiki/User:TUBS

tral role in an expanding maritime nation, the Thames and the Medway became prime spots for recruitment and impressment during the Second and Third Dutch Wars of 1665–1667 and 1672–1674 respectively ()Earle1998 and this geographical imbalance is reflected in verse "Poor Londoners when coming home they / Surely will be pressed all / We've no such fear when home we steer, with / prizes under convoy, / We'll frolic round all Bristol town, sweet liberty / We enjoy" (cited in Earle 1998: 202). Hence, even in popular song, the heavy representation of London among the navy was recognized at the time, and thus we can surmise that sailors from other ports were represented in greater numbers in the merchant service and private enterprise. This may explain why the Southwest has become popularly associated with piracy. Individuals' depositions attest to the agency of Welsh men in pirate vessels, e.g., one letter dated 27 July 1699 from a navy commander describes how the pirate captain he encountered "was a Welshman on Glammorgan shire, his name John James" [CO 5/1411/638]. We know that Henry Morgan, Howell Davis and Bart Roberts were Welsh; Ben Avery was from Devon and Edward Teach from Bristol ()Bicheno2012 and this trend of West Country pirates was driven into the popular imagination through the Devonshire setting of the fictional *Admiral Benbow* Inn of Black Hill Cove and the presumed Devonshire accents of characters in Robert Louis Stevenson's (1883) *Treasure Island*. An association perpetuated by the subsequent Hollywood tradition of West Country accents among pirates in the age of sail, represented as an elongated and rhotic back vowel for comedic purposes. In sum, and acknowledging the potentially erroneous and simplistic influence of popular fiction, certain regions may have been more heavily represented in different types of vessel; Londoners in the Royal Navy, southerners and westerners in privateering and piracy, and northerners in the merchant service.

The National Maritime Museum's "Nelson Navy Nation" exhibition proclaims that an average of 51% of sailors in the British Royal Navy were English over the period of 1688 to 1815. Recruits from the other countries around the British Isles included crew from Ireland (19%), Scotland (10%), and Wales (3%). Qualitative evidence from individual letters and depositions corroborates the presence of sailors from these regions in naval, merchant and privateer fleets. Captain Sharlands informs the Admiralty in a letter dated 13 April 1673, "for yet my dwelling is in Dublin in Ireland" [ADM 106/288/25], the defendant in one trial of 16 August 1727 declares in his defence that "he came of a good family his father being a Merchant in Dublin" [HCA 1/99/8], and among the court documents of another trial 17 of the 23 men accused of turning pirate are described as "Irishmen" [HCA 1/13/11]. Both Cork (Ireland) and Sandwich in Orkney (Scotland) are listed as places of origin for two of the names among a crew of 16 men on trial [HCA 1/99/177], and Claire McLoughlin (2013) stresses the importance of how Irish and Scots neutrality may have facilitated trade between warring kingdoms as well as highlighting the ingenuity of Scottish merchants who took advantage of the situation in the early seventeenth century, thus potentially equipping English-owned vessels with Scottish crews for commercial advantage. However, depositions of British sailors between the period of 1665 and 1720 suggest that although Scots sailors were the largest minority of those deposed (92 depositions), they were still significantly outnumbered by English sailors (1,241 depositions), based on HCA 13/75–86 tabulated in Earle 1993: 81. This suggests that overall the National Maritime Museum's assertion that a majority of sailors were English still holds true.

3.9.3 Sailors not born in the British Isles

The English merchant service of the early colonial period employed significant numbers of sailors born outside of the British Isles, a trend that motivated one of the clauses in the Navigation Acts of 1651 requiring at least three quarters of the crew in specified inter-colonial trading vessels to be British. However, the meaning of "British" was reinterpreted under the scope of the Commonwealth to include any person born in any territory of the British Empire, typically of European descent but also including peoples of African and Indigenous descent. This might explain how Bermudian vessels could still be in compliance with the Navigation Acts when, in 1740 "black seaman occupied more than a quarter of the berths on most sloops [and by 1743]...at least half of the crew aboard all four Bermudian vessels in port were black" (Jarvis 2010: 148). The reality was that many of these African-descended workers, if born in Bermuda, were considered "British" under the terms of the commonwealth. This extended interpretation of what it meant to be British permitted merchant vessels to continue sourcing crew from various colonial locations around the expanding empire, most specifically the colonies of North America and the Caribbean. The navy also benefitted from the cheap labor derived from impressment in these regions; Adkins and Adkins explain, "anyone born before the [United States] Declaration of independence in 1776 was formerly a British subject" (2008: 51) and therefore not only acceptable for employment as a British crewmember aboard merchant vessels, but also eligible for naval impressment. The presence of these American-born British subjects is evident in archival documentation. Various depositions refer to American places of origin, e.g., one deponent who is described as coming from Boston, New England [HCA 1/99/177], another who is described as "going from Virginia to North Carolina the place where he Lives" [HCA 1/99/6], and a third who describes "his house in Carolina" [HCA 1/99/5]. These colonial recruitment grounds were rich pickings. Although colonial towns were small by comparison to trading towns like London, Liverpool and Bristol, they were necessarily more oriented to the sea. Jarvis estimates that sailors made up 20 to 25% of Boston, New York, and Philadelphia's residents compared to only between 2 to 4% of London or Bristol's population, and places like Nantucket depended so heavily on the whaling industry that the majority of residents were likely to have been able seafarers (Jarvis 2010: 259). Similarly, Walsh's work on the composition of the merchant fleets of Salem, Massachusetts indicates that appreciable numbers of mariners listed in the Corwin account books from 1667–1678 lived in Salem or neighboring coastal towns in Essex County (Walsh 1994: 32–33). Such data indicate the significant contribution of sailors born in the colonies to British naval and merchant ships in the early colonial period and also serve as a reminder that we cannot assume that a "British" subject of the early colonial period was born in one of the countries of the political UK as we might assume today.

In addition to the wider scope of the term "British" that permitted recruitment from the colonies, both merchant and naval vessels routinely enlisted foreign crewmembers, and took on foreign servants, passengers and non-paid workers. Indeed, this context may have provided the background to one witness testimony about a British vessel that "there was no Englishman on board besides the captain" [HCA 1/52/100]. Qualitative data from court depositions attests to the commonplace nature of mixed crews in the British service, e.g., George Bougee describes how his crew acquired a doctor of unnamed nationality, "a greek and French boy... a negro man...[and] one Dutch negro man with his owne consent" in addition to "16 or 18 negroes" found among the cargo and a "negro man" that came on board to trade and was forced to remain [HCA 1/12/2]. Michel Angelo's 1666 travel journal notes, "the people aboard were of several nations, as *Indians, Portuguese, English, Dutch, Spaniards,* and *Indian* slaves who followed their masters" [445f.1/509], and Captain Thomas Cavendish "took with him *Santa Ana*'s pilots, the Portuguese Nicolas Rodrigo and the Spanish Tomas de Ersola, as well as three Filipino boys - and two Japanese brothers" (cited in Bicheno 2012: 209). Letters and depositions refer to sailors from Copenhagen, Denmark [HCA 1/14/201], Ostend, Belgium [HCA 1/99/177], and sailors from Germany who "hath been from Hamburge Eighteen years Constantly in the English Service both of Kings & Merchants" [HCA 1/98/262]. The nationalities, names and ports of origin of the many undocumented workers will never be known but we can also assume that they had a similar international representation.

Multinational crews may have resulted from what Fusaro describes as the common maritime practice of outsourcing crew recruitment, vessel hire, and sometimes entire enterprises dating back to the Eastern Mediterranean trade of the late fifteenth century (2015: 8, 17). Particularly in the merchant service, foreigners were very useful because many were exempt from navy impressment, thus potentially leading to a situation in which British merchant fleets were manned by a majority of non-British sailors during periods of conflict. Earle explains how crew shortages in merchant vessels were solved by enlisting men commonly exempt from impressment, specifically "a combination of old and young Englishmen, Swedes and Danes, Germans and Dutchmen, Italians, Greeks and Portuguese, Hungarians and Poles, Cypriots and Maltese" (Earle 1998: 203). Indeed, the very fact that the 1651 Navigation Acts needed to legislate for inter-colonial merchant vessels to maintain a majority of British crew indicates that it was common for such vessels to have a composite foreign majority. Yet even after the Navigation Acts restricted foreign sailors, there are indicators that records may have been falsified to reflect compliance, e.g., "virtually all East Indiamen [...] sailed with a *suspiciously standard* crew of 75 British subjects and 24 foreigners". (Earle 1998: 202–203, emphasis added).

Political divisions may have been less important than the needs of the ship when it came to enlisting crew, and thus, despite intermittent conflicts with the Turkish, Dutch, Spanish and French throughout the early colonial period, sailors of these nationalities were commonplace in British owned and operated vessels. Deponent Edward Wye perhaps sums up the situation well in his testimony, "he did not love to undertake an Enemyie, and though they were Turks they were as good Men as they [the English]" to manage the ship [HCA 1/52/133]. Petty officers were also recruited from the opposition, e.g., one witness testimony referring to "a Dutch surgeon who being sometime among them advised them" [CO 5/1411/97]. Similarly, despite racist slurs directed at the French, such as the threat of one deponent that "he would throw all the French men he could meet withall into the sea" [HCA 1/52/133], repeated testimony and documentary evidence attests to the commonality of French crewmen on British vessels, e.g., among the records of one 1722 trial for piracy, although the sailors' names are not accompanied by their nationality, the list of the 168 accused includes French names such as "Piere Ravon, Ethier Gilliot, Renee Marraud, Reney Froger Gabie, Renel Throby, Mathurm Roulape, and Pierre Shillet" [HCA 1/99/3/3]. In a separate list of 56 men acquitted of piracy, nearly a third (18 men) are listed under the heading "names of the french men" [HCA 1/99/3/180] and a ratio of just under a half of one small vessel's crew are French, described by one deponent, "a pinek about 100 tuns 14 men in her 6 or 7 of them french" [HCA 1/12/1].

Pirate crews of the early colonial period, often recruited by force, coercion and opportunism, may have included significantly more international representation than in naval and merchant vessels in that they were not subject to the same restrictions dictated by the Navigation Acts of 1651. Court records show that sailors under suspicion of piracy were a mixed group, e.g., one crew had a majority of Frenchmen, but with three Dutch, two Martinicans, and one English, Norwegian, Swedish, and Afro-Caribbean sailor [CO 5/1411/826–7], other crews include Greeks [HCA 1/99/94], Dutch [CO 5/1411/98] and Scots [HCA 1/99/120] and many had significant numbers of free workers of African descent, e.g., the testimony of one accused pirate explains "the total of the men on Board were 152 of which 52 were negroes" [HCA 1/99/14]. Moreover, worthy of note are the number of depositions that refer to groups of French sailors in pirate crews, e.g., the prisoner who escaped with five French men [HCA 1/99/99], another group who "went in the Boat 1 Eng and 5 or 6 French men" [HCA 1/99/167], and the testimony of one recruit who expresses his intention, "being in earnest with Roberts to carry Some French Men with them" [HCA 1/99/157]. The fact that all of the above depositions referring to French crew derive from the 1722 colonial records may correlate with the increased collaboration among communities of English and French sailors, hunters, and woodsmen (remembered better as buccaneers) after Spanish authorities began to eject them from their possessions in the Caribbean around the 1660s.

By way of contrast, other pirate crews actively sought English recruits and discriminated against other nationalities, e.g., one deponent testifies that "he was brought from this Dutch Galley according to the law amongst them of taking all English out off [of] foreign Ships" [HCA 1/99/124]. Another witness testifies that "twas against their Rules to take a foreigner" [HCA 1/99/88] and a captive of pirates who thanks providence when pirates took his vessel, "he had expressed himself extremely glad, because he had heard the Pyrates would accept of no Foreigners he being a Dutch man" [HCA 1/99/20]. It seems, however, based on witness testimony that it was specifically Irish recruits that were not desired by some pirate crews. One Irishman claims, "they refused because of this Country" [HCA 1/99/124] and another potential but unwilling recruit explains "he had advised him to pass for an Irish man, as he best Pretene to be rejected of them" [HCA 1/99/142]. However, it may be that–far from a general trend–these depositions all refer to one community of pirates operating around North America's 13 colonies with a specific grudge against Irish recruits, as suggested by the testimony, "it was against the Pyrates Rules to accept of [Irish men], because they had been formerly cheated by one Kenedy an Irish Man who run away with their money" [HCA 1/99/86]. In short, although some pirate crews may have been international and actively sought foreign recruits, other were potentially selective and thus the individual nature of the crew demographics in this community becomes extremely difficult to generalize.

3.10 Language abilities

3.10.1 Monolingualism

Evidence suggests that English was the primary language aboard British ships and in wider inter-colonial trade situations. This is understandable in situations such as that of Edward Whittaker, when asked about the number and nationality of men on the ship his crew had encountered, replied "About forty or fifty *most of them English*" [CO 5/1411/27, emphasis added]. Indeed, despite the prior discussion about the potential international composition of early colonial crews, archival data on sailors' nationality between 1665 and 1720 based on depositions in Admiralty court records [HCA 13/75–86] indicates that over 80% were English and therefore can be assumed to have been native English speakers (Earle 1993: 81, Table 4). With such a majority of English speakers on board, it is a logical deduction that English was the shipboard language of instruction, discipline and social communication aboard British owned and operated vessels, and any foreign-born sailors would have had to learn English. This deduction is supported by the many depositions of foreign nationals in the British court system without the use of translators and also Earle's statement that "language was not a major problem, most foreigners being able to understand sufficient English to do their jobs" (1998: 202). Also many commanders were monolingual in English, such as the captain of the *Swallow* who spoke a West Devonshire dialect and relied on interpreters for international communication (Earle 1998: 21). The widespread use of English among British crews also explains the Admiralty's suspicion in one court case where it was reported that "the prisoner pretended he could not speak English" [HCA 1/99/88], and another Judge's dismissal of a court interpreter with the command "let him make his owne relation [in English] himself" [CO 5/1411/96]. Clearly, it was assumed that if a sailor was capable of serving in a British vessel, he was also capable of speaking English. In such a context, it becomes clear why popular stereotypes of sailors support the idea of them being monolingual English speakers, as illustrated in the following description of a sailor who "regards the customs and languages of foreign countries with a fine scorn, not unmixed with suspicion. He does not understand them; he refuses to learn their speech" (Fox Smith 1924: 8). Such monolingualism was also potentially perpetuated by the use of English as a lingua franca among Dutch-operated Caribbean entrepôts such as St Eustatius, Curaçao, and St. Thomas. (Jarvis 2010: 355). Individual deponents testify as to how English was widely known among Dutch sailors, e.g., "wee mett wth a Dutch ship [...] whoe hailed us wel having Inglish" [HCA 1/12/2] and "her master was Cornelius Jacobs who was a Dutchman & her Company were all English and Dutch and spoke English" [HCA 1/14/140]. Thus, English-born sailors could effectively command or serve on either naval or trading vessels in the Atlantic and Caribbean using only their native English.

Yet this shipboard English that monolingual sailors spoke and learned was not necessarily equivalent to any variety spoken on land. The variety spoken at sea was likely to have significant dialectal influence from not only London, but also the northeast and the southwest, potentially also including transfer from Cornish and Scots that were spoken in these regions. The number of Scottish, Welsh and Irish recruits serving on the ships would have also created a situation of wider language contact that potentially led to linguistic leveling (see Trudgill 1986: 90–103). Adkins and Adkins recognize that in addition to foreign accents from learners of English, "the variety of speech of men from different parts of the British Isles were extra obstacles to the attempts by petty officers to impose order" (Adkins & Adkins 2008: 12). Indeed, despite the fact that two specific Scotsmen served in the British naval service, the court officials who attempted to question them were unable to communicate; the court record reads, "Charles Mackalerleyn & Daniell Maccay are two High Landers and Spoke such Gibberish that they could not be understood either in English Dutch or French so that they could not be examined" [HCA 1/13/97]. Yet the variety of English that these two men spoke was clearly enough for them to manage communication on board their vessel and they potentially represent a whole group of sailors whose English was unintelligible to those not familiar with the leveled dialect and variation among the ships' communities.

3.10.2 Plurilingualism

Language acquisition would have been a natural consequence of the nomadic nature of those who served aboard sailing vessels in addition to the hazards of capture and forced service in foreign vessels. However, much evidence of the plurilingualism resulting from such situations is circumstantial, e.g., although there is no record of Patrick Murphy's linguistic abilities in his court record of 1696, given his experiences of impressment to the Royal Navy from his native Ireland, serving aboard British ships for five years, and subsequent capture and imprisonment among French privateers four years [HCA 1/14/37], it might be assumed that he was probably a native Irish speaker who also acquired English and French. It is also fair to assume that the "severall English Interloapers" captured and taken to serve a French vessel [HCA 1/12/4] acquired at least a functional knowledge of French, as did all the "vast numbers of English [...] that have been taken prisoners at Sea, and are forced to Serve in the Sea Service in France" [HCA 1/13/106]. Likewise, although there is no record of their language abilities, it may be assumed that some British sailors belonging to Dutch ships spoke some Dutch, e.g., John Harvey, described as "English man belonging to the Dutch shipp called the St. Peter" [HCA 1/9/16] and four British sailors who enlisted from Holland [SP 89/25/229]. Similarly, one may surmise that the four Englishmen who served a Portuguese master alongside his Portuguese crew and forty Portuguese passengers spoke at least basic Portuguese [HCA 1/99: The American: Weekly Mercury No. 617, Oct 21–Oct 28 1731]. Such men who acquired foreign languages, either willingly or not, then became a useful commodity in international waters. David Creagh deposes how he was "kept and Detained by force and Violence and compelld to serve as interpreter on board a french Privateer... the captain whereof had taken him in a Poroquez [Portuguese] ship" [HCA 1/13/104] and Cornelius Franc claims that he was taken by pirates who "would not part with him because he could speak severall languages" [CO 5/1411/60]. Thus, language acquisition may have actually been an occupational hazard of life at sea for the common sailor.

Sailors' foreign language abilities were also an advantage to international collaboration. The Caribbean (Figure 3.3) and particularly the Caribbean colonial context at the turn of the eighteenth century (Figure 3.4) was not a dominantly Anglophone region, and most ports shared trading routes with other colonial territories including those of Spain, the Netherlands, France, and Denmark. As a result, fluency in French, Dutch and Spanish would have been useful in bargaining with foreign merchants in free ports.

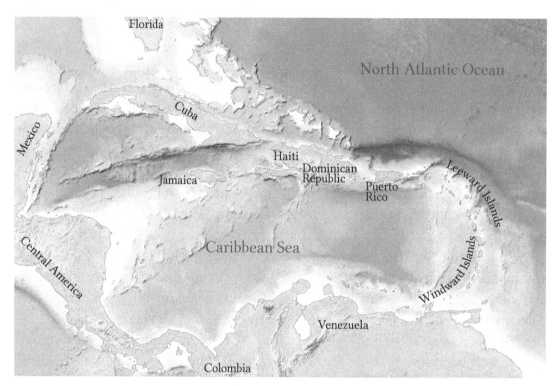

Figure 3.3: Contemporary map of the Caribbean. CC-BY-SA https://commons. wikimedia.org/wiki/User:Nzeemin, adapted

Plurilingualism benefitted not only commanding officers who might be interested in illicit trading not sanctioned by colonial embargoes, but also individual sailors who often carried items to barter or sell on the journey, a practice encouraged to mitigate the impact of wage arrears and promote a more incentive-based

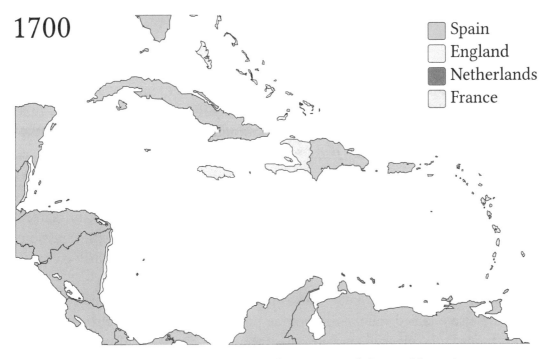

Figure 3.4: Political Map of Central America and the Caribbean in 1700.

system (Jarvis 2010: 148). Furthermore, Jarvis describes the Atlantic commons[5] as incubators of "polyglot seasonal communities, made up of English, Scottish, and Anglo-American men, Indian women, and Hispanic African runaways and slaves" (2010: 220); Fusaro explains how difficult it is to determine the nationality of commercial shipping in the seventeenth century given the range of national interests and crew on board (2015: 5); and Bicheno shows how navigational technology, shipbuilding practices, and trade routes were transferred among Spanish, Portuguese, English, Dutch and French fleets (2012: 113). Such collaboration would have necessarily required communication and therefore some level of plurilingualism in maritime communities such as evidenced in the fact that St. Croix's *Royal Danish American Gazette* printed stories in five languages (Jarvis 2010: 138). Evidence, albeit circumstantial, of such international collaboration abounds in the archival records, e.g., the logbook of the *St. Andrew* that refers to "the signal being made foure saile of Hollanders Came into our fleet" [ADM 52/2/2]; a witness deposition that describes "a french pinck 10 or 11 English men & 3 french boyes on board and theire they joined forces" [HCA 1/12/4]; another

---

[5]The "Atlantic commons" refers to the public resources of the whole Atlantic region that were not explicitly owned, settled or regulated by any one nation at the time, e.g., salt deposits, shipwrecks, coastal forests, maritime trade routes, and sea-life such as whales, turtles, fish, and reefs (see Jarvis 2010: 185–256).

testimony from a commander who explains how "two Spaniards came... he not only gave them leave so to doe but also invited them on board his sloop & treated them very kindly" but when they robbed him, "he saw two Dutch Sails and made up to them and told them what had happened' [HCA 1/99 Jamaica, Aug 23 1738]; and William Wilkinson's 1690 communication with Royal African Company that pirate crews "passed by both French, Dutch, Brandenburgers, Interlopers, either *making merry with them as their Allies*, or not daring to take notice of them as Enemies" [BL/74/816/m/11/36/2, emphasis added]. In addition to documentary circumstantial evidence, we know that certain groups were embedded in international commerce, such as the Sephardic Jews, who "traded within and across national boundaries" (Jarvis 2010: 20) and likely added their linguistic contribution to the plurilingual context of international commerce in the early colonial Atlantic.

Pirate ships were more likely than others to generate plurilingual environments and also enabled sailors with ample time to converse to acquire new languages. Indeed, plurilingualism became, at the time, a marker of guilt and complicity in piratical activity, as illustrated by J. Moreland's testimony, "must I be hanged that I can speake all languages" [CO 5/1411/56] and the accusation that one prisoner heard his captors "profanely Singing at suppertime Spanish and French Songs out of a Dutch Prayer Book" [HCA 1/99/139]. Atlantic historians Linebaugh and Rediker describe the pirate ship as "motley — multinational, multicultural, and multiracial" (2000: 164) and colonial historian McDonald, explains how "pirates served as important cross-cultural brokers in the early modern world" facilitating collaborative efforts among logwood cutters and local indigenous populations in colonial America (2016: 1). Pirate crews also notoriously rejected national allegiance, described by one administrator, "they are governed by no laws of nation" [CO 5/1411/44], an attitude corroborated by the logbook of the *Essex Prize* in the 29 August entry for 1698 which describes how "they [the crew of the *Essex Prize*] could not liarn by any means which way he was bound or from whence he [the pirate ship] came for they all told you they were bound to sea" [CO 5/1411/691]. This rejection of national allegiance, demonstrated visibly with the black ensign, was also likely demonstrated linguistically with the rejection of European standard forms of speech (Delgado 2013: 157–158). This rejection potentially took the form of new dialect genesis, code-switching, and the rejection of a single lingua franca, characteristics that pirates potentially transferred to their freebooting havens in places like Port Royal, Jamaica; Ile Sainte-Marie, Madagascar; Tortuga, Haiti; and the Isle of Wight, England, described as "a hub for corsairs of all nations" (Bicheno 2012: 41).

Among the profusion of circumstantial evidence that sailors were plurilingual, occasional direct evidence also attests to sailors' language abilities. In a rare statement about linguistic abilities in court documents, a description of Charles Macarly states, "the examinant speaks English Irish and a Little Flemmish" [HCA 1/13/96]. Also, Earle's extensive work on the demographics of English Sailors 1570–1775 cites evidence of Nicholas Lawrence who, despite being illiterate, "has been so much abroad as to be able to speak French, Spanish, Italian, Portuguese" and his shipmate Peter Breton could "speake French and English and a little of the Lingua Franca" (1998: 21). Earle also cites information on the Bicknell brothers, who served on the privateer *Swallow* and both spoke Latin, French, Dutch, and "a little broken Spanish and Portuguez" (1998: 21). One sailor working at the end of the eighteenth century describes the plurilingual tradition of the seas in his astonished reaction to naval recruitment aboard British naval vessels, "to the ear was addressed a hubbub little short of that which occurred at Babel. Irish, Welsh, Dutch, Portuguese, Spanish, French, Swedish, Italian and all the provincial dialects between Landsend and John O'Groats" (cited in Adkins & Adkins 2008: 11). Thus, contemporary accounts indicate that not only English dialects from around the British Isles were likely to have been present aboard ships, but also a range of languages, most notably from seafaring European powers yet also potentially from regions of the littoral Atlantic.

Evidence of French, Spanish, Portuguese, Dutch, Italian, and also unspecified African languages are attested to in depositions, letters and logbooks, in addition to Latin that most upper-class people would have been exposed to through formal education. Perhaps not surprisingly, given the geographical proximity of France and Spain and also the importance of these countries in the definition of the religious and political ideology of Britain at the time, French is the language most frequently named in accounts of on-board bilingualism, followed by Spanish. Indeed, speaking French had been a maritime tradition reinforced in the sixteenth century as French corsairs inspired the first waves of Elizabeth I's privateering ventures led by Drake, who "became the heir of the French corsair tradition [and] [...] must have spoken French fluently" (Bicheno 2012: 113). Moreover, as Adkins and Adkins note, up until the eighteenth century, "French was not only the language of England's principal enemy, but the language of trade and politics in many parts of the world" (2008: 22). Certain accounts indicate that it was the commanding officers who spoke French, e.g., one passenger account dated 1666 describes the captain's language abilities, "he spoke to them in French, because they had put up white colours" [445f.1/511] and Captain Vaughan engages one man who "can speak nothing but French" and another who "speaks Walloon & French and no other language" [HCA 1/13/95]. The officers' language abilities, most probably a result of formal schooling, was then potentially extended by contact with other languages in the rich environment of the plurilingual seas. For instance, one ship's clerk is described in court documents thus, "he speaks French and Latin and some few words in Dutch but cannot speak yet any other language" [HCA 1/13/96]. The clerk most likely learned French and Latin through formal schooling, but the fact that he spoke basic Dutch seems to imply a more recent acquisition, Also, the use of the words "cannot speak *yet* any other language" (emphasis added) implies that the court officials anticipate further language acquisition as a result of his presence on the ship. Most able seamen, unlikely to have gone through formal education, may have also acquired languages by contact, e.g. the 1696 witness testimony of 46-year-old John Morphey who "hath sailed to and from severall places by the West Indies... and the reason why he can now speak a little French is because he sailed for the most part amongst other sailors [...] onboard a french privateer" [HCA 1/53/9]. Such language acquisition may have been a natural process for many sailors who were in frequent contact with foreigners, as illustrated (albeit on a much smaller scale) by a journal of one passenger who notes how African natives of the coast "were to carry us to one of their towns, which in their language they call *libattes*, as we shall always call them in this relation" [445f.1/492]. So, even in this much more restricted context of linguistic borrowing, there is nonetheless an indicator that wider language transfer was happening that was potentially ubiquitous among multinational crews.

The extent of foreign colonies in the New World and the consequent emergence of a plurilingual transatlantic trade meant that language abilities were pivotal skills for many mariners of the age, as shown by the crew of the English *St. Peter*, who are described as "speaking Spanish & after that Dutch to them in the Canoa" [HCA 1/9/14]. And on a wider scale, the merchant fleets of an entire nation were served by the language abilities of their enlisted crew. Fusaro's research into seventeenth-century Venetian court records "provides a powerful impression of the international composition the crews of the ships involved" (2015: 16). She concludes that foreign seafarers in Venetian fleets, many of whom were English, had considerable linguistic knowledge based on the fact that only in rare cases did any of them need interpreters in Italian courts (Fusaro 2015: 17). Contemporary allusions to interpreters also attest to the value of language abilities in contexts of trade, e.g., John Everett, deposed in court 1700, is described as "having been then shipped [from Curaçao] [...] to go with him as Pilot and Linguister in the sloop... to trade amongst the Spanish" [SP 42/6/53]; Diego Hossa, a native of

Bahama Island, described as a "negro belonging to capt Higgingbotham" is later referred to as "a linguist or Spanish interpreter" [HCA 1/99 Bahama Islands 1722] and, in a Letter dated 11 January 1697 addressed to Capt Cornelis Jacobs or Capt Samuele Burges, "a mollatto", presumed to have travelled with privateer crews, is described as a person who "Speacks verry good English & Dutch" [HCA 1/98/75]. Moreover, in the absence of an interpreter, some crews sought to train one, such as the crew of one Portuguese vessel described in Arents' journal, who:

> finding it impossible for them to discover any thing more, because they understood not one another, resolv'd to set sail with the first wind [...] they thought good to bring two of them along in the Vessel; in hopes that they might learn the Portuguese language, or that there might some child be found out that might understand what they said. [Arents/361 *The Six Voyages* 1678: 84]

On the other hand, for English crews, trade with foreign nations was either heavily regulated or entirely banned and so knowledge that a sailor could speak foreign languages could potentially be used as evidence for their prosecution, e.g., in one court hearing, testimony is given against the five British men accused of contraband trade, "this said vessel commanded by Solomon Middleton who hailing you in Spanish and some of you making answer Espaniols" [HCA 1/99 Bahama Islands 1722]. African language skills were also viewed with suspicion, e.g., in the case of William Child accused of inciting a negro revolt on board because he "had been talking to the Negroes in Angolan Language all Night" [HCA 1/99/82, 28 March 1722]. A map of Africa by Aaron Arrowsmith submitted as part of a manuscript sent to the "British Association" in 1802 (Figure 3.5) although it dramatically illustrates the lack of knowledge of any territory beyond the coastal and river-basin areas of the African Continent, might provide some evidence of areas that experienced greater language contact with Atlantic maritime communities.

The two areas on the Atlantic coast for which more details are provided (both expanded) correspond roughly to the far west coastal areas of modern-day Senegal, the Gambia, Guinea-Bissau, Guinea and Sierra Leone and the more southerly Angola. This may suggest that the Niger-Congo language family was more heavily represented in Atlantic maritime communities during the period under study, specifically Fula and Mande languages on the far west coastal regions and Bantu languages of modern-day Angola, and potentially also Kru, Kwa/Igbo and other Volta-Niger languages of the West African coast that connected the two regions.

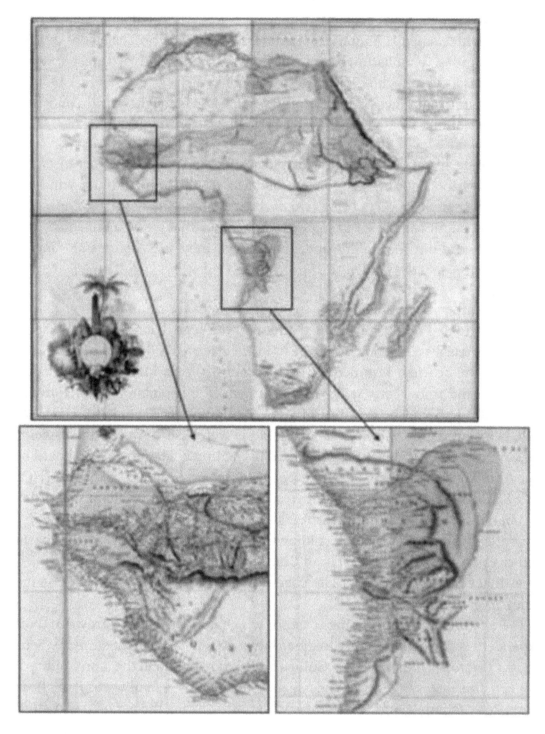

Figure 3.5: Historical map of Africa from a manuscript sent in 1802 written by Aaron Arrowsmith (with added regional inserts).

The details provided for South Africa and Pacific regions (modern-day Mozambique and Madagascar) may suggest that Khoisan was present but certainly implies that pacific varieties of languages of the Bantu family entered the maritime language contact situation (Figure 3.6). In sum, English-speaking sailors often had foreign language abilities that would have been considered unusual for those in professions on land, whether that meant extensive single-word borrowing, a basic competency for trade, or near-native fluency.

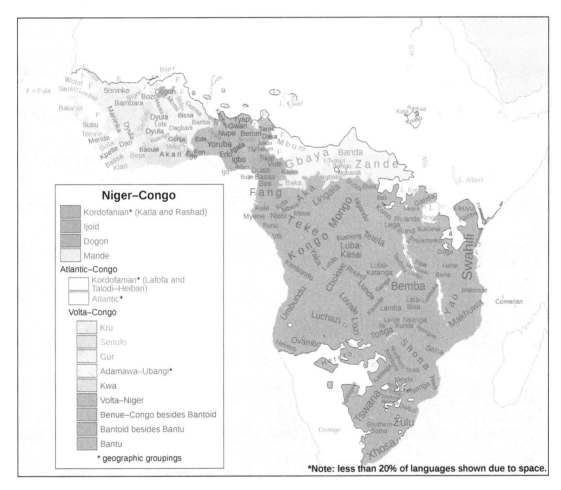

Figure 3.6: Map of the Atlantic-Congo languages within the Niger-Congo language family. © Eric Gaba CC BY-SA 4.0

3.11 Literacy

Despite their spoken competency, most sailors were not proficient in reading or writing in any language. Linguistic skill but poor literacy is illustrated in one deposition of a sailor, "sent to sea at a very tender age as cabin-boy and had no education [...] he could never read a word in a book...[but] he has been so much abroad as to be able to speak French, Spanish, Italian, Portuguese" (cited in Earle 1998: 21). Indeed, most working class people in Britain were illiterate before the Elementary Education Act of 1870 made schooling compulsory, and common seamen were no exception to this general trend (Adkins & Adkins 2008: 345). One rare court record of the testimony of John Morphey in 1696 includes an explanation "that he was examined at Plymoth and that he cannot write" [HCA 1/53/9], and in a context when the illiteracy of sailors would have been assumed, this may only be provided to explain why the deponent did not put his mark on the document. Some type of personal mark would have been a routine procedure for enlistment and was also expected in court documentation to corroborate a testimony written by a court clerk. Pervasive examples of such personal marks in the court documentation include the shaky crosses penned by anonymous seamen unaccustomed to holding pens, legible initials, and also full names signed with a flourish (see Figure 3.7). Yet, even in consideration of Earle's claims that "some two-thirds of ordinary foremastmen and over 90 percent of men who held any type of office in a ship could sign their names" ()Earle1998 the large quantity of testimonies marked with the letter <x> or initials compared to those signed with a legible name support the previous claim that the majority of sailors were functionally illiterate.

Figure 3.7: Examples of personal marks corroborating testimony in seventeenth century depositions and documents prepared by or on behalf of sailors, sources: 1. HCA 1/98/85; 2. HCA 1/101/220; 3. HCA 1/98/173; 4. HCA 1/98/62

Certain sailors who would have been expected to have some degree of literacy are, for instance, all commanding officers, the master, boatswain, purser, carpenter, shipwright, and boys first class. The duties of such positions would have required functional literacy, e.g., the shipwright's assistant who needed to prepare a certificate relating to the condition of the timber for Commander Beach [ADM 106/288/35]. Earle further explains, "a boatswain [...] had to be able to check manifests, read bills of lading and give receipts for merchants' goods delivered aboard" (1998: 21) and sailors could be disciplined or lose their position if unable to complete the tasks of their rank, e.g., the Boatswain of the *Elizabeth* who was dismissed because he "write very indifferently, very slow, could not spell" (cited in Earle 1998: 21). Carpenters were required to be literate, but more importantly to perform extensive calculations, as were ships' officers in charge of determining nautical speed, distance covered and latitude. Thus, numeracy determined competency for many sailors more so than literacy and this is reflected in the educational provisions for wealthy families' children during the seventeenth century. Young boys on the threshold of service at sea were commonly removed from grammar school and placed in specialized occupational schools that were often run by accountants or retired seamen, bypassing the more traditional curriculum in Latin, rhetoric and grammar. Instead these boys were trained in the more practical skills of record keeping, mathematics and navigation (Earle 1998: 22).

Indeed, such skills were paramount if the recruit had ambitions for a naval career and, as a result, numeracy and literacy rates were high among officers. Nonetheless, even literate officers were less exposed to texts and had fewer demands on them to read or write in comparison with standards of today.[6] To illustrate, in the 1700 trial of a Newfoundland chief officer of forces [SP 42/6] various ship masters were alleged to have read and signed a fraudulent certificate, yet, in their defense, Captain Fairbourne explains that "most of them declared that mr. B. handed the certificate to them, and that they were ignorant of the full contents thereof" seeming to suggest that their literacy was not equal to the comprehension of the full document. In another case, a literate sailor who witnessed the crime being tried in a court case in 1731 sent a letter to the court to serve as his testimony, yet this same letter is described as being "conceived in Terms not very intelligible" and therefore the author is sent for "to explain the meaning" [HCA 1/99/9]. Miscomprehension may have been perpetuated by id-

---

[6]A comparison with the compulsory education of a wealthy nation in the twenty-first century is intended, with full acknowledgement of varying global standards of literacy and compulsory schooling.

iomatic language usage, local dialect and non-standardized spelling,[7] but both these examples suggest that sailors considered literate by virtue of their abilities to read and write may not have been able to read or write across a wide range of dialects, registers or styles as we might determine full literacy today.

In lieu of formal schooling, a common seaman may have learned basic literacy the same way that they learned languages, i.e., among crewmates in leisure hours. Jarvis supports this supposition by observing that "seafaring both facilitated and promoted reading: circumatlantic passages provided sailors with ample reading time, and their visits to major seaports helped them procure books" ()Jarvis2010 a claim which supports Earle's observation that "schooling was important, but a sailor's real education began at sea" (1998: 22). Certainly, a small number of functionally literate lower-ranking sailors were likely to have been in great demand when it came to reading and responding to letters from home, and some sailors, no doubt, pressed these scribes to learn how to communicate with loved ones in their own hand. Some personal letters, or copies of such letters, written by common sailors survive in the Admiralty's court papers, e.g., one letter produced as evidence against John Seaman and described "with the hand writing of the defendant [...] beginning with those words Deare father and ending with those words your obedient sone [...] Seaman" [C 22/710/50] and four letters brought as evidence against Alexander Wyatt "who owned them to be in his own Hand Writing" [HCA 1/99 Bahama Islands 1722]. Other evidence survives in miscellaneous documentation, e.g., a series of short letters regarding the will of John Read in relation to his wife [HCA 1/98/92–96] and a personal letter dated April 13 1699 from "Abraham [surname unintelligible] [...] serving aboard Captain Kidd's vessel to his wife Margaret expressing "my Love to you and to our Child" [HCA 1/98/172]. The fact that some letters from literate wives also survive in the records speaks to the anticipated literacy of crewmen, e.g. one wife who writes simply to her "Deare And Loving husband" [HCA 1/98/116] and another who gives evidence of a continued communication in her comment "I have sent you two letters before this and have Received One" [HCA 1/98/118]. Some surviving seamen's journals also contain samples of writing, e.g., the images and notes in Basil Ringrose's journal, dated 1682 [The National Maritime Museum, exhibit P/32] and the comments on Charles II's return from exile in 1660 in Edward Barlow's journal, in which the surprisingly literate seaman describes how

---

[7]Variation in spelling would have been the norm during the early colonial period in question (1620–1750) before standardization of prestigious dialects were codified in prescriptive grammars of the eighteenth century and disseminated in the compulsory education of the nineteenth century.

people saluted the returning king "as though they were all glad to bear him up and have the happiness to welcome home the true sovereign [...] for whom the land had so long grieved" [The National Maritime Museum, exhibit JOD/4f.24]. In conclusion, although numerous indicators suggest that the majority of common seamen were illiterate, rates of literacy among officer ranks were high and there is also evidence that some common sailors were literate, potentially for the purposes of their jobs, and these likely served as readers, writers, and teachers to illiterate crewmates.

3.12 Number of sailors on the ships

Determining the likely number of sailors on ships during the early colonial period in the Atlantic and Caribbean is feasible, but only through analysis of incomplete and fragmentary data. Muster rolls detailing crew lists for British naval vessels did not appear until the mid-eighteenth century (Litter 1999: 125) and the Lloyd's registers of vessels that may have also detailed crew numbers was not established until about the same time (Litter 1999: 191). However, individual ships kept records on their crews, some of which survive in Admiralty archives, and from such miscellaneous records it is possible to make valid assertions about population demographics aboard individual vessels. Based on 22 vessels for which I found first-hand accounts (in the same document) of both the ship size and the size of the crew for Atlantic or Caribbean voyages, there was an average of 115 men in a 21-gun 239-ton vessel, or to express the data in terms more suited to the contemporary manning requirements, the equivalent of 6.39 guns per man or 2.35 tons per man (see Table 3.4). These figures are comparable to the late-sixteenth century optimum of one man per two tons of ship's weight for long voyages (Hawkins, cited in Bicheno 2012: 127), the only changes being that in the seventeenth and eighteenth centuries, larger ships were built with more guns and therefore larger crews were needed to equip them, culminating in the 100-gun warship of Nelson's navy enlisting an average of 837 men (The National Maritime Museum, "Nelson Navy Nation" exhibition).

Large crews were a feature of ships which had a high crew turnover due to death, injury, disciplinary measures and desertion, and because of this, "overcrowding generated the diseases that were the greatest danger on long voyages" (Bicheno 2012: 78). Additionally, in periods of heightened conflict, overmanning ships became a necessary procedure in the anticipation of seizing vessels and equipping them with a functional crew. This tendency to recruit large crews was consequently exaggerated in pirate crews, as suggested by one witness testimony

Table 3.4: Number of crew in transatlantic and Caribbean vessels based on first-hand accounts in the National Archives and Merseyside Maritime Museum holdings

Guns	Tons[a]	Men	Guns/Man	Tons/Man	Source document
44	499	84	1.9	5.9	HCA 1/53/13
40	454	80	2.0	5.7	HCA 1/53/12
18	204	65	3.6	3.1	HCA 1/98/9
18	204	65	3.6	3.1	HCA 1/98/258
40	454	150	3.7	3.0	HCA 1/98/265
22	249	90	4.0	2.8	HCA 1/98/3
22	249	90	4.0	2.8	HCA 1/98/263
12	136	50	4.1	2.7	1045.f.3/1/15
26	295	130	5.0	2.3	CO 5/1411/631
26	295	130	5.0	2.3	CO 5/1411/690
16	181	80	5.0	2.3	CO 5/1411/99
12	136	70	5.8	1.9	CO 5/1411/636
18	204	110	6.1	1.8	HCA 1/98/11
18	200[b]	110	6.1	1.8	HCA 1/98/262
8	90	50	6.2	1.8	CO 5/1411/691
14	158	88	6.2	1.8	HCA 1/99/9
4	45	30	7.5	1.5	CO 5/1411/636
70	794	650	9.2	1.2	HCA 1/53/18
10	150[b]	110	11	1.4	HCA 1/52/94
10	113	120	12	0.9	HCA 1/98/7
10	113	120	12	0.9	HCA 1/98/256
4	45	66	16.5	0.7	HCA 1/52/176
Average 21	239	115	6.39	2.35	

[a]Conversions based on an estimated 11.35 tons/gun derived from 58 warships for which we have tonnage and gun capacity (Bicheno 2012: 353, 358–361).
[b]Tonnage given in archival record (not estimated)

of 28 March 1722, in which one deponent describes "a Boat which they Supposed *by the number of Men in her* were Pirates" [HCA 1/99/24, emphasis added]. Furthermore, warships operating in the transatlantic waters had significantly increased crew for the requirements of navigation and defense. Such large ships weighing between 220 and 760 tons operated with an average crew of 278 (including troops) based on 28 late sixteenth-century English warships for which we have this data (Bicheno 2012: 355). However, extensive variation among vessels would have been determined by the size of the vessel, the type of voyage, the preferences of the captain, recruitment procedures, availability of workers, the anticipated crew depreciation, cargo requirements, and the age, defense system and navigational rigging of the vessel. Small crews served the short-range trading vessels of the wider Caribbean, for instance, "four to eight men were generally sufficient to man a [Bermuda] sloop" (Jarvis 2010: 123) and only ten men were needed to man the 20-ton 3-gun Pinnace *Black Dog* listed for Royal hire and registered in London (Bicheno 2012: 352). Comparatively, the largest crews of the warships could exceed 500 enlisted men, e.g., the 340 crew and 160 troops (500 total) aboard the 760-ton 42-gun Royal Carrack *Triumph* ()Bicheno2012 the evidence of one testimony of a ship of "70 gunns and abt 600 or 700 men" [HCA 1/53/18], and the note in the Boatswain's log of the *St Andrew* to have "hammocks delivered to the men [...] five hundred" [ADM 52/2/3]. However, even given these large crew numbers, the estimated numbers of people aboard any vessel are likely to be extremely conservative in light of the assumption that slaves, servants, women, and non-enlisted children were not counted as they entered the ships through means other than official enlistment and did not appear on wage registers or crew manifests.

3.13 Summary

This chapter re-defines the word "sailor" to refer to all sea-going workers of the early colonial period under study and presents sections on demographics with full acknowledgement of the limitations and complexities of data collection and analysis. Recruitment of sailors included voluntary enrollment; conscription; and the assignment of impressed, indentured, enslaved, and detained populations. Most sailors in lower ranks would have been enlisted via methods involving some degree of coercion, manipulation, or outright force and were routinely kept at sea for long periods without shore leave for fear of desertion. Although popular stereotype assumes that all sailors were male, a minority of women worked on ships as crew, collaborators, and service providers. Most sailors were young, going to sea in their early teens and serving typically until the age of around fifty with an average crew age of around thirty. Poor hygiene, putrid food, overcrowding, and lack of clean water, as well as hard labor, exposure to environmental risks, and wounds caused by disciplinary action or military conflict, resulted in high sickness and mortality rates. Sailors had strong family ties and many served alongside fathers, uncles and sons at sea. Furthermore, and contrary to popular stereotypes, sailors commonly married and had children, and their wives were active in maritime communities, sometimes accompanying their husbands to sea. Ranks determined social status at sea and composed a rigid hierarchy: the privileged upper class, the trade and military middle class, and the seamen of the largest lower class, potentially supplemented by a sub-category of undocumented, unpaid, or forced workers. Theoretically, wages were paid and could be supplemented by various means, but in reality, sailors' wages were perpetually in arrears and paid intermittently and insufficiently if at all, a situation that commonly led to conflict, mutiny, and thus potential imprisonment and death. Most sailors born in the geographical British Isles were English, followed by the Irish, Scots and Welsh. London-born sailors were most heavily represented in naval vessels, coastal northerners in the merchant service and coastal southerners and westerners in privateering and piracy. The Commonwealth's extended interpretation of what it meant to be British meant that sailors were often recruited from British territories, including the Caribbean and the 13 colonies of North America but were also heavily recruited from the sea-going nations of Europe. English was the default language aboard British ships and so some sailors may have been monolingual. However, more commonly, English-speaking sailors had foreign language abilities that were acquired directly from language contact in their maritime communities and were essential in the context of the transatlantic trade. On the other hand, plurilingualism may have been an occupational hazard as it exposed common sailors to capture for the purposes of interpreting and also suggested they were guilty of piracy considering that language contact and therefore language acquisition was perceived as more profuse aboard such vessels. The majority of sailors were illiterate; yet certain positions would have required some degree of functional literacy. Moreover, officers were likely to have had comparatively high levels of literacy and numeracy, and some common seamen may have learned basic literacy among crewmates in leisure hours for purposes of personal communication. Relating to numbers of men on the ships, there was a conservative average of 115 men in a 21-gun 239-ton vessel comparable to the sixteenth century optimum of one man per two tons of ship's weight for long voyages. However, crew sizes were increasing throughout the period under study due to the use of larger ships and piracy.

4 Speech communities

This is the second of two chapters with a focus on socio-historical data that respond to research questions about the sailors and their speech communities. This chapter on the speech communities specifically attempts to characterize the immediate and extended contexts in which sailors were likely to work and socialize. The data presented support the claim that the speech communities of English-speaking sailors were extensive and robust enough to develop distinct features of speech likely to have been recognized by those outside the community as a distinct sailors' variety. The data also speak to how language transfer and change may have been affected by the social networks that bound these communities and maintained their distinct language variety. After a discussion of General Considerations, the chapter continues with two main sections in which data is presented. The section on Insular Ship Communities presents data on sailors' duration at sea, autonomy and violence, social order and disorder, subgroups and social cohesion, the role of alcohol, and shared ideologies and leisure activities. The subsequent section, dealing with Wider Maritime Communities, presents data on profuse maritime activity, convoys and communication, the maritime economy, corruption and theft, sailors on land, and contact with port communities.

4.1 General considerations

The fact that most linguists have neglected to address the nature or importance of maritime speech communities is perhaps not surprising. Not only do these speech communities fail to fit into a traditionally defined geographical region or single social stratum, but their composition has also been obscured by centuries of non-existent, falsified, and fragmentary record-keeping. Even in the context of managing the records of a single nation's trade activity and using only one language, records are often woefully inadequate to reflect the real nature of trade and communication, e.g., Cook's investigation into seventeenth century litigation against a captain in the English coastal shipping trade indicates, *"almost one third of the working runs escaped the official records in the normal pattern of trading"* (2005: 15, emphasis added). Even in consideration of specific ports, record-keeping was typically unofficial and subject to private publication. For example, London shipping was unofficially reported in local pamphlets like the *Lloyd's List* (first published c. 1764) circulated among clients of the Lloyd's coffee house that served as a center of maritime information and insurance. These lists contained selected commercial information and details of vessels arriving at ports in England and Ireland. It was not until 1760 that the underwriters who frequented Lloyd's of London combined to form an association with the aim of producing a more complete Register Book of Shipping, circulated since 1734.[1] Likewise, although Liverpool's shipping was subject to a series of Acts of Parliament requiring that details of vessels be registered, such record-keeping was haphazard up until the Registry Act of 1786.[2] Thus, the sources of information on shipping movements and crew composition that might inform research on maritime speech communities, if they existed at all before 1750, were localized, selective, privately published, and almost invariably lost to the archival record.

The problem of insufficient data is magnified exponentially in the context of inconsistent record-keeping in transatlantic commerce that was conducted in various languages and ranged across multiple ports operated by different European nations on four continents. Jarvis' detailed study of Bermudan maritime activity concludes: "London missed much of what happened in the colony" (Jarvis 2010: 461). And this could be said of most of the colonies of the time, given that imperial record-keeping primarily targeted large bulk shipments of goods and was silent on the abundant maritime activity in local trade and the logging, salvage, turtling, and salt-raking trades of the Atlantic commons that sailors actively concealed from the Board of Trade's custom officials. As a result, Jarvis claims that "much of the North American coast and virtually the entire Caribbean had permeable and blurry maritime borders" (Jarvis 2010: 462). In addition to these blurry areas of imperial oversight, even when records were kept, there was often little verification of their accuracy. For example, one letter from a Virginia court trial details how easy it was to evade port charges with falsification of docking registers: "they give her [the ship] the name of the *Alexander* [...] at other times they will change her name, and call her the *providente-galley*" [CO 5/1411/631]. In short, I acknowledge that empirical data is limited on this subject. Therefore, the following sections on the common characteristics of maritime communities are based largely on qualitative data, in an attempt to characterize the real communities that were often absent from the quantifiable data of the official records.

---

[1]Merseyside Maritime Museum Archives & Library. (2010). *Lloyds Marine Insurance Records* (Information Sheet: 52). Retrieved from http://www.liverpoolmuseums.org.uk/maritime/archive/sheet/52.

[2]Merseyside Maritime Museum Archives & Library. (2010). *Liverpool Ship Registers* (Information Sheet: 50). Retrieved from http://www.liverpoolmuseums.org.uk/maritime/archive/sheet/50.

4.2 Insular ship communities

Working aboard an early colonial vessel was no day job; sailors lived at sea and the vessels they lived on were comparable to small towns. One passenger on a voyage from Europe to Africa in 1666 notes in his journal:

> The ship was like *Noah's* ark, for there were aboard it so many several sorts of beasts, that what with the noise, and the talk of so many people as were aboard, we could not hear one another speak... [the ship] looked like a castle on the sea. [445f.1/509]

It was common for men to "run away to sea" ()Jarvis2010 the very expression suggesting that the vessel was primarily a destination rather than a means of transportation. Similarly, in a letter dated 30 July 1699, "they would not liarn [learn] from whense they came, nor whither they were bound, for they all told him yet his way *bound to sea*" [CO 5/1411/631, emphasis added]. Indeed, the wooden sea-going vessels of the early colonial period were communities in every sense of the word which could be just as large and complex as on land, e.g., one ship's captain, stressing the large nature of the ship and its sizable population, complained that "I was informed there was a surgeon belonging to the ship but never saw him till I returned from Newcastle" (cited in Brown 2011: 48). These floating communities, just like those on land, had their own rituals of social identity and order in addition to language practices that were unique to their context.

4.2.1 Duration at sea

The time that workers were expected to remain on a vessel was a key determining factor in the formation of a sea-going community identity. When sailors could no longer return home after a day at sea or a week's short trading journey around local coasts, the notion of what their "home" was may have radically shifted from a port-based traditional notion of house and family to the assigned quarters or hammock and mess mates of their vessels. As trade and naval operations extended across the Atlantic, and particularly after the English involvement in the slave trade increased after the Royal Charter of 1562, more sailors found themselves serving on transatlantic journeys, described as "an ocean voyage that could last from five weeks to three months" (Brown 2011: 107). So, even if a ship sailed directly to a single port across the Atlantic, then spent minimal time managing cargo and sailed directly back to the same home port, the journey would still take an average of two to six months. However, the reality of shipping practice meant that sailors were likely to be away from land much longer than this.

Figure 4.1: The Atlantic Trade Winds in January and July, adapted from Encyclopaedia Britannica.

Even small sloops that might be expected to return to home port more frequently than larger vessels did not necessarily do so, but instead, as Jarvis explains, "made several round trips between North America and the Caribbean during the summer and fall seasons before returning home" (2010: 111). He goes on to say that although small vessels did not typically make one transatlantic voyage per year as the larger ships did, they nonetheless were at sea for long durations as they made multiple short voyages "at least two or three and in some cases as many as fourteen round-trips in a single year" (Jarvis 2010: 125). The common practice of stopping in multiple ports on circum-Atlantic journeys rather than travelling to a single destination and back again increased time at sea, and this was not only for reasons of legitimate trade but was also necessary for collecting food provisions, wood, and water and enabling enterprising captains to take advantage of international entrepôts of trade, which evaded harsh duties on export and import goods. In addition, the circum-Atlantic pattern of trade winds favored sailing vessels that set circular navigational courses (see Figure 4.1).

Such circular navigation developed the trade system of taking manufactured goods out of Europe: collecting spices, gold and slaves in African ports; bartering for flour, meat and lumber in the Americas and Caribbean; and bringing cotton, fur, lumber, and tobacco back to Europe on the return leg. Such circum-Atlantic trade routes are evidenced in seventeenth century records. For example, one sailor's account of his international movements:

> [the deponent] sailed from England being bound for Jamaica, and arrived at Jamaica in may following... and stayed in Jamaica about a month...[then]

> [...] he made a tripp over to new Yorke, where he staied two months or
> thereabouts [...] he sailed again with the said shipp to Jamaica [...] he sett
> saile from Jamaica being full laden with sugar cottons and other wares...
> but in his passage to London he mett with foule weather and lost his fore-
> mast and threby was forced to putt into Boston in new England where he
> arrived on or about ....August last past and staid there until he had fitted
> the said ship, which being done he sailed from Boston [...] for London, but
> in his passage he lost his rudder was forced into [...] the West of England.
> [HCA 1/52/20]

Circum-Atlantic journeys, such as the one described above that navigated
around extended trade networks, were invariably prolonged by storms and in-
constant weather, as well as by the time required for checking, loading and unloading cargo, and provisioning and maintaining the ship. These voyages thus
required crews to spend significantly more than a few months aboard the vessel.

It is possible to calculate a rough average of the average sailor's duration at
sea, although doing so necessarily obscures the differences between the types
of vessels, types of voyages, and ranks of the crew that likely created very different profiles for different groups of people. Yet, with this caveat in mind, it is
possible to calculate an average time at sea of 15.73 months (or one year, three
months and 23 days) based on 53 first-hand records that were sourced from witness testimony in court records and comments in private letters and journals
(see Figure 4.2). This average duration that individuals reported at sea is corroborated by the data in 84 logbooks that generate an average voyage duration of
14.46 months, or one year, four months and 14 days (see Figure 4.3). Furthermore,
these two sets of data also align with data cited in secondary sources, such as the
comment describing the duration at sea for the crew of the late sixteenth century
ship *Harve*, "They had been gone for over fourteen months" (Bicheno 2012: 124).
Hence, the triangulated data suggests that a typical sailor in the transatlantic
trade could expect to spend at least one year and a quarter continuously serving
at sea at any one time.

However, we should not suppose that after a voyage of over a year, sailors returned to their homes on land. Compelling evidence suggests that many sailors
signed on for (or were forced into) consecutive voyages that might have taken
them away from life on land indefinitely. For example, many of the data composing Figure 4.2 about individual durations at sea come from court trials of sailors
accused of piracy who merely state how long they had been serving on the vessel from which they were arrested, e.g., "has been about 18 mos with the Rogues"
[HCA 1/99/135] and another sailor who was "taken [...] 19 months ago [and] [...]
had not had any Opportunity Since of Escaping" [HCA 1/99/105].

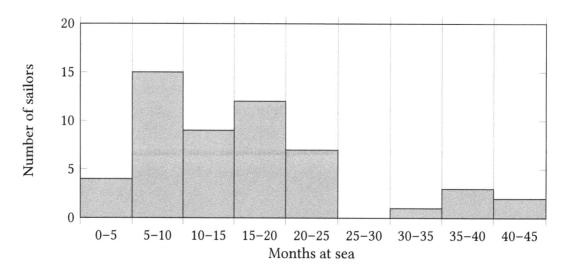

Figure 4.2: Individual time at sea based on witness depositions, letters and journal
Sources: 445f.1/485,486; DDB6 8/4; HCA 1/101/124; HCA 1/13/96; HCA 1/14/17,19; HCA 1/52/20; HCA 1/52/48; HCA 1/9/63; HCA 1/98/252,259,56,57,9; HCA 1/99/102; HCA 1/99/104,105,109,114,116,117,120,121,125,127,128,130,131,132,133,135,140, 146,150,155,157,159,162,165,167,170,72,73,80,86,88,89,90,93,94

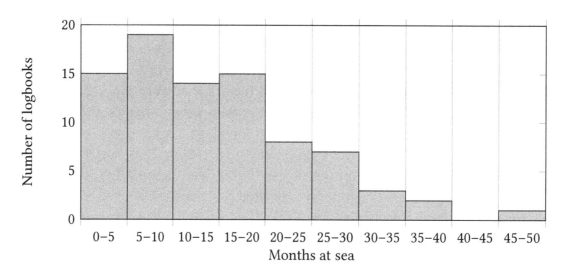

Figure 4.3: Duration of voyages based on ships' logbooks
Sources: ADM 52/1/11; ADM 52/2/1–9; ADM 52/3/1–13; ADM 51/4322/1–6; ADM 51/3983/1–4; ADM 51/3954; ADM 51/3946/1–6; ADM 51/3946/1–13; ADM 51/4170/1–10; ADM 51/3797/1–8; T/70/1215

Thus, it is likely that these individuals had served at sea for longer than their stated duration because this only reflects the time spent with the crew of the most recent vessel they were on. Additionally, and as previously discussed in §3.2, low-ranking sailors were routinely "turned over" from one vessel to another before reaching home ports. This practice kept men at sea for much longer periods of time that the actual sailing routes or military postings lasted (Adkins & Adkins 2008: 365). For example, John Stretton describes consecutive voyages starting with his employment at New York for a voyage to Virginia, and then after to England, Holland, New York again, and Philadelphia Bay, before terminating his term of service in Hamburg [HCA 1/14/140]. Likewise, another sailor is appointed in New York and sails to Jamaica, Lisbon, and back again to New York before heading off to Antigua and then again to North America, including ports on the St. Lawrence river [HCA 1/98/15].

Furthermore, many of the lowest-ranking sailors were denied shore leave for fear of desertion. Sailor testimonies describing the strict enforcement of this rule range from statements attesting to how one ship's master "would not suffer me to go on Shore" [HCA 1/99/5] to the consequences of breaking such mandates, as when the "Master went to the mate and gave him a blow on the face with his fist asking him what he did ashoare" [HCA 1/52/45]. So, it appears not to have been uncommon for sailors to be at sea for years without enjoying shore leave, let alone returning to the home port they had disembarked from. Indeed, the situation was often so repressive that some sailors chose to risk death in the water or upon unknown shores rather than stay aboard any longer, e.g. in the 1700 trial of John Houghling, Corneluis Franc and Francois Delaune, one witness testifies, "I saw three or four jump into the water expecting they would make towd the shore I wan to meet them but only one came [ashore]" [CO 5/1411/39]. Additionally, the fact that sailors were so rarely on land caused problems for the courts, e.g. the petition of David Creagh in 1675 claims that he knows many men who might be able to testify to his innocence, "but being seafareing men he cannot hope to find them always on shore, nor to have the benefitt of their Testimony [...] they being bound for sea" [HCA 1/13/104]; and also the complaint of a plaintiff who was awarded restitution from one sailor, but laments "he believed he shou'd never come to England to pay it" [HCA 1/99/97]. In short, although transatlantic trips could be theoretically made in a few months, it was more likely that voyages took more than a year and additionally likely that sailors served on consecutive voyages, potentially without shore leave, thus creating alternative and relatively stable societies at sea that may have been periodically re-populated, but were invariably composed of workers who spent the greater part of their lives off shore.

4.2.2 Autonomy and violence

Many of the floating communities operating in the murky waters of early colonial trade were largely autonomous as a result of the inability of imperial Britain to effectively regulate them and the existence of international networks of contraband trade and communications that enabled them to operate on the captain's authority. Indeed, a captain might appeal to the men to recognize his own authority regardless of British law, as if the insular communities of the sea were somehow self-regulating and therefore subject only to internal justice and authority. For example, in the late sixteenth century, Francis Drake appealed to the crew, "My masters, you must judge for yourselves whether or not this fellow has tried to undermine my authority… let they who think this man deserves to die hold up their hands" (cited in Bicheno 2012: 140). The type of power that captains like Drake asserted created a pseudo-democratic microcosm of the contemporary British nation-state aboard ship,[3] and this system of government was what enabled insular communities of pirates, freebooters and buccaneers to manage and regulate social order in societies that were marginalized even within the maritime world. The benefits of such insular autonomy were twofold: firstly, it enabled captains to do as they pleased without concern for home legislation, and secondly, it offered the British government a degree of plausible deniability when such captains were engaged in international raiding against supposed trading allies or in nefarious activities that were in the government's interest but which it could not openly support. For example, William Wilkinson, mariner of London, explains how English Captains working for the African Company were allegedly sent to seize merchant ships and cargos regardless of nationality:

> other Commanders have had a share of the Ships and Cargos that have been so illegally seized… and their business has been to destroy and devour the Ships and Estates of English Subjects, and share them as their own… who ought to protect their Merchants Ships in trade. [BL/74/816/m/11/36/3]

Fusaro explains how some captains abused the concept of an onboard democracy owing to the fact that many co-owned the vessels they governed (2015: 23). This emboldened many commanding officers to assert feudal authority over what they considered to be their property (including the workers) with a type of coercion that Ogborn describes as "state-sanctioned violence exported from England" (cited in Fury 2015: 4–5). Furthermore, such appropriation of absolute power often went unchecked by courts in Britain whose judges were politicians rather than defenders of the law. Fusaro explains that the priority of the courts at the time was to protect trade, and therefore, "sentencing was not necessarily in line with strictly operational, or literal, interpretation of existing laws and customs" (2015: 23). Free traders, whether they operated strictly within the existing British

---

[3]Drake is described as "pseudo-democratic" because even in his seemingly democratic appeal to his crew, the men he addressed knew their expected complicity in the execution of Thomas Doughty and how unwise it would have been to speak against the wishes of the aggressive and assertive young officer poised to take command.

laws or not, were often given the freedom of the seas, and their superficial acknowledgement of legal processes, custom and duties is well represented in the contemporary description of how such private trading vessels would operate, "looking one way and rowing another" [BL/J/8223/e/4/27/3]. Captains' disdain of trading regulations frequently prompted response from colonial territories, e.g., a joint petition to British administrators written in August 1709 by proprietors of Barbados bemoans "the Liberty given to Separate Traders; which, unless remedied in time, is like to prove fatal, not only to us, but to the *British* Trade upon the aforesaid Coast" [BL/J/8223/e/4/27]. In such a context, captains' abuses of power over their poorest workers was a minor concern, particularly as such people were perceived as worthless and idle by their home government anyway.

Tyrannical captains and superior officers, although of little concern to home authorities, were the target of regular complaint by sailors. Abuses of power were so common that even some in authority recognized the dangers of power imbalances, e.g., Captain Samuel Burgess writes, "I was never known to be Shart or Severe with any Mann tho I had the advantage soe to bee" [HCA 1/98/57], and Samuel Pepys, in his diary of 1666, comments that pilots "dare not do nor go but as the Captains will have them; and, if they offer to do otherwize, the Captains swear they will run them through" (cited in Lavery 2009: 75). However, based on the profusion of depositions detailing abuses of power by those in command, we can assume that the concerns of those such as Burgess and Pepys were outweighed by the desires for power that persuaded others to perpetuate the status quo. Some of the recoverable grievances brought to court included mild complaints of "ill usage" [SP 89/25/229], "garrulous language" [ADM 52/1/8], and "being continually abused by an Idle master who was drunk every day" [E134/34Chas2/Mich36]. Yet more commonly, sailors presented complaints of physical threats from superior officers, e.g., threats to cut a sailor's ears off for lack of compliance with orders [HCA 1/99/24; HCA 1/99/98], one Quartermaster's threat to throw a sailor overboard for waking him when he should have been on duty [HCA 1/52/124], and another sailor's concern that because of "the ill Usage of Capt. Williams [...] [he] was in continual Fear of his Life" [HCA 1/99.618]. Furthermore, evidence indicates that these were not idle threats. Table 4.1 below provides excerpts from ten testimonies brought before court with a specific complaint and describing physical violence, and Table 4.2 provides excerpts from eleven testimonies evidencing physical violence that resulted in the death of the victim.

Furthermore, when complaints were made, sailors' concerns were dismissed outright, as one seaman found out when he took his complaint of being beaten by the ship's carpenter to the captain, who "called him a Drunken Rogue and

Table 4.1: Samples of court testimony detailing physical abuse from superior officers

Complaint	Details of physical abuse	Source
Torture, Imprisonment	"clapt upon his leggs abt 8 or 9 pound weight [...] put into the stocks, where he lay 37 houres and after he had indured imprisonment for 46 days"	HCA 1/52/47
Violence	"their Captain [...] beat them Severely when they Disobeyed"	HCA 1/99/10
Violence	"The Quarter Master of the Pyrates beat him and forced him in again"	HCA 1/99/18
Violence	"it was out of his power to deny without hazard of beating"	HCA 1/99/31
Violence	"he was beat very much [...] denying their Order"	HCA 1/99/32
Violence	The Boatswain "beat the Crew, for not being brisk enough"	HCA 1/99/41
Severe beating	"gave him more blowes and kicked him [...] blowes around the head, till the blood ran down from his nose and face"	HCA 1/52/22
Severe beating	"Comander fell on him and beate him very violently with his Cane"	HCA 1/52/127
Severe beating	"his head broke, and a hearty drubbing [...] Several Months unable for Duty"	HCA 1/99/72
Severe beating	"very sick with severall wounds the captain had given him on the back"	HCA 1/14/201

bid him be gone to his Hamock" [HCA 1/52/22]. Others who tried to voice their concerns in court were similarly silenced, such as the sailor who complained by letter that there was too little value placed on common sailors' lives and was hauled before high court to explain himself, publicly retract his complaint, and apologize [HCA 1/99 Philadelphia, Oct 15 1731, 9–10]. Another sailor finds so little justice that his last act of life after receiving a mortal beating from the ship's chief mate is to write a letter of testimony to the only person likely to care:

> Ever Loufing wief these lines is to arkquint you that I Lying more like to die than to lief desiring you to remember my kind love to my three Cussons: and so Lying in this condission throw the means of the Cheaf mat of the Ship Bengdall marchant: Rodger Nubery be knowd: so I Laying my Death to the Sadd Rodger Nubery: hear I seal my John Morris. [HCA 1/52/51]

Table 4.2: Samples of court testimony detailing physical abuse from superior officers that resulted in death

Complaint	Details of physical abuse resulting in death	Source
Cruelty leading to suicide	"the said George Rowe did soe Barbarously & Cruelly use [him] [...] throwing himselfe [...] into the Sea to avoyde his Masters Cruelty"	HCA 1/11/110
Beaten to death	" beat him [...] and with his foote or knees or both stampt upon him and bruised his stomach with such violence [...] soon after dyed"	HCA 1/11/111
Beaten to death	Lieutenant George Bing stands trial for beating a sailor under his care to death with "a Cane" [Acquitted]	HCA 1/12/111
Beaten to death	"beate him and threw him downe headlong on the Quarter Deck upon which the said Robert Day fell sick and dyed about three weekes after"	HCA 1/52/127
Beaten to death	"John Rogers received blows from his Captain, allegedly causing death"	HCA 1/52/41
Beaten to death	John nightingall, "a great many blows on the Head, very black & blew"	HCA 1/52/148
Beaten to death	"[the captain] took a cane of moderate size [...] and gave the Deceased two or three Blows about the Head and Shoulders" [Acquitted]	HCA 1/99/8
Beaten to death	John Morris beaten "severall times very violently [...] he struck all of his teeth out of his head [...] laid for about 5 weeks and then died" [Guilty]	HCA 1/52/48
Beaten to death	"many bruises [...] his being beaten might be the occasion of his death"	HCA 1/52/176
Executed	"the Prisoner with two more [men] were sentenced to Death for attempting an Escape from them, and that the other two were really Shot for it"	HCA 1/99/50
Executed	"Were for deserting sentenced to Death over a Bowl of Punch"	HCA 1/99/125

It is worth noting that all the testimony presented so far relates to the treatment that sailors received from their own superiors. In addition to such shipboard violence was the ever-present threat of capture by foreign or pirate vessels and a continuation of cruel and unusual punishments such as being burned with lighted matches [HCA 1/9/3], blindfolded and hung by a rope [HCA 1/9/15], cut around the anus [HCA 1/99 Jamaica 1738–1739], and even having sexual organs twisted [HCA 1/99 New Providence 1722], or cut off and stuffed into the mouth [HCA 1/99 Agostinho, July 8, c. 1721, 4]. Suffice to say, living aboard autonomous sailing vessels of the early colonial period, in which superior officers regularly used violence to subordinate lower-ranking sailors, required great mental and physical strength. It also contributed to the insularity of the speech community as subordinate seamen sought protection (and coping strategies) from the collective.

4.2.3 Social order and disorder

In addition to the cruel and unusual violence that sailors suffered at the hands of captors and their own tyrannous officers, they were also subject to corporal and capital punishment under the British naval law. Rules aboard ship were harsh and punishable by a range of inventive sanctions up to and including death,[4] e.g., Edward Collins was forced to wear a basket of shot around his neck for an hour to make him confess to the stealing of personal items [HCA 1/9/83], Edward Abbot was lashed 40 times "furiously & violently....about the face, back, head & shoulders" for asking for bread, a punishment for which he died three weeks later [HCA 1/9/137–8] and an unnamed sailor accused of attempting to jump ship "was put on Shore on Some uninhabited Cape or Island [with] a Gun Some Shot a Bottle of Powder, and a bottle of Water to Subsist or Starve" [HCA 1/99/109]. Indeed, the scope of potential offenses and the energy with which punishments were administered led to a 1749 revision of the Naval Articles of War that described acceptable punishments for different types of infractions. As part of this revision process, captains were reminded that punishments should never be assigned "without sufficient cause, nor ever with the greater severity that the offence shall really deserve" (cited in Adkins & Adkins 2008: 209) which, in itself, highlights how much of a cultural phenomenon excessive and undeserved punishment had become by that time. Further testimony to this phenomenon is recoverable from the popular songs of the day, such as the 1691 ditty entitled "The Sea Martyrs or The Seamen's Sad Lamentation for Their Faithful Service, Bad

---

[4]It is worth noting that some scholars believe that although the legal code in England was harsh, it was more flexible in practice than in theory. See Fury 2015: 17.

Pay and Cruel Usage" which set to verse a well-known trial in which a group of common sailors organized themselves to petition for improved conditions and pay only to be accused of mutiny and put to death (cited in Palmer 1986: 58). Such cases are also evidenced in witness accounts, e.g. one case c. 1667 in which "Eleven Englishmen came together to complain to the captain that they were not allowed water enough to drink" [445f.1/510]. In this case, the captain's response was to punish the apparent ringleader by placing him in shackles with two sentinels over him until they reached port, at which time he was presumably taken to stand court martial for mutiny. Comparable events detailed in the court proceedings of March 28, 1722, describe an suspected ringleader, who was "set on Shore here by the said Capt Chaloner Ogle for his Tryal" [HCA 1/99/170]. And courts martial were not an unusual occurrence in the naval fleets of the period, e.g., the logbook of the *Albemarle* refers to four separate trials in as many months between January and April 1697 [ADM 52/1/5]. Thus, sailors were subject to ad hoc disciplinary measures determined by the captain as well as the consequences of formal legal proceedings, making harsh disciplinary measures a regular hazard of life for sailors of the early colonial period.

The time that sailors spent waiting for a trial was a punishment in itself in addition to the potential horrors of a guilty verdict. Petitioners were often detained upon a whim for long periods and in poor conditions without formal charges, e.g., Timothy Branoth had already served three years in a naval prison at Marshalsea upon what he could only assume was "a False and Malitious Suggestion [...] of which your petitionr is altogether Ignorant and Innocent off" when he humbly requested that he "may be Tryed or Discharged that he may be att Liberty to provide for his Starving Family" [HCA 1/14/28]; also a petition sent to the court on behalf of John Murphy who admits that he is wholly ignorant of the law, yet "Yor Petitionr doth not know what his Indiction is nor what is Charged against him... he doth not know what to doe" [HCA 1/14/27]. And when sailors finally stood trial, the consequences of a guilty verdict could be severe, e.g., the court records for 28 March 1722 saw 91 sailors stand trial, of whom: 52 were executed, 20 were sentenced to seven-years servitude in Africa, 17 were sent to Marshalsea prison, and two were granted a respite. None were acquitted [HCA 1/99/181]. In fact, although juries were formed and regulated to offer the common man a fair trial, there is still evidence to suggest that their decisions were foregone, e.g. in one trial the judge makes his intentions clear by urging jurors to "reflect upon the [...] ill consequences of acquitting the guilty" [CO 5/1411/80]. A guilty verdict and a sentence of death was a public spectacle intended to deter others, and this deterrent started with the rhetoric of the court:

> Ye and each of you are adjudged and Sentenced to be carried back to the
> place from whence you came from thence to the Place of Execution, and
> there within the Flood Marks be hanged by the neck till ye are Dead, Dead,
> Dead [...] After this you [...] are to be taken down and your Bodys hung in
> Chains. [HCA 1/99/169]

British naval law was not unique in its harsh treatment of sailors either: Gage
explains how contemporary Spanish ships endowed their officers "with full Commission and Authority to imprison, banish, hang and execute all delinquents"
(1648: 15). In short, the international waters were replete with floating, autonomous yet repressive communities in which common sailors were the typical
victims of excessive disciplinary measures intended to ensure their compliance
and subordination.

In such a context of brutality and injustice, it is perhaps not surprising that
collective resistance offered the common sailor some form of protection. Captains of the period routinely complained of "mutinous disobedient men" [HCA
1/101/147], and owners cautioned the commanders appointed to care for their private trading vessels to "be always on your guard against insurrections" [D/Ear-
le/1/1]. Bicheno's work on Elizabethan trading and politics at sea offers the simile
"naval command during the Renaissance was akin to herding cats" (2012: 112), cit-
ing the observations of contemporaries such as Drake, who bemoaned the recurrent problem of managing subordinates, "I know sailors to be the people most re-
sentful of authority in the world" (cited in Bicheno 2012: 142). Indeed, Linebaugh
& Rediker (2000) claim that sailors composed one of the dangerous heads of the
hydra that capitalism engaged to destroy.[5] The description in one court record
of 1669 that attests to the binary opposition of peaceful masters and rebellious
crew seemingly mirrors the sentiments echoing through the philosophy behind
British legislation at the turn of the 1700s:

> the Rioters aforesaid with drawn sword, & other weapons, assaulting —
> beating, wounding, & Bruising, and at last throwing quite overbord Henry
> Tomishire, Edw. Hearle and others who then were, and for severall weeks
> before had been in the peaceable and quiett possession of the sd [said] ship.
> [HCA 1/101/319]

The testimony of common sailors additionally speaks to the perpetual threat
of revolt that might be equitable to peasant revolution in the microcosm of shipboard polity, e.g., a case in 1679 was brought before the Admiralty for a sailor

---

[5]See chapter 5 "Hydrarchy: Sailors, Pirates, and the Maritime State" (Linebaugh & Rediker 2000:
143–173).

charged with killing his superior officer "after the officer had highly provokd & challengd him" [HCA 1/101/329] and another in 1687 "for suspicion of the murder of our Capt Piro by dunking him in the sea" [HCA 1/13/11]. Given the circumstances, it is unlikely that either of these two men acted alone. In other depositions, sailors' intentions to formalize an uprising are even more obvious, e.g., two sailors were overheard asking "whether twas not better to endeavour the rizing a new Comp[any] than to go to Cape Coast, and be hanged like a Dog" [HCA 1/99/83 28th March 1722], and "he heard the said Williams say that if he could get three or four good hands and an artist [a tradesman] he would not be afraid to turn pyrate" [HCA 1/99 Williamsburg, Aug 14 1729]. Given the abuses and lack of possibility of redress that sailors faced on a daily basis on the early colonial ships of the transatlantic, it is perhaps no surprise that there was a concurrent period of rebellion and resistance that is remembered with simplified idealism as the "golden age of piracy".

Responses from ships' officers to combat the agency of collective rebellion, in addition to silencing potential dissenters, took the form of permitting localized squabbles and also mandating participation in public rituals of punishment. The difficulty of punishing collective agency is illustrated by the court records of one trail in the Bahama Islands 1722, in which various witness statements are taken. The case concludes with all but one of the defendants convicted and sentenced to death, followed by a memorandum explaining that everyone was acquitted because they needed workers to prepare for an imminent Spanish invasion [HCA 1/99]. In contrast, isolating and silencing individual dissenters was the most effective means to divide and conquer collective agency and also helped courts to convict sailors in an age before prisoners might be assumed innocent until proven otherwise. For instance, many mariners who refused to recognize the authority of their commanding officers, and by extension, the courts of the Admiralty, did the only thing they could in defiance: they remained silent. One court record of a trial in 1687 describes three men who refused to enter a plea "whereupon the court told them the danger of standing mute, and that if they would not plead, the Law took it for granted they were guilty" [HCA 1/12/111]. Other testimonies describe sailors who refused to participate in trials, e.g., Joseph Benedict, who "hath nothing to say for himself or against himself" [HCA 1/14/201], and Robert Mason, whose supposed deposition "he refused to sign" [HCA 1/14/201]. Perhaps it was this culture of silent complicity that motivated a legal clause in piracy accusations that a person could be guilty by knowledge or association in lieu of testimony or confession [SP 42/6]. Other, more immediate means of subduing sailors involved prompting a cathartic relief of tension. This was done by turning a blind eye to petty complaints and squabbles, e.g., quarrels over private property ownership [HCA 1/99/81]; verbal complaints when ordered to duty [HCA 1/99/26]; physical fights over the pecking order [HCA 1/99/25]; and conflict over assigned sleeping quarters [HCA 1/53/48]. Yet a more effective method of prompting catharsis and relieving the tension in the shipboard community was achieved through mandating participation in public rituals of punishment such as administering lashes. In this context, Fury describes the interactive justice system of the early seventeenth century merchant fleets of the East India Company; she explains that communal justice was necessary because "those in positions of authority had to shore up the fissures in the community and thus the need for rituals, religion, and reconciliation" (Fury 2015: 17). Such public rituals included a punishment known as being "lashed through the company" in which men were sentenced to one or more lashes from everyone aboard the vessel, or the fleet in extreme cases. As a punishment for attempting to run from the ship in Sierra Leone, one sailor "received two Lashes from every Man in the Company as a Punishment" [HCA 1/99/45]; another offender similarly suffered "2 Lashes thro the Company" [HCA 1/99/109]; and "William Williams was lashed by Every Man in the Company" [HCA 1/99/114], both for attempted desertion. Yet the punishment was also administered for lesser offenses such as one sailor's presumed intoxication, e.g. "the Company whipped him because of his Liquor" [HCA 1/99/159]. Another punishment called "running the gauntlet" involved tying the offender's arms and forcing him at knife-point to run the length of the ship lined with his crewmates armed with knotted rope that they used to beat him repeatedly and violently as he passed, a practice abolished in 1806 (Adkins & Adkins 2008: 215–216). So, by selectively permitting minor conflicts among the crew and promoting cathartic release of anger in a controlled manner that also served as a deterrent, those in authority were able to patch up potential fissures in social order that might give rise to more collective dissent.

4.2.4 Subgroups and social cohesion

Undoubtedly, many transatlantic vessels of the early colonial period were engaged in the massive forced migration of human beings via the slave trade, yet there was also a brisk business in passenger transit around the British colonial holdings. Subgroups of maritime travelers were potentially large, e.g. missionary Thomas Gage describes passengers that included "30 Jesuits, a Dominican mission of 27 Friars, and 24 Mercenarian Friars" ()Gage1648 and among a fleet the numbers could be even higher, e.g., one convoy of three ships "carried passengers to the number of one hundred" (Hawkins, cited in Bicheno 2012: 96–97).

Even when passenger numbers were small, they could still potentially outnumber the crew, e.g., "The ships Company being about 15 in number and all the Passengers in her being 21 in number" [HCA 1/52/100], and on larger vessels, passengers could make up such a large group that they disrupted maritime work, e.g., one witness describes "the noise of the passengers, which oblig'd the captain to draw his sword to drive all those under deck who could not help, but only served the hinder the sailors" [445f.1/516]. These passengers of the early colonial period are extremely difficult to trace however, as the Passenger Acts that would record their movements did not start until 1842.

Despite the scarcity of recoverable data that attests to large-scale passenger movements, passenger transit was an important part of the maritime economy. Passengers treated as cargo were sold and paying passengers bolstered the ships' coffers, e.g., the "7 french men on board the said ketch they paying their passage to Capt Prout on board" [HCA 1/12/2] and the "rich Portuguese merchant... who was returning to *Lisbon* with all his family, that is, wife and four children; gave a thousand crowns for his passage" [445f.1/509]. Regular passenger transit around colonial holdings was not only beneficial for the captains receiving their fare but also motivated stronger local economies by maintaining reciprocal trade and barter systems that lessened islanders' dependence on exports from Britain. For example, Jarvis explains how Bermudian mariners operating small vessels "so regularly shuttled between St. Eustatius, St. Martin, St. Christopher, Anguilla, Antigua and other British sites that they essentially operated an inter-island taxi service" (Jarvis 2010: 168). Furthermore, in addition to slave populations, passengers who may have travelled without paying, such as religious missionaries, indentured servants, and economic migrants, were often critical to the development of local workforces and community identity in their colonial destinations. Litter explains, "Passengers, some of whom were emigrants or indentured servants, were carried regularly to North America and the West Indies from about 1660 onwards" (Litter 1999: 45). These passenger groups, described collectively as "the poor, the ambitious or the persecuted" (Litter 1999: 45) composed an essential part of the labor force around Britain's colonies, for instance, after the siege of Limerick in 1691, the military articles of surrender coerced the persecuted Irish poor "to leave the Kingdom of Ireland [...] to go beyond the Seas" and work the land in British territories [HCA 1/13/122]. Ships also provided free transit for military personnel, e.g., "we took in Soldiers to Carry to Languard Fort [...] in the morning received other Soldiers on board to carry back" [ADM 52/2/6], and a description of "47 soldiers on bord [...] 31 Dutch officers (now at Howth) [in transit] for Holland" [ADM 52/2/6]. Also, in an age of routine prisoner exchanges, there were often recently liberated soldiers to return home, e.g., Captain Vaughan testifies that he took on board "English Men & Prisoners of Warr in France [...] to be sett on shore in England" [HCA 1/13/98]. Depending on the different languages and varieties of English that such passenger groups spoke, in addition to their inclination to identify with and accommodate to the maritime speech community, they would have affected the composition of shipboard speech communities and potentially adapted modes of communication for their own purposes.

In addition to working on board ships,[6] women also frequently travelled and lived at sea as guests or passengers. Some of these women were the wives and partners of working sailors, yet others may have travelled with family groups or as part of an indentured or slave cohort. Enslaved and indentured women in transit aboard the ships are rarely noted in official documentation of the era beyond a number tally in a cargo column, but reference to the presence of more privileged officers' wives is recoverable from contemporary records such as court testimony and private accounts. Sometimes these women are mentioned with accompanying details, e.g., "Elizabeth Tengrove that was a Passenger in the Onflow" [HCA 1/99/80], but most often the passing references to their presence on board do not provide any details e.g., "a woman which was a passenger abord the said English shipp"[HCA 1/101/372], "an English woman, that was aboard" [HCA 1/99 in The Tryals of Agostinho, no. 4], and in one rare logbook reference, "much wind putt [...] mens wifes on shore" [ADM 52/3/12]. Some women attest to their own presence at sea by giving testimony in court, such as Sybill Nicholls, wife of Captain Edward Nicholls, who was deposed on July 17 1661: "she toulde the said waterman that she was fearfull of going through bridge by reason it [the sea] was something rough" [HCA 1/9/22]. And Palisnce Bibar, wife of seaman Gibs Bibar, who was deposed on January 15 1696 and whose testimony about the captain's behaviour and hearing the Spanish enemy vessel also confirms her presence at sea [HCA 1/14/56]. In addition to these English wives, indigenous Indian and African partners were also potentially smuggled on board. Diana Souhami's award-winning biography of Alexander Selkirk's abandonment in 1704 envisions how William Dampier's crew bartered and forced such women into becoming sex workers:

> They had their Delilahs or Black Misses, hired for a trinket or a silver wrist band. More often it was rape, unwanted offspring and abandonment. Tawny coloured children of uncertain English paternity were born on board ship to black slaves. (Souhami 2013: 19)

The practice of women giving birth at sea, albeit unusual, is not unheard of in maritime history. Adkins and Adkins' work on the maritime communities of the

---

[6]See §3.3 Gender for a discussion of female crew and non-paid workers.

late eighteenth century claims: "It was not unusual for women to give birth during a battle, as the noise and stress of the situation tended to induce labour. Nor was it unusual for women to have their children with them" (Adkins & Adkins 2008: 176). Hence, although it was unlikely to be a large subgroup of the maritime community, a company composed of women (and potentially also their children) may have also contributed to speech practices at sea.

As discussed in Chapter 3, the largest group in most maritime communities was undoubtedly the lower-class working sailor. The necessary proximity in which enlisted men worked and lived meant that mutual dependency was commonly accompanied by emotional and physical intimacy. Indeed, the kinship or brotherhood of the seas is a common theme and the stereotypical representations of homosexual sailors abounds in maritime fiction and popular iconography.[7] Despite the harsh punishments in place for any proven acts of sodomy brought before the authorities, those managing social order among predominantly male ships' communities often accepted that repeated sexual abuse of child, subordinate, and female workers was to be expected–a sentiment acknowledged in modern scholarship, e.g., Bicheno's discussion of a court martial in the late sixteenth century in which the steward of the *Talbot* was hanged for sodomizing two cabin boys "which is odd, because that's what cabin boys were for" (2012: 188). Yet, it was likely that some familiar and intimate shipboard relationships became sexual in nature leading to consensual yet covert homosexual acts, although these are extremely difficult to quantify given the taboo that prompted contemporaries to either sensationalize, or conversely ignore and under-report, the phenomenon.

Regardless of whether such intimacy was manifest in physical means, sailors undoubtedly shared a kinship bond as a result of working and living in close proximity for the lengthy durations of their service at sea. The working men of a vessel were commonly referred to collectively by the name of the ship (Adkins & Adkins 2008: xxxiv; Palmer 1986: 44), but sailors referred to one another as "brother" e.g., in one letter from a commander to a peer in another vessel, dated 1698 [HCA 1/98/47], and used the terms "brotherhood" or "band of brothers" more extensively to encompass the entire crew, particularly among pirates, e.g., the description of one man "used by the Brotherhood for a Rogue" [HCA 1/99/157]. Walsh explains how, on smaller vessels, familial closeness was a requisite of the physical work: "such craft did not permit much physical separation [...]

[7]See the novels of Julien Viaud (a.k.a. Pierre Loti); the scholarship of Burg's (2007) *Boys at Sea* and (1995) *Sodomy and the Pirate Tradition* and Turley's (2001) *Rum, Sodomy and the Lash*; Klara's (2013) article on gay iconography in marketing, entitled "Perspective: Hey Sailor".

moreover, because much work was shared, there could be little social distance" (Walsh 1994: 35). He goes on to say that on the smaller craft like ketches, sloops and schooners, crews might only number five to six men: a master, a mate, a boy, and two or three seamen (p.35); a number that was optimal for synergy and additionally reflected a type of family unit. Whaling vessels, described as the "nursery of seamen",[8] similarly contained family-like units of six to seven men, often required to work in silent unison to get the harpooner within a few meters of his prey.[9] Larger vessels created similarly small units of men by mandating "mess" groups with the fundamental purpose of managing meals and food rations, yet these groups which ranged from around eight to twelve members also facilitated the formation of familial bonds as the men in each mess took turns as cook for the group and were also responsible for each other's daily wellbeing and conduct (Adkins & Adkins 2008: 75). The groups were composed with the additional intention to distribute sailors with a range of different ages, skills and years' experience among the crew as a means to disseminate knowledge throughout the company and also promote networks of loyalty that might discourage homogeneous rebellions. The messes served to disseminate orders and were envisioned as a series of self-governed units, each with its elder that served as a representative of the group. Fury explains that when officers were managing shipboard accusations and assigning punishments, "leaving the judgement in the hands of the respected men on the ship [i.e., the mess elders] was key to legitimizing it as a broad-based verdict which could be "sold" to the shipboard community in the short-term" (Fury 2015: 4). Officer Samuel Leech describes how these messes functioned aboard a large ship, "the crew of a man of war is divided into little communities...[that] eat and drink together, and are, as it were, so many families".[10] Leech also attests to the value of these groups for discouraging desertion, as "many... were kept from running away by the strength of their attachment to their shipmates" (cited in Adkins & Adkins 2008: 68). This observation is borne out by one testimony of how a captain granted shore leave but only "trusted

---

[8] Cited from a display in the British National Maritime Museum located in the "Atlantic Worlds" exhibition and visited on Nov 22, 2015.

[9] There were, however, crew requirements distinguishing between larger and smaller vessels. Large whaling vessels often had to leave their European and American ports under-crewed with the intention to complete the requisite crew number en-route. Africans (Kru-men) and Pacific Islanders are also particularly noted for this practice. The recruits picked up en-route would form an important component of the shipboard community in addition to those workers who shipped out with the vessel from a home port.

[10] Cited from a display in the British National Maritime Museum located in the "Atlantic Worlds" exhibition and visited on Nov 22, 2015.

on shore at Annabone *only one of a mess*" [HCA 1/99/114 emphasis added], suggesting that desertion was drastically minimized if only one man per mess was permitted off the vessel at any one time. Hence, mess groups were not only functional for practical reasons like distribution of rations and information but also actively promoted familial bonding, and so increased social cohesion and crew retention.

The intimacy and kinship that characterized crews was most pronounced in times of difficulty when survival may have depended on it. Pirate crews that depended on plunder for many of their basic necessities grew accustomed to self-management and especially allocating shares in community goods, e.g., one witness testimony describes how "they Plundered and took all the cloaths they could, and shared the same" [HCA 1/99, Jamaica Aug 11 1740]. Another crew, facing starvation, and "being ardently desirous that at least some one of them might survive to carry home the news of their misfortune [...] cast lots which of them should be killed to serve for food to the other" [445f.1/486].[11] In combat, a unified crew was also a more effective fighting unit, and many witness testimonies reflect sentiments of unity in the face of violent conflict, e.g., witness Joseph Wood describes an invading pirate crew: "I heard them say they would live & dye together" [CO 5/1411/37], and upon capture one sailor explains: "it were as good for them to be blown up & dye altogether in the shipp" [CO 5/1411/102]. Indeed, such social cohesion enabled men to face horrifying violence and retribution with almost joyous unity, e.g., new recruits who are welcomed by the crew "Saying cheerfully and unanimously that they would live & dye with them" [HCA 1/9/155]. Yet, such collective agency was not always instinctive; successful pirate crews forced gang-unity through intimidation and initiation rites, e.g., the description of how one mariner joined the crew when a group surrounded his hammock with swords in their hands and threatened to slice him if he did not stand by them [HCA 1/53/43]. Yet once these gangs were formed, they maintained fierce insular unity. In the event of capture, gang members often depended on each other for their lives, whether that meant pleading to the officers of another vessel or making representation in courts, e.g. one sailor's dangerous position, "he was a dead man if this examinant should presente or give Information against him" [HCA 1/53/9], and another's relative safety, "he was confident of him being intimate accuaintance [...] he would not see him wronged in anything and all of the rest said the like" [HCA 1/101/408]. Indeed, it was on pirate vessels that consent and unity in action may have been most critical to social order. This

---

[11]This plan was abandoned however when the captain, who insisted upon casting his lot with the men, was selected to become the next meal.

may explain why instead of functioning in small and inflexible mess units, pirates were encouraged to consider the whole crew as one mess–their extended family, e.g., the testimony of one accused sailor claims, "he messed with the captain, but withall no Body look'd on it, as a Mark of Favour, or Distinction, for every one came and eat and drank with him at their Humour" [HCA 1/99/59]. Moreover, such equitable practices were mirrored in the signing of ships' articles voting customs that also took place among pirate crews,[12] in which even a captain was considered no more than an elected representative, e.g., "As to the title of Captain it was nothing for every man was alike which was plain" [HCA 1/99/72]. In such contexts, the petition of a captain is no weightier than any other man's vote, e.g., one commander describes how he tried to save his ship: "I begged for her but it was put to the vote and carried for the burning of her and burnt she was" [CO 5/1411/34]. At other times, officers are described as "accompliced with the rest of that Pyratical Crew" [HCA 1/99/170], e.g., "the Commander and the major part of the Company Voted to Sail about the Cape of good hope" [HCA 1/98/263]. Yet the casting of the vote is still an important act, and one without which decisions could be challenged and commanders deposed. Hence, pirate crews (although notoriously difficult to research) might have provided the best models of social cohesion at sea.

In the merchant fleets, there was a degree of individual protection in group agency that emboldened some sailors to act against repressive regimes at sea, e.g., the enlisted men of the East India Company, knowing the value of their labor, lobbied as a collective (sometimes successfully) with the threats of work stoppages and strikes to save shipmates and adjust the trajectory or the time-frame of a voyage (Fury 2015: 15). In a more severe example among the same company, when the men were discovered to have murdered the Master John Lufkin after an on-board dispute and were demanded to reveal who killed him, the crew answered: "One and all of them" (cited in Fury 2015: 11). In lieu of killing their commanding officer, crews might also band together to accuse a superior officer of some crime and thus remove him, as Captain Thomas Oxinden claimed in a letter to the Admiralty dated Aug 28 1667 [HCA 1/101/317]. Collective action provided some degree of safety in numbers, a sentiment reflected by the wording of official statements, e.g., "Ye have all of you been wickedly united...[acting] in a wicked combination" [HCA 1/99/3/2–3], and one court testimony describing

---

[12]See Rediker's scholarship on Atlantic pirates in the golden age, specifically chapter 4 "The New Government of the Ship" (2004: 60–82) and Jarvis's discussion of the traditions of "maritime republics" that go back to the medieval Rules of Oléron (*Rôles d'Oléron*) named for the island of Oléron (off the coast of France), the site of the maritime court associated with the most powerful seamen's guild of the Atlantic (Jarvis 2010: 121).

"Severall of the mariners who were in a confederacy together" [HCA 1/53/42], the words "united", "combination" and "confederacy" implying civic alliance. In light of such examples, the brotherhood of a crew appears, at best, as a workers' union and, at worst, a group of political activists and rebels; and perhaps, given this continuum, it is clear why sometimes collective agency was tolerated as a form of early modern bargaining in the workforce, but at other times was condemned as outright mutiny.

Collective agency provided a kind of pseudo-legal support group for the common sailor who was not likely to receive any such help within the High Court of the Admiralty. Personal letters and witness depositions attest to the tenderness and care with which sailors composed their last will and testament before crewmates or wrote another's will for him as he lay dying, often binding the pseudo-legal documents with their own personal mark and the initials or signatures of shipmates, e.g., the last will of Cornelius Dorington, which begins "I give and bequeath to my loving friend Capt Sammuell Burgess a Gold ring" [HCA 1/98/87], the last will of Joseph Jones, who leaves his worldly goods to his shipmates [HCA 1/98/108], and the unusual joint will of Francis Reed and John Beavis, signed by both men, that declares, in the event of an accident to either, "what gold, silver or other thing whatsoever" shall lawfully become the legal property of the other, explained by the preamble "Be it known to all men [that these two are] in Consort ship togeather" [HCA 1/98/193]. In a modern context, such a document sounds distinctly like the mutual testimony of a monogamous couple and prompts the comparison of a consensual and loving relationship between the two men that they have attempted to legitimize among the crew despite the outlawed nature of their affections in wider society. In short, familial mess bonds among crews facilitated shipboard management and discouraged desertion but may have also gone some way towards legitimizing alternative sexuality and certainly enabling larger networks of collective agency among crews that not only increased the chances of survival and successful negotiation of better conditions at sea, but also provided a much-needed pseudo-legal support network in a context when the common sailor was considered lazy, rebellious, and ultimately expendable.

4.2.5 The role of alcohol

Drinking alcohol with crew mates was the most popularly recognized social event among crews of the early colonial period. Such practices were recognized in wider society as comparable with drinking a toast to success, e.g., the imagery of celebration represented in the popular song "Lustily, Lustily", as mariners celebrate a successful voyage: "We will return merrily [...] /And hold all together as friends linked in love, / The cans shall be filled with wine, ale and beer" (cited in Palmer 1986: 3). Yet the real reasons for consuming alcohol in maritime communities were far more complex. One of the reasons for the excessive consumption of alcohol was the unusually malignant supplies of water that were the only other liquid available to drink.[13] Gage recommended drinking fermented beer, rum or wine as preferable to water as he cautioned his crew against "drinking after them too greedily of the [local] water (which causeth dangerous Fluxes, and hasteneth death to those newly come...) wee should fall sick, and die there as hundreds did" (Gage 1648: 24). Bicheno explains, "All levels of society knew that water, unless from a pristine source, was bad for your health [...] it's safe to say that while the ale remained drinkable everyone aboard was at least mildly inebriated at all times" (2012: 11). Indeed, because alcohol was a safer option to water and hard manual labor in exposed and oftentimes tropical conditions generated thirst, there are frequent references to alcohol consumption in official records. Examples of references in logbooks include: the cargo details of the *St. Andrew*, in 1693 that notes "touke in 30 tunns of Beere this day" [ADM 52/2/2], and "we have been clearing our hould this morning in order to take in 60 tons of beere" [ADM 52/2/3]; the evidence of using alcohol in barter exchanges with the *Albemarle* in 1692, in which the author describes how the crew performed a service "for the *Royall fauvor* but they had no rum for us!" [ADM 52/2/3]; and the surprisingly short and direct entry for the *Pideaux* in 1732 that reflects on a day of leisure, "fair pleasant we excuse; all Drunk" [HCA 1/99/39]. Jarvis explains that a naval sailor of the early colonial period was entitled to 16 gallons of rum per year (Jarvis 2010: 178) perhaps because commanders knew that in spite of extensive hardships at sea, if sailors could maintain their alcohol rations, they would probably continue working.

The drinking culture on ships, unsurprisingly, created some problems as men could legitimately drink at work and oftentimes did so excessively. References to the intoxication of individuals feature in court cases, e.g. one unnamed sailor who the witness claims "he never see him Sober Scarce, or fit for any Duty" [HCA 1/99/44], another who "had made himself drunk with two bottles of brandy, and was not sober again in three days" [445f.1/510], "Stephen Thomas- Deposeth that he was allways Drunk" [HCA 1/99/26], and "Henry Glasby, that he was as brisk and as often Drunk as the Rest of the Company" [HCA 1/99/108]. More shock-

---

[13] The tradition of drinking ale or some form of fermented liquid instead of water for reasons of local pollution is commonplace throughout history (see Salzman's *Drinking Water: A History* 2013). It is not surprising that this tradition passed from general European populations to transient populations and European colonies in the New World in the context of unsecure water supplies.

ingly, there are similarly frequent references to the intoxication of the whole crew, e.g., "the men were drunk when they went on board" [CO 5/1411/101], "they were very Careless in that point, often being all Hands Drunk, and no Body fit for Duty" [HCA 1/99/91], and the description of one severe mistake, in which:

> they were all drunk with Rum and Palm Wine, that words arose and they went to fighting... then being very drunk they fell asleep, and she [the ship] drove out to Sea: that after making the Land again, they mistook the Danish fort for the [fort] of the English. [HCA 1/99 Cape Coast of Africa, Feb 4 1734, 5]

In such a context, it is clear why the navy tried to punish excessive drinking with imprisonment in iron shackles, flogging, and, if a serious crime were involved, court martial (see Figure 4.4). Yet, interestingly, even if a court martial was called, men might be shown leniency for inebriation, e.g., one court verdict that acknowledges diminished capacity: "yet in regard to their being Drunk, and consequently then not altogether capable of judging Right and Wrong, the Court was inclinable to shew mercy" [HCA 1/99 Cape Coast of Africa, Feb 4 1734, 6]. Therefore, it is no surprise to read testimony from other men hoping for similar mercy to excuse their intoxicated actions e.g., "he was drunk and that when he came to his senses he was sorry" [HCA 1/99/23], "any Irregularities he might commit, was the Drink" [HCA 1/99/40], "it was Drink and over Perswasion of the others that engaged him to it" [HCA 1/99/165], "he was drunk when he did consent" [HCA 1/99 Bahama Islands 1722], and "do's not deny his firing a Gun, but excuses it for being Drunk" [HCA 1/99/135]. However, despite a few cases, men were held accountable for their actions while drunk on duty; the ability to hold your drink was considered a part of the job.

Drunkenness was a cultural phenomenon that manifested itself in all ranks aboard ship, not just with the common sailor. Because drinking alcohol served a social function, and reinforced group identity ()Fury2015 the commanders, captains and officers of maritime communities also regularly consumed alcohol, and also often to excess. Examples of drunken officers in court testimony include, "After they had drunke togeather a while Capt Rigby & George Freebound went on board their vessells againe" [HCA 1/9/3], and "the said captain was so very much in drink that he never was afterwards (according to this Deponent's best observation) big help" [HCA 1/14/56]; passenger journals describe "the Captain was a very Furious man, and frequently in Drink; so that I could not have opportunity to speak with him" [445f.1/27]; and logbooks corroborate, "Our captn being drunk did quarrel wth me" [HCA 1/99/62], "master drunk at noon" [HCA

Figure 4.4: "In irons for getting drunk" Colored etching by George Cruikshank https://commons.wikimedia.org/w/index.php?curid=62587613

1/99/65]. Drunken commanders could pose a serious problem to the social fabric of a shipboard community. For example, in an extended court case against Nicholas Reymer, commander of the ship *Lucy*, in a trial dated June 20th 1682, a witness explains:

> Reyner was verry Idle & most commonly in drink & he does believe that his seamens disorder were chiefly occasioned by his sole debaucherys & ill carriage... the dissasters & damage hapened to the shipp Lucy [...] were chiefly occasioned by the carelessness & disorder of said Reymer & his company... before & after the shipp was aground said Raymer was ashoar drinking to excesse. [E134/34Chas2/Mich36]

Qualitative data about intoxication among the commanding ranks prompts the supposition that the harsh treatment sailors experienced at their hands, detailed in §4.2.2 and tabulated in Table 4.1 and Table 4.2, may have been directly related to their lowered inhibitions as a result of being drunk. However, aside from a few specific cases, we are unlikely to know the true extent of and damage caused by the drinking culture amongst commanders and officers of the period, as these privileged few controlled the records and were unlikely to acknowledge blame nor leave evidence that would prompt investigations into their own accountability.

Pirate commanders, and indeed the entire crew of pirate vessels, are commonly characterized by excessive consumption of alcohol. Although, in extreme circumstances, a sailor might lose his allocation of seized goods if he was physically incapable of participating in its capture, e.g., one sailor described as "so Drunk they cut him often out of his Share" [HCA 1/99/171], more commonly, alcohol served a vital role in social order and cohesion. Notorious pirate captain Edward "Blackbeard" Teach recorded in his personal log the dangers of sobriety among his crew:

> Such a day, rum all out — our company somewhat sober — a damn'd confusion among us! — rogues aplotting — great talk of separation. So I look'd sharp for a prize — such a day took one, with a great deal of liquor on board, so kept the Company hot, damn'd hot, then all things went well again. (cited in Bicheno 2012: 121)

Court depositions explicitly associated an inclination for drinking with piracy and accusations were often accompanied by a comment on how much the accused commonly drank, e.g., "for he was a drunken Fellow" [HCA 1/99/103], "he fell to Drinking and became one of the Company" [HCA 1/99/104], "[he] was allways Drunk" [HCA 1/99/116], "he was [...] very much given to Liquor and was as forward as others at going on Board of Prizes" [HCA 1/99/171], "he knew no more of him than that he loved Drinking" [HCA 1/99/63], and "Deposeth him to be a very Drunken Fellow" [HCA 1/99/158]. Conversely, the case for the defense often pleaded, at best, sobriety, e.g., "Swear him to have been a very Sober, civil Fellow no way mischievous" [HCA 1/99/121], and "never heard him Swear, never given to Drink, and calld Presbyterian for his Sobriety" [HCA 1/99/151], and at worst, coerced inebriation "the pyrates whom he presently Saw were forcing Drink upon him as afterwards they wou'd Some Cloths" [HCA 1/99/147]. The true nature of the situation might be best seen through the eyes of one sailor who made his defense against being accused of drinking with a pirate crew: "As to Drinking he Says t'was a Common Fault among 'em, and he knew of no other Company he cou'd keep in that Place" [HCA 1/99/120]. In reality, it may have been that drinking to excess was simply a part of maritime culture, and if sailors were to adapt and accommodate to their peers and enjoy the benefits of collective agency and representation, then there was really no alternative than to accept social drinking as part of the lifestyle.

Maritime communities used alcohol ritualistically to affirm social unity and mark complicity in agreements such as recruitment deals and trade negotiations, few of which were certified by written contacts. Fury (2015) provides evidence of two extreme circumstances in which alcohol was used as a social bonding agent aboard the voyages of the East India Company. The first occurred during the voyage of the *Ascension* 1608–9 when Coxswain Nicholas White was convicted of sodomizing the Purser's Boy, William Acton, and was sentenced to hang; the crew passed among them "a cup of wine shared for his farewell" at his execution (Fury 2015: 10). The second example occurred on the ship *Good Hope* in 1609 after an uprising led to the murder of Master John Lufkin and, as a result, the men "helped themselves to his provisions, carousing and drinking, toasting each other" (Fury 2015: 13). Although superficially there is little connection between these events, the use of alcohol in both serves the role of uniting the crew in a gesture of solidarity against what was considered a severe punishment in the first example, and as in a gesture of celebration and complicity in the mutinous act in the second. The act of drinking itself served to demonstrate solidarity, as one commander demonstrates in his pledge: "he would not see him wronged in anything and all of the rest said the like Whereupon he called for a bottle of brandy & Drank wth them and tould them he would make them all men and officers" [HCA 1/101/408–409]. The drinking of the brandy in this example acts to validate the pledge, similar to how taking an oath might, or signing a document, if the contract were written. Likewise, the following description of post-trade inebriation seems to be an important part of validating the exchange of goods and strengthens the ties between trading partners for the possibility of future agreements:

> One day, a small French sloop came to trade with the English owner of the plantation. The French smugglers (about fourteen or fifteen men) loaded three barrels of brown (pardo) sugar, eleven sacks of cotton, and one barrel of indigo dye onto their ship, and then left the loaded ship moored while they and the Englishmen they had traded with all got Drunk. (Hatfield 2016: 15)

Alcohol served to validate trade agreements, and so the taverns and private drinking houses that supplied the alcohol used to validate these deals were not just places to socialize, but offices of maritime business. In the court records relating to one piracy trial in Rhode Island and Providence Plantation in 1725, the entire courtroom seems to have moved into a local tavern; the court clerk notes "Whereupon the Court adjourned to the *Three Mariners* Tavern... and Opened by proclamation" [HCA 1/99/5]. Yet more commonly, local taverns were not the domain of the administration but rather grassroots maritime communication hubs, e.g. one commander's proposition to enter into negotiations with another: "the said Brock would be glad to Drinke a Bottell of wine with the said Le Fort that he might have his company" [HCA 1/52/137]; and one letter from a sailor's wife that instructs him: "your letter for george herring to be left Mr. Richard merrys here the sine of the *green dragon* nere Shadwell doce [dock] in London" [HCA 1/12/87]. In addition to their role as places of information exchange, taverns were also centers for negotiation on contraband trade that was not subject to the monopolies of the Navigation Acts or the restrictions of other European trading regulations. As such, they proliferated in islands that were centers of news networks and trading routes, e.g., "proportionally, at least one in fourteen Bermudian households operated as a part-time tavern" (Jarvis 2010: 294). Hatfield's work on illegal slave trading by English pirates in the late seventeenth century as described in Spanish Sanctuary Records suggests the cross-cultural nature of drinking rituals accompanying trade. She notes that "the French smugglers and English planters caroused together in addition to trading" (Hatfield 2016: 17). The international and therefore outlawed nature of such trade may explain why colonial government records abound with regulations against and prosecutions for unlicensed taverns e.g., Barbadian legislation in 1652 "to prevent frequenting of taverns and ale-houses by seamen", and two years later, the act "prohibiting persons from keeping a common ale-house, or tippling-house, selling any liquors or this country-spirits, to be drank in their houses or plantations without a license".[14] Such legislation may have been an attempt to restrict the flow of information and operations in illegal trade much more than an effort to increase island-wide sobriety, and suggests that local authorities also knew the important role of alcohol in maritime trade negotiations.

The most extreme and spiritual use of alcohol in maritime ritual relates to preparations among the crew before anticipated combat. One witness testimony reports "after they had been Drinking all Day togeather towards the evening [...] to get all together and seize upon the goods" [HCA 1/9/8], and Fury's research includes a footnote relating to how the crew of the *Golden Dragon* drank to each other in a gesture of forgiveness for any wrongdoings and as an act of solidarity before battle (HCA 13/30/108v, cited in Fury 2015: 10). The act of drinking before conflict is also referred to in the witness testimony of how one captain and his company prepared for imminent battle "Drinking Rum and Gunpowder" [HCA

---

[14]First legislation dated Jan 10 1652 and the second in the Acts of 1654, both retrieved from the Catalogue of Acts 1642–1699, The Barbados Department of Archives, St. James.

1/99 *The American: Weekly Mercury* No.618, Oct 28–Nov 4 1731]. Interestingly, this ritual has historical parallels in Obeah war rituals. Boukman Barima, Professor of Atlantic History and the African Diaspora at Jackson State University, explains:

> Obeah's war rituals survived the erosion of time and were passed like heirlooms between successive generations of freedom fighters as in the practice of consuming rum mixed with gunpowder. Rebels throughout enslavement when they took oaths to pledge their loyalty to each other and their revolt drank this liquid admixture to seal their pact. Binding oaths with liquid concoctions occurs in several West and Central African societies, for instance, in Fanti swearing ceremonies for Omanhene, Asafohene and other leaders this was an essential rite that summoned "the gods to witness" the proceedings and if the person dishonored their pledge "the drink would cause injury or death". (Boukman Barima 2016: 20 with in-text citations of Shumay's [2011] *The Fante and the Transatlantic Slave Trade*)

The use of alcohol in Obeah war rituals to seal a pledge mirrors the role of alcohol in preparations for combat in maritime, and specifically pirate communities, and therefore might also attest to the African cultural influence on such crews. The potential African spiritual influence is even more pronounced when we consider that "common protocol for preparing and hosting rum and gunpowder rituals always demands an adept Obeah man as master of ceremony" (Boukman Barima 2016: 8) suggesting that multicultural crews not only maintained, but also looked towards such spiritual leaders in times of crisis. Hence, regular consumption of alcohol in maritime communities was not just an act of celebration and a necessary replacement for repugnant water supplies, but also served an important role in promoting social order by promoting complicity and unity, regulating trade agreements, and expressing spiritual connectivity in times of distress or anticipated conflict.

4.2.6 Shared ideologies and leisure activities

Sailors were not known for being particularly pious, but the communities they lived in were bound by strong shared ideologies–oftentimes categorized as superstitions, folklore or myths–that manifested themselves in ritual and storytelling. Fantastical beliefs relating to the inherent risks of sailing and the desire for fortuitous sailing conditions date back to antiquity, and sailors of the early colonial period would have tried to derive meaning from omens and portents in the same way as generations of those that went before them. Bassett explains in his book on *Legends and Superstitions of the Sea and of Sailors*:

monsters abode in the waters, gods of monstrous shapes ruled them, en-
chanting sirens, horrid giants, and terrible dragons inhabited the islets and
rocks, and on the dry land beyond, there dwelt strange enchantresses, fire-
breathing hulls, dwarfish pigmies, and man-eaters....Thus sailors as well as
landsmen, in all ages, have been prone to indulge in fancies of all kinds con-
cerning the winds and waves. Such notions are naturally directed to the
weather, the object of so much care and solicitude to the mariner. (Bassett
1885: 12)

Eyers asserts that "sailors remain a notoriously superstitious lot" (Eyers 2011:
5) and his book on nautical myths and superstitions covers material on well-
known lore of the sea such as mermaids, the flying Dutchman, evil spirits and
ghosts of those departed. Yet, evidence of explicit folklore is rare in archival documentation owing to the nature of the beliefs that were typically transmitted in
oral traditions and considered inappropriate to or unworthy of official records.
More commonly, official records include references to orthodox religious observations such as the entry "this day being sabath day our Capt was not willing to
saile" in the logbook of the *Carlyle* [T/70/1216/9], and the warning by court officials against "being moved & seduced by the instigation of the Devil" [HCA 1/99
Jamaica 1738–1739 & Bahama Islands 1722]. However, there are some references
to the darker side of sailors' spirituality in observations such as how one Spanish
crew:

> began againe to curse and rage against the English which inhabited that
> Island [Bermuda], saying, that they had inchated that and the rest of those
> Islands about and did still with the devill raile stormes in those seas when
> the Spanish Fleet passed that way. (Gage 1648: 201)

This journal entry demonstrates the sailors' belief that individuals could en-
chant the winds and purposefully cause storms, a sentiment famously reflected
in Shakespeare's *The Tempest*, believed to have been written around 1611. Another
series of official records which attest to community beliefs in individuals with supernatural powers derive from a series of witness depositions taken in Virginia
1661, in the case of Robert Clarke [HCA 1/9/51]. Although testimonies do not always align, the majority of witnesses in the case corroborate the beating and ulti-
mate death of Robert Clarke in direct retribution for his necromancy. Testimony
describes how Clarke was chained, beaten, had pins thrust into his flesh and
was kept from sleeping before being ultimately bound and strangled with a rope
around the neck. Deponents explain that his treatment was designed to "beate

the Devill out of him [...] that the devils came often to him and would Speake Softly to him" and "some of the passengers would often call the Said Clarke thiefe & witch & the like", and as a result, "Capt Hobbs Did say that they Should never have faire weather till the said Clarke was hanged" [all citations from HCA 1/9/51 batch]. Interestingly, three deponents testify that Clarke was beaten at his own request, had made a confession that he was a witch, could speak Latin, and was often heard reciting the Lord's Prayer and the Ten Commandments. This suggests that Clarke was an educated man, possibly involved with the church, but who potentially suffered from schizophrenia or some other mental disorder that provoked mass hysteria aboard the ship and tapped into deep-rooted beliefs in supernatural agency on the ships. Certainly, little was known about mental disorder at the time and attacks of epilepsy, aphasia, bipolar disorder, in addition to the effects of degenerative muscle, skin, or mental conditions might very well have been interpreted as something sinister.

Dramatic rites of passage, such as initiation of new sailors when they first crossed the line of the equator, commonly bound maritime communities of the early colonial period, and the shared ideology of such rituals are manifest even today (Bronner 2006). Customs like these expressed solidarities among the crew and part of the initiation of new men involved "learning the ropes" when it came to the rites of passage, and so mariners did not customarily make any reference to these events in letters back home or in the official record-keeping. However, one passenger who was privileged to see the custom aboard a late seventeenth century Portuguese vessel reports that he witnessed an "ancient custom", which served to initiate any sailor crossing the line of the equator for the first time. He describes how the novice sailor was required to give food, drink or some physical gift or money equivalent to the mariners, and if any man did not pay:[15]

> the sailors clothed like officers carry him bound to a tribunal, on which a seaman is seated in a long robe, who acting the part of a judge, examines him, hears what he has to say, and gives judgement against him to be thrice ducked in the sea after this manner: the person condemned is tied fast with rope, and the other end of it run through a pully at the yard-arm, by which he is hoisted up, and then let run amain three times under water; and there seldom sails to be one or other that gies the rest this diversion. The same is practised in passing the straits of Gibraltar, and the cape of Good Hope. [445f.1/486]

---

[15]Such rituals are not anticipated to be monolithic but varying among crews and vessels, as such the description serves as an example of one manifestation of the ritual and is not presented as a model.

The dramatic ritual described when crossing the line includes elements of role play, and specifically the use of costume to reflect the role of the judge, a phenomenon also described and illustrated in Charles Johnson's (1724) description of a mock trial among pirates, see Figure 4.5(a). This practice may have roots in the ancient practices of African and European nations that crowned a king-for-the-day, a role that is still celebrated in carnaval cultures across the Americas and Caribbean islands, and is echoed in the witness testimony of how "the Indian would have command of the vessel and would be called capt: and dailly getting Drunk" [HCA 1/99 Barbados 1733]. Thus, dramatic role play may have been a salient part of maritime ritual, particularly with regards to using costume to invert social order and play out alternative models of authority.

Sailors did not always work; they also enjoyed leisure time at sea. The sizeable crews necessitated by navigational, defense, and loading requirements of the large warships and transatlantic trading vessels nonetheless became superfluous during favorable sailing conditions and in times of absence of conflict at sea. This was even more notable on pirate vessels that maintained a typically larger crew and whose speech community Burg (2001) compares to the "total institutions" of prisons and mental institutions, characterized by significant leisure time and greater opportunities for extensive social interaction. During such leisure time, sailors told stories, played games, enjoyed music, and even staged dramatic performances at sea (Rediker 2004: 155). Such speech acts would have provided an ideal situation for the mixing, leveling and simplification processes of new dialect formation, outlined by Trudgill (1986), and also would have provided opportunities for new recruits to listen to, practice, and acquire features of Ship English.

Spontaneous conversation was the most common type of social contact that individual sailors were likely to engage in on a regular basis, and, in the absence of news, gossip and storytelling were favorite group pastimes–as British illustrator George Cruikshank shows in his "Saturday Night at Sea" (see illustration in Figure 4.5(b)). Participation in storytelling served to strengthen social bonds and maritime traditions, particularly as the repetition of stories also demanded accommodation to the original speaker's performance style. It is also possible that ships' cooks, typically older and/or disabled seamen, may have been a focal point of the storytelling tradition, retelling their experiences at sea and teaching new recruits in much the same way as a village elder might. Officer Robert Wilson describes the role of the cook: "when their work is finished for the day they'll take their pipes, seat themselves in Copper Alley, and spin you a long yard [yarn] ... about what they have seen and done" (cited in Adkins & Adkins 2008: 76). And perhaps it was this very role as the acting village elder that makes the

(a) The mock trial performed by the crew of the Thomas from Anstis, from Captain Charles Johnson's *A general history of robberies and murders of the most notorious pyrates* (London 1724) reproduced in Rediker (2004): 156

(b) "Saturday Night at Sea" by George Cruikshank, an illustration from *Songs, naval and national* by Thomas Dibdin, published in London, England in 1841. https://commons.wikimedia.org/wiki/File:Saturday_night_at_sea.jpg

fictional Long John Silver (a disabled cook) so cruel in his attempted corruption of the novice Jim Hawkins in Stevenson's (1883) *Treasure Island*. Sailors knew, as perhaps did Stevenson, that cooks were the focal point of social life aboard ship, and their potential role in transmitting language features through narratives in a predominantly oral culture was sacred.

As mentioned above, music and games were also integral parts of shipboard leisure time, although these often required equipment and some level of experience or ability. Numerous sea shanties of the era survive, not only because regular rhythms facilitated collaborative work efforts, but also because, as Palmer explains, "sailors would assemble there [the mainmast] in good weather during dog-watches and other free times to talk and exchange songs" (Palmer 1986: xxvii). Repeated references to instruments in witness testimony shows that music featured in the daily lives of sailors beyond vocalizations, e.g., drummers are referred to in various documents [e.g., HCA 1/99/124; HCA 1/14/201; and SP 42/6]. The drum may have served a military purpose, but testimony in cases relating to the forced recruitment of musicians on pirate vessels not only shows that other instruments were on board but also that those who could play them were in high demand, e.g., the accused "took from aubord the Shallop a man belonging to the deponent who Could play on the Violin" [HCA 1/99/5], a captured sailor "begged hard for his release, insisting on his being a decreped little Fellow unfit for their Purpose, but he was a Trumpeter, and therefore they would not hear him" [HCA 1/99/33], and another sailor, "a fidler taken with himself was forced [...] to sign their articles" [HCA 1/99/49].

Similarly, witness testimony shows evidence of equipment used for gaming on board ships, e.g., two sailors arguing over ownership of "Baggamon [backgammon] Tables" [HCA 1/99/81], "Peter Fox abt 25 yeares old [...] quick and ready of speech, very plausable in Company, a great gamer, and Seldom wthout a ball of dyce in his porkett" [HCA 1/101/411]. Diarists also corroborate the presence of games on board, e.g., Edward Hayes's late sixteenth century journal notes, "we were provided of music in good variety not omitting the least toys, as morris dancers, hobby horse, and May-like conceits", on board the 10-ton frigate *Squirrel* in the late sixteenth century (cited in Bicheno 2012: 173), and Dr. John Covel's late seventeenth century journal notes:

> we seldome fail of some merry fellows in every ship's crew who will entertain us with several diversions, as divers sorts of odde sports and Gambols; sometimes with their homely drolls and Farses, which in thier corrupt language they nickname Interludes; sometimes they dance about the mainmast instead of a maypole, and they have variety of forecastle songs, ridiculous enough. (cited in Palmer 1986: 104)

Although captains and officers preached the benefits of discipline and self-restraint, they knew that such games were beneficial to occupy idle hands and discouraged more dangerous leisure activities such as talking politics, for example, the conversation about the relative merits of Oliver Cromwell and Charles II that John Barefoot was overheard debating by one witness [HCA 1/9/68]; firing weapons, as happened when pirates got bored and started firing at the *Whydah* for sport [HCA 1/99/99]; and excessive alcohol consumption, discussed in §4.2.5 corroborated by testimonies such as the deposition that describes the crew of the *Elizabeth*, "Carouzing and Drinking with the Rest of the Pyrates" [HCA 1/99/46]. Officers therefore permitted games and music as controlled social acts that helped relieve tedium during uneventful hours at sea.

Occasionally, ships' captains would permit (and potentially encourage) more structured leisure activities on board such as theatrical performances. There is evidence that even the lower ranking officers were involved in amateur dramatics, writing, rehearsing and performing plays for visiting officials (Adkins & Adkins 2008: 339). Fury refers to "the men included performances of two of Shakespeare's plays afloat and ashore" on the third voyage of the East India Company

1604–6 (Fury 2015: 19). And Gage describes how "for the afternoones sport they had prepared a Copmedy out of famous Lope de Vega, to be acted by some Soldiers, Passengers and some of the younger soft of Fryers" (Gage 1648: 16). However, these were likely to have been rare events compared to the more common social activities of telling stories, playing and listening to music, singing songs, dancing, and gambling that fortified the social fabric of the insular ship's community.

4.3 Wider maritime communities

In addition to the insular ship communities that each sailor belonged to, a wider maritime community encompassed and connected all of the vessels at sea, in port and in river-trade, and also extended to the port and littoral communities in contact with sea-going vessels through local trade, employment opportunities or the service industry. These communities had characteristic features that potentially affected the acquisition and transfer of Ship English and the nature of its internal change. These features included the profusion of maritime contact and the nature of contact in ship-to-ship exchanges, the economic profile of the community that supported a culture of theft and the operation of clandestine networks, and the frequency and nature of contact with port communities.

4.3.1 Profuse maritime activity

Shipping for defense and trade purposes has always been important in Great Britain, surrounded on all sides by the sea. Even as far back as 98CE, a Roman trader described its major port town of London as "a busy emporium for trade and traders" (Tacitus 1913), and in the fervor of early colonial manufacture, industry, discovery and international trade, London was defined by its connectivity by sea routes to colonial and foreign locations. Bicheno explains that the population of London trebled during the sixteenth century and in the early seventeenth century, and the docks of London became "one of the most crowded places on earth [...] [when] an estimated 75,000 lived in the square mile of the city – which would put it among the top ten most densely populated cities even today" (Bicheno 2012: 13). In fact, the Thames was so busy that the lightermen, whose job it was to move cargo and thus make the boats lighter, and watermen, employed to move people and transit goods across the river, made frequent complaints about the congestion around the vast system of docks, wharfs, and warehouses, e.g., in one petition, two London watermen complain that "by reason of shipps & other vesssells continually Lying & incroaching upon the said staires [landing place] are not onlely greatly hindered in their dayly Imployments but also much [...] in their boates which are often splitt & broken by such vessells" [HCA 1/11/109]. Such complaints led to the 1667 bill under penalty of fine "that no shipp or vessell shall [...] obstruct or hinder the passage of any lighter or vessell passing to or from the said dock" [IICA 1/11/140] and speak to the problems that London's maritime service providers had to face on a daily basis in the bustling port.

The importance of the sea in terms of military defense is self-evident for an island-kingdom[16] for whom the seas became "a moat defensive" in the words of the dying fictional John of Gaunt in Shakespeare's *Richard II,* (c. 1595, 2.1). Bicheno (2012: 24) explains that "with hundreds of ports and no place more than 70 miles/112 kilometers from the sea, what we might call 'maritime awareness' was a constant in English history". Even at sea, it was a numbers game, (Adkins & Adkins 2008) explain, "the war at sea was one of attrition, with the navy of each side preying on merchant shipping to starve the enemy of supplies, reduce prosperity and thereby limit the capacity to wage war" (p. 231). A profusion of maritime activity was thus actively encouraged by competing European sea-going nations of the time, and this naturally led to frequent contact between foreign ships in the open waters, evidenced by first-hand testimony, e.g., "[we] Chased a french man of warr" [ADM 52/2/8], "there was 16 Saile of french" [DDB6/8/4], "a fleet of ships of 14 Saile Supposing them to be a french fleet" [ADM 52/1/8], and "severl Duch Mercht Shipps with a Man of war came in" [ADM 52/2/5]. Frequent contact between ships also happened in busy ports, e.g., a passenger describes the port at Cadiz in 1666:

> full of an infinitive number of ships, galleys, barks, caravels, tartans, and other vessels, which I was assured at the time amounted to an hundred sail. Just at the entrance of the harbour we saw twenty-five ships of an extraordinary bulk. There is a continual resort of ships from all parts of the world, even from the *Indes*; and it is usual there to see thirty or forty sail come or go out in a day, as if they were but little boats. [445f.1/511]

Such international traffic, in addition to the transatlantic slave trade that began on a large-scale in the mid-seventeenth century, caused crowding in trading zones and the shipping lanes of the open seas because prevailing ocean currents and winds determined ships' navigation and created international sea-highways that all vessels were obliged to use (Adkins & Adkins 2008: xxxiv and refer back

---

[16]An island-nation after the British loss of Calais in 1558.

to Figure 4.1) As such, and according to the British National Maritime Museum's information on shipping lanes, "they also determined the nature of maritime trade and social interaction" (Atlantic Worlds exhibition, Nov 22 2015).

Shipping, critical to the home-based defensive and trading hubs of England, was perhaps more crucial to interconnected colonial settlements. Since the fifteenth century rise in the cod market, the annual fishing migration to Newfoundland saw the English and French fight over control of the port settlements. And with the sixteenth-century demand for oil to use in lamps and bone for manufactured goods such as corsets, umbrellas, shoe-horns, and fishing rods, whaling activities increased in international waters and prompted conflict over the ports that lay on whaling migration routes. The seventeenth-century land grab in the Americas and the Caribbean and the plunder of labor from Africa saw associated movements of officials, merchants, missionaries, military, workers, settlers and captives across the waters and around the colonies. The military presence needed to secure these new colonial holdings meant that the mid-seventeenth century was a time of exponential maritime growth for Britain. Linebaugh and Rediker explain: "the Navy had 50 ships and 9,500 sailors in 1633, and 173 ships and 42,000 sailors in 1688" (Linebaugh & Rediker 2000: 146). The number of ships continued to grow, reaching more than five times the size of the mid-seventeenth century fleet with 939 ships registered in 1815 (The National Maritime Museum, "Nelson Navy Nation").

This period also saw a growth in the range and connectivity among colonial ports. This is perhaps best illustrated by a summary of the shipping news in *The American: Weekly Mercury* [no. 617–618] covering the period of two weeks from October 21 to November 4 1731, in which 79 percent of the vessels in port were arriving from, or bound to, colonial territories compared to twelve percent from/to foreign ports and only five percent heading from/to Great Britain (see Table 4.3). Ships such as the *Antelope* were kept in constant transit around the colonies, e.g., logbook entries from 10 June 1690 to August 3 1691 detail consecutive voyages around Montserrat, Nevis, St. Christopher, Santo Domingo, Antigua, Barbados, Martinique, Rhode Island, Guadalupe, and Carlisle Bay, covering a period just over one year [ADM 52/1/7]. Such voyages were reflective of a phenomenon in which colonies became more autonomous and leveraged the trading commodities, workforce, and defensive capacities that local trading partners could offer before seeking to engage with the customs regulation and high duties that trade and transit with Britain incurred. However, the statistics recovered here are only a partial account of all the traffic that was operating among the colonies. The smaller craft that were critical for day-to-day operations and essential in the inter-colonial networks of trade and communication often by-passed British record-keeping efforts. Jarvis explains that large ships were much less common compared to the ubiquitous smaller vessels of intercolonial traffic, and he presents a table of vessels clearing North American ports in 1772 showing only 2,149 large topsail vessels (just under 30% of the total traffic) compared to 5,047 smaller sloops and schooners (over 70% of the total traffic) (2010: 122 123, Table 4).

He also comments that, even when vessels registered with British authorities, "harried customs officers had neither the time nor the resources to verify information in the registers that mariners presented" (Jarvis 2010: 159). Hence, and accepting the difficulties of data collection in a context of covert trade and falsification of customs records, records suggest that colonial ports saw intense maritime activity, much of which was inter-colonial in nature rather than transatlantic.

Profuse activity around colonial ports attracted contraband trade and piracy, which created additional traffic in the shipping lanes. Gage's description of a colonial port in the Spanish Americas in the mid-sixteenth century shows how a typical "sea towne" was populated: "some very rich Merchants dwell in it, who trade with Mexico, Peru, and Philippines, sending their small vessles out from Port to Port, which come home richly laden with the Commodities of all the Southerne or Easterne parts" (1648: 88). And in such a context, it is clear why British sailors seeking the easy pickings of the Spanish Empire in South America were attracted to the commodity-rich and defense-poor port towns of the colonial Atlantic. British colonies were also targets for foreign raids and the attempts of pirates who rejected any national alliance. In the late seventeenth century, Virginia Governor Francis Nicholson was so keen to secure safe shipping that he offered bounty money for the capture of specific pirates, and "if it was not allowed in the publick Accounts, his excellency was pleased to say, he would pay it him self" [CO 5/1411/644]. Indeed, the first bill (of eight discussed) to be approved in the colony of Virginia on 22 May 1699, was the "bill for restraining & Punishing pirats and Privateers". This bill was discussed and approved before the other seven bills relating to such important issues as: export duties on food, treatment of colonists, regulation of the judicial system, treatment of wildlife, and the regulation of the economy. It appears that the administrators, although concerned about the local food supply chain, the well-being of settlers, and the economy, put greater emphasis on the proliferation of piracy suggesting that it was a concern that required their immediate attention. The issue of piracy was also discussed in full assembly only four days later on 26 May before the less-urgent matter of a bill against "unreasonable killing of poor" [CO 5/1411]; and it

Table 4.3: Summary of shipping information for New York and Philadelphia covering the period of two weeks (Oct 21-Nov 4) in 1731, based on data in HCA 1/99, *The American: Weekly Mercury* (no. 617–618)

		Port/Status of vessel						Total	Total (per category)
		New York			Philadelphia				
		Clearing customs	Outward bound	Cleared customs	Clearing customs	Outward bound	Cleared customs		
British Colonies	Antigua		2		1	2		5	28 (49%)
	Barbados		1		1	1	1	4	
	Bermuda	1	1	1	1	1	1	6	
	Dublin					1		1	
	Gibraltar						1	1	
	Jamaica	1	1	1		2	2	7	
	St. Kitts			1	1	1	1	4	
North American British Colonies	Amboy		1	1				2	17 (30%)
	Boston	1		1	1	1		4	
	Burlington				1			1	
	Cape Fear						1	1	
	Maryland						1	1	
	N. Carolina	1						1	
	New London		1		1			2	
	Newfoundland				1			1	
	S. Carolina				1	1		2	
	Salem				1			1	
	Virginia				1			1	
Foreign	Curaçao (Neth)	1	1	1				3	7 (12%)
	Lisbon (Port)		1				1	2	
	Madera (Port)	1			1			2	
Britian	Bristol	1						1	5 (9%)
	Great Britain		1					1	
	London	1		1	1			3	
	Total	8	10	7	13	10	9	57	

was not until the following month that the assembly met to discuss "a bill for building the capitol & the city of williamsburg" [CO 5/1411/77]. It seems that the administrators of Virginia knew, as did their contemporaries, that without first safeguarding the shipping lanes, there was no point in developing the settlement.

4.3.2 Convoys and communication

Transatlantic vessels frequently travelled in convoys for protection against foreign and pirate attacks, and communication among these convoys was a regular feature of language contact in maritime speech communities. Of the 27 recoverable references to a specific number of vessels sailing in convoy with a majority of British sailors, the average number is 22 ships per convoy. The highest number is 92 [DDB6 8/4], but this seems to be an exception to the trend of convoys numbering between 15 and 30 ships that were most common in international waters (see Figure 4.5).

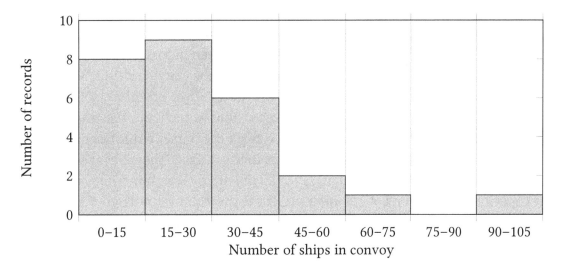

Figure 4.5: Number of ships sailing in convoy based on witness depositions, logbooks and journals

Sources: SP 42/6, DDB6 8/4, CO 5/1411/664, ADM 52/2/5–8, HCA 51/3983/1, ADM 52/3/7, 13, ADM 51/4322/4, ADM 51/3954, HCA 1/99/26, HCA 1/99/3/6, HCA 1/98/45,47, DDB6 8/4, MMM BL/Egerton 2395/0003, Bicheno 2012: 183, Gage 1648: 11, 15

Much larger groupings of ships were possible in port, e.g., "an hundred sail" and "five hundred [...] fishing boats" [445f.1/511]; however, since such references do not necessarily imply that any of the vessels sailed in convoy, they are not included in the data composing the graph in Figure 4.5. The vessels that evidence indicates did sail in convoy with others were potentially made up of mixed groups at sea, both in terms of vessel size and vessel type, including merchant and naval vessels e.g., "above 22 sail with 3 merchant Ships & Sloopes" [ADM 52/1/7], "seven ships & one sloop going after & 10 long ships" [HCA 1/99/26], and "seven large and 22 small ships" (Bicheno 2012: 183). The common maritime practice of sailing in convoys for safety and increased force in the event of attack was also evident among foreign nations, e.g., "16 Saile of french" [DDB6 8/4], and "the Dutch were being about 60 Sayle of men of war" [ADM 52/2/5]; and also in groups composed of international allies, e.g., "the *Assurance* with 12 English Marchant men 2 dutch men of warr & 30 saile of marchant men" [HCA 51/3983/1]. Just like the naval and merchant traditions they grew out of, pirate communities also collaborated in convoy (Esquemelin 1678; Rediker 1987: 268), making the type of collaboration something that characterized all types of transatlantic maritime communities during the early colonial period.

Some fleets may have sailed in perpetual and planned convoy, but many convoys formed at sea without prior organization. Bicheno explains how throughout the sixteenth century, maritime activity evolved "from shoal to school" (2012: 51), and as part of this development, ships started sailing in convoys more. He gives examples of some of the planned convoys of the late sixteenth century in which "articles of consortship" established spacing between ships at about six miles / ten kilometers from each other on a south-north axis (Bicheno 2012: 305). However, in the seventeenth century, and with the profuse maritime activity that came with multitudes of private traders now able to navigate the transatlantic passage, convoys were not always planned from the outset but formed as opportunities arose; or, as one contemporary succinctly puts it, "they met at sea" [HCA 1/14/203]. For this reason, willingness to sail in convoy was sometimes mandated in captain's instructions, e.g., one letter from the Admiralty dated 5 December 1699 to Captain Aldred, Commander of the *Essex Enterprize*, instructs Aldred to "give Convoy to any other ships or vessels of his Majestys subjects bound your way, which shall be ready to sail with you, or you shall meet with, as far as your way shall lie together" [CO 5/1411/657]. Instructions like these confirm that convoys formed impromptu at sea and likely lasted as the participants found mutual benefit in shared passage, as described in one witness testimony regarding a vessel from Newfoundland that was "willing to Consirt wth us in our Design and soe Proceeded wth us" [HCA 1/12/1]. Journals and logbooks show evidence of how vessels left convoys after they ceased to be beneficial, e.g., "the eight Galeons took their leave of us, and left our Merchant ships now to Shift for themselves" (Gage 1648: 15), "this morning mett three East India Shipp which we toke In our Convoye" [ADM 52/1/1], and "we lost Company of 10 ships & Supposed they Staied moord" [ADM 52/2/8]; note that in the last quotation the word "supposed" indicates that there was no prior agreement and that the ships composing the convoy sailed independently. It was therefore possible that multiple convoys were operating in the busy sea-lanes and that vessels could effectively tack from one to the other, as illustrated by one sailor's observation: "wee have sayled & Loggd *upon severall Covoyes* 44 miles" [HCA 51/3983/1, emphasis added]. Such networks of convoys potentially gave rise to a kind of maritime underground railroad for rebels, escaped slaves and indentured workers, a suggestion that might explain the deposition of Alexander Wyat, who testified that two sailors promised to get him away from Havana to France [HCA 1/99 Bahama Islands 1722], another runaway who "got on Board a Dutch Ship" [HCA 1/99/171], and a letter regarding "a mollatto" that ran away and whose likely movements are described:

> he gott to Road Island and perhaps is gon from thence with som of the pryvateers that fitted out there for the Gulph of Porlya [...] If hee bee, it's not unlikely but he is or has been att the marys or Maddagascar. [HCA 1/98/75]

The proven existence of such maritime railroads undoubtedly requires further research, but the common maritime practice of sailing in convoy that was observed throughout the period under study certainly indicates that encounters at sea and consequent impromptu convoys between vessels formed a wider community of sailors on the open waters.

The practice of forming unplanned convoys necessitated communication between vessels, if nothing more, to establish an unknown vessel's purpose and destination in addition to the captain's disposition to sail in consort. As a result, records of the era are replete with notes relating to chance encounters with ships and efforts to communicate with them, e.g., "one day we discovered a ship, and it being our captain's duty to know what she was, he made all the sail he could" [445f.1/511], "we espied a ship [...] being within 3 leagues of it we tackt & speak with the ship" [ADM 52/1/7], "[a ship] bounde for Newfounde Lande: one of our fleet speak with them" [ADM 52/2/8], and "we had sight of a ship and about three she Bore to us [...] to speak with us" [T/70/1216/13]. In order to initiate communication, crews often used signals that would be transmitted over larger distances, such as flags, guns, and fanfare, e.g., "putting out English colours invited the *Maliver* to come and pate [talk]" [HCA 1/53/13], "to give notice to our fleet [...] wee fired 3 gunes Distance and [...] a muskett" [HCA 51/3983/1], "hee Came upon us at a distance & spread his Dutch collors then wee fired a gun [of salutation] at him soe hee Came unboard us" [HCA 51/3983/1], and "the other vessels bore up to us, and gave us a consort of drums and trumpets, saluting us with three huzza's all the sailors gave, taking the signal from the boatswain's whistle" [445f.1/510]. If the vessels were broadside or near enough, then sailors might call to each other from deck to deck or across the gunports, e.g., "[a sailor] did what hee could to speak with mee, being within halfe a mile of mee" [ADM 51/3954], "they hailed him and they spoke with one another" [CO 5/1411/99], and "the whole morning was spent in friendly acclamations and salutations from ship to ship [...] Sea greetings" (Gage 1648: 201). Yet sailors also frequently used small craft to visit each other's vessels, described as "visiting each other with their Cock-boates" (Gage 1648: 15). Officers, in particular, were required to visit other ships as part of proper custom and in order to collaborate with other officers in the fleet, as illustrated by the references: Captains Snapes and Hawkes daily came on board and returned to their own ships [SP 42/6], "this morn a Councill of war on board the *Dutches*" [ADM 52/2/5], and "a Consultation of Flagg officers held on board the *Britania*" [ADM 52/2/5]. Yet the common sailors also had opportunities to pay their peers ship-visits, albeit without the ritual pomp, e.g., "one Mariner of the ship called *St. Francisco* being more [ad]venturous than the rest, and offering to swimme from his ship, to see some friends in another not farre off".[17] (Gage 1648: 21), and Abel Taylor's testimony that "2 or 3 times every day that weather would permitt [them to get] on board [another ship]... and this he declared was practized as well at sea as at Malago & in other parts & that he hath known" [SP 42/6/29]. Adkins & Adkins suggest that crew visits were a common form of leisure: "although the seamen were only occasionally given shore leave, they were generally permitted to visit other nearby ships on Sundays" (2008: 349). Ship-to-ship contact provided the networks by which many sailors kept in touch with their families, e.g., one wife's expectation that "this [letter] will God Willing Come to your hands by the ship *Katheryn*" [HCA 1/98/58], and was also a means to seek and disseminate news of maritime movements, e.g., "in the evening speak with the *Katherine* Yatch who told us the Flemmings were gone to the Westward" [ADM 52/2/6], "a small pinke came up with us & said shee saw the *Assurance* tack in the night" [HCA 51/3983/1], and "Last night Arrived a Small bark & a sloop for the Antego that brings news of the *Garsey* being taken" [ADM 52/1/8]. In fact, getting news from other ships was so common that when it did not happen, it was more likely to be noteworthy, e.g., in the logbook of the *Antelope* 6 March 1691 "this morning arrived here a hag boat from London [that] brought little or noe news at all" [ADM 52/1/8]. And although we only

---

[17]This attempt was not very successful however, as the swimmer became "a most unfortunate prey to one of them [sharks] [...] who had devoured a leg, and arme, and part of his shoulder" (Gage 1648: 21), perhaps explaining sailors' characteristic reluctance to swim.

have witness accounts of such contact between vessels for the majority period under study, later the *Lloyd's List* would report on such "speakings" that were records of communication between ships that met at sea. In short, interpersonal and symbolic communication among the vessels in convoys served a vital function in maritime collaboration; it provided opportunities for sailors to socialize, organize, and collaborate in a way that strengthened the networks of maritime connectivity across open waters, and potentially also aided language transfer around these extended communities, in stark contrast to the literary trope of the lone boat at sea sailing for months without contact that Samuel Taylor Coleridge popularized in his (1798) *Rime of the Ancient Mariner.*

4.3.3 The colonial maritime economy

Fishing and cargo-shipping formed the basis of Britain's trading economy with foreign neighbors since the first sailors crossed the channels to modern day Ireland and France, and with the advent of more reliable transatlantic passages in the sixteenth century, sailors forged the intricate mercantile networks of international commerce on a much greater scale. In 1562, and with the backing of Elizabeth I, Hawkins challenged the Iberian monopoly on the slave trade when he shipped African captives to Hispaniola, and Charles II furthered Britain's involvement in this form of human trafficking with a charter to the Royal Adventurers of England Trading into Africa in 1662 (Brown 2011: 105). Around the same time, Britain was fighting the Dutch for commercial supremacy off the south coast of England, culminating in the Navigation Acts of 1651 that were explicitly designed to maintain trade monopolies in the face of international free markets (Brown 2011: 41). As the British stronghold on colonial commerce increased, so did its role in the transit and sale of human cargo around the Caribbean and Americas. For example, Liverpool's first known slave ship set sail in 1699 and carried 220 captives from West Africa to Barbados, and by 1750 slaving voyages from Liverpool dominated the trade, significantly outnumbering those from London and Bristol, controlling over 80% of the British trade and more than 40% of the European market by the turn of the century.[18] Various depositions of the seventeenth century refer to the infrastructure of this trade around the Atlantic, specifically "factories" and "agents" in West Africa that functioned not only as horrific sites of brutality and abuse, but also created points of commerce [HCA 1/12/2–4]. These points of commercial contact involved language contact, potentially giving rise

---

[18]Merseyside Maritime Museum Archives & Library. (2014) *Liverpool and the Atlantic Slave Trade* (Information Sheet: 3). Retrieved from http://www.liverpoolmuseums.org.uk/maritime/archive/sheet/3.

to the development of what Hancock describes as a "Coastal English" (Hancock 1986; Delgado & Hancock 2017).

In addition to trade in foodstuffs, manufactured goods, and human trafficking, sailors were also essential in maintaining the economies of war by moving large numbers of troops, equipment, and captives during regional wars. For example, Taylor's diary gives details of maritime involvement in the 1691 surrender of Limerick:

> to facilitate the Transporting of the Troops, there General will furnish 50 Ships, and each Ship Burthen 200 Tuns... and also give Two men of War to imbark the Principal Officers , and serve for a Convoy to the Vessels of Burthen....And if there be any more Men to be Transported, than can be carried off in the said 50 Ships [...] where they shall remain until the other 20 Ships are ready, which are to be in a Months time; and may imbark in any French Ship, that may come in the mean time. [HCA 1/13/122]

In addition to legitimate maritime transit and commerce, sailors also supplied colonies and regions around Great Britain by keeping open channels of smuggling for contraband, which was often hidden in vessels with false bulkheads, hollow spars, and adapted cavities between decks.[19] In this context, sailors made the most of opportunistic trading, as described by one witness: "wee sailed along the coast and fell in with the river Sesters and theire wooded and wattered and Traded wth the negroes for fresh provisions" [HCA 1/12/2]. It was precisely this type of ad hoc trading that potentially led to the development of English pidgins around the multilingual coastal regions of the Americas, the Caribbean and Africa. Illegal trading became so intense around pirate havens like Port Royal, Tortuga, Providence and Madagascar that the collusion of any unknown vessel was assumed, prompting one captain leading a trading voyage around Jamaica in 1698 to go to the trouble of getting a letter bearing a seal from the governor that assured all readers of "his just and lawfull affairs" and urging port officials to give his ship free access [HCA 1/98/53]. However, lawful affairs were not everybody's intention, and heavy-handed measures against piracy were taken in the early colonial period to limit damage to the local economy caused by proliferating networks of contraband. In fact, upon close attention to the wording of trials against pirates, it seems that the authorities were far more concerned about the hazard to the economy that these people presented than the protection of basic human rights, as illustrated in the wording of one statement used

---

[19]Merseyside Maritime Museum Archives & Library. (2010) *History of Rummage* (Information Sheet: 73). Retrieved from http://www.liverpoolmuseums.org.uk/maritime/archive/sheet/73.

to open proceedings in a piracy trial in Barbados in 1733: "the crimes of piracy, felony, robbery, & murder committed on the sea are most odious and detestable, *being destructive of all trade and commerce*" [HCA 1/99 Barbados 1733, emphasis added]. Yet, all sailors of the early colonial period performed critical service roles in the British and regional economies not only when they operated under legal jurisdiction, but also when they developed prohibited networks of debt, credit and communication, which shaped both economic and linguistic developments in the decades and centuries to come.

Mariners operated largely on barter economies because coined money was limited and often useless in the context of unregulated international trade. British legal tender was so scarce that sometimes the payment of debts in cash appears to be a notable event, e.g., court cases that refer to "two hundred pounds lawfull money" [HCA 1/9/7], "five pounds payd him in money" [HCA 1/9/64], and "paid him in money" [HCA 1/9/67]. Some trials show evidence that Spanish currency was used, e.g., court proceedings, relating to the theft of "a certain kind, Or pieces or species of money comonly Called pieces of eight to the value of One hundred pounds of lawful money of great Britain" [HCA 1/99/7], and description of trade in Tunis using "some Spanish doubleloons [...] knowing how scarce money was" [SP 42/6]. Yet, more commonly witness statements attest to barter economies in lieu of monetary exchange, e.g., the voyage that took on slaves, flour, beef, and sugar in Antigua to trade for stickfish and wood in Curaçao [SP 42/6], the exchange of "one negroe man slave and five shift for anchorage and seventy pieces of eight in lieu of a barrell of serviceable powder" [HCA 1/98/77], and the invoice of dry goods consigned to Capt Samuel Burgess with the instruction "to sell for my more advantage [or] [...] to lay it out in Such goods or merchandise as you shall think will turn to the best advantage here" [HCA 1/98/143]. There is evidence that salt may have been the preferred currency in Atlantic barter economies when the access to and value of European currencies collapsed at various points in the early colonial period (Jarvis 2010: 400). Dampier gives a first-hand testimony of how this might have worked in maritime trading: "I told him I had not Mony, but would exchange some of the Salt which I brought from Mayo for their Commodities. He reply'd, that Salt was indeed an acceptable Commodity" [1045.f.3/1/31: 30]. Furthermore, Adkins & Adkins suggest that the use of food items and clothing as currency was also a common feature of trade both in port and among crew (2008: 97, 122), e.g., four sailors testify how their captain paid them in shoes and stockings with the explanation that they could trade with these items as if they were money [SP 42/6], and another testimony explains, "if the said master would not give them five crownes he would take 1000 hundred fish for the said shott" [HCA 1/101/431]. Interestingly, the use of salt, clothes or foodstuffs as currency may have some connections with trading economies in Africa that bartered with cloth and shells [445f.1/491–2; Hogendorn & Johnson 2003]. It may very well be that sailors' participation in barter economies and their use of dry goods and provisions as currency in trade was something reinforced by contact with West African societies, much like their use of language may have accommodated African forms of speech.

Systems of credit, debt and loan also served to enable trade and strengthen Atlantic networks of reciprocity. Often, credit was extended in partial payment alongside barter deals, e.g., one letter to the British ambassador to Spain explains how "money is not to be got at Havana for the Negroes", instead, they sold on credit and took crops as a percent of the debt (O'Malley 2016: 20). At other times, one party would loan money to enable trade under conditions of return, e.g., merchant Robert Balle testified in 1682 that he lent commander Nicholas Reymer various sums of money for ship repairs, under the understanding that when the ship put into port in London, the money would be repaid [E134/34Chas2/Mich36], and rope maker Samuel Sherman testified in 1636 that he lent the Boatswain of the *Andrew* some money that he repaid in rope and barrels of tar "as pawne for his debte untill the examinnat has recovered his wage to paie him" [HCA 1/101/221, 224]. Yet, in spite of sailors' promises to be "punctuall & just in the payments" [HCA 1/101/546], many parties ended up in court when they failed to pay debts or when they attempted payment in unacceptable terms, such as Captain Williams' hand-written twenty pound note that was rejected because "Notes of Hand signed at Sea were not valid" [HCA 1/99* *The American: Weekly Mercury* No.618, Oct 28–Nov 4 1731]. Yet when merchants, captains, vessel owners and service providers complied with their debt obligations, they constructed international webs of commerce based on trust and mutual benefit that perpetuated local economies and laid the foundations of emerging international economies.

4.3.4 Corruption and theft

Despite their massive contributions to European and colonial economies, sailors of the colonial Americas, Caribbean and Africa operated cultures of theft, in which ideologies of personal gain were more commonplace than conscientious acts of nation-building. Indeed, such ideologies proliferated in the British colonies themselves among corrupt governors and officials operating public and clandestine networks dedicated to personal gain and often at the expense of others. Even though the mother country provided an abundance of models and examples of criminal and unethical practices, Fusaro (2015) explains how these colonial spaces were ideal regions which favored autonomy and enabled self-interested parties to operate nefarious schemes at a distance from imperial oversight. Examples recovered from the archives include: Bermudian councilors debated British mandates and voted on whether or not to enforce clauses they disliked (Jarvis 2010: 55); governors of Martinique and Guadeloupe encouraged captains to ignore strict rules against trade with France and bring slaves into their labor force (O'Malley 2016: 9–18); corrupt officials in Anguilla, Nevis, and other British islands gave vessels permission and protections to unload contraband cargoes openly (Jarvis 2010: 173); and officials in Newfoundland took bribes to reserve port spaces, operated complex scams to dupe sailors from their pay, took settlers and natives hostage for ransom, and forged "certificates of clandestinity"[20] among illiterate ship masters to cover for their own abuses of authority [SP 42/6]. The reference to a distinct "coast price" in one witness testimony describing "the goods...[that] amounted to the Value of Twenty Pounds at the Coast Price" [HCA 1/99 Cape Coast of Africa, Feb 4 1734, 4] also implies that coastal regions were subject to potentially inflated prices that included bribes and semi-official "taxes" on imported goods that no doubt went directly to government officials. Sir Robert Robinson, Bermuda's governor from 1687–1691, was one local official who personally benefitted from such suspect practices. Robinson made "a small illicit fortune from bribes, fees, and embezzled duties and public funds" (Jarvis 2010: 70), and was one of the many unqualified and incompetent colonial administrators characterized by upholding unscrupulous, discriminatory, and self-interested practices. His background as an ex-navy captain, like many colonial governors, also illustrates the profound links to corruption among maritime communities and colonial administration.

The maritime culture of theft and self-interest negatively impacted the British government's hold on colonial commerce. But ironically, it was fifteenth and sixteenth century British corruption that prompted many of these ideologies among maritime communities in the first place. Bicheno explains how the House of Tudor, and specifically Elizabeth I's state, was dependent on traditions of piracy, which enabled the monarch to collect unofficial taxes on traffic in illicit goods to fill the national coffers. As a result, sixteenth century state-sponsored piracy in the form of corsair activity and privateering proliferated, and private pirate-

---

[20]Although no surviving examples of "certificates of Clandestinity" survive in the archive, various references to them in the series SP 42/6 suggest that they were letters of agreement to unlawful practices that were passed around specific ships' officers to mark their agreement and complicity in nefarious activities. In this same document series, certain illiterate officers testify to signing the certificate without knowing what it was and others testify to not having seen or signed any such certificate.

entrepreneurs such as Sir Walter Raleigh and George Clifford, Earl of Cumberland, operated with the queen's knowledge and approval (2012: 134–328). The very fact that Francis Drake was knighted in 1581 in England but remains known as a pirate in the Spanish-speaking Caribbean indicates the range of conflicting ideologies related to the service of sailors. [21] Moreover, that the exploits of such men no longer feature on British schools' curricula speaks to the fact that they were "the sharp-edged products of a far more abrasive age" (Bicheno 2012: 327). As a result, in 1603 James I inherited a pirate nation whose allegiance to Britain was far weaker than its allegiance to profit, and consequently more cargoes and ships were lost to British pirates preying on their home state than to foreign attack during the Spanish wars (Bicheno 2012: 328). The monarch's efforts to regulate and reign in the renegade maritime communities consequently led to all-out war at sea in the seventeenth century, which only began to settle after the state's complete rejection and suppression of piracy in the early eighteenth century.

Cultures of theft and abuses of power not only prevailed in the British and colonial governments but also much more specifically among the naval administration and regulating bodies of the merchant services. Bicheno explains that "the self-financing power vested in the Admiralty Commission invited the extortion and other abuses that came to characterize the office" (2012: 158), and Lincoln further explains that by the time of Pepys' administration, reforms to stop fraudulence in the Admiralty, and specifically in shipboard accounting, were long overdue because of a culture in which "national duty and private gain were not mutually exclusive" (2015: 145). Naval spending was directed to preferred contractors and commonly involved deals susceptible to nepotism, bribery and fraud. In such a context, it is understandable that naval commanders, captains and senior officers often bypassed legal or moral protocols to make a profit, e.g., senior officers taking cargo such as cloth, raw hides and sugar for private sale and stealing bags of money [SP 42/6]' a superior officer instructing a subordinate to make holes in the bottom of a heavily good-laden ship to feign the sinking of the ship, scare away the crew, and allow him free-access to the cargo [HCA 1/12/84]; a quartermaster helping himself to crew supplies [HCA 1/99/90]; a lieutenant forging official documents [ADM 106/300/54]; a captain bribing officers to keep quiet about what they had seen [HCA 1/99/130]; a captain submitting unsigned

---

[21]Born in England, I learned about "Sir Francis Drake" in school and through cultural transmission. I was shocked to hear him referred to as "The Pirate Drake" in an English-language commentary accompanying a video in San Juan's *El Morro* when I first arrived in Puerto Rico in 2006.

and incomplete customs documents [CO 5/1411/653]; and the common practice of pursers skimming off provisions (Adkins & Adkins 2008: 32). For such reasons, attempts to combat corruption were necessary, e.g., instructions to one captain that explicitly forbade him from taking his pick of the cargo before any captured prize was officially processed [HCA 1/9/19]; a letter thanking the naval board for money and assuring them that the officer in charge would "see to prevent any abuse" [ADM 106/300/91]; an opening statement in court explaining "the duty of Masters of ships, and the great trust that is put into their hands, upon the account of their Merchants and Owners; and what damage and Frauds and Felonies at Sea do bring upon all Foreign Trade and Commerce" [HCA 1/12/111]; and a letter sent to captains from one governor's office promoting "a due observance of the several acts of Trade made for preventing frauds & regulating abuses" [CO 5/1411/618]. Corrupt officers, the self-described "Gentlemen of fortune" [HCA 1/99/6], abounded in a maritime culture of corruption. As such, it is not difficult to see how armed piracy evolved in the late seventeenth and early eighteenth centuries in reaction to officious legislation that attempted to regulate and reap national profits from the accepted and individually gainful practices of earlier times.

Sailors stole for personal gain but also for survival. Given the maritime culture of theft that permeated the administration and commanding ranks of the vessels, it is not surprising to see evidence of individual counts of theft among the common men, e.g., one letter describing a crewman who "was robbed on Saturday last at night of about six pounds seventeen shillings" by some of his peers [ADM 106/288/46, 48]; a deposition about another sailor who is convicted of "the Embezzlement of sundry Goods out of the Longboat belonging to the Servant of Bristol" [HCA 1/99/6]; and a logbook entry "this morning [...] Jacob Annis was whipped at the Maine Yeard for Breaking open a Chest and Takeing out moneys" [ADM 52/3/7]. The "chest" referred to in the previous citation was the only individual space permitted to the common sailor and the theft of personal items, referred to as the "hauling and Plundering of Chests" [HCA 1/99/105], occurred with enough frequency when ships were captured at sea that one captain comments "there was not an honest man in yarmouth", a common recruitment site for seamen [HCA 1/101/431]. Yet sailors were not necessarily interested in money or items to sell. They also plundered chests for essential items, such as clothes that were difficult to acquire and impossible to manufacture at sea, e.g., "the prisoner in Particular has Some of his cloths [...] of which he returnd only a shirt" [HCA 1/99/93]; "he was shifted with a shirt he knew was not his own" [HCA 1/99/99]; "Did make away as likewise your petitoners Sons clothes" [HCA 1/11/110]; and "taking from the said John Wingfield his wearing apparel" [HCA 1/99/170].

Theft at sea happened on an individual and collective scale. Individuals stole what they could for personal reasons, e.g., "they saw him rummaging their Surgeon's chest [HCA 1/99/81], and "they went into a cabbin and tooke a piece of cold beef and Cabbidge and some Bisketts" [HCA 1/53/68]. Crews also plundered captured vessels for the necessary materials to keep their vessels and their workers functional, e.g., records attest to crews targeting ships and plundering captured vessels for such things as: food and provisions [HCA 1/99 Bahama Islands 1/22]; sails and canvas [HCA 1/99/50; HCA 1/99/125]; rigging, anchors and cables [CO 5/1411/631]; and masts, yards, ropes, cords and tackle [HCA 1/101/351]. Captains were also keen to recover any materials found afloat or washed ashore that might be gainfully used, as illustrated in the need for a man "eimployed to looke after stolen or drift goods" [ADM 106/288/33]. Thus, although many crews and individuals may have been motivated to plunder for personal gain, there is significant evidence that theft at sea was also motivated on a larger scale by necessity in harsh conditions.

Rather than envisioning a simplistic division between piracy and legitimate trade, there seemed to have existed a continuum that ranged from violent theft, through forced trade and coercion, to free but non-legitimate commerce that formed an important part of local colonial economies. Indeed, the following letter dated 1690 seems to indicate that conflict and plunder was only a last resort for the pirates around New York who preferred sustainable farming or trading over armed conflict. One trader describes, "having his ship plundered by them [...] But in a short time had a farm common and traded with them" [HCA 1/98/47]. Potential trading partners may have been initially presented with violence to motivate international trade in a context of imperial monopolies, e.g., the sailors who "burnt a towne called Meofe because the inhabitants would not come downe to traffick with them" [HCA 1/53/10]; an incident when a crew encountered "the Negroes unwilling to Trade freely with him [...] [so] the said Collins shot among them and killed one" [BL/74/816/m/11/36/2]; and the captain on the same voyage who settled a trading difference by seizing the master of the town and dragging him to the shore before cutting his head off [BL/74/816/m/11/36/2]. Yet, shows of force like this may have been performative and economically strategic. Leeson's work on the economics of pirate organizations (2007; 2008) indicate that pirates used violence as a form of intimidation to achieve their goals in negotiation rather than as an objective in its own right, and if they could instill enough fear in their potential trading partners to achieve the upper hand, then a suggestion of violence was all that would be necessary to achieve maximal profit with a minimum expenditure (in terms of effort and lives lost) in conflict. Indeed, pleading that trade was forced was a common excuse that local town officials could claim in the event that their complicity in contraband trade was identified, particularly if the "pirates" (i.e., trading partners) had made some public show of force. Bicheno explains how such acts gave Portuguese towns an alibi in consensual negotiations with English traders in the early colonial period that explained "not only evading the Spanish royal tax but also saving the greater loss of time and wastage involved in sailing against wind and current to Saville" (2012: 78). Thus, if the majority of local officials and traders were willing accomplices, as Bicheno suggests, then the shows of violence that seem to define a modern concept of piracy were no more than expected customs of trade negotiations in the context of the early regional economies.

4.3.5 Sailors on land

Sailors often had no choice but to stay ashore due to abandonment or punishment. Enlisted men were abandoned in port if it was not deemed strategically or economically viable to retain them in the ships. Certainly, a crew needed a full complement to operate and defend the vessel, but fewer men on board meant savings in provisions and wages and also reduced the number of men who could claim a share in prizes. Men were abandoned in port towns and remote islands indiscriminately, e.g., John Lewis' 1684 testimony that he shipped "to Carolina and was there Cast Away" [HCA 1/12/5]; Alexander Selkirk's 1704 abandonment on the uninhabited Pacific island of Juan Fernandez (Souhami 2013);[22] and English sailors recruited in Lisbon in 1731 who "were to bee put on shore [at Tercera, a remote island in the North Atlantic Azores archipelago] without any prospect of getting back to Britain" [HCA 1/99 Philadelphia, Oct 15 1731]. Other sailors were forced to remain ashore as punishment. Imprisonment might be sentenced in a foreign jail, e.g., "George Ogle who dyed in Bombay prison" [HCA 1/52/100], and "English Men & Prisoners of Warr in France" [HCA 1/13/98]. However, convicted men were more gainfully used as unpaid workers under the system of indenture or slavery, e.g., the 19 men convicted to serve [as laborers for] seven years [HCA 1/99/174]; the group of men convicted to serve five years "at any of their Settlements [the Royal African Company] on the Coast without the benefit of wages" [HCA 1/99/175–6]; the sailor Nicholas "by just & lawfull meanes becom a slav to mee my heirs & [...] during his Naturalle Life" [HCA 1/98/72]; and potentially the runaway servant who "has been a Sailor" [HCA 1/99 *The American: Weekly Mercury* No.617, Oct 21–Oct 28 1731]. Thus abandoned, imprisoned, enslaved and

---

[22]Selkirk's abandonment and survival story was published by himself and his contemporaries giving rise to Defoe's seminal narrative *Robinson Crusoe*, published in 1719, for which the island is now named.

indentured sailors potentially composed at least a small number of coastal and island populations.

The most common reason for men to be left on shore related to their health. Logbook entries indicate this routine practice, e.g., "this morning Putt the Rest [of the men] a Shore in the Vanguards Smack Being in all so sick & wounded" [ADM 52/2/9], and "Sent our Longboat ashore with 15 sick men for Plymouth" [ADM 52/3/12]. Sometimes these recovering crewmembers returned to duty, e.g., "our tent and sick men came aboard from the shore" [ADM 52/2/3], "Went to Chatham for water & for men that had been sick ashore there" [ADM 52/3/12], and "fell sick and went ashore where he continued for a whole month and after he came on board again" [HCA 1/52/22]; yet others were left indefinitely. Brown's (2011) research on sickness and health at sea explores the frequency and manner in which commanders left sick and injured men on shore and explains how major British ports were commonly provided with medical facilities and asylums for the care of such patients since before the seventeenth century (p.33–36). Yet, these institutions were not well funded, and if the men could not pay for their care then they often found themselves destitute and unemployable. Pepys' observations from the administration of the Admiralty notes,

> having been on shore, the Captains won't receive them on board, and other ships we have not to put them on, nor money to pay them off or provide for them... [so] the sick men that are recovered, they lying before our office doors all night and all day, poor wretches. (cited in Brown 2011: 55)

The numbers of sick, wounded, disabled, aged or otherwise rejected seamen suffering from extreme poverty in British ports was such a problem by the end of the sixteenth century that Drake and Hawkins set up a universal medical aid scheme known as the Chatham Chest, yet this scheme suffered from corruption, underfunding and incompetent management and was ultimately discontinued (Brown 2011: 43). But the multitudes of incapacitated sailors abandoned in British ports were in a preferable situation to the conditions that thousands of sick and injured sailors faced when they found themselves abandoned in foreign ports. Circumstances permitting, in the event that they were not picked up by a passing vessel after recovery, these sailors might have been accommodated in private houses, or they may have been assigned some type of work in the local community. However, they may have ended up in local workhouses or indenture systems if they were unable to pay for care as a guest or function in the new location as integrated settlers (Brown 2011: 57–59, 113). This custom of abandoning sailors in ports became such a problem that by the eighteenth century legislation in Barbados "required shipmasters to deposit money as a security against them abandoning their sick in port" (Lambert, cited in Brown 2011: 113). Apart from the humanitarian impact of such treatment, the linguistic result of such widespread abandonment of sailors meant that they could have potentially formed adstrate language communities in foreign ports that influenced internal change.

Many sailors willingly left the service of sailing vessels to escape harsh conditions at sea and brutal treatment, particularly if they had been forced into service in the first place. Deserters could be ranked officers, e.g., "Moses Dawson [...] Surgeon deserted" [HCA 1/98/15]; but were more likely to be lower-ranking seamen. Many of these lower-ranking seamen escaped in groups, e.g., "2 or 3 that had made their Escape" [HCA 1/99/105], and another sailor who plotted to carry out "concerted measures with the three last named Persons for making their Escape" [HCA 1/99 *The American: Weekly Mercury* No.617, Oct 21–Oct 28 1731]. Although the loss of a few seamen was expected attrition, a larger number could seriously impede the ship's operations, e.g., the logbook of the *Swallow* commenting that "last night 22 of our men ran away [and so] [...] wee had not Enough to Saile our ship" [HCA 51/3983/1]. In response to such hazards to commerce, colonial governments were urged to issue proclamations against assisting runaway sailors, e.g., in April 1643 there was a British proclamation forbidding ale-house keepers and innkeepers "to harbour or entertain any seamen, watermen, and co., prest into any of His Majesty's or merchant ships employed in the service" (cited in Lavery 2009: 50); and Francis Nicholson, governor of Virginia, issued a proclamation in 1699, specifically in response to a complaint from one commander that several of his seamen were concealed by townspeople. The order was issued to "strictly forbid all his majesteys loving subjects, that they doe not entertain, harbour, or conceal any of the seamen belonging to the sd ship *Essex Prize*, which allready have, or here after shall absent them selves from his majestys service" [CO 5/1411/667]. The fact that townspeople were doing this suggests that an extended network of maritime sympathizers (including family members, professional acquaintances, ex-sailors, and friends) might have formed an extended community around the ports of the colonial territories that potentially provided additional opportunities for language contact and feature transmission to take place.

Some sailors went to sea with the specific intention of migrating, or may have chosen to settle in a specific region as their circumstances changed. Depositions include examples of sailors leaving the profession in a state that appears to be a kind of retirement, e.g., "they are going aboute there lawfull nations and further saile not" [ASSI 45/4/1/135]; "he was gone beyond Sea, and knew not when he would return" [HCA 1/14/150]; and one sailor's deposition that "they mett with one Kidd, a pirate who there [in Puerto Rico] lay becalmed" [SP 42/6]. Other sailors may not have been able to retire but actively sought a different profession. As service-towns sprang up around the trade routes, sailors may have found that working in port settlements as a chandler's assistant or apprentice in trade may have paid better, or at least more regularly, than their sailor's wages. Moreover, coastal towns that evolved because they were strategic locations for provisioning or defense rather than points of exporting local commodities may have been almost entirely populated by sailors and military personnel before local markets were established, e.g., the operational base that Raleigh attempted to set up in Virginia from which to intercept the Spanish *Flotas* (Bicheno 2012: 301). Similarly, the small seasonal towns that sprang up to service and house the workers of the fishing, turtling, logging and salt-raking trades in places like Newfoundland, Jamaica, Virginia, Belize, Honduras, Yucatan, and Turks were likely to have been populated if not entirely by sailors, then certainly by workers very familiar with maritime culture (Draper 2016: 3–4; Jarvis 2010: 185–256). Furthermore, the international port settlements that specialized in recruiting crews, fencing plunder, and buying and selling contraband also provided plenty of itinerant work for enterprising individuals who were abreast of maritime movements and knew how to balance supply and demand. McDonald provides a wonderfully nautical metaphor for such settlements in his description of how English sailors, and more specifically pirates, "stubbornly clung to the Honduran littoral latter like barnacles on a whale" (McDonald 2016: 15). Dutch entrepôts with comparatively easy paths to naturalization also particularly attracted sailors, e.g., one sailor's revelation that "the major part of men now on Board Did Designe to have setled here on the Cape Good Hope in hopes that the Dutch would have protected them" [HCA 1/98/25]. Settling in an emergent port town with international protections certainly seemed to be a preferable option to a life of hardship and near-starvation at sea, as illustrated in one journal writer's reflection on the prospect of settling in India:

> A League from the Fort is a fair Town, that grows bigger and bigger every day. When the *Holland* Company arrives there with their Ships, if any Soldier or Mariner will live there, they are very glad of it. They have as much ground as they can manage; where they have all sorts of Herbs, and Pilse, and as much Rice, as as many Grapes as they can desire. [Arents/361, The Six Voyages, 1678: 206]

As a result of such motivations, settler populations that had previously worked at sea may have formed distinct language communities in foreign ports. They may even have influenced the direction of language change or founded new varieties, as happened in Palmerston Island after a small groups of sailors, with their female passengers and children, founded a settlement on the tiny Pacific island in the 1860s.[23]

4.3.6 Contact with port communities

Port communities thronged with service providers that had intermittent and selective contact with sailors via small craft. Industries such as ship brokerage, stevedoring, porterage and chandlering had multiple sub-industries that maintained, serviced and supplied the vessels of the British naval and merchant fleets. There were also a host of service providers that serviced and supplied the needs of sailors that populated these vessels, such as inn-keepers, money lenders, religious leaders, prostitutes, washer women, small-goods traders, medical professionals, slop-dealers, and clothes-makers. In Britain, these service providers most likely spoke English but in the Caribbean and the Americas the majority of these maritime service providers were free or enslaved men and women of African heritage (Jarvis 2010: 259), and as such, this demographic composed a rich source of potential language contact. Additionally, although the majority of these workers would have been based in port or coastal communities, many visited the vessels using bum-boats, lighters, or the "severall Smacks [that] came aboard with provisions" [ADM 52/2/6], and thus service providers interacted directly with the men who lived aboard. Indeed, it was for transit to large vessels, in addition to the local needs of fishing and transport, that many indigenous populations maintained a fleet of canoes, described by Gage as "above two hundred thousand of these little boats [...] wrought like a kneading trough, some bigger than others according to the greatness of the body" (1648: 50).

Undoubtedly, some of these service vessels brought free and coerced sex-workers to the sailors. For such reasons, large ships were equipped with a "whip", a hoist attached to the main yard for lifting people on board who were not expected or able to scale the rigging. Sea shanties attest to the custom of permitting women on board when ships were in port, specifically to attend to the pressed men who were not permitted shore leave, e.g., "All in the Downs the Fleet lay moored, / When Blackeyed Susan came aboard", in a shanty attributed to John Gay (1685–1732; cited in Hugill 1969: 17). Gay's shanty alludes to the naval custom of draping

---

[23]Rachel Hendery's (2013) work on Palmerston Island English (p. 309–322) details how the first settlers came from maritime communities and how their linguistic heritage gave rise to a variety of English that is unique in the Pacific.

red cords on the port side of the vessel or hanging red petticoats (souvenirs from previous visits) to advertise that the ship was open to sex-workers:

> At anchor see she safely rides,
> And gay red ropes adorn her sides,
> Her sails are furled, her sheets are belayed,
> The crimson petticoats displayed.
> Deserted are our useless shrouds,
> And the wenches come aboard in crowds. (cited in Hugill 1969: 18)

These visits may have lasted for as long as the ships were in port, as suggested by two lines of Gay's shanty voiced in the character of a visiting woman: "When I passed a whole fortnight atween decks with you, Did I ere give a kiss, lad, to one of your crew?" (cited in Hugill 1969: 17). Despite the romanticized representation of monogamous and coy intimacy that this shanty presents, local women and girls who worked the sex-trade in port towns suffered much more caustic realities. Many may have been forced into their profession by necessity after being seduced by sailors, bearing children to them and consequently being abandoned by their families, or choosing prostitution over starvation when a sailor-husband's pay never materialized (Adkins & Adkins 2008: 164–167, 173). Thus, it is entirely possible that these women raised children whose fathers were sailors and who were maintained by earnings from itinerant sailors in a maritime environment that had regular exposure to sailors' speech, both directly, through the mother's profession and the presence of sailors in port, and indirectly, as a consequence of the service-industry. In such a context, it is not far-fetched to suggest generational language transmission of Ship English, although obviously more research would be required to substantiate claims that sailors transmitted features of speech to their (collective) offspring in port communities.

Pilots were perhaps the other most common visitor on large sailing vessels. Pilots worked to help vessels navigate the dangers of coastal areas such as rocks, collisions, wrecks, sandbanks, tides, currents, and fog; and the traditions of their service have been organized in Britain since Henry VIII granted a royal charter for Trinity House, the deep sea pilotage authority, in 1514. Pilots were a necessary and frequent part of maritime life because, while the hazards of coastal waters around Great Britain were not well known,[24] the hazards of unknown coasts

---

[24]Pilots were notoriously secretive and did not share local sketches, observations, maps of landmarks, sea beds, depths, tides and river estuaries (Bicheno 2012: 64); a coastal survey of Britain was not published until 1681 (The National Maritime Museum, Samuel Pepys: Plague, Fire, Revolution, exhibit G218: 11/25).

were even more dangerous. Shipwreck might have meant death through starvation, exposure, or tropical disease if sailors survived the hazards of the water. Bicheno notes that "even the skilled navigator Francis Drake continued to use foreign pilots until the day he died" (2012: 60). As such, contemporary accounts frequently mention pilots, e.g., "Having taken in pilots belonging to the port, as is the custom" [445f.1/511]; "having no Pylote morred againe" [ADM 52/1/1]; "they discharged their pilot" [SP 89/34/128]; and "Polott Came in Board us to Carry us about into the Downes" [ADM 52/2/5]. Pilots and the information they represented were a valuable commodity at sea, illustrated by one court case in which pilot John Houghling explains "the pyrate kept me against my will" [CO 5/1411/42]. And, although they were usually not a permanent part of the crew, pilots certainly functioned as part of the speech community, potentially serving as conduits for language transfer and foreign borrowings as they interacted with a range of international crews and ports as part of their regular working practice.

Vessels spent periods of time docked in port, at which time sailors had exposure to the speech varieties of coastal communities and also exposed those they came into contact with to their own language features. Time in dock was required for such activities as vessel maintenance [HCA 1/99/103], fitting out the ship with equipment and provisions [DDB6 8/4], and unloading cargo and military personnel [HCA 1/9/18], in addition to any unanticipated times that the vessel was taken out of action by events such as unfavorable weather conditions, lack of a crew complement, running against coastal hazards, or enemy attack. It is extremely difficult to retrieve quantitative data from archival records regarding the specific lengths of time that vessels spent in port communities, as even logbooks are sometimes not explicit about this information, and references in letter and depositions are often rough estimates. However, the data available in 16 legible, complete and corroborated records attest to periods of as short as one week to as much as three months in ports, with an average of 31 days or one month (see Table 4.4). And although this average is calculated on a small number of citations, it compares favorably with Jarvis' estimated 34 days that a large vessel needed for a layover in port (2010: 134). However, it is worth remembering that smaller vessels such as sloops that were ubiquitous around the waters of the wider Caribbean and American colonies needed much less time to unload cargos and complete vessel maintenance, and their average stays in port are estimated at 18 days (Jarvis 2010: 134). In addition to these average lengths of stay in ports, vessels were often required to wait in port for anticipated funding to complete repairs or payment obligations, favorable winds, tardy cargos, expected convoys, and companion ships to complete preparations.

Table 4.4: Durations of vessels in port based on 16 sample documents

Citation indicating duration	Days^a	Source
stayed 2 or 3 dayes	2.5	HCA 1/12/2
stayinge there 5 or 6 dayes	5.5	HCA 1/12/2
six or seven daies	6.5	HCA 1/9/18
9 dayes or thereabouts	9	HCA 1/12/84
about 14 or 15 days	14.5	HCA 1/14/205
from 14 to 28 days	21	HCA 1/98/267
Seven and twenty days	27	Arents/361 The Six Voyages 1678: 84
a whole month	30.5	DDB6 8/4
about a month	30.5	HCA 1/52/20
one month	30.5	HCA 1/98/259
a month	30.5	cited in Bicheno 2012: 318
about 5 or 6 weeks	38.5	HCA 1/52/88
6 weeks	42	HCA 1/99/103
staied two months	61	HCA 1/52/20
about two months	61	HCA 1/52/104
3 months	91	HCA 1/98/259
Average days	**31**	

^{a}If a date range is given, number of days is calculated based on a middle point. Note that the average and the median length is almost the same.

One deposition attests to such anticipated delays: "they think to saile in 10 days time but as we have always known fleets to be long in geting redy" [DDB6 8/4]. Acknowledging the likelihood of such delays, the average of 31 days' duration in port may have commonly been extended under local circumstances.

Sailors who were granted shore leave and who expected, and were expected by their employer, to continue their service on the vessel used their time ashore to socialize, negotiate deals, and attend to personal matters. They frequently chose to spend this time ashore in the company of other sailors, e.g., the complaint addressed to Captain John Aldred that "thou be often on shore your self, as likewise your men...[who] commit disorders in the night time" [CO 5/1411/653]; various depositions that describe groups of sailors drinking together in local taverns [HCA 1/99/6; HCA 1/99/7; HCA 1/99/5]; and the witness testimony describing higher-status groups of sailors socializing:

Master & Marryner [...] was With one Captaine Laman at his house in Rathiffe nerve New Church there with one Captaine Thomas Garnitt between six and seven of the Clarke in the morning where was then in company with them one Bawlke & a young man called Thomas *all seamen.* [HCA 1/9/67, emphasis added]

Sailors without their own houses in port towns commonly stayed together in lodgings, e.g., the captain who was seeking "convenient lodging for himselfe and his crew" (Gage 1648: 11), an accused sailor described as being "on Shore dwelling with another of the Crew" [HCA 1/99/45], and the sailors described as lodging together "at the signe of the *New Castle* at the *Armitage*...more of the said parties lodge in the farme house" [HCA 1/9/67]. And it was at such inns, taverns and drinking houses that sailors forged extended maritime networks by communicating news, proposing alliances and sharing stories with each other and with service providers, e.g., "the woman of the house Mrs Whitehouse told Vidal of the Design the Deponent had said to take the Schooner" [HCA 1/99/7], and "an inn-keeper, liveling at the sign of the *White-Hart* and three *Tobacco Pipes*... did inquire of him for one Joseph Passoff who [...] did use to lye at his house" [HCA 1/14/151]. Familiarity and friendship with service providers was facilitated by the common practice of using small groups of sailors to work the same routes, as suggested by the repeated names on port records of Bridgetown, "implying that there was a small cohort of mariners whose primary income was transporting wood between St. Lucia and Barbados" (Draper 2016: 13). Such "small cohorts of mariners" potentially lodged together in port as well as at sea and got to know the communities of the port towns well; indeed, their trade may have depended on it. The interconnectivity of a community that comprised sailors and service providers is evident in court cases such as the trial of Robert Ingo, 27 May 1636, in which a rope maker, a lighterman, a laborer, and two of the sailor's shipmates give witness testimony on his behalf [HCA 1/101/219-220]. Thus, in port, sailors socialized with each other, but depended on service providers for the months that they may have spent ashore, not only to provide bed and board for them, but also potentially to maintain the larger maritime networks that facilitated trade, shared maritime news, and forged trade alliances among divergent crews.

4.4 Summary

This chapter presents common characteristics of the immediate and wider communities in which sailors lived, from the most insular mess group, to the crews of their own vessels, the collective crews of the convoy, the wider brotherhood of the maritime professions both at sea and in port, and finally to all those service providers working and living in port communities. The divergent characteristics and constraints on all of these groupings affected language use and potential transfer both on board the sailing vessels and around the port communities they visited. Among insular ship communities, passengers including women (and potentially their children) travelled and lived at sea, forming subgroups of speech communities onboard sea-going vessels. Yet the largest group in most maritime communities was undoubtedly the lower-class working sailor. A typical sailor could expect to spend at least one year and a quarter continuously serving on a transatlantic voyage and was likely to serve on consecutive voyages, potentially without shore leave, thus leading to long periods at sea. Autonomous communities at sea were prone to tyrannical captains and violent superior officers who frequently inflicted physical harm and even caused the deaths of men working under their care. Common sailors were also frequently the victims of unreasonable imprisonment, excessive disciplinary measures, public rituals of punishment, and cruel and unusual violence intended to ensure their compliance and subordination. In response, collective resistance offered the common sailor some form of protection. Collective agency enabled successful negotiation of better conditions at sea and provided a pseudo-legal support network. The social cohesion that prompted such collective identification among working sailors was facilitated by mess groups and consequent kinship bonding that manifested itself in sentiments of brotherhood and also potentially intimate and/or sexual relationships among the crew. Such sentiments of brotherhood were most pronounced in times of difficulty when survival may have depended on them, but were also prominent in examples of collective activism against repressive regimes that ran the risk of punishment for mutiny. Another method of marking collective agency and complicity is evident in the regular consumption of alcohol. This use of alcohol was not just an act of celebration and a necessary replacement for repugnant water supplies, but also served to regulate trade agreements and express spiritual connectivity in times of distress or anticipated conflict. Sailors also reinforced group identity through shared beliefs in ancient maritime folklore and participation in storytelling, music, gaming and dramatic play, potentially under the cultural leadership of the cook.

Wider maritime communities developed in response to the profuse maritime activity of commerce and conflict in the early period of Atlantic colonial expansion. Colonial ports depended on interconnected shipping and communication that might have maintained strong ties to Europe in the early period, but rapidly became inter-colonial in the context of strict British regulations and developing local economies. Planned and spontaneous convoys of vessels sailed in collaboration around the colonies for safety and maintained strong symbolic and oral communication networks among their crews. These networks provided a social outlet for vessel-bound sailors and also potentially fostered a maritime railroad system for runaways. The maritime economy that these networks maintained – based on a complex system of debt, credit, factorage and barter – was the foundation of emerging international economies. However, it was rife with corruption in an age where ideologies of personal gain in the monarchy, in the government and at the local level were explicit. As these ideologies degenerated into all-out piracy in the early eighteenth century, the tightening noose of the British commercial and judicial system saw a rapid increase in theft at sea, followed by its bloody suppression. However, violent theft was not only a cultural trait, it was also a necessity for many destitute sailors in vessels without the means to maintain their livelihood and was also potentially an expected custom of trade negotiations in the context of the early regional economies. Destitute and incapacitated individual sailors were often abandoned on land as a punishment or for health reasons, but many also deserted or chose to migrate in order to escape harsh conditions at sea. Sailors also had occasional contact with service providers during the time that they attended the vessels and their crews, specifically pilots and sex-workers who spent periods of time aboard the ship. Yet sailors came into contact with more service providers if they were granted shore-leave for the month or so that they were in port to service and provision the ship, in addition to unloading and taking on cargo. During these times, sailors maintained close contact with each other in taverns and communal lodgings and also socialized with service providers to conduct business, share news, and forge alliances. The distinct speech communities created by these alliances and the common cultural traits described in this chapter likely impacted methods of language transfer and the development of internal language change, in addition to reinforcing the distinct language varieties of the extended maritime language community.

5 Noun phrases

This is the first of three chapters that are linguistic in focus and respond to the research questions on the salient markers and characteristics of Ship English. This chapter on noun phrases opens with some general comments on the scope of the data presented and continues with four sections moving from the smallest unit of noun composition to the largest constructions of the noun phrase. The first section on single-word or bare nouns includes a brief discussion of phonology, morphology and lexicon, followed by more focused analysis of genitive forms, plural inflection, and noun head omission. The second section on determiners presents data on number and sequence marking, quantifying mass nouns and articles. The third section on pronouns presents data on personal and possessive pronouns, expletives, indefinite and reflexive pronouns and gives some details about how relative pronouns are used and omitted from modifying clauses. The last section on noun phrase modification presents data on pre- and post-nominal modification and focuses on present participle phrases and the specific linguistic constraints of phrases headed with the participle "being".

5.1 General considerations on scope

The smallest unit of linguistic analysis in this chapter is lexical, starting with the bare noun component of the noun phrase, and the focus of linguistic analysis is syntactic. Yet that is not to suggest that phonological and morphological features did not feature in the corpus nor that there is inadequate material for analysis. The reason such issues are not dealt with in detail in this study derives from a desire to focus on syntactic issues in the knowledge that this area is least represented in the literature on sailors' speech (discussed in Chapter 2) and in no way implies that research in these other areas is either conclusive or comprehensive. Given that the most extensive research into sailors' speech to date is Matthews' (1935) monograph on sailors' pronunciation in the second half of the seventeenth century based on phonetic spellings in ships' logbooks, the scope of this book does not include work on phonology. However, my own research suggests that Ship English has distinctive phonological features and the early findings of that research were presented at the Summer meeting of the Society of Pidgin and Creole Linguistics in Graz, Austria (Delgado 2015). To give a brief overview, notable findings include the realization of front vowels in higher position than anticipated, particularly in pre-nasal contexts, the avoidance of long vowels, and a fricative-plosive interchange that appears to be conditioned by social rather than linguistic factors. However, this book will only present selected discussion of phonology as it relates to the linguistic features under discussion and is not intended to represent the wide range of phonological variants found in the corpus. Morphological issues are also of great interest, yet have been previously addressed, albeit in brief, in Bailey & Ross's (1988) article on the morphosyntactic features of Ship English that focuses on evidence of variation in tense marking and the copula. Like phonological data, selected morphological data in this current corpus will be presented only as they apply to the category of speech under discussion, for example, the morpheme "-s" as it applies to plural inflection and third person singular verb agreement, and the morphemes "noon" and "yest" as they show evidence of free and bound variation in sequence marking. I have chosen not to dedicate sections explicitly to morphology, particularly as early indications suggest that further scholarship is needed to analyze potential morphological constructions and constraints. For example, one interesting feature that requires further study would be the use of pre-nominal "a-" in words such as "a board" [ADM 52/1/8], "a shore" [ADM 52/1/8], and "a back" [DDB6 8/4] compared to the more recognized pre-verbal usage of the morpheme in phrases such as "a Cruising" [ADM 52/2/6], and "a pyrating" [HCA 1/99 Barbados 1733] that has parallels with the <a> prefixing denoting durative aspect in Appalachian English (Hickey 2004: 612; Montgomery 2001: 148).[1] Although morphological features such as those suggested here are interesting, this book does not propose to deal with them in full but only aims to highlight their usage with a specific syntactic feature and flag the phenomena for potential future study.

---

[1]Further research into the morphology of Ship English might also focus on a preference for nominalization over copula or linking verbal constructions such as is expressed in nominal forms using "-ness", e.g., "the same forwardness" [HCA 1/99/45], "the involuntaryness of his actions" [HCA 1/99/51], and "his unaquaintedness with what path they should follow" [HCA 1/99/52]. Study into the use of adjectival superlatives using <est> that also embed into noun phrases when they might have been realized in verbal constructions may also prove enlightening, e.g., "was one of the forwardest in robbing her" [HCA 1/99/37], "he was one of the activest and Briskest among the Pyrates" [HCA 1/99/7], and "they were the activest and Leadingest Men among the Company" [HCA 1/99/39].

5.2 Bare nouns

5.2.1 Morphology and lexicon

Ship English permits a degree of freedom and variation with morphemes that are explicitly bound in other varieties of English, such as the morphemes "noon" and "yest" that are permitted in both bound and free contexts. The morpheme "noon" only survives in modern English in the bound context of "afternoon" and as a free morpheme meaning midday. Yet, in the corpus, the process of nominal compounding using the morpheme "noon" occurs with various referents of time, e.g., "this forenoon" [ADM 52/1/8], "yest noon" [ADM 52/2/5], "this day noon" [ADM 52/2/5], "after last noon" [T/70/1216/12], and "to day noon" [ADM 52/2/5]. This variant usage suggests that the process of compounding happened progressively from a prepositional phrase using the free morpheme e.g., "after noon" [ADM 52/1/7] through progressive nominalization with the explicit use of a definite article, e.g., "in the after none" [ADM 52/2/1], and finally developed the compounded lexeme "afternoon" [ADM 52/2/3]. It is also possible that this lexical change was happening with other free morphemes such as "fore" or "for" (i.e., before) that produced the archaic lexeme "fornoon" [ADM 52/2/3] as an antonym to the term "afternoon". Such variant usage of what we might consider bound morphemes by modern standards is also reflected in the usage of the term "yest" as we know it from the lexeme "yesterday". In Ship English, evidence indicates that a free morpheme "yest" was used in variation with other time referents, e.g., "yester night" [ADM 52/2/3], "yestday noon" [ADM 52/1/5], "yest noon" [ADM 52/2/5], and "yest afternoon" [ADM 52/2/5]. The variation evidenced with morphemes like "noon" and "yest" might be a manifestation of a wider phenomenon in Early Modern English in which the language had become more analytic favoring the use of free over bound morphemes (Millward & Hayes 2012) yet might also suggest characteristic diversity among sailors who resisted nominal compounding with markers of time and instead made use of free morphemes with a range of nominal markers.

Modern linguistic classifications of lexicon are applied throughout this chapter and the following chapters on verbs and larger syntactic constructions, yet discussion of the material in these chapters acknowledges that the variety of Ship English evidenced in the corpus was a manifestation of Early Modern English that potentially used lexical items in ways that are no longer acceptable. To illustrate, the noun "fortnight" deriving from a contraction of the Old English "fēowertyne niht" which became "fourteniht" in Middle English and "fortnight" by Early Modern English, literally meaning "fourteen nights" (*Oxford English*

Dictionary 1989: Vol 6: 102) is used according to its etymology as a temporal noun in Ship English, e.g., "fort night last" [HCA 1/9/64] and "they were taken about a fortnight afterwards" [HCA 1/13/98]. The nominal form was also used in the predicate noun position in copula constructions, e.g., "munday last was fortnight" [HCA 1/13/97] and "yesterday was fortnight last" [HCA 1/9/67]. Yet the lexeme could also be used as an adverbial sequence marker accompanying the copula, typically in an inter-verbial position in a passive verb phrase, e.g., "was fortnight taken in the said barque" [HCA 1/13/97] and "on Thursday last was fortnight met" [HCA 1/9/67]. In this context, the word is potentially used as a contracted from of a phrase meaning "a fortnight ago" in a prenominal position, yet that fact that the specific lexeme "fortnight" can function nominally and adverbially suggests that this was a variant feature of sailors' usage that was not customary with the nominal etymology of the word. Furthermore, this example might suggest that modern day linguistic typology of word constituents[2] may be inadequate to reflect the variation inherent in sailors' speech.[3] In addition to such routine vocabulary, Ship English was likely to have used many words that were specific to the technical equipment or movements of the vessel and crew, thus forming a kind of professional jargon. Indeed, this jargon composes the bulk of the literature on sailors' speech: the maritime dictionaries and word lists (see §2.1.1). There is potential for future research,[4] but as lexicon is not my central

---

[2]The term "constituent" is applied here and throughout this work following Morenberg's definition as "an individual word or a group of words that fill a single slot" (2010: G–341).

[3]I do not propose that the phenomenon of multifuctionality is unique to Ship English; it is a feature typical of non-standardized varieties.

[4]Further research into the lexicon of Ship English might focus on how such words compare to the lexicon of English-lexifier creoles or language universals given the role of mariners in providing for and settling the European colonies in the sixteenth and seventeenth centuries. Future studies might also find interesting data on how existing lexicon developed alternative denotation in sailors' speech communities, e.g., "he was only to be *a husband* for them and not to over charge them" [SP 42/6 emphasis added] in which the lexeme "husband" denotes an agent appointed by the owners to attend to the ship's affairs while in port (*Oxford English Dictionary* 1989: Vol 7: 510), and "the *Lizard* bore NbE" [ADM 52/2/3 emphasis added] in which the "lizard" refers to the peninsula of Cornwall seen from the starboard side of a vessel when sailing for Portsmouth or Plymouth. Studies may also focus on the etymology and usage of nautical words such as the word "slatch", potentially deriving from the word "slack" and dating from 1625 in nautical use to denote a portion of loose rope that hangs overboard or a brief interval of favorable weather (*Oxford English Dictionary* 1989: Vol 15: 659), e.g., "hope [...] wee may have a slatch of a faire wind" [ADM 106/288/30]. Regionalisms such as the northern term "lads" also feature in Ship English and might be a fruitful focus for future research, e.g., "the young Lads had killed the master" [HCA 1/99/10] and "Give way my lads" [445f.1/41]. However, in the context of this chapter, these few examples are briefly presented only to motivate potential future directions of research by indicating areas of interest in this corpus.

concern, I will limit my observations here to an acknowledgement that Ship English was a variety of Early Modern English and as such, there is potential for certain lexical items to align with or show variations on obsolete usage.

Certain nominalizations speak to the multilingual composition of the sailors' speech communities in that they have either been borrowed or influenced by another language, or show modern-day parallels with other languages. For example, the word "rhumb" e.g., "Clear Cours upon severall Rumbs" [ADM 52/1/7], denotes either a rhumb line or a direction on a nautical chart and dates from the end of the sixteenth century (*Oxford English Dictionary* 1989: Vol 6: 870). The word seemingly derives from the Spanish "rumbo" (course or direction) and was potentially transferred to English ships via French usage of the rhumb line in navigational practices. Another word adapted from Spanish was "plate", meaning money and deriving from an anglicized form of the Spanish word "plata" (silver). Words such as "rhumb" and "plate", were adapted from Spanish but other words were borrowed without adaption, e.g., "commanded the Soldadoes" [HCA 1/98/265] "making the best of our way to windard to weather Disseado but gained noe Ground" [ADM 52/1/7]. The two words "Soldadoes" (soldiers) and "Disseado" (i.e., *deseado* or desired) in the previous citations do not appear to be anglicized, and furthermore, the second example "weather Disseado" uses Spanish post-nominal modification rather that the anticipated order of the adjective preceding the noun in standard English: "weather desired" suggesting that the speaker was familiar with Spanish speech and not just Spanish words. Other phonological evidence supports the suggestion that sailors had influence from other languages when speaking English. For example, the loan of the word "Espaniols" [HCA 1/99] to refer to Spanish sailors demonstrates the Spanish-language phonotactic constraint that a syllable may not begin with /s/ followed by a consonant. And if such contexts manifest themselves, e.g., as in the combination /sp/ in words such as "spy", then the Spanish phonotactic constraint dictates that the /s/ phoneme is assigned to the prior syllable in an obligatory process of epenthesis that adds /e/ before the initial /s/ to create an additional syllable (Schnitzer 1997: 85). The word "Espaniols" may also have been preferable to "Spaniards" as it avoids the three-part consonant cluster in the coda of the last syllable "-rds" that features in the Standard English vocabulary. Although orthography suggests that the speakers of Ship English did not default to Spanish phonotactic constraints in general, compelling evidence of this type of epenthesis is suggested by the spelling of the word "spy" in archival documents, e.g., "he espyed a Vessell there riding" [HCA 1/9/67] "they espied a vessell" [HCA 1/9/6], "they espied a boat" [HCA 1/99 Bahama Islands 1722] and "espied a saile and chased him" [HCA 1/9/13].[5] Thus, not only lexical, but also syntactic and phonological evidence suggests that language contact in the speech community, and specifically contact with Spanish, may have manifested itself in Ship English through nominal borrowings and potential phonological and syntactic interference.

5.2.2 Genitives

Further evidence that English-speaking sailors favored syntactic constructions common to Romance languages can be found in the analysis of genitives (typically reflecting possession, partition or agency). Before language change in the Middle English and Early Modern English period developed new ways to mark the genitive case, Anglo-Saxon use of uninflected genitives was commonplace. Although this was certainly not common in the period under study, there are examples of such archaic constructions in the corpus, e.g., "under Holland colors" [HCA 1/10/2] and "the King of Ennglande pape[r]" [CO 5/1411/78]. However, more commonly, the corpus shows examples of the two forms of genitive marking still permitted in modern standard English: either a noun followed by an apostrophe and an "s" morpheme that combines to form a genitive noun, or a noun appearing after the preposition "of" in a prepositional phrase that is genitive in function. The linguistic data in the corpus showed that both forms were available in Ship English, yet, the use of the contracted form apostrophe plus "s" was more unusual. This might attest to the fact that the "-'s" possessive form was a later development in the Early Modern English period that was still in competition with the Anglo-Saxon use of uninflected genitives or the Latin use of prepositional genitive phrase during the period (Millward & Hayes 2012: 266). Perhaps due to the fact that this variant was more recent, its pronunciation was still variable and so sailors may have interpreted the final [s], [z], or [Iz] allophone of an inflected genitive noun as a contraction of the possessive pronoun "his" rather than an inflectional ending, particularly if the noun already ended in a sibilant and the /h/ of the following word was unstressed, e.g., "in Roberts his Company" [HCA 1/99/170], "sailing under Robert's his Command" [HCA 1/99/170], "Roberts his Death" [HCA 1/99/51], and "Robert Clarke Capt Hobbs his Servant" [HCA 1/9/51] which are more likely to have been intended as "in Roberts's company", "sail-

---

[5]The English use of the verb "espy" derives, in part, from a verb form in Old French "espier" dating back to around 1250 that was transferred into Middle English and then potentially reinforced by cognates from other Romantic languages (e.g., Spanish, Portuguese, and Italian) and Germanic languages (e.g., Dutch, Swedish, and Old Norse), (*Oxford English Dictionary* 1989: Vol 16: 383).

ing under Roberts's command", "Roberts's death", and "Robert Clarke, Captian Hobbs's servant".[6] Yet, overwhelmingly, the linguistic data in the corpus showed that the default form of expressing genitive case was through the use of a prepositional phrase. Examples showed this form was used: to indicate possession, e.g., "the luggage of his majties Embassador" [HCA 1/98/271]; to indicate source composition, e.g., "a very hard gayle of wind" [HCA 1/101/473] and "a sudden Storme of wind" [HCA 1/14/107]; to indicate partitive relationships, e.g., "What troopers of horse" [HCA 1/9/105], "the high court of admiralty" [HCA 49/98/106], "the master of the examined" [HCA 1/52/1], "they of the *Sea Flower*" [HCA 1/53/57]; and also to show appositive relationships, e.g., "the River of Thames" [HCA 1/9/64] and "the bay of Chesepeak" [HCA 1/99 Williamsburg, Aug 14 1729]. It appears that the use of the contracted form "-'s" was not favored in Ship English, and although this form was universal throughout Early Modern English period, it seems that sailors may have preferred to mark genitive case with prepositional phrases, specifically because this construction aligned with Spanish, French and potentially other languages that contributed to the linguistic diversity on board ships and reduced the number of variations in cognitive processing.

Genitive case marking using possessive pronominal determiners is common in Ship English, although this sometimes resulted in double genitive marking. Double genitive marking, or genitive concordance, occurred when a pronominal possessive determiner such as "my" "his", or "her" was used in a prepositional phrase "of..." that also marked genitive case, e.g., "some vessel of his" [HCA 1/12/4], and "these few lines of mines"[7] [HCA 1/99 loose letter c. 1730] in which the genitive is marked once by the prepositional phrase headed by "of" and secondly by "his" and "mines" respectively. This construction is most common in the third person form,[8] e.g., "the Comand of her" [T 70/1/11], "Comander of her" [HCA 1/14/17], "the Second Mate of her" [HCA 1/99/144], "Carpenter of her [HCA 1/99/153], and "the Master of her" [HCA 1/99/39]. It may be that references to rank such as these were idiomatic and that the genitive concordance consisting of using a prepositional phrase in conjunction with a possessive pronominal determiner was considered correct usage, as evidenced by the witness testimony "the Master and Mate of her were knocked over board with the Boom at Sea" [HCA 1/99/11] in

---

[6]Millward & Hayes 2012 suggest that this type of orthographic misinterpretation occurred on a wider scale in the Early Modern English period (p. 260).

[7]The pluralization of the first person possessive pronoun "mine" also potentially reflects Spanish morphology i.e., "mio" (sg) "mios" (pl).

[8]Note that examples using the female third person possessive pronominal determiner "her" are debatable as the accusative case "her" is identical to the genitive form, yet they are treated here as representative of the genitive form given other evidence suggesting this construction.

which the words "of her" are inserted superscript, presumably after the original was composed and later revised for corrections. This use of double genitives in Ship English does not appear to follow Peters' claim that such constructions may only be applied to human referents (2007: 162) because the "her" of the previous citations refers to the vessel itself and not a female human. However, this is less problematic in consideration of the maritime custom of referring to the ship (and often naming the ship) as a woman, e.g., "we suposed her [a sighted ship] to be standing the saime Course" [DDB6 8/4]. The gendering of sea-going vessels is explored in Creighton and Norling's *Iron Men, Wooden Women* (1996), including specific details about how, in the seventeenth century, wooden sailing vessels were often gendered female owing to English medieval customs of naming a vessel for the monarch's mistress and referring to the antiquated custom of sailors invoking a deity of the sea — often a woman. Therefore, in the context of maritime culture, it is more understandable that a double genitive, thought to be confined to usage with human referents, is applied to (female) sea-going vessels.

Although genitive concordance often occurred with the third person female pronominal genitive "her" used in "of..." phrases marking genitive case, the same structures are not as common with male or plural referents. Instead, and even when genitive case was clearly implied, the accusative case of the pronoun was preferred, e.g., "him wife" [HCA 1/9/8], "him lights" [ADM 51/4322/4] and "the goods of him" [ASSI 45/4/1/135/5]. There are no examples of third person plural possessive pronouns, either "their" or "theirs" in double genitive constructions in the corpus. Examples of constructions using a third person pronoun referent make use of the accusative case in prepositional phrases, e.g., "pyracies that have been committed under Colour of them" [HCA 1/99/10] and "the pyrate and his consort two ships of them" [HCA 1/99/39]. Thus, we might surmise that it was specifically female pronominal determiners that caused double genitive marking as they combined with the default variant of marking genitive case with prepositional phrases rather than nominal inflection.

The linguistic context that may have prompted the use of variant forms of genitives in Ship English are extremely difficult to derive, more than anything because of the limited number of examples available upon which to base a satisfactory interpretation. However, different forms of marking genitive case sometimes appeared in close proximity in the written records and in documents prepared in the same hand, implying that they were potentially in competition and maximally variable in the speech of individuals rather than regionally or socially distributed. For example, one witness deposition taken on 28 March 1722 reads, "this man as Carpenter of her, and when brought on Board the *Fortune* Carpenter's mate going on Board" [HCA 1/99/153] and includes examples of the Anglo-Saxon uninflected form "*Fortune* Carpenter", the prepositional genitive phrase "Carpenter of her" and the bound "s" morpheme "Carpenter's mate" within the same utterance. Similarly, another deposition taken on 14 August 1729 includes the clause "prisoners took away a new jacket of his mans from his back" [HCA 1/99 Williamsburg, Aug 14 1729] and includes examples of the prepositional genitive phrase "jacket of his mans", and a suggestion of the bound "s" morpheme in the use of the word "mans" although it is not represented orthographically with an apostrophe, it clearly does not refer to the plural "men" but rather a possessive form denoting that the jacket belonged to "his man" i.e., his servant. Although few, such examples show that even by the early decades of the eighteenth century, there was no universal default genitive marker but rather that the historic and contemporary variants available to each speaker were used concurrently, even within the same noun phrase.

5.2.3 Plural inflection

The corpus includes repeated examples of nouns that are pluralized by numerical determiners but do not inflect with an "s" morpheme, specifically regarding units of measurement. Logbooks and witness testimony frequently refer to the number of fathoms[9] that a vessel measured, and most of these entries include a phrase in which the single form of the count noun "fathom" is prefaced with a cardinal number. Sometimes the singular form of the count noun is prefaced with a number that is written out, e.g., "five fathome" and "sevean fathome water" [both citations from HCA 1/9/155]. However, more commonly, authors expressed cardinal numbers in numerical form, e.g., "anchd in 7 fathm" [CO 5/1411/675] and "had 9 fathom" [ADM 52/1/7]. It is interesting that many examples of usage include some variant spelling of the fixed expression "fathom water", e.g., "dropping our anchar in 6 fatham water" [ADM 52/1/6], "sevean fathome water" [HCA 1/9/155], "12 fathom Water" [ADM 51/3797/1], "30 fadam water" [T/70/1215 Oct 15 entry], "in 33 Fathom-water" [1045.f.3/1/16], and "had 50 fathome water" [ADM 52/3/12]. This expression suggests that the phrase derives from an underlying construction including a pre-article composed of a number and "fathoms of" followed by the bare noun "water" whose contracted form is understood among speakers and recipients. Yet, although the use of the uninflected noun "fathom" predominates in corpus examples, there is evidence of free variation, e.g., "wee had som time

---

[9]A nautical unit of length, 6 feet or approximately 1.8 meters, used to measure the depth of water and often measured with a sounding or lead line dropped over the side of the ship.

7 fatham and 3 fatham...[and other times] 5 and 6 fathams" [DDB6 8/4]. The fact that both the singular form "fatham" and the plural form "fathams" are used in the same document by presumably the same author implies that both variants were available to speakers and could be used within the same utterance.

Many of the other units of measurement that are demonstrated to be plural with numerical determiners but without using inflected noun forms also relate to nautical calculations of time, distance and weight. Examples of units of time expressed with an uninflected bare noun include "seaven night last past" [HCA 1/9/63] and "in few day after" [HCA 1/52/75] contrary to the expectation that bare nouns would take the plural form, i.e., "nights" and "days" after a determiner of quantity. Measurements of distance expressed in the unit of length composing 12 inches often used the singular form of "feet", e.g., "about 2 foot in heighth" [1045.f.3/1/25], "3 or 4 Foot high" [1045.f.3/1/27], and "several Foot of Water in the hold" [HCA 1/99 *The American: Weekly Mercury* No.618, Oct 28–Nov 4 1731]. Distance expressed in nautical miles also used the singular form of the bare noun in collocation with numerical determiners e.g., "Laguna was but 3 Mile off" [1045.f.3/1/18], "Dist[ance] 196 mile" [ADM 52/1/11], and "up in the Country 15 mile" [T/70/1216/8]. Weight measurements showing use of uninflected nouns refer to tons and pounds of cargo, e.g., "Burthen about two hundred and fifty ton" [HCA 1/52/103], "got 7 or 8 Tun of Salt" [1045.f.3/1/30], and "Butter [...] 332 pound, Suffolk Chefe 375 pound, Bread in two baggs 179 pound & Rapines 113 Pound" [ADM 52/1/6]. The use of uninflected "pound" as a unit of weight is also reflected in its use as a unit of currency, e.g., "Fifty pound in mony... and for fifty pound more" [HCA 1/14/167]. The linguistic tendency in Ship English to maintain uninflected bare nouns after a determiner of quantity was not unique to sailors' language however, Millward & Hayes 2012, explain that "measure words like mile, pound, fathom, pair, score, thousand, and stone frequently appeared without a pluralizing -s, especially after numerals" throughout the Early Modern English period (p. 167).

It certainly may have been that the tendency to retain unmarked plurals after a cardinal determiner in Ship English reflected wider Early Modern English usage at the time, yet sailors' use of non-traditional and figurative units of measurement to refer to the size and capacity of their communities marked Ship English as distinctive. The number of guns that a ship could carry was often used as a measurement of size, and although there are numerous references to the inflected form of this word in the corpus, there are also a few examples of its uninflected usage with a numerical determiner, e.g., "this ship to have 20 or 24 gun" [T/70/1216/13]. Sometimes units of measurement to count the number of vessels in a company, fleet, or convoy were expressed with singular nouns, e.g., "mett with three East India Shipp" [ADM 52/1/1]. However, the literal unit of measurement "ship" was most frequently inflected, e.g., "two ships" [HCA 1/99/105] and "severall ships" [ADM 52/3/7]. Much more common in the corpus were the frequent examples of uninflected figurative units of measurement to count the number of vessels, specifically the synecdotal use of the singular noun "sail" to refer to a vessel, e.g., "3 sayle more" [ADM 52/2/5], "twenty Sayle of Ships" [ADM 52/3/12], "20 sayle of Merchant Shipps" [ADM 51/4322/1], and "20 Saile of third rates" [ADM 51/4322/4]. The last three examples that include the inflected nouns "ships", "Shipps", and "third rates" respectively suggest that the use of the uninflected "sail" was specific to the pre-article composed of a cardinal number and "saile of" followed by an inflected (and literal) noun such as "ships" drawing comparisons with the idiom "fathoms of water" previously discussed. Yet even when not used as a pre-article,[10] it seems that the lexeme "sail" was uninflected in the context of its use as a unit of measurement, as illustrated by the following two examples in which the figurative unit of measurement "sail" is not inflected yet the literal units of measurement "ship", "sloop" and "leagues" are inflected: "being in number as above 22 sail with 3 merchant Ships & Sloopes" [ADM 52/1/7], and "having discovered four saile about four leagues ashore"[11] [HCA 1/9/155]. In further support of this interpretation, there are no examples in the corpus of the uninflected use of the word "sail" in its literal sense to refer to the plural canvas sheets, instead, when used literally, the noun "sail" takes a plural inflection, e.g., "with Keept topsailes" [ADM 52/2/9]. Furthermore, this distinctive feature of sailors' speech was salient enough to feature in published sea-songs of the seventeenth century, e.g., "Beset with five sail of Pirates" (cited in Palmer 1986: 50) and "Nine sail of ships" (cited in Palmer 1986: 65). Thus, we can surmise that speakers of Ship English used uninflected plural units of measurement that were specific to the speech community in addition to idioms that included plural nouns marked by cardinal determiners but not inflection.

Nouns inflected for plural marking and used for generic referents are common in Ship English, but examples also show that uninflected nominal forms without an article could be used to refer to a generic referent. The phenomenon seems

---

[10] The term "pre-article" is used per Morenberg (2010: 76) and includes several word classes including partitives, quantifiers, multipliers, and fractions that occur before articles or possessives.

[11] The inflected plural "leagues" in this second quotation appears to be an exception to the tendency to use uninflected nouns with cardinal determiners in Ship English. The word is inflected even in contexts where speakers use unmarked plurals for other units of measurement, e.g., the deponent who refers to "13 fathome [...] 20 fathome [...] 26 & 27 fathome" but in the same speech act also says "7 Leagues" [ADM 51/3/12].

to have been particularly applied to turtles (both the animal and its meat) e.g., "sent out Long boat a shore to Cath Turtle" [T/70/1216/8], and "we liv'd on Goats and Turtle" [1045.f.3/1/11]. The use of the uninflected noun "turtle" in a noun phrase in which the word is correlated with the inflected noun "goats" using the conjunction "and" suggests that the lexeme "turtle" is an irregular plural like "sheep" or "deer" that may not have developed a regular inflected form yet, although later the regularization of the plural form adopted the morpheme "-s" to align with the regular pluralization paradigm. Considering the word "fish" and the traditional uninflected plural form "fish" which is now accepted in addition to the newer and regularized inflected form "fishes", the suggestion that the word "turtle" was also an irregular plural appears more plausible. This interpretation furthermore appears to be supported by usage of the word in contexts which are clearly marked for plurality, such as in a position after a cardinal number signifying a plural referent, e.g., "bringing 5 small Turtle" [T/70/1216/8]. Hence, although examples such as "turtle" might suggest that uninflected nouns were acceptable for generic reference, it is perhaps more likely that newly introduced words (given that turtles are not endemic to the waters around Great Britain) were undergoing a process of regularization that had not yet been fully realized.[12]

5.2.4 Noun head omission

Nominals in subject positions, a requisite established by the end of the Middle English period (Millward & Hayes 2012: 274), can be omitted in Ship English. Human noun-phrase subjects can be omitted when the context of the utterance renders the reference to the agent of the action redundant, either because it has been previously established or is obvious from context. In court depositions, singular human subjects of a clause predominantly refer to the speaker (the witness) or the accused, and plural subjects of a clause predominantly refer to the ship's crew or the port authorities. Given so few variants, and considering the context of testimonial speech acts in which the referent is understood from the context of the testimony, witness depositions often omit noun phrase subjects, e.g., "Why he did not goe in her [I, the witness] do not well know" [T 70/1/12], "[I, the witness] was to moore him there" [ASSI 45/4/1/135/4 1650], "[I, the witness] can not tell" [CO 5/1411/640], "[he, the accused] Signed and Shared but never fired a gun at the Swallow" [HCA 1/99/92], "[he, the accused] Did not see any application" [HCA 1/99/129], "Fogg comes on So thick [they, the crew] had Much trouble" [ADM

---

[12] The *Oxford English Dictionary* (1989) states that the word "turtle" was explicitly "a corruption, by English sailors, of the earlier 'tortue'" derived from "tortoise" of French origin that referred firstly to the species (from 1657) and later to the flesh of the species (from 1755), (Vol 18: 722).

52/2/9], "[they, the crew] "burnt a towne called Meofe because the inhabitants would not come downe to traffick with them [HCA 1/53/10], "[they, the crew] Carried aboard the enemy" [HCA 1/9/105], and "[they, the port authorities] have given him a receipt for them" [T 70/1/10].[13] The fact that these omissions reflect spontaneous speech rather than the composition of the court clerk are potentially reflected in one deposition that reads "was killed that [he] thereupon went to the other" [HCA 1/99/4] in which the nominative pronoun "he" is inserted superscript, presumably as a correction or clarification after the original utterance was transcribed.

Nominal subject omission is evident in logbook entries when the human subject of a clause refers to the crew in general terms, e.g. "this morning with Snow & Sleet [we, the crew] Struck yards & topmasts at 5 this morning" [ADM 52/2/3] and "The fogg being Cleared Up [we, the crew] Came to Saile" [ADM 52/2/9]. In addition to redundant human subjects, logbooks also show evidence of non-human nominal subject omission when the referent is obvious from context. Examples of such omission most notably relate to the weather, and more specifically the wind, e.g., "very fresh & hard [wind] from the SW" [ADM 52/1/6] and "this 24 howrs [wind] blew hard and hazey weather winds" [ADM 52/2/9].[14] Similar to the conditions that prompt human subject omission in court documents, the reason for the omission of the non-human noun "wind" is most likely due to the redundant nature of the referent when most logbook entries were expected to open with a report on wind conditions, and also the redundancy of the word "wind" when used in collocation with "gusts" and the verb "blow" which make the meaning clear. Furthermore, the omission in this context is also potentially motivated by the abbreviated style of writing permitted in logbook entries. In sum, both court depositions and logbook entries show evidence of the omission of noun phrase subject heads when the referent is understood from the context or the customary format of the speech act, and the fact that these omissions index shared knowledge is not surprising given that the sailors who composed these speech acts were addressing a very specific, small audience.

Certain linguistic constraints condition the omission of subject noun heads. The speaker's inclusion of attendant circumstances, specifically in the form of a

---

[13] Although these examples may appear debatable out of context, they are sampled from larger legible documents in which the division of utterances are evident from context, e.g., "and upon the Ethiopian coast [nominative missing] burnt a towne called Meofe because the inhabitants would not come downe to traffick with them" [HCA 1/53/10].

[14] It is also possible that the noun phrase "weather winds" that ends the sentence could be the subject and so reflect an inversion of anticipated word order from Subject-Verb-(Adverb) to (Adverb)-Verb-Subject.

fronted participle phrase appears to promote noun subject omission in the subsequent clause. Examples from witness depositions include: "Nott willing to venture our sailes near any factory And unwilling to keep any to brood fachons amongst us [we, the crew] have in the long boat turned to sea all such as were unwilling to stay" [HCA 1/14/206], "the sea growing very high [we, the crew] were forced on a reife of sand and [I, the witness] was forced to cut away our main mast" [HCA 1/12/2], and "Being asked by the Prisoners from what Post the Spanish vessell Came, and whether they had a Commission from the Spanish King, And in what manner the Vessell was fitted out, [he, the accused] Says the Spansih Vessell Came from Porto Prince in Cuba" [HCA 1/99/5]. This construction of a fronted participle phrase giving attendant circumstances followed by a clause with an omitted noun phrase subject is also repeated in journal entries, e.g., "I having not hove the grapling, [he, a sailor] turns me about, saying, What's the matter?" [445f.1/43]. The construction is also evident in logbook entries, e.g., "Sunday at 7 in the morning weighd wth a fresh Gale, and got into the Gulf stream, but the weather being squally [we, the crew] could not hold it, so [we, the crew] were forced to bear up and anchor in 7 fa water" [ADM 52/2/6]. The repetition of this construction in court depositions, journal and logbook entries suggests that omitted nominal subjects after attendant circumstances may have been a widespread feature of sailors' speech.

In addition to the presence of fronted participle phrases that appear to permit subsequent nominal omission, there is evidence that fronted prepositional phrases and adverbial phrases permit the subsequent omission of noun phrase subjects as well. Court depositions include frequent examples of fronted prepositional phrases that permit subsequent nominal omission, e.g., "after a fight of abt 3 quarters of an howr [we, the crew] board" [HCA 1/53/3], and "at sevin [I, the witness] got into the fleet and was ordered to go" [ADM 52/1/1]. And this feature is also evident in logbook entries, e.g., "From yesterday Noone to the no one [we, the crew] have had a moderate gaile" [ADM 52/2/8], and "At 4 in the Afternoone [we, the crew] came to an anchor" [ADM 52/2/6].[15] In addition to these examples of fronted prepositional phrases, court document also show that fronted adverbial phrases similarly permit subsequent nominal omission, e.g., "Ever since [I, the witness] hath been on St. Marys" [HCA 1/98/256], "after a fight of abt 3 quarters of an howr [we, the crew] board" [HCA 1/53/3], and "when they had bin

---

[15]Citations of use here do not imply that the feature was universal or even consistent for individual sailors, for example, the same author of this logbook entry "At 4 in the Afternoone [we, the crew] came to an anchor" later writes, "at 4 in the morning we off weighed" [ADM 52/2/6] showing omission of the nominal subject after a prepositional phrase in the first example and the inclusion of a pronoun in the second.

a fortnight or 3 Weeks att sea [we, the crew] mett with a ship" [HCA 1/12/4]. Thus, whether the fronted phrase is a participle construction, a prepositional construction, or an adverbial construction, it appears that when the attendant circumstance is moved to the start of the utterance, it conditions circumstances that permit subsequent nominal omission in the matrix clause.

Clauses that compose correlative constructions yet do not necessarily include a correlative conjunction also permit the omission of a repeated noun phrase subject in the second of the two clauses. These clauses are best interpreted to derive from an underlying form using the correlative conjunction "and" which precedes the omitted noun subject and are thus represented as such in the following examples, "he was taken [...] against his will, [and he] had a Wife and 3 Children" [HCA 1/99/95], "he says himself he put the Match to the Gun but that it did not go off, [and he] was taken in John Tarton about 5 Mos agoe" [HCA 1/99/167], and "she Fled into the Bushes. [and she] Knows that the two Sloops were one Destroyed and the other Taken, together with her Husband" [HCA 1/99 New Providence 1722]. It may be that the use of correlative conjunctions permitted noun phrase omission in direct object as well as subject positions, e.g., "brought up the money upon deck and divided [it, the money] amongst the Crew" [HCA 1/99/8]. Although examples of object omission were much less notable in the corpus, it is possible that the omission of nominal and pronominal accusative forms in object position were also conditioned by underlying correlative constructions.

Object noun phrases may also be omitted in the direct object position and when they appear as the object complement or the object of a preposition. Direct objects are omitted in witness statements, e.g. "the Murderers...threatened to Put to Death [those people] who should refuse to take it" [HCA 1/99/8] and "they bind them and every [one] of them" [HCA 1/9/7], and they are also omitted in logbooks, e.g., "took in ten thousand [unit measurement] of wood" [ADM 52/2/3]. The last two examples also suggest common omission of noun heads functioning within the pre-article determining phrase of the direct objects. Yet omission is not restricted to this context. Nouns may be omitted when they function as the object complement, e.g., "there was no wind it was a calme [night]" [HCA 1/9/155], and more commonly when they function as the object of a preposition, e.g., "a Small Hoy with petty warrant [officers]" [ADM 52/2/3], "his master having often sent him out on Privateering [voyages]" [HCA 1/99/8 New Providence 1722], and "hoping you are in good [health]" [HCA 1/101/553]. Furthermore, the omission of all three noun phrases after an adjective in the three previous examples shown appear to suggest that nominal omission may have been conditioned using an adjectival modifier in addition to the possibility of conditioning by the presence of pre-articles.

5.3 Determiners

5.3.1 Deictic function

Words with a deictic function, commonly realized in English with the four demonstrative determiners "this" "that" "these" and "those", showed some variant usage and formation in Ship English. Both the singular and plural demonstratives are used with atypical nominal and verbal agreement in Ship English, e.g., the expressions "this Dutch Interloping Ships" [HCA 1/99/105] and "these lines is to arkquint you" [HCA 1/52/51], used in a witness deposition and a personal letter, respectively, show variant nominal and verbal agreement in terms of the singular or plural nature of the subject noun phrase. In the first example, the singular demonstrative "this" refers to the plural noun "ships" and in the second example, the plural demonstrative noun phrase "these lines" is followed by the copula verb conjugated to a third person singular subject. In other examples, redundant demonstratives are in competition with other determiners, e.g., "but these their good designs were discovered" [HCA 1/99/80] in which the determiner "these" and the pronominal form "their" compete in the determiner position. The formation of demonstrative determiners from accusative pronominal forms was also a notable feature in the corpus, e.g., the word "them" in the excerpts "don't you see says he them two ships" [HCA 1/99/105], "he was one of them Pyrates" [HCA 1/99/105] and "t'was too good for them people" [HCA 1/99/110].[16] Thus, although only limited examples of determiner use show in the corpus, they suggest that demonstrative number agreement was not universal, that deictic markers were permitted to compete with other determiners in pre-nominal position, and that accusative pronouns could take a deictic function when used in a pre-nominal position.

5.3.2 Number marking

Post nominal lexemes and indefinite pre-articles denote estimated quantities. Although logbooks made extensive use of symbolic number marking specific to maritime shorthand and witness depositions included roman numerals (specifically to denote ages of deponents) these are not discussed here as they appear

---

[16]This use of accusative pronouns with a deictic function in a pre-nominal position is still a feature of certain vernacular dialects of English.

only in the very specific contexts of nautical and court record-keeping conventions and do not appear to have phonetically realized forms distinct from the ordinal or cardinal variants here discussed. The use of the lexeme "odd", specifically in combination with a round cardinal number marks estimated quantities, e.g., "70 odd men" [CO 5/1411/636], "two hundred sixty odd points" [HCA 1/53/57], and "One hundred and odd pieces" [HCA 1/9/58].[17] However, indefinite pre-articles in a prenominal position more commonly denote estimated quantities in the samples of Ship English contained in the corpus. The word "several" occurs frequently with inflected plurals as we might anticipate from its usage in Modern English, e.g., "we have made severall trips" [ADM 52/1/7], "severall vesells" [ADM 52/3/12], "severall parcells of hulks" [T/70/1216/8], "Severall pasengr boates" [HCA 1/52/88], and "Severall arrived men" [HCA 1/10/2]. Although all the examples above and many more in the corpus precede plural nouns, the pre-article "several" might also take an uninflected noun, e.g., "we fired Severall Shott" [ADM 52/1/7] and "several Foot of Water" [HCA 1/99 *The American: Weekly Mercury* No.618, Oct 28–Nov 4 1731]. The pre-articles "many" and "some" might also precede uninflected nouns, e.g., "and by all the many report" [ADM 106/288/36] and "saw Some Shipp" [ADM 52/1/1], and other quantifying pre-articles also showed this trend, e.g., "a pair of shoe" [HCA 1/99/6], and "a few more shot" [HCA 1/99/14]; yet there are fewer examples of these constructions than the more common phrases with inflected nouns or noun phrases. The majority of bare pre-articles take inflected plurals, e.g., "many Moors Shipes" [HCA 1/98/24], "so many ships being before me" [D/Earle/3/1], "some days in august last" [HCA 1/99 New Providence 1722], and "for some weeks past" [HCA 1/99 *The American: Weekly Mercury* No.618, Oct 28–Nov 4 1731]; and the majority of pre-articles using a prepositional particle "of" also take inflected plurals, e.g., "two pairs of large tops" [HCA 1/9/67], "5 pairs of small pearls colored silk tops" [HCA 1/9/67], and "severall parcells of hulks" [T/70/1216/8]. Yet, as previously identified with words of nautical measurement such as "sail" and "fathom", when such nominals are used as part of a quantifying pre-article phrase, they may not be inflected for plural marking when there is a cardinal number preceding the pre-article, e.g., "60 Sayle of men of war" [ADM 52/2/5], "2 pair of Pistols on" [HCA 1/99/157], "nineteen paire" [HCA 1/9/67], and "Ninety head of cattle Bulls and Cowes" [HCA 1/52/10]. In sum, although it is possible for quantifying

---

[17]The *Oxford English Dictionary* (1989) explains that this usage renders the lexeme "odd" as a rare type of indefinite cardinal number which denotes an unspecified number of lower denomination than the round number preceding it and this usage dates as far back as the fourteenth century (Vol 10: 698).

pre-articles to take uninflected nouns and include uninflected nominal forms in phrasal constructions with the particle "of" (and this was more likely when they denoted a maritime unit of measurement) uninflected nouns do not appear to be a grammatical projection of indefinite quantifying pre-articles but rather a conditioned or free variant.

Explicit number marking in Ship English predominantly makes use of cardinal rather than ordinal numbers in pre-nominal positions.[18] Cardinal numbers were necessary in pre-nominal positions to mark plurality given the fact that bare nouns may have remained uninflected and ordinal numbers were more likely in sequencing and specifically dates. Ordinal numbers used to express dates are commonplace in the corpus, e.g., "the firstt of July" [DDB6 8/4] and "the fifteenth day of July last past" [HCA 1/9/139], "tenth day of Novr last past" [D/Earle/1/2] "the 23rd day of May" [HCA 1/13/97], and "the 10th of February" [HCA 1/99/3/10]. And although the prefixes <st>, <nd>, and <rd> are not always used consistently on numbers ending in either 1, 2, or 3, the sense of denoting ordinal sequence is clear, e.g., "The 22th of July" [HCA 1/9/8] and "the 2d of april last" [HCA 1/98/123].[19] However, many dates expressed in the written records do not carry any type of ordinal marker, e.g., "8 October last" [HCA 1/99/87], "The 21 of October last" [HCA 1/14/140], "The 3 day of May" [DDB6 8/4] and "the 29 of Aprill last" [CO 5/1411/60]. This feature is mirrored in other references aside from expressing dates but where an ordinal number would be anticipated, e.g., "he was 2 Mate" [HCA 1/99/59], "the 7 day we gott up" [DDB6 8/4], and "this 4 day" [DDB6 8/4]. However, given that these documents were composed before the standardization of English orthography and its imposition in public education coupled with the fact that many of the authors may have been only partially literate (see §3.11), the use of cardinal numerals, e.g., "2" may have denoted both the word for the cardinal and ordinal number, i.e., "second" and "two".[20] This interpretation is

---

[18] Although there is a suggestion that cardinal numbers could occur in post-nominal position, e.g., the line "They had not sailed leagues two or three" indicated in the sea-song "A joyful new ballad" (cited in Palmer 1986: 13), there was no significant evidence of this in the corpus.

[19] The variation in ordinal suffix and orthographic representation use may be partially explained by the fact that the words "first" and "second" are not true ordinals, according to the *Oxford English Dictionary* (1989) but rather nominal forms meaning "earliest" and "next" respectively, and as such, they were typically subject to greater variation than the true ordinals which are based on the cardinal forms, e.g., "Three" and "Third".

[20] Although standard spellings for printed text were established by the end of the seventeenth century, there was a lag in handwritten work as literate individuals did not necessarily reproduce standard forms in their private communication (Millward & Hayes 2012: 275). Idiomatic terminology may also account for examples like "Henry Every who was *before* mate" [HCA 1/53/12], presumably meaning "first mate" given the context of the excerpt.

supported by the fact that many of these numerals are preceded by either a definite article, e.g., "the 7 day we gott up" [DDB6 8/4] and "the 29 of Aprill last" [CO 5/1411/60], or a demonstrative, e.g., "this 4 day" [DDB6 8/4] suggesting that they should be spoken as ordinal and not cardinal numbers. Indeed, the apparent use of an ordinal noun for a date followed by a cardinal numeral for a subsequent date in the following example "the firstt of July and the 3 of July" [DDB6 8/4] seems to owe more to orthography than it was likely intended to represent in speech. Yet, having acknowledged the likelihood of misinterpretation of this feature, it is nonetheless evident that some cardinal numbers were used to express dates and common expressions in sailors' writing where we might anticipate ordinal determiners.

5.3.3 Sequence marking

Sequential ordinals such as "next" and "last" are a salient feature of sailors' speech in the corpus and this is likely because deponents were required to specify the dates and sequences of events to recreate projected timelines leading up to an alleged crime. The most prominent sequential marker used in noun phrases was "last", which was used in 118 examples or over two thirds of the sequential determining phrases sampled from the corpus, followed by the idiomatic phrase "last past" which was used in 28 examples or one sixth of the 171 examples collected (see Table 5.1). Less frequent examples of ordinal and temporal markers included the words "past", "since", and "following" none of which composed more than one twentieth of all the samples collected. The most common marker "last" was used most commonly to refer to periods of time such as months, e.g., "in July last" [HCA 1/99/155] and "a little before Christmas last" [HCA 1/9/39]. The second most common referents were specific dates, e.g., "the 20th of Aprill last" [ASSI 45/4/1/135/10] and "the 1st Day of October last" [HCA 1/99/170]; and the least frequent type of referent was a day that was not described with a numerical date but was nonetheless specific, e.g., "on Saturday last" [ADM 52/1/8] and "Ten days before Christmas last" [HCA 1/14/54]. This scale of frequency may relate to the quantity of testimonial material in the corpus, yet given that letters, logbooks, and miscellaneous documents also reflected this trend in ordinal marking with specific types of referent, it may reflect a wider feature of language use. Further support shows in the fact that the markers "last past" and "past" are also most commonly used with periods of time, e.g., "In the month of June last past" [HCA 1/9/63], "at the beginning of March last past" [HCA 1/52/100], and "Febuary Past" [HCA 1/98/66], and "Four yeares past" [HCA 1/14/38]. Significantly fewer examples were found of the temporal marker "last past" used with specific days but without dates, e.g., "Upon tuesday or wednesday last past" [HCA 1/10/9] and "seaven night last past" [HCA 1/9/63]; and there were no examples of the marker "past" used with specific days but without dates, instead all examples were either periods of time or dates. The temporal marker "following" was identified only nine times in the sample material and there was no visible preference for what type of referent was used. The temporal marker "since" was the least used of all the temporal markers studied, yet showed an interesting trend in that it was used exclusively with periods of time, e.g., "about half a year since" [HCA 1/13/98] and "about six months since he was first taken" [CO 5/1411/97] comparable to the usage of the word "ago" in modern speech. Thus, overall, the data show that when using sequential ordinals in time references, "last" is the favored marker and among all variants and periods of time are favored over specific day or date references.

Table 5.1: Frequency and type of sequential ordinals with types of referent in 171 examples

Sampled from collections 1045.f.3, 445f.1, ADM 106/288, ASSI 45/4/1/135, CO 5/1411, HCA 1/9–14, D/Earle/1/2, HCA 1/52–53, HCA 1/98–99, HCA 1/101, SP 42/6, SP 89/25, & T/70/1216.

Type of referent	Frequency by type of sequential marker Number of uses (percentage of examples per marker)					Total
	'Last'	'Last past'	'Following'	'Past'	'Since'	
Period of time	50 (42%)	14 (50%)	3 (33%)	7 (77%)	7 (100%)	81
Specific date	43 (36%)	11 (39%)	3 (33%)	2 (22%)	0	59
Specific day	25 (21%)	3 (11%)	3 (33%)	0	0	31
Total	118	28	9	9	7	171

Sequential markers show trends of usage in relation to estimation with certain markers being used exclusively with estimated times and others seemingly not permissible with estimation. The marker "since" is used exclusively with estimated periods of time in the seven samples of usage recorded in the sample, e.g., "about 3 weeks or a month since" [HCA 1/13/97], "he arrived about two months since" [HCA 1/13/97], and "about three years Since" [HCA 1/14/20]. Comparatively, none of the 18 markers using either "following" or "past" were used with an estimated time period or date suggesting that the combination is either not permitted or unusual in Ship English. The two most commonly sampled markers, "last" and "last past" however, permit estimation, e.g., "about the middle of January last" [HCA 1/99/58], "either on Friday of Thursday last" [ADM 106/288/26], "about the 22nd of June last past" [HCA 1/10/2], and "In or about the month of June last past" [HCA 1/9/138]. Yet estimation was evident in only a tenth of the structures using "last" (12 examples of 118) compared to a fifth of the structures using "last past" (5 examples of 28), so although the numbers of "last past" are fewer overall, the frequency with which they permit estimation is significantly higher than the marker "last" suggesting a general trend.

The placement of sequential markers in predominantly post-nominal position was also a feature of their usage. The majority of all the 171 examples taken to study sequential marking, and all of the markers using "last past", "following, "past" and "since" were in post-nominal position, e.g., "The 9th day of Aprill last past" [HCA 1/14/140], "we came thence latterly the 5th following" [SP 42/6], "this 3 weeks past" [ADM 106/300/52], and "about five months since", [HCA 1/13/97]. The most commonly used marker analysed in Table 5.1, the word "last", although it was also used overwhelmingly in post-nominal positions, also permitted pre-nominal usage, e.g., "at 4 Last night" [ADM 52/1/8], "on the last day of September" [HCA 1/98/255], "Last Christmas" [HCA 1/13/96], and "last April" [HCA 1/99/130]. Although pre-nominal examples were few in comparison to the number of post-nominal examples (only 10 examples or 8% of the total 118), the finding is significant in comparison with the complete lack of pre-nominal usage for other markers. Additionally, less-used markers such as "next", were permitted in pre- and post-nominal positions, e.g., pre-nominal "went thither again the next morning" [HCA 1/14/51] and "the next day" [HCA 1/14/201] compared to post-nominal "before March next" [HCA 1/14/20] and "on Wednesday next" [HCA 1/99 *The American: Weekly Mercury* No.618, Oct 28–Nov 4 1731]. The fact that certain words such as "last" and "next" were permitted in pre-nominal and post-nominal positions suggests that either these were the first sequential markers that were showing movement into the determiner position from a more common default post-nominal modifying position as part of a wider process of language change, or that such variation was potentially conditioned and specific to Ship English.

5.3.4 Quantifying mass nouns

Mass nouns, specifically referring to the weather, were common in Ship English. Climatological phenomena such as rain, wind, and lightning are often referred to with the mass determiner "much" or "some" to denote quantity, e.g., "the weather cold the last night some Raine" [ADM 52/2/5], "fair weather for the most part som raine" [ADM 52/2/8], "very much Rain" [ADM 52/1/7], "with mutch littning and Raine" [DDB6 8/4], "we had much winds" [ADM 52/1/4], and "wee had mutch Westterly winds" [DDB6 8/4]. The word "gust" referring to a localized strong current of wind although commonly treated as a count noun in modern English appears to have also been used as a mass noun in Ship English, e.g., "blowing hard in gust" [ADM 52/1/7] and "with Gust and Rain" [ADM 52/1/7], although it may be that the use of the uninflected form in the last example might have been conditioned by correlation with the mass noun "rain" as there are also examples of how the supposedly mass noun "rain" is inflected for plural marking in correlation with the inflected form "gust", e.g., "very hard gales with much Raines" [ADM 52/1/1]. Hence, it might be that the grammatical correlation that requires the same nominal constituents (i.e., inflected noun + inflected noun) takes precedence over inflectional morphology at the lexical level based on whether the noun is a mass noun or a count noun.

Abstract nouns commonly expressed in mass form could be realized as singular count nouns and with plural inflection in Ship English. For example, the word "evidence" is realized as a singular count noun determined by the singular demonstrative "this" in the example "this evidence that have been already produced" [CO 5/1411/33], and the noun is explicitly inflected for plural marking in conjunction with a cardinal number in the example "three evidences" [HCA 1/9/51]. The plural inflection of this word is similarly realized alongside indefinite pre-articles, e.g., "more evidences wou'd have appeared" [HCA 1/99/36], "produced Several evidences in their Behalf" [HCA 1/99/69], and "I have a great many evidences" [CO 5/1411/41]. Other abstract and mass nouns common to court proceedings such as "advice" and "information" are similarly expressed as count nouns, e.g., "The Advices Your Honour is pleased to favour us with" [HCA 1/99 *The American: Weekly Mercury* No.617, Oct 21–Oct 28 1731], "an information" [HCA 1/14/150], and "his only informations" [HCA 1/99/42]. Additionally, other common mass nouns such as "work" and "money" are realized as singular count nouns or inflected plurals in the corpus, e.g., "this provision must be a work of some time" [BL/Egerton 2395/0007], "takeing out moneys" [ADM 52/3/7], and "confes, where their moneys was" [HCA 1/9/18]. Such evidence appears to suggest that categories of mass noun and count noun were not mutually exclusive and that certain lexical items could be realized as uninflected mass nouns in addition to being used as count nouns with plural inflection and singular-referent articles and pre-articles.

Determiners specific to mass nouns such as "much" "little" and "small" are frequent in Ship English. The use of the determiner "much" in correlation with mass nouns in both logbooks and witness depositions appears to be common in the context of indicative modality, e.g., "Much Thunder lightning and Raine" [ADM 52/1/1], and "with much Rain" [ADM 52/1/7], and "he saw much blood" [HCA 1/101/405]. And this usage is particularly pronounced in reference to the wind, e.g., "much wind all the night" [ADM 52/3/12], "very mutch Raine and wind" [DDB68/4], and "much wind" [ADM 52/1/10, ADM 52/2/3], although other abstract nouns and adjectives such as "trouble", "afraid" and "out sailed" show similar usage of the determiner "much" in the context of indicative modality, e.g., "they had much trouble to gett [a pilot]" [ADM 52/2/9], "but were much afraid of us" [T/70/1216/9], and "the Dutch frigatt who we Much out Sailed" [ADM 52/2/9]. This usage in the context of indicative modality appears in contrast to the common native usage of the word when it is conditioned by interrogative modality or negation in phrases such as "Is there much wind?" or "there wasn't much wind". Other examples such as the use of "any" in indicative modality in the example "they had sold any timber" [HCA 1/9/53] (meaning that they had sold *some* timber) suggests that constraints assigning determiners to specific modalities was not as strict as we might anticipate in contemporary standard varieties of English.

The determiner "small" is used with uninflected mass nouns to denote a small amount, e.g., "small drizzling rain" [ADM 52/2/3] and "some small Raine" [ADM 52/2/5] in addition to its use as an adjective with count nouns, e.g., "small Arms" [HCA 1/98/271] and "a Small Hoy" [ADM 52/2/3]. This determiner is also commonly used with uninflected mass nouns to denote a small amount, e.g., "little or noe news" [ADM 52/1/8] and "little sugar to be had" [T 70/1/9]; yet examples show that the determiner "little" is almost universally used with the nominal "wind", e.g., "blowing unconstant sometime little wind" [ADM 52/1/7], "Little wind and much lightning" [ADM 51/3946/6], "foggy at the forenoon at afternoon little wind" [ADM 52/2/2], "feare weathr but Little wind" [T/70/1216/10], and "Little wind" [ADM 52/3/12]. However, the predominant use of the determiner "little" with the noun "wind" does not condition the noun to appear in an uninflected form as a mass noun but also permits inflection and use of the nominal as a count noun, e.g., "little winds" [ADM 52/2/5], "littel winds" [HCA 1/99 Log Book Pideaux 1731], "and little winds" [DDB6 8/4]. And this usage seemingly extends to other typically mass nouns, e.g., "our monys being little and not enough" [T 70/1/10]. Therefore, we may surmise that although the determiners "much" "little" and "small" are commonplace in Ship English, they each have specific constraints reflating to modality, use with mass and count nouns, and lexical projection that do not seem to be universal among the determiner class.

5.3.5 Articles

Variation in the use of indefinite articles does not feature heavily in the corpus, but examples of their usage may suggest some features of phonological realization and the customs of marking for indefinite and specific referents. One example of the indefinite article "a" used in a prevocalic position in the phrase "he hath been a Eye witness to many Moors Shipes" [HCA 1/98/24] may suggest that in certain contexts, the pronunciation of the article was realized as a vocalic attachment to a prior closed syllable. To illustrate, the excerpt "been a Eye" from the previous citation may have been realized phonetically as /bɪnʌaɪ/ in which the article "a" is realized as an unstressed vocalic nucleus (specifically, a caret) attached to a second syllable that re-assigns the final coda /n/ of the syllable "been" as the onset of the newly created syllable that the article attaches to. The syllable division, in addition to the unstressed caret would help avoid potential cacophony with the rising diphthong at the onset of the word "eye". However, such conjecture is nonetheless dependent on specific preferences for vocalic realization that are extremely difficult to determine from written samples. Another feature of indefinite article usage suggested by examples in the corpus is that they were permissible in pre-nominal position with generic abstract referents, e.g., the abstract nouns "courage", and "prey" and the abstract adjective "french" in the examples "the capt of the Pyrates bid me have a good courage" [CO 5/1411/35], "those men should become a Prey" [BL/74/816/m/11/36/1], and "Being a french men" [HCA 1/14/38]. Furthermore, in addition to indefinite articles being permissible for generic abstract referents, they also appear to have been acceptable for specific singular referents (more commonly denoted with the definite article), e.g., "Ships Company espying in a morning Severall pasengr boates" [HCA 1/52/88] and "he looked upon a chart and shewd us way they were to go" [HCA 1/99 The Tryals of Agostinho, July 8, c.1721, 7]. In both previous citations, the specific "morning" and the specific "chart" might be anticipated to have been referred to using the definite article "the" prior to the noun. Thus, although examples of such usage are not extensive, they certainly suggest accepted (if potentially localized) variation in usage.

Omission of articles, both indefinite and definite, is a much more prevalent feature in the corpus than variant usage. The following four examples taken from a witness disposition, two letters, and a journal entry omit the indefinite article: "he was [a] very good man" [D/Earle/3/1], "about [a] fortnight before" [HCA 1/101/46], "Within [a] few days" [BL/Egerton 2395/0003], and "they have [a] variety of forecastle songs" (cited in Palmer 1986: 104). Other examples omit an article that could have been realized as an indefinite or a definite article depending on context: "[a/the] great quantity of goods" [HCA 1/53/12], "I could not have [a/the] opportunity to speak with him" [445f.1/27], "This morn: had [an/the] order to go for Plimouth" [ADM 52/1/1], "gave him [an/the] account", and "on [a/the] promise that" [HCA 1/99 Bahama Islands 1722]. Other examples of omission are clearly referring to specific vessels or parts of the ship that would typically select a definite article, e.g., "his majesteys ship [the] *Essex prize*" [CO 5/1411/653], "last night at 12 umoored [the] ship" [ADM 52/1/5], "command was then given to shorten [the] saile" [HCA 1/9/155], "winds [...] last night struck [the] yards & topmasts" [ADM 52/2/3], and "we gett [the] Anchor aboard" [ADM 52/3/7]. Such usage is mirrored in specific references to ranks and concrete nouns, e.g., "he was [the] Boatswaine[s] Mate of an English ship" [IICA 1/53/10] "he was absent from [the] house" [HCA 1/101/425], and "I went [...] for to selle at [the] ffartory" [T/70/1216/13]. It may have been that the abbreviated nature of ships logbooks and court documents rendered articles unnecessary, as we might infer from the lack of a definite article to refer to the "prisoner" in the example "whether he ever saw [the] said prisoner" [HCA 1/99 New Providence 1722]. However multiple examples of ships logbooks and Admiralty court documents that make use of the definite article seem to contradict the suggestion that the omission was associated with the accepted styles of the written modes, e.g., "after they of the *Briganteen* had plundered the said ship the *Sea Flower* and taken out of her what they thought fitt they coming again about the sd *Briganteen* put the mast of the *Sea flower*" [HCA 1/53/57]. This example shows definite article usage in all of the phrases that refer to both ships and the equipment of the ship, and even uses the definite article in the expressions "the said ship" and "the sd *Briganteen*" that are explicitly marked as formal courtroom utterances. Another possibility to explain the omission of articles is that the expressions in which articles are omitted are idiomatic, e.g., the expression "made [an/the] oath" [CO 5/1411/640] in a letter circa 1697 that is repeated almost exactly in many other unrelated documents e.g., "made [an/the] Ooath" in a witness deposition in 1700 [SP 42/6]. Indeed, whether it was because of idiomatic usage or characteristic variation, the omission of articles is salient in a range of documentation that includes witness testimony, personal letters, logbooks and journal entries written by or on behalf of mariners.

It appears that rather than something that was conditioned by linguistic constraints, the omission of articles was a free variation for many speakers of Ship English. This assertion is based on a number of documents written in the same hand, and so therefore assumed to be by the same person, showing variation between the use of articles and their omission with similar nominal forms in comparable structures and in a single speech act, e.g., the author of one logbook uses the definite article for "the wind" but then omits the definite article prior to the cardinal direction "west" in the entry "att 10 att nightt the wind came to [the] west" [DDB6 8/4], and the author of another logbook uses multiple definite articles (both orthographically represented as "ye" and "the") for weather and compass point directions in addition to referring to the ship's cargo hold, but then omits the anticipated definite article when referring to the ship's decks in the entry "This 24 houres ye wind from the WS to the SO and back to ye SWbW Stored downe into ye hould betwixt [the] decks" [ADM 52/2/3]. In another example, a logbook entry includes the excerpts "the long boat came a boord with provisions...[and] yesterday afternoon [the] long boat went to pagan Crook for provisions" [CO 5/1411/712] using the definite article for "long boat" in the first clause but omitting it in the second. Two pages later, this same author uses the same syntactic construction as the second clause which omitted the definite article, but this time the definite article is present, "yesterday afternoon the long boat came from york" [CO 5/1411/714]. Such free variation was also a common variant in court documentation, e.g., the omission and then use of the definite article prior to the noun "prisoner(s)" in the example, "[the] prisoner having nothing more to say. The Prisoners were ordered to withdraw" [HCA 1/99 New Providence 1722]. Although it is possible that logbook authors might have purposefully oriented themselves towards formal court language in logbooks, it may also have been that clerks of the High Court of the Admiralty acquired variant maritime usage from exposure to multiple examples in sailors' speech through their job requirement of having to write sailors' depositions.

The definite article was permitted with specific semantic fields and appears to have been conditioned by adverbial gerund phrases and to avoid null categories in the determiner position. Gerund phrases may take a definite article in Ship English, specifically when used in adverbial constructions, e.g., "order to *the having* of her secured" [CO 5/1411/653 emphasis added],[21] and "by *the not keeping* their apparel sweet and dry, and *the not cleansing* and keeping their cabins sweet" (cited in Brown 2011: 64). However, even in constructions not subordinated by adverbial markers, gerunds may be preceded by definite articles, e.g., "meaning as this Deponent understood, *the Running-away* with the Pink" [HCA 1/99 *The American: Weekly Mercury* No.618, Oct 28–Nov 4 1731]. In addition to using definite articles with gerund phrases, Ship English also permits the use of definite articles with newly-introduced and generic referents, e.g., one sailor's explanation of how wooden ships are damaged because "*the worm* comes in... [hulls] being much dammaged by *the worm*" [CO 5/1411/651]. Following Hawkins' (1978) classification of definite article usage in English, unless the reference to "worms" was anaphoric, associative, or indexed some kind of previously-established shared knowledge, then the use of the definite article noun phrase "the worms" rather

---

[21]Italic font emphasis is added to all examples of noun phrases with definite articles in this paragraph.

than the generic plural "worms" is atypical. Yet, the use of definite articles in such contexts is common, particularly with abstract nominals, e.g., "the Discouragement which these proceedings bring to *the Navigation*" [BL/74/816/m/11/36/1], "of *the Cash* he hath not one penny" [HCA 1/98/259], "taking *the command* over them" [HCA 1/99 Cape Coast of Africa, Feb 4 1734, 4], and "not being perfectly versed in *the English*" [HCA 1/99 The Tryals of Agostinho, July 8, c.1721, 7]. Furthermore, temporal references permit the use of definite articles, specifically in logbook entries, e.g., "The wind was moderate all *the morning*" [ADM 51/3797/1], "the weather cold *the last night* some Raine" [ADM 52/2/5], "Little wind all *the night*" [ADM 52/2/5], and "with a fresh gale of wind all *the 24 hours*" [ADM 52/2/5]. It may be that time references in logbooks required an explicit determiner and if no other determiner was used, the definite article served to avoid a null constituent.[22] Yet, the definite article was also used in ways common to Early Modern English such as referring to locations, e.g., "being bound for *the Barbados*" [T/70/1215 29th Oct] and "designing for *the Havana*" [HCA 1/99 Bahama Islands 1722] and in certain idiomatic expressions, e.g., "the Master would not agree to this, but kept *the Sea*" [445f.1/33]. Thus, although definite articles followed many of the accepted usage constraints that we might see in other varieties of Early Modern English, it appears that Ship English also permits the definite article with specific abstract and temporal semantic fields and in the linguistic contexts of gerund phrases and otherwise null determiner categories.

5.4 Pronouns

5.4.1 Heavy use of pronominal forms

The corpus shows heavy use of pronominal forms including nominative, accusative and genitive case variants in a single phrase or clause. Court depositions show particularly heavy personal pronoun usage in short excerpts, e.g., "he was sorry he was sick, and could not goe with him, he taking a Laced Hat away" [HCA 1/99/38] including three instances of the singular male third person nominative form and one instance of the accusative form; "Capt Fairbourne, to whom I delivered the letter you sent me for him...presented a salute from him" [SP 42/6] including two instances of the nominative form and three instances of

---

[22]The suggestion that Ship English preferred multiple determiners over null constituents in determiner position is further supported using demonstratives alongside possessive pronominal determiners, e.g., the appearance of "this his" in the testimony "sufficient force to defend this his colony & dominion" [CO 5/1411/630] and competing determiners, e.g., "this last 24 hours wee had the wind variable between the NNWt and NEt" [ADM 51/3983/1].

the accusative form; and "the Quarter Master called him out of the Boat Several times, which he not obeying presently, beat him severely for, in his sight" [HCA 1/99/166] including one instance of the nominative form, two instances of the accusative form, and one instance of the genitive form.[23] Furthermore, many pronouns are redundant in their linguistic contexts, such as pronouns used to refer to human subjects who are also named in an adjacent noun phrase, e.g., "Mr Harley he's got 203 cheeses" [HCA 1/101/541], "him who is Your loving Fried Fra. Nicholson" [CO 5/1411/652], "him the Deponent" [HCA 1/99/3, HCA 1/99/5, 1/99/7], and "He(e) this deponent" [HCA 1/9/10, HCA 1/14/17]. Prenominal redundancy also features in the idiomatic expression "on board of…" or "a board on…" followed by an accusative pronoun (typically "him" but also potentially "them" and "us") and was repeated numerous times in the corpus, e.g., in HCA 1/98/182, CO 5/1411/98, CO 5/1411/99, 445f.1/34, ADM 52/1/7, ADM 52/1/8, and HCA 1/99/80. This idiomatic structure makes use of a prepositional phrase with an accusative object of the preposition yet the structure is redundant in most cases as the vessel boarded is made clear in context e.g., "fall with the said fisher boat and remained them a board on him" [HCA 1/101/431] and "this same Moody was one of the Pyrates, that came on Board of him in the Boat" [HCA 1/99/37]. Interestingly, the last example also makes use of a double marked nominal "Moody…one of the pyrates" in addition to the double marked object "on Board of him… the Boat" further suggesting the nature of heavily marked nominal forms in Ship English. Redundant prepositional phrases of agency including pronominal objects of the preposition and grammatically unnecessary markers of the indefinite object also feature in the corpus, e.g., "was Burnt by us" [ADM 52/1/1], "his own confession to him" [HCA 1/99/22], and "I can demonstrate to you" [BL/74/816/m/11/36/2]. In short, although sailors' speech was characterized by heavy pronominal use, many instances of personal pronouns are redundant in context suggesting that they were customarily used in acts of over-specification.

---

[23] Although case marking is discussed under the assumption that classifications follow the same parameters as modern usage, there is some data to suggest that variation was permitted or the constraints which selected case marking were not as fixed as we might anticipate, e.g., one logbook entry reads, "meridian morinlgo beard from we", [HCA 1/99/29]. The verbal marker "beard", most likely to be a past form of the nautical term "to bear" with a regularized inflection, projects a prepositional phrase "from we" expressed with a nominative case pronoun "we" and not the anticipated accusative case "us".

5.4.2 Possessive pronouns

In addition to the possessive pronouns that mark genitive case marking (also discussed in §5.2.2), pronominal forms that function as determiners in noun phrases, e.g., "his" and "your", commonly occur in collocation with gerund phrases. One sailor's letter shows this structure in a prepositional phrase of reason, "thanke you for *your sending* us the Navy-Yacht" [ADM 106/288/30 emphasis added]. In this specific example as well as others, the possessive pronominal determiner might have been omitted without affecting meaning and this suggests that when gerunds are used in Ship English, they involve linguistic constraints that select determiners. Furthermore, these pronoun and gerund constructions often function in lieu of subordinating clauses, e.g., one witness deposition includes the phrase "*his getting* a certificate clandestinly sign'd by sevll masters of ships in this land" [SP 42/6 emphasis added] that opens with a prenominal possessive determiner "his" and forms a noun phrase with the gerund "getting a certificate" that is itself modified by the phrase "clandestinly sign'd by sevll masters of ships in this land". This construction forms a lengthy noun phrase that might have been expressed as a subordinated clause, "[because] he got a certificate clandestinly sign'd by sevll masters of ships in this land". Other examples with emphasis added to the constructions in question are "[he] knows nothing of *his being* ashoare" [HCA 1/99/8], and "[I] don't Remember *his going* Particularly on Board" [HCA 1/99/91]. In both these examples, the pronominal determiners "his" preceding the subsequent gerund forms "being" and "going" avoid the need for a secondary relative clause and instead embed the information in the primary clause. Both examples might be expressed as compound sentences using the relative pronoun "that", e.g., "he didn't know *that* he was ashore" (for [he] knows nothing of *his being* ashoare], and "I don't remember *that* he went on board particularly" (for [I] don't Remember *his going* Particularly on Board). Yet, speakers and writers of Ship English consistently show an avoidance of such relative clauses and instead prefer to build complex matrix clauses with multiple embedded noun phrases.[24] Although further research would be needed to confirm these constraints, the examples presented here suggest that determiners were not only acceptable but also potentially necessary in gerund phrases expressing attendant circumstances and

---

[24]Millward & Hayes 2012 explain that Early Modern English favored long and heavily subordinated constructions that emulated Latinate style that built upon older native traditions of cumulative, paratactic sentences that were never completely lost (p.188, 275–276). It may be that the complex matrix clauses with multiple embedded noun phrases of Ship English derive from the Old English preference for cumulative, run-on clauses which were reinforced by more recent preferences for subordination.

that this contributed to a wider phenomenon of compounding complex matrix clauses rather than using subordinating clause structures.

Possessive pronouns such as "yours", "mine", and "hers" are not frequently used in the corpus, but do occur in some personal communications. One letter begins "yours of the third I received on Saturday" [CO 5/1411/647] and because this is the opening line of the letter, the possessive pronoun "yours" has no antecedent and so the reader can only assume the author meant "your letter". This use of possessive pronouns without a prior antecedent is repeated in other letters among sailors, e.g., "I received yours of the Second of october 1693" [HCA 1/98/56] and "hopes may hear from you in answer to ours" [T 70/1/12]. This type of usage may have been a dialectal or idiomatic variant specific to personal communication in Early Modern English among the literate classes, but it does not appear in either of the two widely circulated epistolary narratives of the seventeenth, specifically James Howell's *Familiar letters* (1645–1650), Aphra Behn's *Love-letters between a nobleman and his sister* (1684–1687). However, this use of possessive pronouns without a specific anterior referent does make an appearance in eighteenth century fiction, specifically Samuel Richardson's widely popular epistolary novel *Pamela...* (1740), e.g., "we had not read through all yours" and "I see yours is big with some important meaning" (both examples from Letter XXXII). Yet the usage is not frequent and does not appear at all in the same author's nine-volume *Clarissa Harlowe...* written only nine years later, suggesting that although the feature was an acceptable variant in contemporary English, it was certainly not common, even among the specific groups of people who used it. Literate sailors who used possessive pronominal forms without specific anterior nominal markers may therefore be one of the small groups for whom this usage was acceptable as early as the seventeenth century.

5.4.3 Expletives

Pronominal expletives are commonly used with references to the weather but can be omitted in reference to intangible referents. Logbook entries often include references to the weather using the expletive marker "it" (indicated with italic emphasis), e.g., "This 24 hower we have had *it* for the moss part Calme" [ADM 52/2/10]. "*it* began to raine to raine have been little wind" [ADM 52/2/3], and "this morn *it* came to WNW a very hard Gale" [ADM 52/1/1]. This is even more common with references to wind conditions, e.g., "*It* blew a hard gale" [ADM 52/3/12], "*It* continued a fresh Gaile" [ADM 51/3797/1], and "*It* was soe much wind [...] wee were forced to lay under our Maine Sayle" [ADM 51/4322/1]. References to storm conditions use similar constructions, e.g., "All last night *it* blew a Storme" [ADM 51/3954] and "last night *it* began to blow and this morning it encreasing to a Storme" [ADM 51/3954]. Yet, in contexts with no tangible referent such as wind, rain, or a storm, expletives are infrequently used or omitted completely, e.g., "I suppose [it] was in regard [of] so many" [CO 5/1411/41] and "in March last [it] was two years he sailed out of the River of Thames" [HCA 1/14/201]. Thus, we might surmise that although expletive pronouns are evident in the corpus, their use was localized, or at least preferred, with tangible referents rather than being used to function as the grammatical subjects of existential constructions.

5.4.4 Indefinite pronouns

Indefinite pronouns are not common in either witness depositions, logbook entries or personal communications, instead, sailors used adjectives to indicate generic referents. References to a sizable but indefinite group of people (most commonly an entire or partial crew) often include the particle "all" to index large but indefinite numbers, e.g., "Ye have all of you been wickedly united" [HCA 1/99/3/2] and "we thought all that you had been sick" [HCA 1/101/541]. The phrases "all of you" in the first citation and "we...all" in the second might be understood as "everybody" or "everyone", yet instead of using the indefinite pronouns that were fairly recent developments in Early Modern English, sailors seemingly preferred to use personal pronouns such as "you" and "we" respectively alongside a modifying particle. This same strategy is evident with the use of the term "every" that does not always compound to form an indefinite pronoun but can function as a modifying adjective particle with subject pronouns, e.g., "requested that you and every [one] of you" [HCA 1/98/53]. The assumption that the nominative form "one" exists in the underlying structure of the previous example is based on other examples of usage, e.g., "every one that take it will make use of their time" [ADM 106/288/31] and "every one came" [HCA 1/99/59], in which the phrase "every one" is not conceptualized as a single pronoun but rather a noun phrase composed of "one" modified by the adjective "every".[25] Yet, Millward and Hayes explain that in the Early Modern English period it was acceptable to use "every" as an independent pronoun meaning "all" rather than solely as a pronominal adjective (2012: 264) and the *Oxford English Dictionary* (1989) states that the particle "every" was commonly used as an adjective in collocation with nouns like "one" and "body" to create indefinite noun phrases up

---

[25]Note that this is in contrast to the indefinite pronouns "everything" and "somebody" that do appear written as one lexeme in the corpus, e.g., "hacking everything" [HCA 1/99/126] and "somebody had stole the boat" [HCA 1/99 Bahama Islands 1722].

until 1820 with orthographically joined examples of the words not appearing until the eighteenth century, e.g., Defoe's use of "everybody" (cited in the *Oxford English Dictionary* 1989, Vol 5: 466). It seems that although conjoined forms were becoming acceptable in the period under study, sailors continued to mark indefinite nouns using adjectival particles and pronominal forms, or to use particles such as "all" and "every" as independent pronouns themselves.

Like constructions using "all" and "every", phrases with explicit negation or interrogative modality were also constructed with adjectival particles that could function as independent pronouns. References to zero people (i.e., nobody) and zero items (i.e., nothing) were commonly denoted with the particle "none" functioning as an independent pronoun, e.g., "if you maet none" [CO 5/1411/657], "could find none at all" [T/70/1213], "eaten by none else" [1045.f.3/1/28: 25], "could get none" [HCA 1/9/155], and "there being None in Stores" [ADM 106/288/32]. There are examples of the usage of the particle "any" as an independent pronominal form, e.g., "nott any that wee did like" [T/70/1213], "if they did not meet with any to go" [HCA 1/99/6], and "if any such there be" [CO 5/1411/649]. Yet, the word "any" was more frequently used in sailor's speech as an adjectival particle, most commonly with the word "person", e.g., "he did noe hurt to any person" [HCA 1/9/67], "nor shall carry off this land any Persons" [HCA 1/9/7], and "nor with any other person" [HCA 1/9/63]. The use of the particle "any" with the nominal form "one" was also evident, although whether this was considered in its underlying form as either a noun phrase composed of an adjective and noun, or a pronominal lexeme is unclear — and orthographic spacing seems to imply that both interpretations are valid, e.g., "I lay not this as an injunction upon any one" [445f.1/22] and "did no harm to any of them, nor never Intended to Kill anyone" [HCA 1/99/11]. The interpretation that the construction "any...one" was used as an indefinite pronoun is supported by similar and repeated constructions of the word "any...thing", e.g., "neither he nor any of the others understand any thing of navigation" [HCA 1/99/11], "Did you heare him say any thing" [CO 5/1411/29], and "but did not before know anything of them" [HCA 1/13/92]. So, although the particles "none" and "any" are both used as independent pronouns in the same way as "all" and "every", they were also used by sailors as indefinite adjectives in apparently free variation.

5.4.5 Reflexive pronouns

Reflexive pronouns in the corpus are sometimes used in ways that align with common usage, yet they also have variation that was not common in the Early Middle English period. Sailors used reflexive pronouns typically when the object of the sentence is the same as the subject, e.g., "I...haveing no mony nor frinds to help my selfe" [HCA 1/12/36], "he thought himselfe in ill companie" [ASSI 45/4/1/135/4], "he would defend himselfe" [HCA 1/52/46], "wee doe not wrong our Selves" [HCA 1/9/13], and "seamen belonging to the sd ship *Essex Prize*, which allready have, or here after shall absent themselves from his majestys service" [CO 5/1411/667]. Yet, even though the use of reflexive pronouns had been established since Middle English in the object position of a sentence that referred back to the nominal subject (Millward & Hayes 2012: 263), sailors commonly omitted anticipated reflexives and instead used accusative personal pronouns, e.g., "John Wingfield Swears him[self] to have been a Loving Man" [HCA 1/99/38], "he said in defense of him[self]" [HCA 1/99/48], "he really believes him[self] to have been the instrument of saving her" [HCA 1/99/50], "he had confessed to him[self] a great deal of sorrow" [HCA 1/99/50], and "George Freeborne took upon him[self] to be a Man of War" [HCA 1/9/14]. It seems that this was a salient feature of sailors' speech as it is represented in a popular sea-song of the early seventeenth century, "John Dory bought him[self] and ambling nag" (cited in Palmer 1986: 1). Yet more commonly than replacing the reflexive pronoun with another pronominal form, evidence from the corpus shows that sailors used reflexives in contexts where they were not typical, such as to show genitive case, e.g., "it is the opinion of my self" [CO 5/1411/647], and to refer back to a subject that was not the subject of the anterior clause, e.g., "he took in the water, and likewise my self again" [CO 5/1411/639], meaning that he (the accused) took caskets of water on board and also took the witness (i.e., "me") on board again. However, the most common variant usage of reflexive pronouns in the corpus of Ship English was in the subject position of a clause where a nominative (subject) form of the pronoun would be more typical e.g., "to day my self made [...] survayed 5 butts in the hold" [ADM 52/1/6], "himself was beat, and forced from a good Employ" [HCA 1/99/80], "himself came to us" [T 70/1/10], and "Yesterday My Self with the Rest of the Foresignts Company were turned over" [ADM 51/4170/2]. Although not reproduced in full here, these examples were taken from larger legible utterances in which it was clear that the subject of the previous clause was not the same as the referent indicated by the reflexive pronoun, as in the example "the prisoner should go when himself [i.e., the witness] did" [HCA 1/99/48]. So, although reflexives sometimes followed common usage patterns in sailors' communities, they were not semantically restricted to refer to the same subject referent of the clause in which they appear, nor were they grammatically restricted to the object position of the clause.

Sailors routinely used reflexives after certain verbs of personal expression. Specifically, verbs with a semantic link to oral expression often took a reflexive direct object, e.g., "he had expressed himself extremely glad" [HCA 1/99/20], "he expressed himself sorry for it" [HCA 1/99/133], "he lamented himself under this condition very much" [HCA 1/99/70] "was bemoaning himself" [HCA 1/99/167], "gave orders himself" [HCA 1/99/72], "he says himself he was forced from the Sloop" [HCA 1/99/93], and "he says himself he put the Match to the Gun" [HCA 1/99/167]. This phenomenon may speak to a localized retention of prior transitive verb structures (taking a reflexive pronoun when the direct object was the same as the subject) in sailors' speech when most English speakers in the in Early Modern English were moving away from this pattern towards intransitive verbal expression in the same context (Millward & Hayes 2012: 263). Certain verbs, such as "behave", were typically expressed with the older transitive grammatical form in Ship English and the verb invariably took a reflexive pronoun when the direct object was the same as the subject, e.g., "he haveing behaved himself so unjustly to them" [SP 42/6], "he behaved himself scandalously", [SP 42/6], "behaved himself dutifully enough" [HCA 1/99/112], and "he hath behaved himself very diligently" (cited in Brown 2011: 49). Other verbs such as "feel" also show the same expression as transitive verbs with reflexive direct objects and similarly connect to the semantic field of personal expression, e.g., a ship doctor's journal that records an interview with one of his patients "asking him when he was at stool, and how he feels himself" (cited in Brown 2011: 48). Limited examples of this structure were evident with verbs that did not connect with the semantic field of personal expression, e.g., "[he] overslepte himself" [HCA 1/99/7] but most had some kind of link with oral or physical expression, suggesting that the retention of the older forms of transitive verbal structures that permitted reflexives was conditioned by semantic rather than linguistic factors.

In addition to their potential semantic conditioning with retained transitive verbs, reflexive pronouns were also commonly used to stress human agency and intention in a context where so many sailors' actions were restricted. Expressions associated with emphatic agency commonly relate to sailors' voluntary recruitment in opposition to the coercion of the press, e.g., "[he] shipped himself on board" [HCA 1/12/5], "he left her [his former ship] and shipt himself second mate and Gunner, on board of the Ship *Succession*" [HCA 1/99 *The American: Weekly Mercury* No.617, Oct 21–Oct 28 1731], "[he] Shipped himself" [HCA 1/13/97], "[he] Listed himself" [HCA 1/13/97], and "[he came] in order to enter himselfe on board" [HCA 1/53/68]. In the context of witness depositions and court records it was also important to mark sailors' willingness in collaboration with pirates, and this was often done through the use of reflective pronouns to mark agency, e.g., "the whole fleet birthed themselves in their divisions & moor'd" [ADM 52/2/6], "[the crew] did as they wou'd themselves never observing him" [HCA 1/99/50], "through his means he made himself away" [HCA 1/11/110], "Capt Every but would have united himselfe with Capt Esq..." [HCA 1/53/14], and the partially-legible fragment "& went himself in the" [...] [HCA 1/53/32].[26] Markers of agency were also important to stress sources of information in a largely oral culture of knowledge transfer, and this was often done using a reflexive pronoun in a modifying prepositional phrase, e.g., "he says of himself that..." [HCA 1/99/79], "he said little for himself" [HCA 1/99/42], "He say'd for himself that..." [HCA 1/99/28], and "he says for himself he has been only 5 Months with them" [HCA 1/99/165]. When used as an emphatic marker of agency, a reflexive pronoun is permitted in a post-nominal position that re-asserts the noun phrase subject, e.g., "Roberts the Commander of the Pyrate Ship, also himself told him..." [HCA 1/99/21], and "He himselfe had caused it to be done" [HCA 1/9/155], and "Robert Steewed himselve did resolve to be revenged upon the master if it cost him his life" [HCA 1/101/425]. The occurrence of a reflexive pronoun in post-nominal position features in the line "The sea itself on fire" in a seventeenth century sea song (cited in Palmer 1986: 67) and appears to attest to the salience of this type of structure in sailors' speech. Reflexives were also permitted in non-restrictive modifying phrases, e.g., "he was flourishing his Cutlass [...] and cryed out [...] *himself being then just wounded*" [HCA 1/99/29, emphasis added], and "I am very much concerned to hear of any disorders committed at Kikotan, *more especially my self*, which I am an utter strangor for" [CO 5/1411/654, emphasis added]. In sum, Ship English permitted reflexive verbs as markers of emphatic agency in contexts in which reflexive pronouns were grammatically not required, notably as direct objects in verbs that may be expressed intransitively, in post-nominal positions that repeated the subject, and as part of modifying phrases.

5.4.6 Relative pronouns

The word "which" is the most common relative pronoun evident in the corpus for both human and non-human referents. Non-human noun phrase referents commonly attach a relative clause headed with "which", e.g., "saw a fleet to Cerousd which was our officers came from Plymouth" [ADM 52/1/1] and "The[y] called for the Pump handle, which was the instrument used to kill the rest" [HCA 1/99/9]. Human noun phrase referents also commonly attach a relative clause headed with "which", e.g., "men which die yearly...the old Man which he found" [BL/74/816/m/11/36/2], "a woman which was a passenger" [HCA 1/101/372], and

---

[26]This last fragment is particularly interesting as "go" has rarely been used as a transitive verb in English but there are reflexive varieties of the verb "go" in Spanish and Portuguese (*ir-se*, meaning to go away or leave), suggesting that the adoption of this form might also speak to language context. It is important to note that some of these statements may also have been meant emphatically, an interpretation discussed in more detail below.

"two slaves which was purchased with Gun powder" [HCA 1/98/29]. Indeed, the relative pronoun "which" is much more common in the corpus when referring to human referents than the pronoun "who" that was equally available to speakers of Early Modern English, e.g., "especially to the inhabitants, who, he that commends after the men of warr are departed has chiefly to deal withal" [SP 42/6]. Thus, we can surmise that for any noun phrase referent, either non-human or human, the default relative pronoun choice was "which" in modifying clauses and phrases.

The relative pronoun "which" could potentially eliminate the head noun of an antecedent noun phrase and thus appear to take a determiner, or could appear with a determiner in its own nominal construction. The relative pronoun "which" sometimes appears to eliminate an antecedent noun head, e.g., "those [people] wch came up to Day" [ADM 106/288/30], "he told one [person] which was nigh him" [HCA 1/99/59], and "three [ships] which gave us chase being french" [ADM 52/1/1]. In the three examples listed above, if the underlying noun heads (assumed to be, "people", "person", and "ships") are not realized then it might appear as if the relative pronoun "which" is the noun projection of the determiners "those", "one" and "three", an unlikely grammatical occurrence given that a relative pronoun typically replaces an entire noun phrases in any relative clause. Instead, what seems to occur is that the use of the relative clause permits the noun head of the matrix phrase to be unrealized, and this may have been common in situations of oral communication when the referent was understood. Yet, the possibility of the relative pronoun potentially taking a determiner in its own right, although anathema to modern-day speakers, was potentially acceptable to sailors of the early colonial period. Examples include the quantifying determiner "all" in the letter excerpt, "to *all which* I shall wait yor excys [your excellency's] orders & directions therein" [CO 5/1411/651 emphasis added], and the repeated examples of definite article determiners in depositions such as "and upon *the wch* day" [HCA 1/52/6, emphasis added], and journal excerpts, e.g., "several were kill'd on Shoar; *the which* added much to my sorrow...they bad me go in; *the which* I had not freedom to do...*the which* I knew very well" [445f.1/20,27,36, emphasis added].[27] Thus, whether the relative pronoun created linguistic conditions in which the noun head of the antecedent phrase could be unrealized, or if the

---

[27]Similar rare examples are evident in historical usage. Evidence of "all" as a determiner features in the example "The Italian, French, and Spanish: *all which* in a barbarous word" dated 1613. Additional evidence of "the which" in historical usage also shows the structure functioning as an adjective, e.g., "the which copies" c. 1447, as a pronoun, e.g., "the which I had almost forgot" c. 1682, as a compound relative c. 1523, and as a pronoun specific to people c. 1338 (*Oxford English Dictionary* 1989: Vol 20: 224–225).

relative pronoun could take a determiner in its pronominal form, it nonetheless created conditions in which it could acceptably follow a determiner.

The word "which" could also function as a demonstrative determiner with or without a repeated noun antecedent. This feature occurs in court records when a witness is talking about some pistols and explains, "one of *which pistolls* appears now" [IICA 1/99/7, emphasis added], it occurs again in the opening phrase of one day's proceedings, "*Which day* appeared personally Thomas Colston" [HCA 1/14/17 emphasis added], and it also occurs in published writing for a wider regional audience, "they met a Sloop at Sea from Boston bound to Maryland, the master of *which sloop* came on board" [HCA 1/99 *The American: Weekly Mercury* No.618, Oct 28–Nov 4 1731, emphasis added]. Two of the examples, specifically the record of court proceedings and the publication *The American: Weekly Mercury*, feature in a formal context, potentially suggesting that the feature may have been conditioned by register. However, examples of the word "which" functioning as a determiner are few and do not suggest the kind of salience as evident in instances of the word functioning pronominally in relative constructions that are much more common in the (presumably) unplanned speech of witness depositions.

When functioning as a relative pronoun in the modifying clause of a noun phrase, the word "which" may be deleted, even when it refers to the subject of the matrix clause. Relative phrases functioning as nominal modifiers in which the relative subject pronoun is omitted are evident in the corpus, e.g., "to day came in a Brigginteens [which] have forced in from the Buoy" [ADM 52/2/5], and "this morning arrived here a hag boat from London [which] brought little or noe news at all" [ADM 52/1/8].[28] Contemporaries identified the phenomena of omitted relative pronouns in sailors' speech; repeated examples occur in the sea song "Lustily, Lustily", e.g., "Here is a boatswain [which] will do his good will" (cited in Palmer 1986: 3). It is notable that the example in this line of the song, a structure that is repeated in all three lines of the short stanza, indicates that even though it is the logical subject, the relative pronoun occurs not as in the position of the explicit subject of the sentence but in the complement position of the expletive construction "Here is". This very specific usage is also evident in the corpus, e.g., "There are more yet [which] have been sent to lie at these places" [BL/74/816/m/11/36/3] in which the relative pronoun fills the complement slot of the expletive construction "There are". Furthermore, it is not only in the context of logical subjects that relative pronouns are omitted from positions in the cor-

---

[28]The default relative pronoun "which" is provided in square brackets to indicate the underlying construction of the relative clause from which the phrase is derived.

pus, there are also repeated instances of omitted relative pronouns that serve as modifiers to a noun phrase functioning as direct object, e.g., "we had a lighter [which] came aboard" [ADM 52/2/7], "Capt Fairbourne, to whom I delivered the letter [which] you sent me for him" [SP 42/6], and "nor knows any Body acquitted [which] can speak for him" [HCA 1/99/90]. Similarly, relative pronouns can be omitted when they serve as modifiers to a noun phrase functioning as the object of a preposition, e.g., "In the Manner [which] has been related" [HCA 1/99/105] and "he shifted himself in a shirt, [which] was not his own" [HCA 1/99/98]. There was no clear pattern of linguistic conditioning that the corpus examples indicated, yet it is possible that omission of the relative pronoun may have been more common when strong verbs (i.e. irregular verbs in Modern English) featured in the relative construction, or when the relative construction included an auxiliary verb of modality or aspect.

5.5 Noun phrase modification

5.5.1 Types and placement of modifiers

Bare nouns and noun phrases are frequently modified in the corpus and one of the most common methods of modification is the addition of adjectives in prenominal position, e.g., "*Faire cleare* weather" [ADM 52/2/11, emphasis added]. Yet variation was permitted and modification using past and present participles as adjectives could be placed in pre- or post-nominal positions, e.g., (all with italic emphasis) "Severall *arrived* men" [HCA 1/10/2], "a most dreadfull woman *abused*" [HCA 1/101/429] and "two buts of beer *Stinking*" [ADM 52/2/3]. In addition to participle adjectival forms, Ship English permitted noun forms to take adjectival function, e.g., (all with italic emphasis) "Anne Foster then *Servant* maide" [HCA 1/101/429] "a twine or *rope* yarn" [HCA 1/9/51], and "*China* Ware which they took out of a *China* Ship" [HCA 1/98/265]. Further supporting the interpretation that adjectival words took nominal form rather than adjectival form is the fact that they can be pluralized, e.g (all with italic emphasis): "Contry *Marchts* Ships" [ADM 52/2/5], "A colsultation [consultation] for *flags* officers" [ADM 52/2/5], and "Showed his *Hollands* Colours" [HCA 1/9/9]. Although the pluralization of nominal adjectives may derive from language contact, it may also indicate an underlying genitive function as in "Merchants' ships" (the ships of the merchants), "flags' officers" (the officers of the flags), and "Holland's colours" (the colours of Holland). However, examples such as "In Company with *others* Persons" [HCA 1/10/105, emphasis added] appear to suggest that the nominal form "others" is pluralized in its own right and not as a derivation from an underlying genitive form as it would imply "the persons of the others" rather than its most likely meaning "other people". Thus, although it is not clear as to exactly why nominal forms, and specifically pluralized nominal forms, are permitted in pre-nominal position with adjectival function, the corpus materials attest to their use in sailor's speech alongside variation in the placement of participle adjectives either pre- or post-nominally.

5.5.2 Present participle phrases

Speakers of Ship English frequently use modifying present participle phrases. These present participle phrases commonly follow a noun phrase that they appear to modify, e.g., "**the wether** *continuing hasy* stode sometimes of sometime on" [ADM 52/1/1],[29] "There **the winds** *blowing hard* drove the ship to sea" [HCA 1/14/201], and "**he** *standing hard*" [HCA 1/98/270]. However, present participle phrases can also precede noun phrases, e.g., "This day at 9 in the moring *having feare weathr but Little wind we* came to saile" [T/70/1216/10] and "*Haveing Soe convenient an opportunity I* thought my selfe bound to give your honor notice" [HCA 1/9/4] in which the present participle phrases precede the pronominal subjects "we" and "I" respectively. Indeed, certain examples of orthography suggest that these phrases function as non-restrictive modifiers at the sentence level rather than functioning as embedded adjectival noun phrase modifiers, e.g., the parenthesis and the comma use in the excerpts, "which **the deponent** (*showing some fear at*) he answered" [HCA 1/99/84] and "**William Batten** Master of the Experiment A Merchantship, *now Liveing at Wapping*" [HCA 1/13/107]. The parenthesis and the comma usage in these examples suggest that the phrases are not bound within the noun phrases "the deponent" and "William Batten" but rather should be considered as non-restrictive modifiers with freedom to move into different locations in the sentence/utterance. Furthermore, the interpretation of such phrases as non-restrictive modifiers at the sentence level rather than nominal modifiers aligns with their common function as sentence adverbs. The adverbial nature of many of these types of structures is apparent through their frequency of stative verbs, e.g., "there are **Publick Houses** *scattering by the wayside*" [1045.f.3/1/18], "**Josiah Johnson** *belonging to the same ship*" [HCA 1/99/69], "**all the men** *now belonging to the said Burger*" [HCA 1/98/23], and "**he** *having deserted her*" [HCA 1/99/165]. The number of phrases that also include non-essential

---

[29]This and all subsequent examples include participle phrases emphasized in italics and the adjacent noun phrases emphasized in bold to draw attention to structure.

but relevant background information also attests to the adverbial nature of the structure at the clause level, e.g., "**the Pyrates** *wanting his water*" [HCA 1/99/110], "**the examinant** *imagining that it was stolen goods*" [HCA 1/101/220], "**they** *denying that they had sold any to him*" [HCA 1/9/53], "**Capt Warren** *finding the Pink to sail heavy* left him" [HCA 1/98/267], and "**The Pyrates** *having Seized their ship at Whydah January last*, forced those on Board" [HCA 1/99/77]. Thus, although the frequent present participle phrase structures evident in the corpus might all be interpreted as noun phrase modifiers, they could also function at the sentence level by providing attendant circumstances, specifically in giving information that might be relevant in court testimony.

The significant number of present participle structures in the corpus is notable and these structures also appear to combine freely with other modifying phrases. The most common combination of modifying phrases happens with similar constituents, (i.e., another post-nominal present participle phrase) and these occur with or without coordinating conjunctions or subordinating clause structures, e.g., "**The count** *knowing him to be an old offender, having served the Company of Pyrates as Quarter Master till he was turned out by them* very readily found him Guilty" [HCA 1/99/36], "**the Pyrates**, *hearing he was a Taylor*, and *wanting Such a person very much*, did oblidge him" [HCA 1/99/28], "**they** *having the command of his small Arms* and *lying in the Great Cabin* and **he** *having in the whole vessel but 12 men and boys*" [HCA 1/98/271], and "he had **former accuaintence** *being page to earle of Winselsea who being then in very good apparell having good store of mony* entertayned him" [HCA 1/101/408]. The post-nominal placement of the present participle phrases in all of these examples serves as the common default, and this tendency is repeated when the correlating modifiers are prepositional phrases, past participle phrases, or present participle phrases, e.g., **Moody and the Cooper of the Pyrate [ship]** *having their Pistolls about them & in search for that purpose* came to this..." [HCA 1/99/97], and "**A Servant of Masr John Smiths called Richard the Tanner** was **one** *haveing a light Candle*" [HCA 1/9/51]. In short, most modifying participle phrases in the corpus are post-nominal and although they may potentially embed into the noun phrase as adjectives, many also combine freely with other modifying participle phrases and prepositional phrases that also take an adverbial function at the sentence level.

There is some evidence that the present participle phrase could function as the complete predicate of a clause although the main verb lacks a finite. This phenomenon is most explicit when the subjects of adjacent clauses differ, leaving no possible interpretation that the participle phrase is a modifier, e.g., "and **he** *owning that he had 12 passengers which he brought from St. Marys* I slopp'd him and sent for mine" [HCA 1/98/270]. This example is a three-clause excerpt in which the first clause composes the subject "he" and the predicate "owning that he had 12 passengers" that has its own embedded relative clause "which he brought from St. Marys". In this example, the tense-less participle "owning" appears to serve as the main verb of the subject "he" in the matrix clause and thereby suggests that present participle structures could potentially assume main verb status. In another example, the excerpt "**they** *tarrying longer* the said Le Fort sailed away" [HCA 1/52/137] combines two clauses with the implication that the first clause "they tarrying longer" is subordinate to the second clause "LeFort sailed away" with a meaning that is equivalent to "...because they tarried [i.e., stayed/waited] longer, LeFort sailed away". This example and others similar to it suggest that the clause formed with the present participle was marked as subordinate to the matrix clause that was expressed with a finite verb. This interpretation that present participles compose clauses marked for subordination is further supported by excerpts in which participle phrases are coordinated with clauses in logbook entries, e.g., "**we** *saying by our drums as the day before* and went for them" [T/70/1216/9]; they are also coordinated by parallel structures at the sentence level in court depositions, e.g., "we ware forsed to run to Anckor Againe **we** *finding we Lost ground*" [T/70/1216/11]. The structure is even evident when the noun phrase subject is omitted in logbook entries, e.g., "Saile with Keeft topsailes [we] *haveing Showery Blowing weather*" [ADM 52/2/9]. In short, present participle phrases could function as main verbs in a subordinating clause predicate in addition to their capacity to function as adjectival noun phrase modifiers and adverbial clause modifiers (comparable to Modern English), and these potential realizations potentially contribute to the high frequency of the structure in the corpus.

5.5.3 Phrases headed with "being"

Present participle phrases in a post-nominal position and headed with the word "being" are a salient feature in the corpus and appear in all registers and modalities sampled. The present participle constructions follow the same usage patterns as identified in the previous paragraphs for all present participle phrases, specifically: they can modify noun phrases, e.g., "**the winds** *being contrary*" [HCA 1/53/12]; they can function as non-restrictive modifiers at the sentence-level, e.g., "Then **it** *Being high water* Slack Come to Saile" [ADM 52/2/9]; and they can function as predicates in subordinate clauses, either with or without an explicit nominal subject e.g., "**he** *being a Centry* beat one of their Ships Company" [HCA 1/99/139], and "they forced him [**he**] *being unwilling*" [CO 5/1411/97]. However, the present participle phrases headed with "being" are so salient in the corpus that their usage deserves specific attention. For example, in a letter of just one page [HCA 1/98/254] four present participle phrases occur and three of them are headed with the word "being": first, "about three weeks after his arrival **his vessel** *being fitted for his home ward bound voyage* then came in there the Beckford Gally", second, "**she** *being burnt by the Natives*" third, "**Capt Burges** *being there* she got her passage", and finally "**all the men** *now belonging the Burges Shippe*" [HCA 1/98/254]. In one courtroom deposition, a speaker used three present participle phrases in the same utterance to modify a single noun phrase, two of which are headed by the word "being": "**your prisoner** *beinge a Marryner*, and *goinge in the Good Shipp the Katherin of London*, and *beinge beyond the Seas out of the Shipp* a difference fell between the prisoner and one Richard Chubb" [HCA 1/101/209]. This profusion of present participle phrases headed by the word "being" suggests that it was a preferred structure for expressing attendant details and stative verbs in ship communities.

There is evidence to suggest that the present participle phrase headed by the word "being" was also used in a way that is comparable to modern day usage of linking verbs such as "appear" and "become" that can take a predicate noun or predicate adjective. In the corpus, participle phrases headed by "being" could take a bare noun e.g., "**The 16 Day of** July *being Monday*" [DDB6 8/4], "**a Discovery** *being Death* to them" [HCA 1/99/92], and "**William Cornelius**...*being skipper* in the said Shipp" [HCA 1/9/3]. And more complex noun phrase predicates could include determiners, adjectival components, adverbial components, and coordination e.g., "**one quarter** of what his Excelecy at present has, *being two ounces of Cinnamon*" [CO 5/1411/654], "his only **Informations**, *being old Slander*" [HCA 1/99/42], "**Tuesday** *being the next day after Christmas day*" [HCA 1/52/1], "**he** *being then Boatswain of her*" [HCA 1/99/75], and "Spoke with **them** att 7 in the morning *being the Archangle & two Mercht men*" [ADM 51/3797/6]. Comparable to modern linking verb structures, participle phrases headed by "being" could also take a bare adjective predicate, e.g.," [...] **Pond of fresh Water**... but *being stagnant*, 'tis only us'd for Cattle to drink" [1045.f.3/1/19], "**the cooke** *being dead*" [HCA 1/101/405], and "At 6 last night **the flood** *being made* we weighed [anchor]" [ADM 52/3/12]. However, the adjectival constituents following a prepositional phrases headed by "being" are more commonly adjectival phrases that included adverbial components, prepositional phrases with potential genitives and coordination, e.g., "**it** *being late in the evening*" [T/70/1216/8] "**The English army** *being landed and possessed of the Brass works*" [BL/Egerton 2395/0003], and "**the Commandr** of the said Vine pink *being hindered of his Voyage*" [HCA 1/98/267].

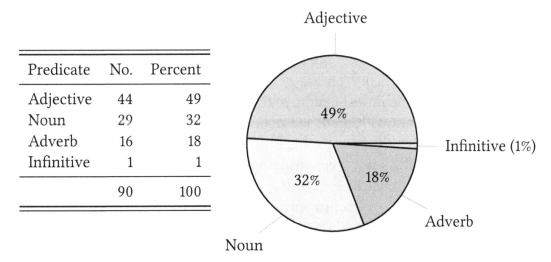

Predicate	No.	Percent
Adjective	44	49
Noun	29	32
Adverb	16	18
Infinitive	1	1
	90	100

Figure 5.1: Distribution of predicate types used with a sample of ninety present participle phrases headed by the word *being*
Sources: ADM 51/4322, 3797, HCA 1/101, Brown 2011, T/70/1216, MMM BL/Egerton 2395, CO 5/1411, HCA 1/52, ADM 52/2, HCA 1/53, T/70/1/10, HCA 1/98, HCA 1/99, 1045.f.3/1, D/Earle/3/1, HCA 1/13, HCA 1/14, DDB6 8/4, HCA 1/9, & HCA 1/10

Interestingly, the "being" phrase permits the use of another present participle adjective after the present participle head (just like a modern linking verb does) despite the doubling-up of present participles, e.g., "**wee** *being rideing*" [ADM 52/2/1], "**his help** *being wanting*" [HCA 1/99/109], "**depot** *being then belonging*" [HCA 1/9/39], and "**The capt & Lieut** *being standing together*" [HCA 1/9/155]. In terms of frequency, the use of an adjectival constituent (expressed as either an adjectival, past participle, or present participle phrase) with the present participle head "being" was the most common type of usage in the corpus with nearly half of the constructions in a ninety-count sample showing collocation with adjectival predicates (44 counts) compared to only around a third (29 counts) of collocation with noun phrases (see Figure 5.1). Yet both combinations are common, and the versatility of the construction may explain why the present participle phrase headed by the word "being" features so heavily in the corpus.

In addition to the ability of the present participle phrase headed by the word "being" to take predicate nouns and adjectives, it could also take predicate adverbs, specifically prepositional phrases that are adverbial in function. And this capacity draws parallels with the finite use of the copula in modern English.[30] Examples of such usage from the sample include: "**we** *being in the trade wind*"

---

[30]The use of "being" as a copula form is also implied in examples like "the Dutch were being about 60 Sayle of men of war" [ADM 52/2/5] in which the finite verb "were" also takes a participle "being" in an utterance with stative meaning.

[DDB6 8/4], "**they** *being in a sloop*" [CO 5/1411/97], "**wee** *being at an anker in 30 fathom*" [ADM 52/2/1], "so many **ships** *being before me*" [D/Earle/3/1], and "**John Smith** the Msr *being upon the quarterdeck*" [HCA 1/52/41]. Although the usage of the present participle phrase headed by the word "being" with an adverbial predicate had the fewest counts in the sample (only 16 counts compared to 29 and 44 when used with predicate nouns and adjectives, respectively) the numbers were still significant with this type of usage representing nearly one fifth and 18 percent of the total constructions sampled (see Figure 5.1). Hence, the present participle phrase headed by the word "being" could be considered as a kind of common linking verb or copula in Ship English, used with predicate nouns, adjectives and adverbs.

Notable features associated with the present participle phrase headed by the word "being" include the use of a genitive pronominal form preceding the phrase, the placement of adverbs before the predicate, and the tendency for the phrase to assume the function of a subordinate clause. The use of a genitive pronominal form (here emphasized in bold) preceding the "being" phrase seem to suggest that the phrase itself is nominal in function, e.g., "to justify **his** *being forced*" [HCA 1/99/84], "since **his** *being with the pirates*" [HCA 1/99/165], and "Haveing heard nothing before of **his** *being dead*" [HCA 1/9/51]. This interpretation aligns with the use of the "-ing" word as a gerund and is further supported by examples showing the phrase used as the object of a preposition and as a nominal subject, e.g., "told him nothing of **his** *being to go with them* till the last Day" [HCA 1/99/114],[31] and "**his** *not being suffered to go on Board of Prizes* makes him incapable of judging" [HCA 1/99/153]. Another feature of the "being" phrase is that it permits an adverbial particle (here emphasized in bold) after the present participle and before the predicate, e.g., "Joseph Anderson *being* **still** *their command*" [HCA 1/12/4], "the Spaniards men *being* **all** *in the Army*" [HCA 1/99/9], "ago he *being* **very** *poor*" [HCA 1/13/97], and "he *being* **so** *Complaisant*" [HCA 1/99/132]. And, although not as common as one word adverbs, prepositional phrases functioning as adverbs are also permitted to occupy this space in the phrase, e.g., "[I] was very glad to see one of the King's Ships, *being* **before our coming** *afraid* of Pyrates" [1045.f.3/1/23]. The "being" phrase also shows a tendency to assume the function of a subordinate clause, specifically showing a relationship between cause and effect that might be expressed with a conjunction like "because" or "so" in Modern English, e.g., "we were obliged [to trade] there *being little sugar*

---

[31]This example is also the only evidence of the infinitive predicate used after the present participle "being" that was found in the sample and composes the one percent of the graph in Figure 5.1.

to be had" [T 70/1/9], "we found the Stock broke we *being forced to Cutt our best bowar* Cable" [ADM 52/2/5], "**this morning** *being fair weather* we heeld & scrubbd our Shipp" [ADM 52/2/6], and "but Doth not believe they will be able to fit her out againe **their** *being so few men here*" [HCA 1/98/30]. The subordination of the "being" phrase is explicit in the example "**Tho: Ashley, Stephen Bales and John Lother** *being English men & Prisoners of War in France* were taken on board" [HCA 1/13/98] in which the main clause predicate "were taken on board" includes a finite copula, which itself may have been expressed as "being taken on board" in a subordinate position. The complexity of such subordination rules, in addition to the constraints that appear to govern genitive pronominal collocation and the placement of adverbs before the predicate shows that the use of the present participle phrase headed by the word "being" is conditioned by both linguistic and syntactic constraints in the corpus. This ultimately contributes to the claim that sailors' speech is characterized not only by the highly-popularized phonological assumptions connected with the profession and its technical jargon, but also by the frequency and constraints of specific words and nominal constructions that, combined, begin to show the bigger picture of Ship English as a comprehensive variety of the language.

5.6 Summary

In terms of morphology, Ship English resists nominal compounding with markers of time and instead permits use of free morphemes with a range of nominal markers. Lexical distinctiveness is well represented in the literature on sailors' speech but further research might expand our knowledge of how multilingual environments motivated lexical, morphological, and phonological feature transfer. Ship English marks genitive case with noun compounding, possessive pronominal forms, inflectional morphology, and prepositional phrases; and these variants occur concurrently in free variation. Double genitive marking occurs when a pronominal possessive determiner is used in concordance with a prepositional phrase and this is most common in idiomatic descriptions of rank that index a female vessel. Uninflected bare nouns are retained, even when marked as plural by a cardinal determiner, and these frequently occur regarding units of distance, time, and weight measurement. Other uninflected nominal forms referring to generic subjects may derive from words that were recent additions to the lexicon and had not yet undergone morphological regularization. The omission of nominal subject heads occurs when the referent is understood from the context of the speech act and alludes to shared knowledge, yet nominal head omission is also linguistically conditioned by the presence of a fronted participle, or a prepositional or adverbial phrase. Additionally, correlative clause constructions also permit the omission of the nominal head in the second clause. Object noun phrases may be omitted in the direct object position and when they appear as the object complement or the object of a preposition and are potentially conditioned using an adjectival modifier or the presence of pre-articles.

Demonstrative determiners were permitted to compete with other determiners in pre-nominal positions and accusative pronouns could take a deictic function when used pre-nominally. Ship English predominantly makes use of cardinal rather than ordinal numbers in pre-nominal positions but number agreement was not universal between determiner and noun constituents, many of which remain uninflected in plural contexts. Sequential markers occur in predominantly post-nominal positions and although the distribution of temporal markers shows that specific lexemes are preferred in pre-nominal positions and for estimated time referents, the most common marker is "last". Categories of mass and count nouns are not mutually exclusive with various mass nouns having the capacity to be inflected for plural nominal aspect and take a determiner specific to count noun usage. Determiners specific to mass nouns are common in the context of indicative modality yet specific usage appears to be governed by constraints that are not universal among the determiner class. Articles are subject to significant localized free variation and omission that is potentially conditioned by linguistic and semantic context in addition to stylistics common to the written mode.

The corpus shows heavy use of pronominal forms including nominative, accusative and genitive case variants in a single phrase or clause, yet many instances of personal pronouns are redundant in idiomatic expressions, prepositional phrases of agency, double marked nominal phrases, and when they function as grammatically unnecessary indefinite objects. Possessive pronominal determiners commonly occur in collocation with gerund phrases that express attendant circumstances and have the effect of building single complex clauses that are characteristic in the corpus. Literate sailors used possessive pronominal forms without specific anterior nominal markers in their personal communications, and logbooks show that pronominal expletives are preferred with tangible referents rather than being used to function as the grammatical subjects of existential constructions. Indefinite pronouns are not frequent in the corpus, instead, Ship English marks indefinite nouns using adjectival particles that may compound with nominal forms but can also function as independent pronouns in free variation. Reflexive pronouns were not semantically restricted to refer to the same subject referent of the clause in which they appear, nor were they grammatically restricted to the object position of the clause. Used in variation, reflexives could occur in genitive case, they could assume the subject position of a clause, and they were permitted in post-nominal modifying phrases. Their use was most common with certain verbs of personal expression where they were specifically used as markers of emphatic agency. The word "which" is the most common relative pronoun evident in the corpus for both human and non-human referents. This pronoun created conditions in which it could acceptably follow a determiner, although it is unclear whether this was the result of an antecedent noun head being unrealized or if the relative pronoun could take a determiner in its pronominal form. The word "which" could also function as a demonstrative determiner, potentially conditioned by genitive case or formal register. Omission of relative pronouns is permitted when the relative construction modifies the object or the subject of the matrix clause, but the conditioning for such omission is not clear from the corpus examples.

Noun phrase modification frequently occurs as a single-word adjective in a pre-nominal position, but nouns with adjectival function and participle adjectives can also modify noun phrases and may occur in either pre- or post-nominal positions. The use of present participle phrase modifiers occurs with salience and high frequency in the corpus and, although these might all be interpreted as noun phrase modifiers, they could also function at the clause level by providing attendant circumstances. Furthermore, when they assume an adverbial function, these present participle structures combine freely with other modifying participle phrases and prepositional phrases that also take an adverbial function at the sentence level. The most common type of present participle phrase in the corpus was headed by the word "being" which could be considered as a kind of common linking verb or copula in Ship English and was used with predicate nouns, adjectives and prepositional phrases that were adverbial in function. Usage of this present participle phrase headed by the word "being" permits a genitive pronominal form to precede the phrase and permits the placement of adverbs before the predicate, and the phrase also shows a tendency to assume the function of a subordinate clause (albeit without a finite verb) of a matrix clause with a finite verb.

6 Verb phrases

This is the second linguistic chapter with a focus on the salient markers and characteristics of Ship English. This chapter on verb phrases begins with the simplest realization of any verb constituent as a single word and continues with the expansion of the verb phrase as it incorporates tense, modality and aspect. Subsequently, §6.1, verbs in Ship English, opens with a discussion of how the variety favors a [non-specific verb + specifying nominal complement] construction in which the syntactic verb serves to introduce a nominal form in the direct object position which expresses the core event of the sentence.[1] This sections then presents data on phrasal verbs and negation markers. The second section, 6.2 on tense, discusses present and past tense variation and features a discussion of the potential role of the Northern Subject Rule, [2] and the manifestation of Narrative Present in performative speech in addition to the presentation of potential linguistic constraints on salient zero-inflection and the use of infinitive forms. The third section, 6.3 on the copula and auxiliary "be", presents data on variation in the inflectional paradigm and discusses how the verb "be" is used and omitted in various contexts including those with aspectual meaning. The last section, 6.4 on auxiliaries, presents data on inflectional variation and uses of auxiliary verbs such as "have" and "do" as they are used in interrogative, indicative, and conditional modalities with details on how they express aspectual meaning.

---

[1] Also know as a light verb construction.

[2] The Northern Subject Rule, described by de Haas (2006) as a unique variation in verbal endings specific to Northern dialects of British English that involves variation in verbal endings according to type and position of the subject. She explains, "Finite verbs adjacent to a pronominal subject (excepting 2SG thou and 3SG, which always take -s) take a zero ending, whereas finite verbs adjacent to a nominal (Determiner Phrase or DP) subject or not adjacent to any subject take an -s ending" (de Haas 2006: 111).

6.1 Verbs in Ship English

6.1.1 The [non-specific verb + specifying nominal compliment] construction

As discussed in chapter 5, the data indicate that Ship English favors heavy nominalization. This section shows how verbal constructions promote this perception by relying on [non-specific verb + specifying nominal complement] constructions, in which verbs retain their syntactic function, but nominals carry more semantic load compared with prototypical "heavy" verb constructions. For example, "the first man they gave torment to" [HCA 1/9/16] rather than "the first man they tormented", and "[they] Spyed a Sayle and gave him chase" [HCA 1/9/13] rather than "they spied a sail and chased him". Furthermore, this usage is found in sea shanties and so speaks to the frequency and salience of the construction in cultural forms of expression, e.g., "Give ear unto the mariners" (shanty in Hugill 1969: 6). Other verbs such as "use" and "offer" are used with similar syntactic function that favor the description of the event in nominal form as the direct objects, e.g., "he used some threatenings" [HCA 1/99/22] rather than "he threatened", and "any one that offered any hurt or violence to Clarke he would make him suffer" [HCA 1/9/51] rather than "any one that hurt...Clarke". The use of nominals, most frequently in the position of the direct object, to express events means that speakers can rely on semantically less-specific verbs. This consequently means that the original direct object is demoted to another nominal position, for example an indirect object, e.g., "to have satisfaction made him" [HCA 1/99/1], "Would not return him any answer" [HCA 1/52/133], and "to make him dishoner" [HCA 1/9/8]. The pronoun "him" in all three examples above might be expressed as the direct object of a verbal form which is semantically specific enough to actually denote the central event of the sentence on its own, e.g., "to satisfy him", "to answer him" and "to dishonor him". However, "him" is expressed as the syntactic indirect object in all three Ship English examples because the direct object position is already occupied by the nominal forms specifying the central event of the sentence, i.e., "satisfaction", "answer", and "dishonor". Similarly, in the example "the prisoner was put commander of the small sloop" (meaning that he was given command) [HCA 1/99 New Providence 1722], the use of the semantically non-specific verb "put" necessitates that the direct object position be occupied by a nominal form that specifies the actual central event of the sentence "command" which forces "the small sloop" (what is commanded) into the position of the object of the preposition in an adverbial phrase. In short, sailors' preference for the [non-specific verb + specifying nominal complement] construction means that the sentences they used favor relatively non-specific verbs and make ample use of event nominalizations.

The verb "make" is the most commonly used verb in [non-specific verb + specifying nominal complement] constructions in the corpus. It often denotes that an event comes to pass or is caused to happen, and this event is subsequently expressed in nominal form , e.g., "in order to make trade" [HCA 1/99/4], "he made a resistance with a cutlass" [HCA 1/99/9], "make information against them" [HCA 1/99/7], "Freebourne made answer" [HCA 1/9/6], and "Letts goe and make an end of the fellow" [HCA 1/9/51]. Here the events "trade", "resist", "inform", and "answer" are expressed in nominal form in the direct object positions following the usage patterns discussed in the previous paragraph. Yet the verb "make" is worthy of individual discussion as it not only permits a noun phrase object, but also a prepositional phrase indicating a direction or manner of movement, e.g., "she made away from him" [HCA 1/9/18], "the informant made to her" [HCA 1/52/124], and "this examinant made for Cape Charles" [HCA 1/9/13]. Indeed, this sense of movement may explain the idiomatic usage in the corpus that associates the verb "make" with travel, transit and arrival, e.g., "we made the Island" [1045.f.3/1/16], "he made the best of his way" [HCA 1/98/254], "they made what saile they could after them" [HCA 1/53/12], "he designs to make his escape" [HCA 1/99/51], and "Make all the dispatch you can" [HCA 1/101/553]. These sample clauses with the verb "make", whether they are expressed with nominal or prepositional complements, all illustrate the preference for the [non-specific verb + specifying nominal complement] construction in Ship English and is a salient feature of the corpus.

6.1.2 Phrasal verbs

Phrasal verbs in the corpus show a tendency to be expressed as fixed expressions, in which the verb and the particle need to be adjacent. These expressions resist the insertion of an object noun phrase or pronoun between the main verb and the satellite particle. The majority of phrasal verbs occur without separation of the verbal particle(s) and satellite particle(s), e.g., (with emphasis added) "by *breaking downe* her misson mast" [ADM 106/288/40], "[he] was presently *sent for up* by the said Taylor" [HCA 1/9/39], and "when they *got up* the anchor" [HCA 1/99/6]. A few examples show that it was permissible to insert a direct object noun phrase between a verb and a satellite particle, for example the separation of "fetch out" in the example, "he *fetch'd* the captain's charts *out*" [HCA 1/99/7]. Indeed, when the direct object of a transitive phrasal verb is a pronoun, we would anticipate it to be expressed in a position separating the verb and the satellite particle, e.g., "they *whipped* him *up* again" [HCA 1/99/7]. Yet phrasal verbs in Ship English appear to resist even this type of separation. Instead, the direct object is more commonly expressed after the complete phrasal verb, regardless of whether it is a noun phrase or a pronoun, e.g., (with phrasal verbs italicized and direct objects in bold for emphasis) "*call abroad* **him**" [E134/34Chas2/Mich36], "*took away* out of his packett **his Sealed ring**" [HCA 1/9/18], and "they *let go* **her anchor**" [HCA 1/52/2]. Thus, although phrasal verbs permitted separation of the verb and the satellite particle, it was common to keep both or all parts of the phrasal verb together without separating them with either a nominal or pronominal direct object.

6.1.3 Negation

Negation can be marked in a variety of ways in Ship English, the most common of which was the use of the negative particle "not" after a finite verb.[3] Modern day speakers of English are accustomed to the particle "not" used with "be" used as an auxiliary verb, and this type of modern-standard usage was evident in the corpus (all examples emphasized), e.g., "Our Ankor *was not* no sounder" [T/70/1215], "the country and his colonies *was not* under his command" [CO 5/1411/101], and "the Prisoner was not only never on Board" [HCA 1/99/156]. Standard modern usage also requires "do-support" in the negation of verbs expressed in the present tense indicative mood, e.g., "he *does not / doesn't* work", and this type of standard usage was also evident in the corpus, e.g., "he *did not hear* it" [HCA 1/99/5], "The English *did not row*" [HCA 1/13/96], "he *did nott thinks* itt convenientt" [ADM 52/2/3], and "Porter complained that they *did not work*" [HCA 1/99/8]. The verb "do" is also used as an auxiliary with indicative verbs despite the fact that the conjugation of the auxiliary, particularly with third person singular subjects, does not always align with modern-day standard usage, e.g., "Capt Rigby *doe not* nor shall *carry off* this land any Persons" [HCA 1/9/7], "Captain Sharp *don't forget* to Speak for us" [HCA 1/99/30], "he *don't know* that the prisoner had any money" [HCA 1/99/10], and "[he] *do's not know* what ship" [HCA 1/99/99].[4] However, this type of negation using "do support" and the "not" marker for simple verb

---

[3]The most common pre-verbal usage of the negating marker "not" occurred in phrases headed with "being", e.g., "he did not Duty *not being well*" [HCA 1/99/108] and "the merchant ship *not being gon* into York river" [CO 5/1411/702].

[4]The use of "doth" in negation is rare in the corpus and mostly seems to derive from the speech acts of judicial representatives in court records and not the sailors themselves, e.g., "he doth not know of any corespond[ance]" [HCA 1/14/140], "Doth not know the ships name" [HCA 1/14/140], and "whose name he doth not remember" [HCA 1/14/203].

phrases in the negated indicative mood had a low frequency in the corpus and may only reflect recent changes in the direction of Early Modern English. Much more salient was the use of the particle "not" immediately after the verb and without any auxiliary marker. Examples of this type of negation appear in logbooks, e.g., "wee *weighd nott*" [ADM 52/2/6], and "But [we] *found not* A man in har [i.e., her]" [T/70/1215], in journals, e.g., "I *hope not* so" [445f.1/26], and "I *got not* in till the next Day" [1045.f.3/1/22]; and in private correspondence, e.g., "they *had not* those termes" [CO 5/1411/39], and "I *doubt not*" [BL/74/816/m/11/36/1]. Yet, it was most common in witness testimony, e.g., "he *intended not* to sell the said rope" [HCA 1/101/224], "She *remembers not*" [HCA 1/9/51], "He *cared not* what the master did" [HCA 1/9/139], "I sent for him aboard but hee *came not*" [HCA 1/9/4], and "he *had not* opportunity of getting away" [HCA 1/99/165]. This type of negation was even more pronounced with the verb "know", which showed up in negated statements repeatedly in the corpus in both past and present tense, e.g., "he *knew not* the design of the others" [HCA 1/99/5], "he *knew not* when he would return" [HCA 1/14/151], "he *knew not* but that he might prosecute him" [HCA 1/52/46], "He *knowes not* of any Nutmeggs or Cloves" [HCA 1/12/78], "whose names I *know not*" [BL/74/816/m/11/36/3], "I *know not* of any methods" [CO 5/1411/655], and "He *knows not* nor ever heard" [HCA 1/9/51]. However, negation with the "not" marker was versatile and permitted syntactic variation; for instance, it occurs in a position separated from the verb by a pronominal direct object (emphasized in bold), e.g., "wee *saw* **him** *not*" [HCA 1/12/2], "yet [we] *made* **him** *not* Bear for our company" [T/70/1216/13], "he *has* **it** *not* for himself" [HCA 1/99/51], and "They *found* **it** *not* safe to hazard" [ADM 51/4322/4]. Indeed, "not" was the most versatile and the most common negation marker in the corpus, and based on a sample of 204 items (see Figure 6.1), accounts for more than half of all negated verb phrases. In sum, although the salient "not" negation marker was used in a manner comparable to modern-day usage of the verb "be" and with "do-support", it was more frequent in a variant post-verbal position without any auxiliary marker. [5]

The second most common negation marker in the sample was the word "never" which was used both to mark categorical denial over time (as in standard modern usage) and to mark the negation of a simple verb form with no aspectual meaning. Given that the term "never" derives etymologically from the negative particle "ne" (meaning "no") and the adverb "ever", the most transparent meaning of the negative marker is one associated with a durative aspect and the most logical context is with a situation of zero-possibility with a cumulative quan-

---

[5]Negation using "not" with auxiliaries of conditional modality also feature in the corpus, but are discussed in §6.4.3 Modal Auxiliaries.

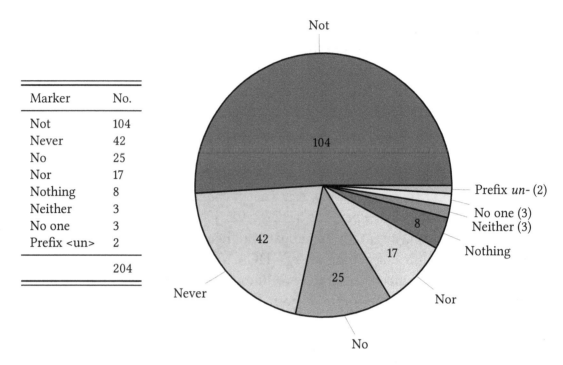

Marker	No.
Not	104
Never	42
No	25
Nor	17
Nothing	8
Neither	3
No one	3
Prefix <un>	2
	204

Figure 6.1: Distribution of negation markers used in a sample of 204 verb phrases
Sources: 1045.f.3/1, 445f.1, AC WO 16–16/8–16, ADM 51/4322, 3983, 3954, ADM 52/1, 2, BL/74/816/m/11/36, CO 5/1411, DDB6 8/4, HCA 1/9, HCA 1/11,12,13,14, HCA 1/52, HCA 1/98, 99, 101, Palmer (1986). SP 42/6, T/70/1215.

tification over time, i.e., something that has categorically not happened up to and including the present moment. This meaning is evident in the corpus (all marked for emphasis), e.g., "he did not hear it Read, nor *never* heard that it was read" [HCA 1/99/5], "he had *never* been arrested of any ill action" [HCA 1/99/8], "was *never* till now taken" [HCA 1/13/95], "was *never* before seen by him" [HCA 1/13/92], and "*Never* had any acquaintance or discourse with nor ever saw the said Prock or Richard [...] before" [HCA 1/52/133]. However, less than a quarter of the "never" negation markers in the sample, only 10 of the 42 items sampled, had the meaning "no(t) ever", see Figure 6.1.

The majority of examples of "never" were used with specific durations of time or to negate indicative past tense situations. The marker "never" used to negate specific durations of time and that frequently occurs with adverbs such as "(un)til" or "since" is comparable to negation in perfect aspect or with preterit verbs in modern standard English. For example, "he *never* was at attacking any Ship, Since he has been among them" [HCA 1/99/80] is comparable to perfect aspect negation in modern-day usage, i.e., "he *had not attacked* any ship since he had been among them". In contrast, "he *never* knew the prisoners till taken in the boat" [HCA 1/99 Bahama Islands 1722] is comparable to preterit negation in modern-day usage, i.e., "he *didn't know* the prisoners until taken in the boat". Even more common than this, however, was the use of "never" to negate events with little or no evidence of durative aspect, e.g., "[on] July the 16th 1720, [he] owned he helped travessing a Gun but *never* fired" [HCA 1/99/78], "he knew very well he had *never* signed the Articles" [HCA 1/99/62], "he *never* see him Sober Scarce" [HCA 1/99/44], and "Shows [shoes], stocking, which *never* cost about [...] shillings" [SP 42/6]. Some examples of this type of indicative past tense negation are only ev-ident in light of the context of the utterance, e.g. the defendant who claims he "did *never* see any letter" [HCA 1/98/255] is clearly referring to a specific letter at a specific time and not "any" letter at any previous time in his life (as would be implied by the use of "never" meaning "not" + "ever"). Similarly, when John Barefoote, Yeoman of the powder room of the *Antelope* during April of 1663, tes-tifies that he "*never* had any discourse with Nathaniel Paintor Armourer in the *Anthelope* nor with any other person in the said shipps Gunroome" [HCA 1/9/63] he is most likely referring to a specific conversation on a specific day (and hence, preterit negation) rather than the idea that he "never" spoke with the armorer of the vessel nor any other person in the gunroom — an unlikely claim given that his job was to store and manage the gunpowder. Thus, whether it is evident from the linguistic context of the clause itself or the wider socio-historical con-text of the speech act, the majority of negated statements using "never" appear to denote indicative past negation and not any kind of durative aspect that we might associate with a lexeme that derives from the negative particle "ne" and the adverb "ever".[6]

The third and fourth most common negation markers in the sample were the words "no" and the conjunction "nor", which sampled at 12 and 8 percent of the total number of examples, respectively (see Figure 6.1). The negative marker "no" was most typically used in a prenominal position before a direct object or object compliment and took the function of a zero-marking determiner, e.g., "wee hav-ing noe boate" [HCA 1/12/2], "we found noe ground with our hand line" [ADM 52/1/7], "he thought himself no robber" [HCA 1/99/23], "Being able to get no im-ploy" [HCA 1/13/97], and "He knew of no offense that he had done therefore would ask him no pardon" [HCA 1/52/14]. This method of negation functions in accordance with the previously discussed tendency in Ship English to favor nom-inalization using light verbs, e.g., "Wee tooke no harme" [ADM 51/3983/1], "The Governour was a board of us but made no stay" [ADM 52/1/8], "but knows of no Sharing they made" [HCA 1/99 New Providence 1722], and "no vessell come-

---

[6]It is worth noting that this past indicative use of the adverb "never" without durative aspect is still found (in addition to other variant uses with varying degrees of aspectual meaning) in modern-day non-standard English dialects (see Lucas & Willis 2012).

ing that year could make noe prize" [HCA 1/98/262]. The negative marker "nor", instead of being used in a pre-nominal position after an inflected verb, often preceded a non-finite verb, e.g., "he nor seeing them come out nor dealing with the master" [T 70/1/10] and "nor being neither this Deponent" [HCA 1/14/51]. However, the more customary use of "nor" as a negating conjunction frequently occurs in the corpus and often functions to conjoin constituents that already have negation. Such negative concord was a salient feature of sailors' speech that manifests itself in popular songs about life at sea, such as the seventeenth-century song "Another of Seafarers" that includes the line "Nor have no room" (cited in Palmer 1986: 6). The simplest example of negative concord in the corpus is the word "nor" used to conjoin two negated verb phrases, e.g., "He knows not *nor* ever heard" [HCA 1/9/51] and "he ...did *not* bye them *nor* had *not* any conferences" [HCA 1/101/221]. In addition to concordant markers of negation occurring in the same phrase, strings of negated clauses are also common in the corpus, for instance, the witness statement "But knows *not* what it was, for he did *not* hear it Read, *nor never* heard that it was read, *nor* knows *not* how the Vessell was fitted out" [HCA 1/99/5] includes 6 negation markers, "not" (used three times both in a post verbal context and with "do support"), "nor" (twice), and "never" (once). The conjunction "nor" functions to join three negated clauses, firstly, "for he did *not* hear it Read", secondly, "*never* heard that it was read", and lastly "*nor* knows *not* how the Vessell was fitted out" and all of these are prefaced by another negated clause "But knows *not* what it was" making a string of four negated clauses. A few times, the negative particle "nor" occurs as part of a correlative conjunction with the word "neither", e.g., "he *neythor* aske any price of the said Sherman for the said goods *nor* the said Sherman never asked him if he would sell them or not" [HCA 1/101/224]. Yet, even in these few instances, the clauses that are conjoined often include negative concord within the conjoined structure, such as in the example, "*nor* the said Sherman *never* asked him if he would sell them or *not*." This type of negative concord may have been a feature of Ship English, but it was not distinctive from other varieties of English. The phenomena of negative concord in non-standard varieties of English is widespread around the modern-day Atlantic (van der Auwera 2016), and (Kortmann & Lunkenheimer 2013) attest to 80% negative concord among global varieties of English . Thus, negative concord, specifically using "no" in a prenominal position and joining negated phrases or clauses with the conjunction "nor", is a salient feature of Ship English, but this is not surprising given its occurrence in Old English and its persistence throughout history up to the modern day in variant negation systems throughout the Anglophone world.

6.2 Tense

6.2.1 Present tense variation

Logbooks, letters and depositions alike show variation in inflection patterns for present tense indicative modality, specifically an absence of inflection with singular third person subjects. The following examples show uninflected finite verbs (emphasized by italics) with singular third person noun phrases (emphasized in bold) "**moderate weather** *blow* fresh" [ADM 52/2/3], "**Our boat** *goe* in to Black Slakes" [ADM 52/2/9], "**all shipping** that *come*" [BL/Egerton 2395/0007], and "**the boat** *want* for wood" [CO 5/1411/712]. One specific witness deposition taken in Grand Bahama Island and dated 1722 shows inflection as a superscript particle (see Figure 6.2) suggesting that the original statement may not have included the inflection but it was added at a later stage in the court clerk's revisions. In addition to the examples of verbs used with singular third person noun phrases, there is also evidence of zero inflection with singular third person pronouns, e.g., "**whoever** *see* one first" [HCA 1/99/143], "He swore that **he** *know* no negroes" [T 70/1/5], "**He** *know* of no commission" [HCA 1/9/10], "**he** *know* not" [HCA 1/101/219], and "**He** well *know* Joseph Passof" [HCA 1/14/150]. Examples appear to connect the zero inflection with negation and specifically the verb "know", suggesting that this variation may be conditioned by linguistic constraints or favored specific lexemes in idiomatic phrases, however, the potential role of the Northern Subject Rule might also affect the selection of zero inflection with third person pronominal subjects (see de Haas 2006).

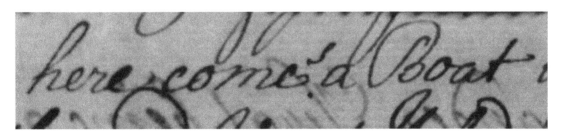

Figure 6.2: Excerpt from a deposition showing superscript inflection with a third person singular noun phrase in present tense indicative modality [HCA 1/99 Bahama Islands 1722]

The Northern Subject Rule may also account for examples of atypical inflection with plural third person subjects and when the verb is not adjacent to a subject. In the corpus, some plural third person subjects that are expressed as noun phrases (emphasized in bold) take an inflected verb (emphasized in italics), e.g., "**the barracks** *tooks* fire" [SP 42/6], "**severall papers** which *comes* herewith"

[SP 42/6], and "**which accts** plainly *demonstrates* the tricks" [SP 42/6]. The last two examples show the inflected verb in a position that is not immediately adjacent to the noun phrase subject, and perhaps this was a conditioning factor in the use of inflection with third person subjects. Yet, whether it was due to the Northern Subject Rule, or another conditioning factor, the atypical inflection with plural third person subjects in Ship English — particularly when the verb is not adjacent to a subject — was salient enough to be recorded in seventeenth century sea-songs, e.g., "They cried **Englishmen** *comes*" (from "A joyful new Ballad" cited in Palmer 1986: 16), and "**Brave sailors** that *sails* on the main" (from "Sailors for my Money" cited in Palmer 1986: 31). Thus, although the constraints of the variation within inflectional paradigms are not entirely clear, sailors of the period were known to inflect verbs in ways that did not follow conventional contemporary standards.

In addition to variation in present tense inflection, there is also evidence of present tense use in past contexts. Logbook entries clearly marked for past context make use of verbs inflected for the present indicative tense, e.g., (with italic emphasis), "Last night the wind *proves* Westerly" [ADM 52/2/9]. Witness depositions feature the use of present tense more heavily despite the fact that the statements are marked for past context by the nature of their narrative content and also by the use of other preterit verbs (emphasized in bold), e.g., "Then the Captain *goes* upon the Half-Deck again, and **call'd** to his Man" [445f.1/23], and "the mariner **Lay** and there *talkes* with the men" [HCA 1/101/217]. Indeed, the use of inflected present tense in past contexts in alteration with preterit forms may be a manifestation of the narrative function of witness statements. Fleischman explains, "the NP [Narrative Present] is a spontaneous use of the PR [present tense] that occurs consistently in *alternation* with tenses of the P [past] and is linked to a performative mode of *oral* storytelling" (1990: 258, author's italics). Witness statements are certainly a modality of oral storytelling and in this context, alternation from past to present forms may have helped sailors bring immediacy — and thereby credibility — to their performances in court. The same use of Narrative Present tense features in journal writing, e.g., Angelo and De Carli's published work, "A Curious and Exact Account of a Voyage to Congo in the Years of 1666 and 1667" that narrates events alternating between present tense forms (in italics) and past tense forms (in bold):

> In a little time *comes* the Lieutenant, and *says* to one of them, Go down to thy Quarters; his answer **was**, I *can* Fight no more; The which **was** what he looked for; for he **was** our greatest Enemy. Then he *goes* to the captain, and *makes* the worst of it, saying, Yonder the Quakers be altogether, and

> I *do not know* but they *will* Mutiny, and one *says* he *cannot* Fight; then he **ask'd** his name and **came** down. [445f.1/23]

Although the use of the present tense is understandable in the representations of direct speech in this excerpt, narrative phrases also use present tense to provide immediacy for the reader. So, although we might anticipate that the oral performance of witness testimony be more likely to show evidence of the Narrative Present, examples suggest that sailors also alternated between past and present in logbooks and journals, potentially reflecting their oral and performative culture (discussed in Chapter 4, Section 4.2.6 on shared ideologies and leisure activities).

6.2.2 Past tense variation

Variation in past tense marking was one of the most salient features in the corpus. There are many examples of regular inflection with weak (i.e., regular) verb stems, (emphasized by italics) e.g., "we *stopped* our ship" [ADM 52/2/5], "he *answered* that he does not know" [HCA 1/13/94], and "he came afterwards & *robbed* her" [HCA 1/99/41]. Even with non-standard orthography, many examples of verbs imply pronunciation of the regular past tense suffix <ed>, e.g., "[he] *call'd* to his Man" [445f.1/23], "wee *stopt* the Ebb all the flett *Ankerd*" [ADM 52/2/1], "wee *waid* [weighed] Anker" [ADM 52/2/1], "Both his pistolls *mist* [missed] fire and did not go off" [HCA 1/52/137], and "*kist* [kissed]... *tript* [tripped]" [HCA 1/99/11].[7] However, there were also many examples of weak finite verbs that were not inflected in a regular preterit form despite being contextualized in the past tense (by virtue of their narrative content and/or the past inflections of adjacent verb phrases). Excerpts from depositions illustrate this phenomenon (emphasized by italics), e.g., "he *fetch* some wine and & beer" [CO 5/1411/47], "He *hoyst* sayle & went from that place" [HCA 1/52/41], "The Carpenter... came up, and *answer* to the captain" [HCA 1/52/41], and "[the men] *board* and *board* in which severall men were killed" [HCA 1/53/3]. Note that in the last three examples the unmarked forms are used in collocation with the preterit forms of strong verbs, "went", "came", and "were", respectively, which not only mark the past context of the excerpt but also show that unmarked forms were not universal in individual speech acts or for individual speakers. Similarly, excerpts from logbooks also

---

[7]In addition to these accepted regular forms of preterit weak verbs, the use of "-th" inflections were also acceptable in the Early Modern English period, e.g., "who *giveth* him dayly wages" [HCA 1/101/219] and "[he] *saith* hee did" [HCA 1/9/3], although they were not a dominant form in the corpus.

include frequent uninflected weak verbs in the past tense, e.g., from the logbook of the *Pideaux*: "this morning we *lift* him again" and "he *lift* the vessel" [HCA 1/99/53] and from the logbook of the Albemarle: "at 9 at night wee *anker* in 30 fathom water", "in the afternoon we *fetch* 3 boat Loads of Ballast", "at night we weighed & *fill up* the boy", and "We *Bury* overboard another Wounded" [ADM 52/2/1,6,8,9]. Although a number of the examples from logbooks follow prepositional phrases marking time, this is not considered to be a linguistic constraint of unmarked preterit forms as there are also many examples of weak verbs with regular <ed> suffixes in this context. In short, it appears that Ship English permits free variation between regular weak preterit forms and unmarked preterit forms, and this can occur across a range of registers, modalities, and linguistic contexts.

Strong verbs (i.e., irregular verbs) presented the most variation in past tense marking. There are many examples of strong preterit forms in the corpus, e.g., (with italic emphasis) "and [I] *spoke* with him" [CO 5/1411/700], "They *took* and plundered and *took out* some rice & sugar" [HCA 1/52/75], and "he *saw* the prisoner have a Sword" [HCA 1/99/72]. Yet, numerous examples also attest to variant methods of marking the preterit. In some excerpts, past participles are used as preterit forms of strong verbs, e.g., "he *seen* him cut her cable" [HCA 1/99/73], "he *seen* him go on Board" [HCA 1/99/96], and "[we] *Rid* all night" [ADM 52/2/6].[8] Other excerpts show alternative irregular preterit forms, e.g., "I *writ* from Leverpoole" [445f.1/46], "I am informed of a letter you *writ*" [HCA 1/98/66], and "we *kam* to Anankor" [DDB6 8/4].[9] The most common inflected variant however was a regularized form of a strong preterit that was marked with a regular <ed> suffix, e.g., "He should not be *hurted*" [HCA 1/99/9], "[I] *quitted*" [HCA 1/99/12], "he *waked*" [HCA 1/99/4], "she went out and *catched* the Swallow" [HCA 1/99/150], and "[he] *threw'd* the Dept. against the Ladder" [HCA 1/99/152]. The last example is particularly interesting as it marks tense twice, once in the form of the anticipated strong preterit form "threw" and again with the regular inflection "-ed" common to weak verbs. This example appears to corroborate the double tense marking that Bailey and Ross found in logbook entries: "we *bored* the yards"

[8]According to Blake (2002: 95) the preterit and past tense forms were encroaching into each other's syntactic space in the Early Modern English period and so this type of variation may have been common at the time. Furthermore, this usage remains common in some modern non-standard varieties (Cheshire 1994: 125).

[9]The preterit in the example "we kam to Anankor" [DDB6 8/4], is somewhat problematic and depends on the speaker's realization of the orthographic 'a' which appears to be [æ] but could just have likely been realized as the diphthong [ɪ] or another allophonic variant acceptable in contemporary usage.

(1688: Sloane 3671) and "we *tookt* in the Virgins Prises" [ADM 51/4298 1692] (cited in Bailey & Ross 1988: 204). It also potentially corresponds with the type of concordant past tense marking in examples using an auxiliary verb, e.g., "*Did found* Robert Clarke" [HCA 1/9/51] that marks past tense once in the auxiliary verb "did" and again in the strong preterit "found". There were no discernable linguistic constraints that governed selection of past tense realization, and some documents written in the same hand show free variation in similar linguistic contexts, e.g., the journal of mariner and merchant Bryan Blundell (1687–1754) that includes the phrase "[the wind] *blowed* very hard" and also "the wind *blu* very hard" [DDB6 8/4] showing examples of the regularized past tense form and the irregular form by the same author.

Just like their weak counterparts, strong verbs also frequently occur without any past tense marking, and this was the most common variant realization in the corpus for this type of verb. Strong verbs in witness testimony narrating past events frequently show zero marking, (emphasized by italics), e.g., "hee well *know*" [HCA 1/52/1], "*strike* him severall bloes about the head" [HCA 1/11/74], "He left one & *Bring* one to us" [ADM 52/2/9], "he *say* that" [HCA 1/98/24], and "he was a Brisk Fellow [...] and *tell* Roberts" [HCA 1/99/132]. Strong verbs in logbook entries relating to recent events in the past tense also show frequent zero marking, e.g., "Longboat in a Violent Gust *break*" [ADM 51/3954], "The wind *blow* fresh" [ADM 51/4322/1], "we *gett* 32 punsh [punch] & 31 butt ashore" [ADM 52/1/8], "wee *give* Our ship" [ADM 51/3797/1]. Although the frequency of zero-marked preterit strong verbs is significant for a range of verbs both in logbooks and witness depositions, there were some trends that suggest a higher usage with specific verbs. The verb "see" was sampled with zero past tense marking 21 times (significantly more than any other verb) throughout the corpus, e.g., "I *see* him put it under his left arm" [HCA 1/99/7], "he *See* him go over the Side" [HCA 1/99/147], "he *see* him cruelly beat to make him go" [HCA 1/99/147], "hee *see* George Freebound" [HCA 1/9/3], and "In Hasting Bay wee *see* Severall French Shipps" [ADM 52/3/7]. Four counts of zero marking with negation imply a possible condition, e.g., "he never *see* them any more" [HCA 1/99/110], "never *see* him in Arms" [HCA 1/99/133], "never *see* any Letter" [HCA 1/98/20], and "Gott about the mast but *see* nothing but three small Topsails" [ADM 52/3/7]. However, there is little evidence that this specific verb is conditioned by any specific factors that select zero preterit marking and the strong preterit form is equally represented in the corpus (including in phrases with negation) e.g., "had never saw a Prize taken" [HCA 1/99/8], "wee saw him not" [HCA 1/12/2], "At two yesterday [...] *saw* our fleat" [ADM 52/1/1], "he *saw* the prisoner have a Sword" [HCA 1/99/72], and "he run away when he saw twas the Kings Ship" [HCA 1/99/96]. Thus, the lexical item itself rather than the linguistic context of its use appears to select a preference for zero marking, although zero marking occurs with a range of verbs and is not restricted to specific lexical items like the verb "see".

The verb "run" was the second most heavily occurring strong verb with an unmarked preterit form, sampled 18 times in the corpus. Every one of the 18 examples occur in the context of a phrasal verb (emphasized in italics) e.g., "he *run up* the shrouds" [HCA 1/99/9], "*Run out* to the buoy" [ADM 52/2/5], "they *run* her *on* ground" [HCA 1/99/10], and "he Saw the Kings Colours he *run down*" [HCA 1/99/78]. As in the last example, many of these unmarked phrasal verbs occur in contexts where other strong preterit forms and weak preterit forms are explicitly marked for past tense (marked in bold), e.g., "when he **Saw** the Kings Colours he *run down*, **Confessed** he had been on Board" [HCA 1/99/78], and "we **shote** his maine yard Down but he *run over* the officer and *run up* Poldard bay [...] where he **durst** not follow" [ADM 52/1/1]. The satellite particle "away" used with the verb "run" appears to favor zero past tense marking more than any other satellite particle. This is evidenced by the fact that "run away" composes more than half of the recorded samples using the verb stem "run" (10 of the 18 samples),[10] e.g., "John Hardin who *run* away" [SP 42/6], "one of them who run away with the sloop" [HCA 1/99 Bahama Islands 1722], "Kenyou *run away* crying what have you done" [HCA 1/99/7], "he *run away* when he saw twas the Kings Ship" [HCA 1/99/96], and "Some men that *Run away*" [HCA 1/13/100]. Yet "run" (with whatever satellite particle it takes) is not the only verb stem in a phrasal verb that is represented with zero marking in the corpus. Various uninflected verbs with a range of satellite particles also select zero marking, e.g., "We *goe away* Before" [ADM 52/2/9], "The Cable *give waye*" [ADM 51/3797/1], "His Company aforesaid and *take away* his said Vesell" [HCA 1/52/133], "At two yesterday [...] saw our fleat then we *hall in*" [ADM 52/1/1], "A saile *stand out* of the Ba [bay]" [ADM 52/2/9], "We soon *come up with* her" [ADM 52/2/9], "Watts *take off*" [HCA 1/99/145], and "I *come to* an Anchor" [1045.f.3/1/16]. In short, although "run", specifically used with the satellite particle "away", was the most salient example of unmarked strong preterit forms in the corpus when expressed as a phrasal verb, evidence indicates that Ship English permits zero marking in any phrasal verb composition, although certain lexemes might favor zero marking in idiomatic usage.

---

[10]The high frequency of "run away" may, in part, be explained by the nature of witness testimony coupled with the number of court cases related to sailors deserting their vessel.

As discussed in the previous paragraphs, past tense variant forms may be conditioned by certain lexemes such as "see" and "run" or they may be conditioned by verbs used in phrasal verb constituents, yet overall there is no convincing evidence that linguistic or socio-linguistic factors play a role in past tense variation. Instead, variant forms occur in the same linguistic contexts, in the same documents, and in the same handwriting across a range of documents with varying levels of formality and stylistic expectations. For example, one witness deposition includes the statement, "They **took** and **plundered** and took out some rice & sugar and some rigging and then *sink* her" [HCA 1/52/75] in which an unmarked preterit "sink" occurs in a coordinated clause structure with the standard inflected weak verb in past tense "plundered" and also the standard form of the strong verb preterit "took". Logbooks also show examples of zero marked preterit forms in coordinated clauses with standard forms of strong verbs, e.g., "severall of the fleet *break* their Cables & we **lost** our Long boat" [ADM 52/2/6], and "every one **came** and *eat* and **drank** with him" [HCA 1/99/59]. Other logbooks show the same verb occurring in standard and preterit forms in a single speech act, e.g., the verb forms "gett" and "gott" in the excerpt, "We *gett* Anchor aboard [...] we *see* severall ships a stern which **Came** into our fleet ... severall of the fleet **made** Sayle and **gott** into [...] harbor" [ADM 52/3/7]. A longer excerpt from a single witness statement taken at the Rhode Island and Providence Plantation on 9 September 1725 shows similar variation among standard and zero-marked forms of strong verbs by one speaker:

> he [the captain] **told** me he would make me Sign and **sent** for two candles in a plate and **made** me eat them. And then *bid* me go to the Devil for he would force no man then I *see* some of them with Sticks in their Hands & Needles through the end of them I **asked** Jonathan Barney a prisoner on Board what they **were** for. [HCA 1/99/5]

Such evidence of wide-ranging yet non-universal distribution of variant forms in the past tense suggests that free variation is a more probable explanation than conditioned variation.

6.2.3 Infinitives

Ship English permits infinitives in non-standard contexts and also permits their omission when standard usage anticipates them. Infinitives are permitted after participle forms of a verb, for instance, present participles (marked in bold) permit subsequent infinitives (in italics), e.g., "**observing** Shaik Joseph *to hold* a Bag in his hand" [HCA 1/99 Bombay, July 17 1730, 3], and "**finding** the Pink *to sayle* heavy" [HCA 1/98/28]. Yet infinitives after past participles (marked in bold), are more common, e.g., "they mett with a little Dutch shipp **designed** *to go* trade with or among the Spaniards" [CO 5/1411/97], "[he was] **obliged** *to leave* the money he had formerly wrought for (being a carpenter], and was **gone** *to receive*" [HCA 1/99/8 New Providence 1722], "Barbley, about two dayes after **caused** the Saw *to be* brought into his yard" [HCA 1/9/57], "[he was] **promised** *to be* landed in England" [HCA 1/13/97], and "[he] **assisted** *to rob* her" [HCA 1/99/42].[11] Infinitives are also permitted after auxiliary verbs with conditional modality (marked in bold), e.g., "he begged if possible his Ship Mates **cou'd** *to hide* him from the Pyrates" [HCA 1/99/21], "a Lock, and Key which the prisoner **wou'd have** *to belong* to him" [HCA 1/99/30], and "our men **would have** me *to put* them on" [445f.1/45]. Infinitive use after modal auxiliaries also occurs in parallel structures with verbs expressed in their uninflected form (marked in bold), e.g., "for I cannot **doe** what I would *to doe*" [HCA 1/101/423], and "they would **put** the Goods in the Hould [...] and *to send* her in with twelve men" [HCA 1/9/9], suggesting that the uninflected form and the infinitive may have been interchangeable. This suggestion is supported by omission of the particle "to" in some contexts, e.g., "bidding him [*to*] hold his tongue" [HCA 1/9/139], "I humbly thank you for any share you are pleased [*to*] take in my favour" [HCA 1/101/382], "you need [*to*] chuse" [CO 5/1411/658], and "the prisoner bid the deponent [*to*] look for the saw" [HCA 1/99 Williamsburg, Aug 14 1729]. Omission of a complete infinitive form (both the particle and the verb) is permitted when the meaning is evident from context, e.g., "wee met with Shipton again who forced us [*to go*] with him" [HCA 1/99/5], and "believes him [*to be*] one of those who divided his Cloths" [HCA 1/99/140].[12] In sum, and although there were too few examples to make strong claims about the linguistic conditioning of variant infinitives, samples suggest that these verbs without tense were permitted after participle forms and modal auxiliaries but were completely or partially omitted in other contexts; they were also potentially interchangeable with the uninflected form of the verb.

---

[11] This last example "[he] **assisted** *to rob* her" [HCA 1/99/42] may not be a true infinitive but a manifestation of the commonly collocated "assisted to" expression that is seen elsewhere in the corpus prior to a noun phrase, e.g., "**assisting to** the Robbing of his Ship" [HCA 1/99/42].

[12] The omission of the infinitive "to be" is specifically discussed in a later subsection on usage and omission of "be" in this chapter, see §6.3.2.

6.3 The copula and auxiliary "be"

6.3.1 Inflection

The verb "to be" features most predominantly in past tense, and "was" occurs as the most frequent past tense inflection with all types of nominal and pronominal subjects in first, second, and third person.[13] The standard preterit form "were" is evident in the corpus, but is not common, e.g., "we *were* foresd" [ADM 52/1/7], "they *were* in trenches" [ADM 52/1/7], "the Men out of the *Onflow were* Volunteers" [HCA 1/99/112], and "those who *were* active and were minded to recommend themselves for brave men" [HCA 1/99/94] (all italicized for emphasis). Of these limited examples, the most common occurrence of the inflection "were" occurred in statements marked for subjunctive mood, e.g., "except he *were* dead" [HCA 1/9/51], "If he *were* a Hollander" [HCA 1/9/9], "if all *were* of my mind" [HCA 1/99/36], "asked how he would like it, *were* he a prisoner" [HCA 1/99/30], and "ask'd if any vessel were coming from Barbados" [HCA 1/99/6]. Far more common than "were" in all indicative contexts was the preterit form "was" that appears with first, second, and third person subjects (both with noun phrases and pronouns), in singular and plural contexts (see Table 6.1).

In terms of linguistic conditioning, the most salient use of the preterit form "was" appeared in third person plural contexts with a noun phrase (emphasized in bold), and most examples of these were to be found in witness depositions, e.g., "**those men** [...] that *wasn't* immediately on board" [ADM 106/300/25], "they met with **two ships** which *was* pirates" [HCA 1/98/47], "there *was* **three** at first" [HCA 1/99/8], "about **tew of them** *was* gone" [HCA 1/99/126], "Four to one *was* **odds**" [HCA 1/9/155], and "to confes, where **their moneys** *was*" [HCA 1/9/18]. Although various examples of third person plural noun phrases used with "was" appear, very few trends of usage suggest any type of internal linguistic conditioning that selected the preterit form "was" over the alternative variant "were". One potential conditioning factor was the use of a compound noun phrase as a subject that is formed with a conjunction (noun phrase emphasized in bold), e.g., "**8 sayle of English & Dutch** *was* drawn out" [ADM 52/2/5], "Where **his money & Gold** *was*" [HCA 1/9/18], "**my Ledger and hauwl** *was* carried a shore" [ADM 51/3954], "**hee and Captaine Thomas Garnett** *was* taken" [HCA 1/9/67], "**the country and his colonies** *was* not under his command" [CO 5/1411/101], and "**Nutmeggs or**

---

[13]Variation in past tense realizations of the verb "be" is no surprise given the widespread tendency to level the contrast between "was" and "were" potentially owing to the fact that "be" is seen as "a defective verb", with an inflectional paradigm that derives from three distinct and independent verbs in Aryan, Teutonic and Greek (*Oxford English Dictionary* 1989, Vol 2: 1).

Table 6.1: Examples of the preterit "was" used for with first, second, and third person nouns and pronouns, both singular and plural

person		Singular	Plural
1st	**Noun phrase**	n/aª	"My Self and the rest of the Company under my command *was* entered and Musterd on board" [ADM 51/4170/2]
	Pronoun	"I *was* told, no other Trees fit to build with" [1045.f.3/1/27]	"then he made [out] what we *was*" [ADM 52/1/1]
2nd	**Noun phrase**	n/aª	"you also John Jessop *was* lately wicked" [HCA 1/99/170]
	Pronoun	"it may be you *was* not willing at the first" [CO 5/1411/42]	"*was* you [referring to John Houghling, Corneluis Franc and Francois Delaune] on board the pyrate shipp when she was taken" [CO 5/1411/28]
3rd	**Noun phrase**	"the prisoner *was* belonging to Augustino's crew" [HCA 1/99/7]	"those goods *was* to ship" [HCA 1/98/43]
	Pronoun	"after he *was* come on board" [CO 5/1411/99]	"where they *was* carried" [HCA 1/101/220]

ªNot applicable as reference to self (first person) or addressee (second person) using a noun phrase renders it third person.

Cloves that *was* given away" [HCA 1/12/78]. Yet there is no evidence to suggest that the plural or singular nature of either constituent in the conjoined noun phrases affects the choice of "be" preterit as either "was" or "were" and this may signify that the use of the conjunction itself selected the use of "was" rather than the composition of the conjoined noun phrase. Another potential conditioning factor may have been the use of a first person plural pronoun subject "we" as the subject of the clause in which "was" forms the main verb of the predicate, particularly when directly preceding "be", e.g., "**wee** *was* forced soe neare the shoare" [HCA 1/12/2], "**we** *was* forsed to Stand to the Westward" [ADM 52/1/1], "masking what **we** *was*" [ADM 52/1/1], and "agreeable to you as **we** *was* then got out" [D/Earle/3/1]. The salience of this usage is also highlighted by its inclusion in published sea-songs of the seventeenth century, e.g., "As **we** *was* sailing on the main [...] we was in danger" (cited in Palmer 1986: 51). Yet, despite these two potential conditioning factors for selecting "was" rather than the preterit form "were", the frequency and range of variation in the corpus suggests either free variation or a general tendency to select "was" in all contexts rather than complementary distribution of the "was" and "were" forms.

Present tense and infinite forms of the verb "be" feature less frequently than past tense forms in the corpus, but show similar variation. In the present tense, examples of usage show a tendency to level the contrast between "is" and "are", with "is" appearing more frequently with noun phrase subjects in the singular and plural third person forms. Furthermore, this occurred when the "be" was in pre- and post-subject positions and also when it was either adjacent to or separated from the subject, e.g., "here *is* 2 **Merchant men**" [ADM 52/1/8], "**pitch**, which *is* wanting" [5/1411/646], "**The ships** *is* all gone" [HCA 1/101/553], "Give me an account how **all things** *is* in the Contrey" [HCA 1/12/86], "**These** *is* received" [ADM 106/300/12], and "Men which die yearly in those Forts, **whose Substance, Wages, etc.** *is* left for the Company" [BL/74/816/m/11/36/2]. This finding supports Bailey & Ross's (1988) observation that in seventeenth century logbooks "*is* is the predominant plural in many of the logs, with *are* relatively uncommon" (p.201, authors' italics).

In addition to preference for "is", Bailey and Ross also recognize the use of the uninflected verb "be" in finite contexts in the logbooks they analyzed, e.g., "they *bee* well sett people" (1988: Sloane 3833) and "the corkers *be* come to Corke" [ADM 52/78], both cited in Bailey & Ross (1988: 200). The usage of uninflected "be" also seems to characterize representations of sailors' speech in publications such as sea-songs, e.g., "Victuals and weapons they *be* nothing scant", "Her flags *be* new trimmed", and "The dangers great on seas *be* rife" (cited in Palmer 1986: 2,

3, & 6, respectively). Seminal literary works related to sailors also show this type of usage, e.g., "*be* it some Object", "he *be* much O glad", and "you teach wild Mans *be* good" in Defoe's (1998) *Robinson Crusoe*,[14] and "Master Billy Bones, if that *be* your name" (part 1, ch 2), "the slight, if there *be* one, was unintentional" (part 2, ch 9) in Stevenson's (1883) *Treasure Island*. However, although usage of uninflected "be" was evident in the corpus, e.g., "if any such there *be*" [CO 5/1411/649], it was not a regular nor salient feature of present indicative statements as claimed by Baily and Ross's scholarship and suggested by literature representing sailors' speech. Instead, the use of uninflected "be" seems to be restricted to the context of subjunctive or imperative modality that equates with standard usage, e.g., "yet one thing I have to advise you of, that you *be* not ensnared" [445f.1/22], and "*be* not afraid" [445f.1/44]. It may be that popular representations of foreign sailors' speech that potentially suggest a maritime Pidgin have influenced the perceived salience of a variant uninflected "be" feature that is not significantly represented in the extended corpus of this study.

6.3.2 Usage and omission

The verb "be" is not frequently used as the principal inflected verb in the corpus in a way that corresponds to how we use the verb in a non-auxiliary manner in standard modern English. Specifically, the use of the copula as a type of linking verb with a predicate adjective, noun, or adverb does appear in the corpus, but this type of usage is not common, e.g., with a predicate adjective (in bold), "John Jessop *was* lately **wicked**" [HCA 1/99/170]; with a predicate noun (in bold), "I considered to strike them that was next [to] me, which *was* **the weakest**" [445f.1/44]; and with a predicate adverb (in bold), "and we *was* **up in the country**" [T/70/1216/10]. The use of the copula as part of an existential clause is also evident but is similarly infrequent, e.g., "*There was* five hundred thousand cheeses" [HCA 1/12/84], "*itt is* a very hey [high] Iland" [DDB6 8/4], "*it was* stolen goods" [HCA 1/101/220], and "*there was not* any Ship or vessell taken by him or any of his Company" [HCA 1/14/205]. Existential use of "there" plus the inflected copula is not common in the corpus given the propensity of sailors to express attendant circumstances with a present participle phrase headed with being, e.g. "And account *being* given to me by you captn John Aldred" [CO 5/1411/665] "but could not speak with them *being* night and hazey" [CO 5/1411/699], and "The capt & Lieut *being standing* together" [HCA 1/9/155]. Even when expletives such

---

[14]The last two of these three examples from *Robinson Crusoe* are contextualized in the voice of Man Friday and thus potentially aim to illustrate a Ship Pidgin feature rather than a variation inherent to Ship English.

as "there" and "it" are explicit, it is permissible to use a predicate headed by the infinite participle "being" rather than the finite copula, e.g., "weighed [anchor] **it** *being* little wind" [CO 5/1411/694]. In short, linking and existential contexts in which the finite copula might be common in standard usage are evident but infrequent in the corpus of Ship English under study.

In contrast, the finite forms of the verb "be" appear frequently in the corpus as a requisite of passive structures. Sometimes these structures are made explicit by the use of a prepositional phrase of agency (in bold), e.g., "he *was* misused and beat **by the pyrates**" [HCA 1/99/31], "[they] *was* fired at **by a great Spanish shipp**" [HCA 1/9/18], and "the Governers Wife and Daughter of Cuba *were* taken Prisoners **by a Pyrate**" [HCA 1/99/9]. However, more frequently, the omission of such a prepositional constituent obscures the logical subject of the transitive verb that has been rendered in passive form, e.g., "we *are* excused" [HCA 1/99/39], "our Spare Anchor *was* gott aboard" [ADM 52/2/3], "he *was* beat" [HCA 1/99/124], "they *were* not permitted to trade" [HCA 1/9/18]. It is worth noting that "be" in passive structures is subject to the same variation and tendency to level the inflectional paradigm as with any other finite usage (discussed above), e.g., "**[we]** *were* forced on a reife of sand and **[we]** *was* forced to cut away our main mast" [HCA 1/12/2], "**2 ships** that *was* driven from the Virginia Coast" [ADM 52/1/8], and "**they** *was* carried" [HCA 1/101/220]. In addition to inflectional variation, finite "be" omission in passive structures is also a permissible variant, e.g., "Five pounds [was] payd him in money" [HCA 1/9/64], "today [was] Taken out of the George Hoy Tho Harris" [ADM 52/1/5], "found his chest [was] broke open" [HCA 1/99/7], and "they [were] called to go one Boarde" [HCA 1/99/140]. In short, frequent uses of the "be" in passive structures support the general tendency for leveling of the inflectional paradigm but also indicate that "be" omission was an acceptable variation.

The omission of "be", regarding which Bailey and Ross find "zero evidence" in their study of seventeenth century logbooks (1988: 202), manifests itself in a range of contexts in this extended corpus of documents ranging from 1620 to 1750 and composing logbooks, depositions, letters and miscellaneous documents. Interestingly, most of the examples come from logbooks of the late 1600s and early 1700s, e.g., "the wind [is/was] blowing violent & contrary" [HCA 1/12/2], "the wind [is/was] very little or calme" [ADM 52/2/3], "we thought it [is/was] the same" [HCA 1/99/27], "we [are/were] Riding Single till noon" [ADM 52/2/5], "our Long Boate [is/was] employed to fetch water all night" [ADM 52/1/8], "at day light [there is/was] little wind" [ADM 52/2/3], and "fair pleasant we [are/were] excuse[d]; all Drunk" [HCA 1/99/39]. The abbreviated style permitted in logbook writing may have conditioned "be" omission, particularly in stative contexts when used as the main inflected verb and even more so when the meaning was self-evident or routinely referenced such as talking about wind conditions. Omission of "be" was also evident in other types of documents, e.g., the letter that opens, "It [is/was] appealing to me, that it is for his majestys official service" [CO 5/1411/666], and the testimony that states, "information wee have from one that [was] razed with him" [ADM 106/288/42]. Omission of "be" in its infinitive form (i.e., the satellite particle "to" and the base form "be") occurs in witness depositions, e.g., "believes him [to be] one of those who divided his Cloths" [HCA 1/99/140], "happened [to be] in your way" [HCA 1/99/3/2], and "owns himselfe [to be] and Irishman" [HCA 1/53/3]. And, just like the finite omission in logbooks and letters, this type of infinitive omission in courtroom testimony could also have been conditioned by the function of the verb in contexts where meaning is self-evident or routinely referenced such as giving character descriptions (stative or existential copula function) or indicating places (locative function).

6.3.3 Aspect using "be" auxiliary

Finite "be" auxiliaries and present participle verbs are used to mark progressive aspect in the corpus, however the structure permits variation that is not typical in standard usage. Limited examples show standard usage of the finite "be" verb (in italics) with a present participle verb phrase denoting active process (in bold), e.g., "*Edgar* wch *is* now in **Paying** & hope to dispatch to morrow" [ADM 106/288/30], and "his tobacco *was* **throwing** overboard" [CO 5/1411/58].[15] This usage is standard because the finite auxiliary ("is" and "was", respectively) projects a present participle denoting active process ("Paying" and "throwing") and both events are continuous over a period of time (SIL International 2005).

However, comparable to uses of the progressive aspect with a present participle denoting active process, the corpus includes many more examples of this same structure used with participles of verbs that have a stative meaning, e.g., "the prisoner *was* **belonging** to Augustino's crew" [HCA 1/99/7], "I do not know nor never heard that the Master or any of the Seamen *were* **knowing** of it" [HCA 1/9/51], and "it *was* **being** with some officers upon an island sevrall daies without victualls" [CO 5/1411/41].[16] The stative meaning of the participles emphasized in

---

[15]Note that the example "his tobacco *was* **throwing** overboard" [CO 5/1411/58] is expressed in the passive voice and so a standard version might be rendered "his tobacco *was being thrown* overboard".

[16]The combination of the finite "be" auxiliary with a present participle of a stative verb was (and is) not generally permissible in standard usage but was (and still is) acceptable in certain dialects and contexts, (Römer 2005: 113–116).

bold are more suited to preterit verb use in standard English, i.e., "the prisoner *belonged* to Augustino's crew", "...the Master or any of the Seamen *knew* it", and "it *was* with some officers upon an island sevrall daies withouth victualls" [CO 5/1411/41]. Indeed, for this reason many of the progressive aspect structures in the corpus of Ship English might be more suitably rendered in preterit tense in standard usage. Yet, use of a structure composed of the auxiliary "be" and a stative participle seems to have been a feature of sailors' talk, and the fact that it features in popular sea-songs attests to its salience as a marker of their speech, e.g., the line "They *were* the treasure **possessing**" (cited in Palmer 1986: 55). In sum, when sailors used the progressive aspect they sometimes rendered it with a present participle denoting active process (in accordance with standard usage) but more frequently rendered it with

The use of present participles as the only constituent of a main verb structure implies that "be" may have been omitted when used as an auxiliary in an underlying aspectual structure. Interestingly, this type of omission occurs more often with active verbs that would be more suited to the progressive aspectual structure, e.g., "they [were] whispering and afterwards [were] agreeing one with another" [HCA 1/99/112], "he [was] with his Cutlass spoiling and hacking everything" [HCA 1/99/126], "they [were] abusing him" [HCA 1/99/103], and "we [were] Riding Single till noon" [ADM 52/2/5]. Without any finite auxiliary, these excerpts are reduced to phrases headed with a present participle. Yet, it is possible that these phrases derive from underlying progressive aspectual structures with omitted finite auxiliaries, and that would explain how they appear to function as independent clauses of attendant circumstances rather than as modifications of an antecedent noun phrase. This interpretation is reinforced by the fact that many examples of these structures appear in coordination with clauses that have indicative non-aspectual verbs and therefore potentially show a time sequence juxtaposing the progressive duration of one clause with the single time referent of another. To illustrate, the following excerpt from a witness deposition: "they tarrying longer the said Le Fort sailed away" [HCA 1/52/137] can be interpreted as two clauses, the first expressed with progressive aspect and the second with a preterit indicative verb specifically denoting the fact that it occurred later and interrupted the durative event of the first verb, i.e., "they [were] tarrying longer [when] the said Le Fort sailed away". In another example of a letter written by mariner John Morris to his wife, the opening excerpt reads, "Ever Loufing wief these lines is to arkquint you that I Lying more like to die than to lief desiring you to remember my kind love to my three Cussons" [HCA 1/52/51]. If we interpret the two present participles "Lying" and "desiring" to derive from underlying progressive aspectual structures with omitted finite auxiliaries and the three verb constituents to represent three separate clauses, then the excerpt would be interpreted as: "Ever Loufing wief these lines is to arkquint you that I [am] Lying more like to die than to lief [and I am] desiring you to remember my kind love to my three Cussons". This excerpt then expresses three distinct ideas, firstly, the matrix clause, "these lines is[are] to aquaint you", secondly, the embedded relative clause, "that I am lying more likely to die than to live", and thirdly, the subordinating clause, "[so] I am desiring [I desire] you to remember my kind love". Moreover, this interpretation matches the proposed sailors' standard use of the progressive aspect in standard distribution with active verbs ("I am lying") and also demonstrates their tendency to use a marked variation of the same structures with stative verbs ("I am desiring"). Such examples support the suggestion that present participle phrases may have denoted (or derived from) clauses with progressive aspects in which finite "be" had been omitted but are still manifest in the underlying structure.

Variant usage of the verb "be" includes structures that denote completed events and therefore suggest perfect aspectual meaning. These structures are sometimes expressed in the finite present or past tense, e.g., "wee *are* 6 month and 6 days upon our voyage" [DDB6 8/4], "the ship *is* sailed...he *is* run away" [5/1411/646], meaning "we **have been** 6 month[s] and 6 days upon our voyage" and "the ship **had sailed**...he **had run away**", respectively. Other completive events are expressed with the present participle of "be", e.g., "the merchant ship not *being* gon into York river" [CO 5/1411/702], and "news *being* come at that time" [HCA 1/99/9], meaning "the merchant ship **had not gone** into York river", and "news **had come** at that time" respectively. In all of these examples, the verb "be" appears to function the same as the auxiliary "have" does in structures with perfect aspect and suggests that this exchange may have been a variant feature of how "be" was used to denote aspect in Ship English.

6.4 Auxiliaries

6.4.1 The auxiliary "have"

The verb "have" is frequently used to denote perfect aspect in the corpus of Ship English under study, but just like "be", it is prone to inflectional variation. The range of historical forms of this verb available to Early Modern English speakers owes to various dialectal forms derived "largely to weakness and stresslessness of the word in many uses, both as a principal verb and as an auxiliary"

(*Oxford English Dictionary* 1989, Vol 7: 15). However, the four most common to sailors were the two present tense forms "has" and "have" and the past tense form "had" that are still in use today, in addition to the obsolete form "hath" that was familiar to contemporary speakers. The oldest form "hath" (italicized) was used infrequently with a third person subject (emphasized in bold) functioning as an auxiliary verb in perfect constructions, e.g., "**it** *hath* Blowed hard" [ADM 52/2/5], "**our Longboat** *hath* made 3 Tunnes" [ADM 52/2/5], and "**The examinant** *hath* not since seen him" [HCA 1/14/140]. The standard form "had" was more commonly used with all subjects, including third person singular subjects, e.g., "**Bragg** *had* broke two of his ribs" [HCA 1/53/48], and "**[the quartermaster]** had Iron & Beads stole away from him" [HCA 1/12/2], and "**he** *had* got lame" [HCA 1/99/62]. The inflected form "has" was used with third person singular and plural subjects, e.g., "**he** *has* at time Spoke to him" [HCA 1/99/142], "**this month last past** *has* been such turbulent weather: the like has not been all this Winter" [CO 5/1411/654], and "**Our people** *has* no mind to go to sea" [HCA 1/101/553].[17] The non-standard use of this variant with third person plural subjects appears to have been a marked feature of sailors' speech that was represented in the lyrics of sea-songs, e.g., "**Many** *has* searched" (cited in Palmer 1986: 54), and "*Has* not **men** wished and cried" (cited in Palmer 1986: 57). The last variation, the uninflected form "have", was used most notably with third person singular subjects that require the inflected form "has" in standard usage, e.g., "the said **Frederik Philips** *have* manumitted" [HCA 1/98/72].[18] Yet, many examples of the non-standard usage of "have" with third person subjects derive from perfect-aspect verb phrases using the participle "been", (emphasized) e.g., "**Wm Lilburne** *have been* aiding [...] he have ordered us" [SP 42/6], "**the wind** *have been* at SW" [ADM 52/2/1], "**This evidence** that *have been* already produced" [CO 5/1411/33], and "**John Smith** who is and *have been* as badd" [HCA 1/99 Barbados 1733]. The frequency of uninflected "have" with the past participle "been" in collocation suggests that this may have conditioned the variation regardless of the singular or plural nature of the third-person subject.

---

[17] The noun "people" as plural referent with a singular third person verb conjugation "has" reflects the arbitrary designation of count noun and potentially reflects similar singular forms in other Romance languages, e.g., "la gente" in Spanish.

[18] Although the word "have" is here discussed as an uninflected form, it is also possible that speakers/writers were using the third person plural form that takes the same form as the uninflected verb i.e., "have". I acknowledge that the variation of this paradigm may therefore be considered as a singular/plural inflectional paradigm rather than a finite/infinite paradigm. My interpretation of the paradigm as a finite/infinite variation owes to the earlier work of Bailey & Ross in which they describe present tense marking and specifically describe "third singular forms are sometimes unmarked [i.e., uninflected]" (1988: 199).

The perfect structures available to speakers of Ship English correlate with standard usage but permit internal variation such as separation of the auxiliary and its associated verb phrase and deletion or substitution of the auxiliary constituent. Sailors made use of different types of perfect structures permitted in standard usage, for instance: perfect aspect with indicative mood, e.g., "if they *had known* the sloop had been fitted out" [HCA 1/99 Bahama Islands 1722]; perfect aspect with conditional modality, e.g., "they *would have kept* me" [445f.1/27]; perfect aspect with progressive aspect, e.g., "Wm Lilburne *have been aiding*" [SP 42/6]; and perfect aspect with negation, e.g., "they *would not have come* on board" [HCA 1/99 Bahama Islands 1722]. In perfect structures, Ship English permits the separation of the auxiliary verb "have" and its associated participle verb phrase in contexts such as adverbial placement and negation, e.g., "after he *had* **unfortunately** *fell* into their hands" [HCA 1/99/38], and "he *had* **never** *done* it since he had belonged to them" [HCA 1/99/23].[19] It also permits nominals to separate auxiliary verbs and their associated participle verb phrases, e.g., "We the mariners belonging to His Majesty's Ship *James Galley have* **many of us** *been* desperately sick" (cited in Brown 2011: 49). Another variation was the apparent omission of the auxiliary verb, e.g., "John Hardin who [had] run away from a ship" [SP 42/6], "I thought you would [have] been as you promised me" [HCA 1/12/85], and "one of the people who [had] stole or run away with the boat" [HCA 1/99 Bahama Islands 1722].[20] Ship English also appears to permit substitution of the auxiliary verb phrase in passive structures, e.g., the use of auxiliary "be" in "after he *was come* [had come] on board" [CO 5/1411/99] and "he *was beine* [had been] at Martinco" [HCA 1/13/95];[21] So, although verb phrases with perfect aspect are used in syntactic constructions that are predominantly aligned with standard usage, they also permit some internal variation that is not typical.

One of the most marked features of variation in perfect verb phrases is not the auxiliary itself, but what verbal particle it is permitted to select in a perfect structure. Standard English requires the auxiliary "have" to select a past partici-

---

[19]Note that the separation of auxiliary verb and its participle verb phrase was permitted in a range of Early Modern English dialects and continues to be acceptable in modern varieties including standard American English.

[20]It may be that some examples do not have an underlying verb phrase with perfect aspect but instead are manifestations of the preterit forms of verbs without past tense inflection, e.g., the example "John Hardin who run away from a ship" [SP 42/6] might have an underlying perfect structure with a deleted auxiliary, i.e., "John Hardin who *had run* away from a ship" or might be a preterit verb without inflection, i.e., "John Hardin who *ran* away from a ship". In many cases, the context permits both alternatives.

[21]See §6.3.3 for more examples of "be" used as an auxiliary in verb phrases with perfect aspectual meaning.

ple in verb phrases with perfect aspect, and this does sometimes occur in Ship English, e.g., "whether he had not *returned*" [HCA 1/99/52], "We had *been* gone from there aboutt two moones" [T/70/1213], "if they had *known* the sloop" [HCA 1/99 Bahama Islands 1722], "would have *had* an anchor let goe" [HCA 1/9/155], and "had *heard* it talked" [HCA 1/99/153]. However, much more common was the selection of a variant verbal form such as an irregular formation or an uninflected form (marked for emphasis), e.g., "it hath *Blowed* hard" [ADM 52/2/5], "they had *arrive*" [HCA 1/53/66], "wee have sayled & *Logg* 116 miles" [HCA 51/3983/1], and "he had been misused and *beat* and threatened to be shot" [HCA 1/99/97]. The last example includes the uninflected form "beat" in coordination with the inflected weak verbs "misused" and "threatened" and potentially illustrates the common feature of preterit verbal usage in perfect aspect constructions. In other words, although the word "beat" may be an uninflected form of the strong verb, it is also the form of the preterit, as in the standard usage "he beat the prisoner", and this usage supports evidence that it was the preterit forms of the verbs that were used in collocation with the auxiliary "have" in perfect structures and not a distinct past participle form. This interpretation is complicated by the fact that the past participle forms of weak (i.e., regular) verbs are the same as the preterit form, e.g., "I have *answered*" (perfect aspect) and "I *answered*" (preterit) in contrast to strong (i.e., irregular) verbs that usually have different preterit forms, e.g., "I have written" (perfect aspect) and "I wrote" (preterit). Thus, the weak verbs appear to have standard past participle forms as the preterit is inflected with the morpheme "-ed" just as the past participle is in standard usage. However, the strong verbs appear to show marked variation (see Table 6.2), when in fact they may demonstrate the same inflectional paradigm as the weak verbs.

One interpretation of this inflectional variation is that Ship English permitted a preterit verbal form of any strong or weak verb after the auxiliary "have" in a construction marked for perfect aspect, although this was not universal nor conditioned by any additional internal linguistic constraints. This interpretation is one that appears to have been favored by Bailey and Ross whose discussion of preterit forms of strong verbs recognizes "the use of what are now strong preterits as past participles" (1988: 204). However, the data presented above may also be evidence of a collapsing and simplification of the preterit and past participle paradigm system rather than free variation between preterit and past participle forms in perfect structures. Further evidence of this potential simplification of preterit and past participle forms occurs in the variant usage of verbal forms in passive structures with auxiliary "be", e.g., "his head was *broke*" [HCA 1/52/148], "2 new cables that were *hid*" [HCA 1/99/41], "The Anchor and Cable...is *took* up"

Table 6.2: Sample of 11 verb phrases marked for perfect aspect that permit the preterit forms of strong verbs after the auxiliary "have"

Ship English citation (with preterit form marked for emphasis)	Standard past participle	Source document
wee have *rid* her	ridden	ADM 52/2/1
he before had *spoke* through me	spoken	445f.1/35
this day we have *took* out	taken	ADM 52/2/5
[he] had Iron & Beads *stole* away from him	stolen	HCA 1/12/2
had never *saw* a Prize taken	seen	HCA 1/99/8
those who had *fell* into their Hands	fallen	HCA 1/99/51
Make him Lye in Irons till he had *swore*	sworn	T 70/1/5
he had *broke* open his chest	broken	HCA 1/99/7
when he had *hid* himself	hidden	HCA 1/99/52
I had *forgot* to write you	forgotten	AC WO 16–16/8–16
I have *wrote*	written	445f.1/46

[5/1411/645], and "he was *beat* and forced among them" [HCA 1/99/54]. It may be that sailors used a simplified paradigm of verbal forms in which the preterit and the past participle (in both passive and perfect structures) were the same. This would certainly have made it easier for foreign language speakers to acquire correct Ship English syntax and may have been a salient feature of sailors' speech in general during the early colonial period, as suggested by the repeated use of such structures in seventeenth-century sea-songs, e.g., "Many persons of good account were *took*" ("A Joyful New Ballad", cited in Palmer 1986: 17) and "[they] Were *drove* out" ("Sailors for my Money", cited in Palmer 1986: 44).

6.4.2 The auxiliary "do"

The verb "do" is frequently used as an auxiliary verb in the corpus of Ship English under study, but is not prone to significant inflectional variation. Although there were a range of inflections available in the Early Modern English period for the verb "do" (see *Oxford English Dictionary* 1989, Vol 4: 901), this corpus suggests that sailors generally used "did" for the past and "do" for the present tense, with a few infrequent cases of "does" occurring in late seventeenth century and early eighteenth century documents, e.g., "[he] *do's not know* what ship" [HCA 1/99/99, c. 1694] and "he answered that he *does* not know" [HCA 1/13/94 1731]. The archaic form "doth" was similarly infrequent and more associated with court usage than sailors, for instance, one sailors' testimony reads "David Czah who there [did] and still ^{doth} owns himselfe an Irishman" [HCA 1/53/3] in which the words "did" and "doth" are inserted superscript, potentially as corrections to the sailors' spontaneous speech that was transcribed in haste and later revised for accuracy (see also footnote in this chapter for examples of "doth" used by court officials in negated statements). Although sailors did use this archaic inflection of the verb, e.g. "*Doth* believe Really they got their money by pyracy" [HCA 1/98/259], "the other seamen *doth* believe that they were Likewise killed" [HCA 1/101/405], and "He *Doth* suppose that these nine men may have some Riches on board" [HCA 1/98/29], the scarcity of examples of this form in the data suggest that the inflection "doth" was not common. Thus, although the verb "do" appears often in the corpus, it does not demonstrate the same frequency of inflectional variation as other auxiliaries such as "be" or the perfect auxiliary "have".

Verbs phrases using "do" are common in the corpus of Ship English, but the verb "do", rather than functioning as a requisite constituent of negatives and questions (as in standard usage), composes affirmative statements in the indicative mood, which may or may not reflect standard usage to mark emphasis. It is possible that statements may have included the grammatically redundant auxiliary verb "do" as a marker of emphasis, particularly considering that much of the corpus derives from witness depositions that were made in response to direct questions. For instance, the witness that stated, "he *did* attend upon them" [HCA 1/98/267] may have been responding to the direct question "Did he attend upon them?".[22] However, other examples suggest that emphasis was not intended, such as the comments in logbook entries about daily events, e.g., "[we] have taken a strict and carefull survey, and *doe* find that she wants calking inside and outside" [CO 5/1411/662], "The wind from the SSW to the SW *did* blow" [ADM 52/2/3], and "six violent squails of wind and rain all which *did* continue till this day noon" [ADM 52/2/3]. Letters also include this structure in a way that does not suggest emphatic usage, e.g., "as many have and daily *doe* find" [BL/Egerton 2395/0007], "the Royal Company *do* expend yearly 20000l. Sterling" [BL/74/816/m/11/36/2], and "I *doe* so consider" [HCA 1/101/527]. In addition to these contexts in which the verb "do" serves as a redundant auxiliary marker of emphasis or indicative mood, verb phrases with auxiliary "do" (or "do support") function in standard usage to create negated preterit structures from principle verbs that have no existing auxiliary in the indicative mood; they

---

[22]The majority of witness depositions are written in continuous prose and do not include the interrogative contributions of a second speaker, it is therefore extremely difficult to assess the validity of this suggestion although it is logical given the context of the court testimony to assume that witnesses were asked questions.

also serve as auxiliary particles that can be moved to mark the interrogative mood. And both standard uses of the auxiliary "do" are evident in the corpus (emphasized), e.g., for negation, "Both his pistolls mist [missed] fire and *did* not go off" [HCA 1/52/137] and for interrogative mood, "where *did* they take this shipp" [CO 5/1411/97]. However, most structures containing the auxiliary verb "do" do not suggest emphatic usage, nor do they mark negatives or questions, instead they are seemingly redundant auxiliaries of the indicative mood expressed in the affirmative, e.g., "we *doe* assure you" [ADM 106/288/30], "I *doe* wonder" [HCA 1/98/57], "our ketch *did* touch our stearn and *did* us some damage" [ADM 52/2/3].[23] Furthermore, this type of usage is marked in representations of sailors' speech in a range of sea shanties and songs, e.g., "now mind what I *do* say" (cited in Hugill 1969: 51), "I *did* dwell" (cited in Palmer 1986: 4), "Their admiral *did* want to be / Aboard" (cited in Palmer 1986: 52), and "What the laws *did* still forbid" (cited in Palmer 1986: 75). In short, the scope and frequency of the auxiliary verb "do" in depositions, logbooks, and personal statements without explicit emphatic meaning suggests that the auxiliary was commonly used as a component of the indicative mood regardless of negation, interrogative modality or emphatic meaning. Indeed, using a default auxiliary verb for all verb phrases would have arguably made Ship English easier to learn for new recruits for whom English was not native as it meant that if they mastered the verb "do" in its present tense and preterit inflections they could use any other verb in its uninflected form in any simple indicative, negated, or interrogative structure.

However, the use of an affirmative indicative verb phrase with the auxiliary "do" often combines at the clause level with a singular principal verb in preterit form, suggesting that the use of the auxiliary marker was not a default but was used in complementary distribution to create contrast in meaning. To illustrate, the following excerpt includes two clauses, the first is expressed with a preterit verb phrase (in bold) and the second is expressed with a verb phrase containing the auxiliary "do" (italicized): "wee **came** where wee *did take in* the Soulders [soldiers]" [ADM 51/4322/1]. If the use of the auxiliary "do" were a default in constructions with affirmative indicative modality then both verb phrases in the sentence would take it, i.e., "wee *did come* where wee *did take in* the Soulders" and if the default were not to use the auxiliary in the indicative mood, then neither clause would use it, i.e., "wee **came** where wee **took in** the Soulders". Yet the

---

[23]The first two examples: "we *doe* assure you" [ADM 106/288/30], "I *doe* wonder" [HCA 1/98/57] could be interpreted as emphatic usage that may have been customary in formal speech. However, the last example "our ketch *did* touch our stearn and *did* us some damage" [ADM 52/2/3] does not appear to be emphatic and neither do the excerpts from the sea shanties that follow these three examples.

conscious variation within the utterance appears to mark the clauses differently. It may be that the preterit and the verb phrase expressed with an auxiliary are marked for sequence or subordination in the sense that "wee **came**" necessarily occurred first and "wee *did take in* the Soulders" occurred after — and because of — the completed first event. Indeed, this type of subordinating or aspectual interpretation of the complementary verb forms appears to be supported by various examples which express a sequence of events, e.g., "he **was** Drunk when *he did consent*" [HCA 1/99 Bahama Islands 1722] in which the event of being drunk occurs before (and potentially causes) the event of consenting;[24] and "the wind [...] **came** from Dover and **brought** ten tunns of Watter and *did Returne* this day thither againe" [ADM 52/2/2] in which the event of the wind and water coming is completed before they return. The examples given above include verb phrases that are written in the same sequence as they occur, but even when these verb phrases appear in reverse order, the meaning still favors the completive aspect of the preterit verb before the verb with the "do" auxiliary happens, e.g., "And [I] *did heare* that the captain **took** them" [HCA 1/13/97] in which the taking of prisoners occurs before the witness can hear about it; and "before they *did do* it, he **had expressed** himself extremely glad" [HCA 1/99/20] in which the adverb "before" makes it explicit that the expression of emotion occurs before the unspecified event was performed. It appears that in these contexts, regardless of the order of the clauses, the expression of the verb phrase as either a principal verb in preterit form or a verb phrase in past tense with "do support" communicates subordinating and aspectual information that may reinforce the listener's interpretation of the sequence and causation of events.[25]

---

[24]Past perfect constructions typically indicate the sequence of events in standard usage by marking the verb that occurred first (i.e., "drunk" would be the verb marked by past perfect as it occurred first, creating the phrase "He had been drunk when he consented".) Note that the excerpt "he was Drunk when *he did consent*" marks the second of the two verbs (i.e., "consent") and thus demonstrates contrast to standard usage in sequential marking on the second event rather than the first event.

[25]This complex interpretation of how "do support" functions to mark aspectual and/or subordinating meaning in affirmative clauses in the indicative mood when used in conjunction with preterit forms does not necessarily negate the conclusive statement of the previous paragraph, i.e., that "do support" may have been a universal in all affirmative verb phrases to aid the process of acquisition for language learners. Instead, the use of "do" may change with any individual speaker's fluency with the language; learners might have defaulted to a universal use of "do support" without aspectual or subordinating meaning, and native/fluent speakers might have used the available structure to mark subtle distinctions in meaning between verb phrases.

6.4.3 Modal auxiliaries

While most of this chapter's analysis is based on the indicative or unmarked modality of verb phrases in Ship English,[26] this section is dedicated to auxiliaries used in the marked interrogative and conditional modalities. The interrogative mood is briefly addressed in §6.4.2 regarding the auxiliary "do", given that the standard method of forming interrogative modalities uses "do support", as illustrated by the prosecutor who asked witness Joseph Wood, "*Did* you heare the Pyrates talk of blowing ther shipp up?" [CO 5/1411/37] (marked for emphasis). However, it is important to recognize there were relatively few examples of sailors using the interrogative modality in the documents composing the corpus, and this is not surprising given that witness depositions, logbooks, and personal communications are predominantly informative in purpose and therefore disposed to indicative modality. Yet, limited examples show that "do support" was used in interrogative contexts such as the tag question in the excerpt, "he took part of the drink *did* he not?" [CO 5/1411/57] and samples of indirect speech in which a question was asked, e.g., "ask him where *did* they take this shipp" [CO 5/1411/97]. Sailors' use of "do support" in interrogative modality is further supported by its occurrence in sea shanties, e.g., "When I passed a whole fortnight atween decks with you, / *Did* I ere give a kiss, lad, to one of your crew?" (voice of a female character in a shanty attributed to John Gay 1685–1732, and cited in Hugill 1969: 17). Thus, although not attested to in many examples, the use of "do support" to form questions was evidently one option available to sailors of the early colonial period.

Sailors employed a variety of structures to form questions and were not restricted to the use of the auxiliary "do" in interrogative modality. One variation that did not require the use of the auxiliary "do" was to move the main verb to a fronted position before the subject to create a verb-subject construction. Subject-verb inversion is typical of standard usage in Early Modern English, yet the distinguishing factor of sailors' syntax is that the verbs undergoing movement are not auxiliaries but the principal inflected verb, e.g., "how *came* you to say you shot the shott that killed the master?" [CO 5/1411/43]. In other words, the interrogative construction "how came you" shows movement of the principal inflected verb "to come" before the subject "you" rather than the insertion and movement of an auxiliary verb as in the modern standard variation "how *did* you come". The same structure could potentially occur with any principal verb, e.g., "what *lack* you" [445f.1/31]. Yet, this type of construction notably occurs with the verb

---

[26]The subjunctive and imperative moods are addressed briefly in §6.3.1.

"have", e.g., "what colours *had* the pyrates" [CO 5/1411/22] and "*had* you any goods on board" [CO 5/1411/37], suggesting that it may have been conditioned by verb choice, potentially because the verb "have" can function as an auxiliary when used as part of a perfective verb phrase, although it is not doing so in these examples.[27] In these examples, the verb "have" is used as a principal verb meaning to own or possess and thus should therefore be subject to the same paradigm as the other principal verbs for which the "do" auxiliary is inserted and moved. However, the occurrence of the verb "have", immaterial of its function, appears to favor movement of the principal verb rather than the insertion and movement of the auxiliary "do". This potential linguistic conditioning caused by the use of the verb "have" is also suggested by how the structure is used in complementary distribution by court officials in Admiralty trails, for instance, the same prosecutor who asks "what number of English prisoners *had* the pyrates shipp" [CO 5/1411/23] and "what office *had* he" [CO 5/1411/29], showing movement of the verb "have", also asks "*Did* you heare him say any thing" [CO 5/1411/29] and "*did* you leap overboard" [CO 5/1411/30] showing insertion and movement of an auxiliary verb when the principal verb was not "have". The movement of the verb "have" (even when it functions as a principal verb) may have been reinforced by systemic leveling given that this syntax results in the same construction that is used with "be" in interrogative modality (even when used as a principal verb), e.g., "*was* you on board the pyrate shipp" [CO 5/1411/28].[28] Thus, one hypothesis that might be tested with further research is that when forming questions, sailors defaulted to the movement of verbs before the subject if they were verbs that can function as auxiliaries, i.e., "do", "have", or "be", regardless of whether they were used as auxiliaries or as principal verbs.

The standard construction of the conditional mood is common in Ship English but permits verbal omission in ways that are not accepted in standard usage. Ship English incorporates verb phrases marked for modality in conditional sentences that express an event whose realization is dependent on another factor, just like standard usage, e.g., "If he did see any one that offered any hurt or violence to Clarke he would make him suffer" [HCA 1/9/51] and "Terrors of Death (which they said they were sure would be their Position should they refuse)" [HCA 1/99/8]. Most examples of conditional mood occur in the context of a sim-

---

[27]The fronted verb "have" still occurs in a limited set of phrases such as "Have you no shame/decency/compassion?" which appear to signal a dramatic challenge or critique of a person's actions.

[28]This question does not derive from a sailor but a court prosecutor who addresses it multiple times to different witnesses in the trial of John Houghling, Corneluis Franc and Francois Delaune (Virginia, 13–17th May 1700).

ple modal auxiliary (italicized) and a base verb (bold), e.g., "they *would* **pistoll** him" [HCA 1/101/406], "lest the prisoners *should* **force** him away" [HCA 1/99 Williamsburg, Aug 14 1729], and "he *may* **be** att Liberty" [HCA 1/14/28]. Although some examples suggest that either the modal auxiliary or the main verb could be omitted in contexts where meaning was apparent, e.g., "in case of resistance he [*would*] **compell** him by force so to doe" [CO 5/1411/663], "he **had** [*would* **have**] done it if there had been Powder enough" [HCA 1/99/157], "whether he *would* [**go**] to sea" [CO 5/1411/639], and "The Governor bidding them [...] they *would* [**go**] away from thence" [HCA 1/9/18]. Interestingly, various examples of omitted main verbs in conditional structures suggest movement, such as the omission, assumed to be the verb "to go" in the previous examples. The following examples are also assumed to omit verbs synonymous with travel that could also be expressed using the verb "to go" (emphasized in bold), e.g., "you *must* [**head/go**] away 50 Leagues & then you are clear of the sands" [HCA 1/99/22], "Declared that he *would* [**sail/go**] for the North of Cuba" [HCA 1/9/6], and "most of them *would* [**disembark/go**] about noon" [ADM 52/1/7]. In sum, most verb phrases with conditional modality are constructions comparable to standard usage with a single auxiliary and a single main verb, yet either constituent could be omitted, particularly if the main verb expressed movement or travel in a manner synonymous with the verb "to go".

There is little evidence in the corpus to indicate that sailors used expanded modal constructions with either perfect or progressive aspect. Most conditional structures were simple with one modal auxiliary (italicized) and a base verb (in bold), e.g., "we *could* **doe** little good of it" [ADM 52/1/8] and "he *might* **prosecute** him" [HCA 1/52/46]. Rare examples of verb phrases with more than one verbal component after the modal auxiliary include "two or three Passengers...*might* **be heard** to justifie his being forced" [HCA 1/99/85], and "the Purser said he *must needs* **goe** a shore himsefle" [ADM 52/1/8]. Yet neither of these examples suggest an expanded verb phrase; the first example, "might be heard", is explained by its passive status and the second, "must needs goe", is explained by the idiomatic use of the expression "must needs" (surviving today in the form of "needs must") with the word "needs" appearing to form part of the modal auxiliary stem. None of the documentary evidence in the corpus indicates that sailors used expanded modal constructions such as perfect conditionals ("I should have gone") progressive conditionals ("I should be going"), or perfect-progressive conditionals ("I should have been going"). However, certain examples of conditional verbal phrases indicate an underlying assumption of aspectual meaning that would suppose a perfect conditional structure, e.g., "any Irregularities he *might* **commit**, was the Drink that he was a forced man" [HCA 1/99/40]. This example refers to a completed period when the accused was on board an alleged pirate vessel and he wishes to express repentance for any "irregularities" (i.e., crimes) he might have committed in a way that does not incriminate him. However, the perfect conditional "might have committed" is not used, instead the conditional phrase used is "might commit" which suggests that he is talking about potential future events rather than events that are completed. Another example of conditional modality expressed as a simple construction (i.e., auxiliary modal + main verb) yet with completed aspectual meaning in the context of its utterance, is "Harry Gatsby believes he *might* **be forced** at first but since had done as others" [HCA 1/99/93]. This example marks completive aspect with the adverbs "at first" and "since" but does not express the conditional verbal phrase with perfect aspect "might have been forced", instead the construction "might be forced" suggests that the event is extant as opposed to its assumed completive meaning. Other examples show that sailors attempted to express conditional modality and completive aspect in other ways (italicized), e.g., "threatened him in So much that he *had like to have incurid* [would have likely incurred] Some severe punishment about it" [HCA 1/99/93]. The fact that sailors used alternative methods to mark completive conditional modality may suggest that they avoided multiple auxiliaries in verb phrases or may suggest more specifically that the perfect auxiliary "have" was not permitted in coordination with conditional auxiliaries. As a result, most verb phrases with conditional modality are basic constructions with a single auxiliary and a single main verb despite evidence that attests to intended aspectual meaning.

Negation in conditional modality predominantly aligns with the general trends discussed in §6.1, and specifically the section dealing with negation, §6.1.3. The most common negative marker was the word "not" inserted after the conditional auxiliary verb, e.g., "our Ship but *could not* gett her keel out" [ADM 52/1/8], "the captain *would not* wrong me" [CO 5/1411/638], and "what the event is I *cannot* tell" [ADM 52/1/8]. Other negative markers include negation with "no", that was typically placed in a noun phrase constituent or an adverbial phrase (in bold for emphasis) e.g., "I *could* get him **no way** to adhere to me" [445f.1/36], "we *culd* see her **no longer**" [DDB6 8/4], "But *could* get **no more**" [ADM 51/3954], "the Pyrates *would* accept of **no Foreigners**" [HCA 1/99/20], and "[I] *could* see **no sign** of the boat" [HCA 1/99 Bahama Islands 1722]. Less frequent markers of conditional negation include "never" used pre-verbally, e.g., "he **never** *wou'd* go even in his Turn" [HCA 1/99/156] and negative concord using the conjunction "nor", e.g., "The Captain said, I *cannot* sell the King's Victuals. I answered, **Nor** I *cannot* do the King's Work". [445f.1/29], "he *would* do him **no hurt** and **nor** the money in his pocket *should* be touched" [HCA 1/99/8], and "Capt Rigby doe **not nor** *shall* carry off this land any Persons" [HCA 1/9/7]. Overall, negation in verb phrases marked for conditional modality did not always align with standard usage, but is comparable to trends identified for indicative verb phrases.

6.5 Summary

Sailors' preferences for nominalization are evidenced by a tendency to use non-specific verbs which permit the expression of the main event of the sentence in nominal form in the direct object position. Common constructions using "make" suggest an event (expressed nominally as the direct object) that is brought into being or caused to happen, and idiomatic usage of the verb "make" with travel and transit permits prepositional complements. Phrasal verbs show a tendency to be expressed as fixed expressions in the corpus and resist the insertion of an object noun phrase or pronoun between the main verb and the satellite particle. Examples of negation in the corpus demonstrate significant variation, but the most common negative construction is the use of the negative particle "not" after a finite verb regardless of whether it is an auxiliary or base indicative verb without any auxiliary support. The second most common negation marker in the sample is the word "never" which is sometimes used to mark distinct categorical denial over time (as in standard modern usage), but is more commonly contextualized with specific durations of time or to negate indicative past tense situations with no aspectual meaning. Other common negation markers include the particle "no" after a non-finite verb and the conjunction "nor", both of which often compose or join clauses that already have negation. The resultant negative concord is a salient feature of the corpus.

Inflectional variation in verb forms expressed in indicative modality — specifically zero inflection with singular third person subjects — is potentially conditioned by using certain verbs such as "know", by negation and third person pronominal subjects, and/or by observance of the Northern Subject Rule. The use of present tense in past narrative contexts may have reflected sailors' performance culture, but variation in past tense marking appears to be the result of free variation given the range of forms occurring in the same linguistic contexts, in the same documents, and in the same handwriting across a range of registers and modalities. Preterit forms of weak verbs could be either inflected according to the regular "-ed" paradigm or left in an uninflected form, but preterit forms of strong verbs might be expressed as past participles, variant preterit forms, twice-marked irregular stems with regular inflection, or uninflected verbs. Certain verbs such as "see" and "run" appear to select a preference for zero marking and phrasal verbs with a range of satellite particles appear to permit zero marking in the preterit form of the associated verb. Variant forms of infinitives occur after present and past participles and after auxiliary verbs with conditional modality but are omitted in contexts of transparent meaning, and there is also some evidence to suggest that the base form of a verb and its infinitive may have been interchangeable.

The scope of variation permitted in form and usage of the verb "be" marks it as one of the most divergent features of Ship English. In terms of inflection, "was" occurs as the most frequent past tense form of the verb with all nominal and pronominal subjects in first, second, and third person, although compound third-person noun phrases and plural first-person pronouns were the most salient contexts that selected this non-standard past tense form. Present tense and infinite forms of the verb "be" show similar variation, with "is" occurring as the most frequently used present-tense form alongside free variation with non-finite variants such as the uninflected form and the present participle. In terms of usage, the copula does not commonly occur as the principal verb of a clause, but "be" occurs frequently in the corpus as a requisite of passive structures. Variation in these passive structures supports the general tendency for leveling of the inflectional paradigm but also indicates that "be" omission was acceptable, and this type of omission is mirrored in contexts when it is used as an auxiliary in structures marked for progressive aspect. In these progressive structures, auxiliary "be" commonly selects a stative present participle rather than the standard default of an active present participle. There is also evidence to suggest that the auxiliary "be" could mark perfect aspect in addition to progressive aspect.

The auxiliary verb "have" is prone to inflectional variation such as the non-standard use of "has" with third person plural subjects, and uninflected "have" in conjunction with the past participle "been" regardless of the subject, and this may have been an indicator of a collapsed inflectional paradigm. Examples of verb phrases marked for perfect aspect also permit separation of the auxiliary and its associated verb phrase, and deletion or substitution of the auxiliary constituent. However, the most salient variation in perfect verb phrases is not the auxiliary itself, but the fact that it often selects a preterit verbal particle or a form resulting from a leveled paradigm of the preterit and past participle forms.

The auxiliary "do" is not prone to significant inflectional variation but is used in affirmative statements of the indicative mood in ways that mirror its insertion in negative and interrogative modality. Although this might suggest emphasis, repeated usage in contexts without explicit emphatic meaning suggests that sailors commonly used the auxiliary as a component of the indicative mood. Although this may attest to systemic leveling that aided language learners, evidence also suggests that fluent speakers used the auxiliary "do" in juxtaposition to preterit verbs to communicate subordinating and aspectual information. In addition to the standard use of "do support" to form questions, Ship English also permits the movement of the main verb to a fronted position before the subject to create a verb-subject construction common to standard usage. However, the verbs undergoing movement in Ship English are not auxiliaries but the principal inflected verb, and this type of construction is specifically notable with principal verbs that can also function as auxiliaries. Most verb phrases with conditional modality are constructions with a single auxiliary and a single verb form, yet either the auxiliary or the principal verb could be omitted, particularly if the principal verb expressed movement or travel in a manner synonymous with the verb "to go". There is little evidence in the corpus to indicate that sailors used expanded modal constructions with either perfect or progressive aspect, and as such, the conditional mood had a limited scope of usage in Ship English. Finally, negation in verb phrases marked for conditional modality showed variation that was not common to standard usage but is comparable to trends identified for indicative verb phrases.

7 Clause, sentence and discourse level phenomena

This is the third linguistic chapter with a focus on the salient characteristics of Ship English at the clause, sentence, and discourse level. The first section on syntax within the clause presents data on adverb use and placement, inherent variation in the prepositional paradigm, intransitive verb fronting and the use of both direct and indirect objects. The second section on subordination and coordination illustrates the syntactic complexity of Ship English with specific attention to strategies of subordination and coordination. The last section on swearing as a discourse marker explores the role of oath-making and profanity in sailors' speech to mark communicative intent, grammatical modality, individual agency and group identity.

7.1 Syntax within the clause

7.1.1 Adverbs

Ship English makes heavy use of prepositional phrases and one clause might feature several adverbial constituents. The two following examples from depositions illustrate heavy use of prepositional phrases with adverbial function: "That being at Borligne he was hired by the said Capt Vaughan to serve with him as Master in the barge" [HCA 1/13/95], and "a Prisoner on Board of them Swears, he Several times in that Space addressed to him in French, and with Tears bemoaned his being in Such Company" [HCA 1/99/168]. Many of these prepositional phrases with adverbial function occur in the default position of modern standard varieties at the end of the clause, e.g., "and am thies day going with a small vessel for kopon hagen" [HCA 1/101/527] in which the phrases "with a small vessel" and "for kopon hagen" attach to the end of the clause. One-word adverbs could also occur at the end of the clause (italicized for emphasis) e.g., "the tides proved very loe *still*" [ADM 52/2/3], and "they should have Rum *enough*" [HCA 1/99/7]. Adverbial phrases composed of more than one word but not taking a prepositional head also commonly occur at the end of a clause in sailors' speech, e.g., "several times was threatened *very much*" [HCA 1/99/69] and "John Edwards who came *just then*" [HCA 1/9/51]. However, sailors commonly placed adverbial constituents in a range of positions within the main clause whether they were prepositional phrases, single-word adverbs, or adverbial phrases without prepositional heads (Figure 7.1).

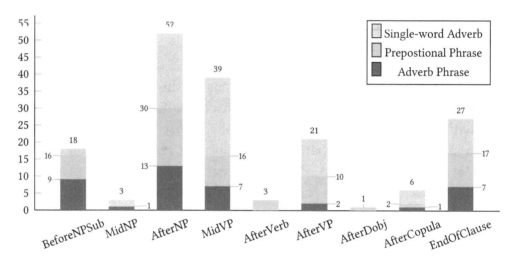

Figure 7.1: Syntactic placement and type of adverbial constituent in 170 examples
Sources: 1045.f.3, 445f.1, Adkins & Adkins (2008) ADM 106, ADM 51/1, 3954, ADM 52/2, Brown (2011) CO 5/1411, D/Earle/1/1, DDB6 8/4, HCA 1/9, HCA 1/12, HCA 1/13, HCA 1/14, HCA 1/52, HCA 1/53, HCA 1/98, HCA 1/99, HCA 1/101, Palmer (1986), SP 42/6, SP 89/34, T/70/1216.

The most common placement for adverbial constituents was after the noun-phrase subject and before the main verb phrase. Prepositional phrases (italicized for emphasis) are regularly placed in this position between the subject and main verb, e.g., "which they *in a short time* did" [HCA 1/52/88], and "The ship Hastings *in the chase* fired about five & twenty Gunns" [HCA 1/52/176]. Although the examples given above are short, sailors also inserted long prepositional phrases in this position between the subject and the verb, e.g., "The Mate *then coming towards him the said John Humphreys* told him" [HCA 1/52/124], and "He *with other who had a potentall Comission to take Spanish goods* did seize on them lately at sea" [HCA 1/9/67]. Single-word adverbs and adverbial phrases also commonly occur in this position between subject and the main verb, e.g., "hee *well* know" [HCA 1/52/1], "he *lately* belonged to a Spanish frigate" [HCA 1/99/5], "doctors of physic in ships *many times* are very careless" (cited in Brown 2011: 47), and "Manuel Guzman *the second time of Landing* was chosen the officer in Chief" [HCA 1/99 New Providence 1722]. Overall, this post-nominal and pre-verbal position was the most common location for all adverbial constituents in the sample, comprising 52 of the 170 examples or 31% of the total and was the most common placement for both adverbial phrases and prepositional phrases with an adverbial function (see Figure 7.1).

The most common placement for single-word adverbs was between an auxiliary verb and a verbal participle.[1] This occurred with do-support in indicative modality, with perfect aspect, and with copula auxiliaries in both progressive aspect and passive constructions, in both indicative and negated statements, e.g., "I did *formerly* present to you" [ADM 106/300/21], "The examinant hath not *since* seen him" [HCA 1/14/140], "hee had *long* swam" [HCA 1/53/3], "I am *soone* going to Sea" [HCA 1/101/356], "Which had been *before* taken" [HCA 1/13/95], "Ship that was *lately* cast away" [HCA 1/12/79], and "used to be *often* meditating on the Godly Books" [HCA 1/99/156]. In this position, these single-word adverbs interrupt the verbal phrase, and this effect is more pronounced when the inserted adverbial is either an adverb phrase or a prepositional phrase, e.g., "Thomas Gardner [...] did *in June last* take from hence [Deptford] an hoyes Maine saile & a quantity of Doales" [ADM 106/288/42], "She was *with many of her Slaves* chained" [HCA 1/99/91], "Juan Boneta Lucrass had *under pretence of that commission* taken Several Sloops" [HCA 1/99/10], and "This informant was *after the sale of the sd ship the Loving Land as aforesaid* put aboard the Gunll of this sd Spanish man of Warr" [HCA 1/53/8]. This interruption is even more pronounced when two or more adverbial interjections are placed in a mid-verbal position, e.g., "Capt Parsons did *in a mornng ab:[about] 9 or ten dayes before Christmas last* call upon this Deponent" [HCA 1/14/54]. In addition to the placement of adverbs between auxiliary verbs and their participles, prepositional adverbs are also permitted to occur after a main verb and before an infinitive creating a similar effect of interrupting the verb phrase, e.g., "he attempted *at Sieraleon* to run away" [HCA 1/99/45], "they were both commanded *in the Boat* to row their Capt on Board" [HCA 1/99/149], and "you are to be carefull *therefore suly* to observe the sd directions" [CO 5/1411/618]. Although this was not a common feature, it could be seen as an extension of the tendency to place adverbials between auxiliaries and main verbs, which is the most common location for single-word adverbs, and the second most common location for all adverbial constituents in the sample, comprising 39 of the 170 examples or 23% of the total (see Figure 7.1).

Further to the most common two placements of adverbial constituents (after the subject noun phrase and between auxiliary and main verb) Ship English permits other placements with no apparent linguistic conditioning by adverb type. Adverbial constituents in the sample often occur after the verb phrase but be-

---

[1]Millward & Hayes claim that Early Modern English in general showed a tendency to insert adverbial modifiers between an auxiliary verb and a past participle (2012: 271–272).

fore the direct object of a transitive verb, e.g., "two of them loosing *each* one leg" [HCA 1/12/2], "and has had *since* no opportunities of escaping" [HCA 1/99/125], "the pyrate gave *to the capt* his longboat" [CO 5/1411/42], "took away *out of his packett* his Sealed ring" [HCA 1/9/18], and "there was by his order put *into a boate belinging to the St. Andrew* 2 coyles of rope" [HCA 1/101/224]. Similarly, linking verbs permit adverbs before nominal or adverbial predicates, e.g., "become *again* our enemy [445f.1/21], and "he appeared *allways* disconsolate" [HCA 1/99/129]. The copula likewise permits adverbs before adverbial predicates, e.g., "Richard Taylor was *a little before* come" [HCA 1/9/39], "He had been *then* dead about foure howers" [HCA 1/9/51], and "Which ship was *abt four years since* run away with" [HCA 1/52/75]. Although the placement of adverbs after verbs and before direct objects or predicates is not common in the sample of 170 sample phrases analyzed, it does suggest that sailors had the option of placing adverbs after verbs regardless of whether the verb in question was transitive, linking, or copula in nature. In short, sailors had the option of locating adverbs in various positions without apparent linguistic conditioning by type of adverbial constituent or main verb type, resulting in patterns of free variation in the corpus.

Contrary to this pattern of free variation, non-finite adverbial clauses are predominantly located at the start of the matrix clauses in which they occur. Although sailors had the option of placing other types of adverbial constituents (i.e., prepositional phrases, single-word adverbs, and adverbial phrases without prepositional heads) at the start of the clause, fronted adverbial placement was much more common for non-finite adverbial clauses than it was for other types of adverbial constituents. Thus, although phrases with fronted single-word adverbs such as "*likewise* says the captain" [HCA 1/99 New Providence 1722] are evident in the corpus, they are not common. Comparatively, sentences with fronted non-finite adverbial clauses occur frequently, e.g., (with non-finite adverbial clauses emphasized in italics) "*upon his threatening to shoot him* he delivered up to him" [HCA 1/99/6], and "*to prevent more of his Impertinence* which she was afraid off went down into the Gun Room" [HCA 1/99/79]. In sum, although we might conclude that single-word adverbs and adverbial phrases have no default placement in Ship English — only a preferred tendency to be placed after the noun-phrase subject and before the main verb phrase or in a mid-verbal position between an auxiliary verb and a verbal participle — when adverbial constituents take the form of non-finite adverbial clauses, they default to a placement at the start of the matrix clauses in which they occur.

7.1.2 Prepositions

Prepositional phrases that are adverbial in meaning are sometimes difficult to identify because Ship English permits the omission of prepositional heads. Prepositional omission occurs with a range of adverbial types, for instance: adverbs of location, "arrived here, [in] his Mars Ship the Tilbury" [SP 42/6]; adverbs of duration, "with Snow [for] most part of the night" [ADM 52/2/3]; adverbs of manner, "wished he had never come [on] the voyage" [HCA 1/99/62]; adverbs of comparison, "never having been looked on [as] a Trusty Man among them" [HCA 1/99/151]; adverbs of direction, "then returned him [to] his owne Brigganteine" [HCA 1/98/258]; and adverbs of relation, "he was examined by the Viceadmiral [about] what Companyes of foote were in the Islands" [HCA 1/9/105]. Furthermore, this type of omission which was common to the transcribed depositions and hand-written letters of sailors was also reproduced in print, for instance, the prepositional omission at the head of the adverb of manner in a maritime pamphlet "On the 26th past arrived here [on] the Snow Susannah, Capt. Landon from Bristol" [HCA 1/99 The American: Weekly Mercury No.618, Oct 28–Nov 4 1731]. Examples suggest that in such cases the prepositional constituents are indeed present in the underlying structure but perhaps the unstressed nature of the prepositions in speech coupled with high levels of partial literacy among mariners promoted omission in written representations.

Idiomatic use of prepositions in specific phrases was fluid and highly variable. This is not surprising given that the Early Modern English period was a time in which numerous dialectal differences manifested themselves and there were many new prepositions entering the language owing to the loss of inflection to indicate grammatical relationship (Millward & Hayes 2012: 268). Limitations of space do not permit a detailed discussion of each preposition here, but some examples are illustrated in Table 7.1.

Certain combinations with the preposition "for" re-occur frequently in the corpus but are not necessarily idiomatic. Phrases featuring the combination "for that" can function as complementizers in the same way that the word "that" can when used alone, e.g., "it is untrue, *for that* Scudmore belonged to, and was on Board the *Ranger*" [HCA 1/99/101]. However, other examples suggest that there is a specific meaning attached to the collocation of the two words that act in the same way that the conjunction "because" functions in Modern English, e.g., "he would not do it without the Captains order, *for that* he knew not whether the Captain would allow it" [HCA 1/52/20]. Indeed, this combination appears to mirror the use of the word "for" as a subordinating conjunction when used alone e.g., "[we moored] In 15 fathome, of water *for* it was Calme" [ADM 51/4322/1] and "we kam to Anankor *for* we had the wind att no [north]" [DDB6 8/4]. At other times, the combination of the two words "for" and "that" might have been coincidental, e.g., "if he was *for that* he would defend himselfe" [HCA 1/52/46]. This example can be broken down to mean that the unnamed subject was "for" something, and the something he was "for" is a clause introduced by the subordi-

Table 7.1: Sample of prepositional variation in idiomatic phrases

Preposition	Excerpt containing idiom	Source
at	Gust at WSW[West South West]	CO 5/1411/706
	Piracy at sea is the same with Robbery at land	CO 5/1411/45
	a longboat at anchor in Shoar	HCA 1/99/3 Cape Coast 1734
	he never was at attacking any Ship	HCA 1/99/80
by	and by the way mett wth a ketch[a]	HCA 1/12/3
	missing the Islands by contrary winds	HCA 1/98/267
for	was for scuttling the Ship	HCA 1/99/22
	for till such tyme	ADM 106/288/40
	hee would go for Yarmouth	HCA 1/52/4
	the fleet went for England	ADM 52/1/1
	gave him for answer	SP 89/25/230
in	evidences in their behalf	HCA 1/99/69
	was concerned in taking away the other things	HCA 1/99 New Providence 1722
on	seize on him	SP 89/25/230
	lay hold on the Captain	445f.1/40
	when on a sudden	HCA 1/99 Barbados 1733
to	wee put to sea[b]	HCA 1/12/2
	the wind came to no [north]	DDB6 8/4
	there was no violence used to the master	HCA 1/53/67
	aiding & assisting to all mastors	SP 42/6
	saw a ship to westward	ADM 52/1/1
	in order to your returning to Engld	CO 5/1411/658

[a]Although the idiom "by the way" appears similar to the way we might express a parenthetical fact in modern English, the usage in this context means a more literal "on route" (i.e., "on the way").

[b]This use of the idiom "put to sea" is still used in modern Standard English, sometimes with the preposition "out" inserted after the verb to create the phrase "put out to sea".

nator "that", expressed as "that he would defend himself", and so the two words "for that", although they appear to combine in the same way as in the previous examples, are functioning separately. In short, although several examples of the combination "for that" feature in the corpus, there is no convincing trend that implies a distinct meaning or an idiom specific to the speech community but rather that sailors used the preposition "for" as a concordant complementizer or a subordinating conjunction.

Much more salient than "for that" was the prepositional phrase "for to" that occurred specifically by allowing the preposition "for" to take an infinitive verb phrase complement, without an intervening subject, as in present-day Standard English (e.g., "for her to give up now would astound me". The variety of verbs with which this collocation occurred suggest that the combination of "for to" was not idiomatic but the result of a syntactic rule permitting infinitive verbs to follow the preposition. Examples of the combination in witness depositions include (with italic and bold emphasis) "it was *for* **to destroy** what cloathes we had" [SP 42/6], "we were forced *for* **to lye**" [ADM 52/2/8], and "and *for* **to satisfie** you" [HCA 1/101/423]. However, the combination was also common in logbooks, e.g., "we waid Anckor and came to sayle *for* **to make** the best of our way" [T/70/1216/12], "after dinner *for* **to goo** to the ground" [T/70/1215 Oct 15], and "Recieved Orders from the captain of the Drake, *for* **to Ride** Commandr in Chief" [ADM 51/4322/1]. Miscellaneous letters authored by sailors also show this syntax, e.g., "a Young Man, willing *for* **to Sacrifice** his life" [HCA 1/101/207], and "All possible Endeavours were rosed *for* **to heare** her off" [HCA 1/9/155]. Further evidence indicating that the underlying structure of the combination was "for" + [infinitive] rather than an idiomatic usage of "for to" is that the structure could be interrupted by adverbial constituents, e.g., the word "strictly" in the excerpt "and them *for* strictly **to examine**" [SP 42/6]. The salience of the "for" + [infinitive] structure is highlighted by its representation in several contemporary sea-songs and shanties that were either authored by sailors or written to reflect their speech, e.g., "I met her walking on the Strand / Dressed up *for* **to beat** the band" ()Hugill1969 "our Lord High Admiral *for* **to pursue** them sought" (cited in Palmer 1986: 8), "The course / intended *for* **to Steer**" (cited in Palmer 1986: 74), and "Pork cut in pounds / *For* **to eat** with our peas" (cited in Palmer 1986: 71). The combination "for to" in documents written by sailors, transcribed for sailors, and representing sailors all appear to confirm that the salient use of "for to" occurs because the first preposition is permitted to take an infinitive complement rather than its occurrence as an idiomatic expression, and this coincides with the usage that Baker & Huber identify as a feature of world-wide English-lexicon contact languages (2001: 201).

The preposition "of" is permitted to combine with other prepositions and often occurs preceding noun phrases and pronouns both with and without genitive function. Before another preposition, examples include "in his Action *of with* the Swallow he Remembers nothing" [HCA 1/99/59], and "and went *of from* the ship" [HCA 1/99/71]. In this latter case, "of" might be an orthographic representation of the preposition "off", which might more commonly combine in such contexts, e.g., "took the Pyrate *off from* beating him" [HCA 1/99/30]. Some of the examples in which the preposition "of(f)" follows "out" and refers to a specific location are acceptable in modern standard usage, e.g., "they took Capt Macfashion & Nicholas Simonds *out of* him [the ship]" [HCA 1/99/7] and "mariners sayld *out off* Jamaica ten years" [HCA 1/98/7]. Sailors seemingly extended this usage of "of" + [location] to include the preposition "aboard", e.g., "we put men *aboard of* the London" [ADM 52/2/13] and "they could not ship any goods *aboard of* any ship" [HCA 1/99/113 loose letter c. 1730]. When the preposition "of" proceeds either noun phrases or pronouns, the structure sometimes carries a genitive/associative meaning, e.g., "two buineshas [businesses] of him" [SP 42/6], "came down the River of Thames" [ADM 52/1/5], and "the articles of the pyrates" [HCA 1/99/48]. Other examples have a partitive meaning, e.g., "hallf *o(f)* an ouer [half an hour]" [ADM 52/2/1], and "one other *of* the men was order'd to go againe on Board" [HCA 1/99/6]. Yet other uses of the preposition appear to have no genitive or partitive function, e.g., the excerpt "He would go *of* himself" [HCA 1/9/139] means that he would go "by himself" or alone; "wee were forcd to buy *of* him or goe naked [...] to buy of him at 10 shillings" [SP 42/6] means "to buy from him;" and "bears witness *of* it" [HCA 1/53/48] means "bear witness to it". Other examples suggest that "of" could function as a subordinator, e.g., "each time *of* the prisoner coming to Cat Island she fled into the bushes" [HCA 1/99 New Providence 1722], or could function as a pseudo-verbal particle after an auxiliary modal, e.g., "they found victualls and sale whar [where] they could *of* it" [HCA 1/53/66]. Although this is a highly marked variant, the use of a preposition as a verb particle is evident with other prepositions such as the word "up" in the excerpt "we have *up* our anchors" [ADM 52/2/6] and these examples may attest to a feature of sailors' speech that potentially extended to a number of prepositions. Further examples of the preposition "of" seem redundant, e.g., "he should accept *of* it" [HCA 1/99/59], "the Pyrates missing *of* him" [HCA 1/99/64], and "the Duch squadrn that Came in yesterday counting *of* about 12 Saile of men of war" [ADM 52/2/5]. Although such examples were few, and there is no significant trend showing non-standard usage of the preposition "of" in Ship English, these excerpts attest to a variation that extended well beyond genitive and partitive functions familiar to modern standard usage.

7.1.3 Variation in SVO order: Verb fronting

Ship English permits intransitive verbs to be expressed before noun-phrase subjects in simple clauses. This structure occurs with independent verbs, with phrasal verbs, and with verb phrases which include auxiliary constituents. Intransitive verbs used independently (i.e., as the sole constituent of the verb phrase) often precede their noun phrase subjects, e.g., (with verbs italicized and noun phrases in bold for emphasis) "*began* **a very Sore Storme of Wind**" [ADM 52/2/3], "if *blows* **any wind**" [CO 5/1411/640], "*appeared* personally **Thomas Colston**" [HCA 1/14/17], "*Stayed* for the stern **most ships** all night" [ADM 51/3954], and "still *continued* **much wind**" [ADM 52/2/5]. When intransitive verbs incorporate a satellite particle they are also permitted to precede their noun phrase subjects, and this is most notable with the verb "to come", e.g., "*came in*: **2 Jamaica Sloops** from Barbados" [ADM 52/1/7], "Yesterday in the afternoon *came hither* **Captn Wm** [William] **Passenger**" [CO 5/1411/659], and "Last night *came aboard* **5: hhs [hogsheads] of beefe**" [ADM 52/1/8]. Indeed, fronted verb phrases using "to come" appear to have been a salient marker of sailors' speech and are recorded in sea-songs of the seventeenth century such as "A Joyful New Ballad" that includes the line "First *came up* **their admiral**" (cited in Palmer 1986: 25). Verb phrases which include auxiliary constituents also precede their noun phrase subjects, e.g., "*was coming* **a soldier** to Cape Coast Castle" [HCA 1/99/28] and "The day following *were landed* **7000 foot soldiers**" [BL/Egerton 2395/0003]. This common feature of verbs proceeding their subject noun phrases appears to be conditioned by the intransitive nature of the verb itself and is unaffected by the composition of the verb phrase as either an independent lexeme, a phrasal verb with satellite particle(s), or a complex verb phrase with auxiliary constituents.

Many of the examples cited in the paragraph above attest to the commonality of adverbial constituents preceding fronted intransitive verbs. Repeated use of adverbs was evident throughout the corpus and may reflect the informative purpose of many of the documents studied, yet it may have also provided the linguistic conditioning that enabled intransitive verbs to assume a position prior to the noun phrase subject. Although some of the adverbial constituents involved do not relate to time, e.g., (italicized for emphasis) "*likewise* says the captain" [HCA 1/99 New Providence 1722], most examples in the corpus where an adverbial constituent precedes a fronted intransitive verbs are adverbs of time, such as the excerpts from the following depositions: "*In the after noon* came in the Tiger Prize" [ADM 52/1/7], "*at seaven in the morning* came in a fine ship" [ADM 52/2/3], and "*Towards the evening* came both on board" [HCA 1/9/3]. Logbooks also show this syntax, e.g., "*In the morninge* Came a little wind" [ADM 51/4322/1], "*This morninge* Came one Board of us: some cannewse[canoes]" [T/70/1213], and "*In the morning* died one of our sea men and *in the After noon that day* died our dorktor" [T/70/1213]. Likewise, journals show the presence of adverbial constituents preceding fronted intransitive verbs, e.g., "*Within few days after* followed the generals" [BL/Egerton 2395/0003], and "*Then* said I to the Men" [445f.1/36]. Thus, the placement of intransitive verbs before their noun phrase subjects was a wide-ranging feature in the corpus that was potentially motivated by constructions where adverbial constituents relating to time preceded fronted verbs.

The placement of verbs before the subject is predominantly associated with intransitive verbs, yet there is limited evidence of this syntax also occurring with linking verbs, transitive verbs, and as part of pseudo-expletive structures. The example "then began I to think" [445f.1/35] shows how this occurs with a linking verb, and "often being all Hands Drunk" [HCA 1/99/91] shows its occurrence with the copula. The examples "don't you see says he them two ships" [HCA 1/99/105] and "the following bills delivered the attorney General" [HCA 49/98/106] also illustrate how verb-subject inversion may occur with a transitive verb, and this even extends to passive constructions, e.g., "today [was] Taken out of the George Hoy Tho Harris, Mr". [ADM 52/1/5]. Expletive structures composing the word "there" and the copula before a predicate noun phrase functioning as the logical subject technically do not permit the verb before the subject which is grammatically represented by the word "there", (in italics for emphasis) e.g., "*there* are the principal ports on each side" [1045.f.3/1/16]. However, variations of this structure in which the word "there" does not function as a grammatical subject, in which it is replaced by an adverbial locative "there" appear to feature verbs occurring before their noun phrase subjects. The examples "*there* hapned a very great storme" [HCA 1/14/16] and "*there* appearing several persons" [HCA 1/99/50] appear to use the word "there" as a grammatical subject, yet the verbs "to appear" and "to happen" are not typical in expletive constructions and so cause the word "there" to be interpreted as an adverb rather than a grammatical subject and this consequently means that the only logical noun phrase subject occurs in a position after the verb. The same kind of effect occurs in the example "for *here* commonly runs a great Sea" [1045.f.3/1/26] in which the word "here" suggests a logical subject in the same way that "there" does in existential structures, but is interpreted as an adverb meaning "here in this place" rather than a pronominal constituent and so the only noun phrase in the clause, "a great sea", occurs after the verb "to run". Even followed by the copula, the word "here" can be interpreted as an adverb rather than a grammatical subject, e.g., "They build with Fig-Tree[s]; *here* being, as I was told, no other Trees fit to build with" [1045.f.3/1/27]. The limited number of examples that show a fronted verb that is either linking, transitive, or used as part of a pseudo-expletive construction may indicate that some sailors extended the scope of intransitive verb fronting. However, given the small number of examples available, it may also show idiolectal variation within the speech community. Research on this specific feature with a larger sample might show that conditioned variations were permitted with verbs that were not intransitive; it might also indicate potential language change within the community as the feature of verb fronting began to widen in its linguistic scope beyond its common intransitive context.

7.1.4 Direct and indirect objects

Evidence from sailors' speech and contemporary sea-songs of the late sixteenth and early seventeenth centuries suggest that direct objects may have been moved to an initial position, i.e. OSV word order. Sailors sometimes expressed direct objects at the start of the clause in which they occur, e.g., (italicized for emphasis) "*this fellow* I did not see" [CO 5/1411/36] and "*this* we will do" [445f.1/37] in addition to the standard expression of the direct object after the subject and main verb, e.g., "we culd see *her* no longer" [DDB6 8/4]. The fronting of direct objects among sailors may have been a salient feature of their speech given that it occurs in contemporary sea-songs and shanties several times. For example, it occurs twice in the late sixteenth-century song "Lustily Lustily" in the lines, "*Nothing* we want" and "*ourselves* we will try"[2] (both cited in Palmer 1986: 2) and it occurs twice in the early seventeenth-century song "Another of Seafarers [...]" in the lines: "*A happy end* I do require" and "*Gentle calm* the coast will clear" (both cited in Palmer 1986: 6). Sea-songs of the period also suggest that sailors were known to place predicate noun phrases at the front of a clause after the copula in the same manner as a direct object might undergo fronting, e.g., "*My eldest daughter* thy wife shall be" (cited in Palmer 1986: 48), yet there is no evidence in the corpus of sailors' speech that attests to this potential extension. Thus, although the evidence from the corpus of Ship English does not suggest the same level of salience that the contemporary sea-songs suggest, evidence shows that sailors did sometimes locate direct objects at the start of the clause.

---

[2]This excerpt is taken from the line "Like worthy mariners *ourselves* we will try" in which the reflexive "ourselves" functions as the direct object of the transitive verb "try" and thus creates the meaning "we will try ourselves" (i.e., put our own actions on trial). Although out of context, the reflexive may appear to function as an emphatic marker (i.e., we *ourselves* will try [to do something]) the absence of an infinitive complement in the clause or an associated verb phrase in the adjacent lines of verse weakens the validity of such an interpretation.

Direct objects might be expressed after a nominal subject and before the main verb in a clause. Sea-songs suggest that sailors might have expressed the direct object of transitive verbs after a pronoun (in bold for emphasis), e.g., "Let **him** *his native soil* eschew" and "To haughty hearts **who** *fortune* seek" (both from the song "In Praise of Seafaring Men", cited in Palmer 1986: 4). In addition, one example of a predicate adjective (italicized) located after a noun phrase and before the copula suggests a similar structure: "**our prayers** *so fervent* were" (from the song "Sailors for my Money" cited in Palmer 1986: 45). Although there was no evidence in the corpus of sailors' speech that attests to direct objects occurring between subject pronouns and verb phrases, some examples in which the subject is omitted shows the direct object occurring before the verb phrase suggesting similar underlying syntax, e.g., "send for the severall men brought in by Captain Legg, and *them* **strictly to examine apart**, and of them enquire whither the said sloop was bound" [SP 42/6/52]. The excerpt in bold "them strictly to examine apart" is interpreted as a clause meaning "you will examine them separately and strictly" and as such, the absence of the subject noun phrase and auxiliary verb is explained by the imperative modality. However, the verb "examine" in standard syntax should precede both the direct object and any adverbial constituent (in that sequence), yet the excerpt "them strictly to examine" expresses the direct object "them" first, followed by the adverb "strictly" and then the verb "examine" showing variant placement of the direct object in the underlying syntax regardless of where the noun phrase subject might have been placed. Further support for this interpretation is suggested by a maritime pamphlet that features two statements in which the subject is omitted (here shown in parentheses) and the direct object of the verb (in italics) precedes the verb: "and then and there *the said ship and her Cargoe* [they] did Piratically and feloniously steal take and carry away" and "*the said Ship* [they] did Piratically and Feloniously sink and destroy" [both from HCA 1/99 The American: Weekly Mercury No.617, Oct 21–Oct 28 1731]. Thus, although supporting evidence is limited, it is possible that variant placement of the direct object after the subject and before the main verb in a clause was permitted, even when the subject was expressed in pronominal form or was not realized in the surface structure.

Limited evidence suggests that direct objects may have been omitted from clauses featuring transitive verbs. The most common occurrence of direct object omission took place in logbooks, and specifically in contexts where the direct object of the verb is self-evident, e.g., "This Day att 10 in the Mouning wee weayed [anchor]" [DDB6 8/4]. Of course, it is possible that the verb "to weigh" is being used as an intransitive verb in such contexts, yet the more common usage of the word (even in nautical contexts) as a transitive verb that occurs explicitly with the direct object "anchor" diminishes the likelihood of intransitive use. Further to the specific example of "to weigh" in logbooks, personal communications and witness depositions also suggest that direct objects could be omitted with other normally transitive verbs. For example, Captain William Hennesey's letter to an Admiralty official regarding a quantity of money that he has yet to receive explains that he is writing "although demanded [the money] of him before" [ADM 106/300/35],[3] the deposition in which the witness explains how pay was promised to the crew but never materialized, even after a promise the captain made "to give the men [extra pay] for extraordinary works" [SP 42/6]. Depositions omit direct objects when they may have been realized as pronouns, e.g., "I made [him] lye downe his sword" [SP 42/6] and "his owne safety & conscience obliged [him] to it after" [SP 42/6 17 Aug 1700]. Interestingly, the second example includes the direct object "him" (here shown in parentheses) written in the margin of the transcribed testimony, presumably added as a correction after the initial testimony was transcribed. Hence, the initial transcription without an explicit direct object might have been more closely reflective of the speech of Henry Atkinson who was making the testimony and potentially more reflective of common speech of sailors rather than the Standard English that court clerks would have been expected to use. In short, such evidence might suggest that sailors not only permitted the fronting of direct objects but may also have omitted them from speech altogether in contexts where the object referent was understood from context.

Indirect objects expressed after the direct object are often used without either the preposition "to" or "for", contrary to standard modern usage that requires a prepositional phrase in contexts where indirect objects follow the direct object.[4] Sailors sometimes expressed indirect objects (italicized) after prepositions (in bold), e.g., "to make room **for** *him*" [SP 42/6] and "to fetch provisions **to** *the*

---

[3]Although the context of the letter makes it clear that the author is referring to payment, there is no explicit reference to a direct object (e.g., "money" or "wages") in the clause that might serve as an antecedent referent.

[4]Millward & Hayes explain that Middle English saw an increase in the use of prepositions to clarify the relationships between constituents of a sentence that no longer carried the distinctive inflections of Old English determining grammatical function. (2012: 178). Regarding the use of prepositional particles with indirect objects, they explain that since Old English, when both indirect and direct objects are present in a clause in the DO+IO order, the construction may occur without a prepositional particle, e.g., Shakespeare's "'twas men I lack'd, and you will give *them me*" (Henry VI, Part 2,c. 1591, 3.1.345). They further stress, "this option is still available in British English, but has been lost in American English, where give me it is acceptable, but give it me is not" (Millward & Hayes 2012: 321).

others" [HCA 1/99 New Providence 1722]. Yet more commonly, when the indirect object occurs at the end of the clause, it is used without a preposition. The archetypical verb that demands a direct object and an indirect object, "to give", shows this prepositional omission most clearly, e.g., "liberty was given *me* to go" [CO 5/1411/28], "Orders will be given *you*" [CO 5/1411/658], "he did not give it *him*" [SP 42/6], and "They had Brandy given *them*" [HCA 1/9/14]. Other verbs that necessitate both direct and indirect objects are expressed with comparable syntax, e.g., "which was granted *me*" [1045.f.3/1/10], "I shall lose all my mony *him*" [HCA 1/101/317], "he brought his privities & showed them *me*" [HCA 1/99/4], and "we had a pilot ordered *us*" [ADM 52/2/9]. It is possible that sailors did not assign a great deal of importance to expressing indirect objects, as exemplified by two court depositions in which they are added in superscript by the court clerk, "his unjust dealings ^to us^ may meet him" [SP 42/6], and "made him lay down his swoard, but gave it ^him^ again" [SP 42/6]. However, even when expressed, indirect objects were not required to follow prepositions when placed after the direct object, as in modern standard usage, e.g., "give **it** *to me*" but were permitted to stand alone as complementary object constituents to the transitive verb.

7.2 Subordination and coordination

7.2.1 Syntactic complexity

The corpus of written Ship English is notable for its complexity in terms of clause subordination and extensive use of adverbial phrases.[5] It may be that such complexity derives, at least in part, from the stylistics expected from formal letter writing during the period. One letter (reproduced in full below) dated 1700 and addressed to the Admiralty is punctuated as a single sentence:

> My lords of the Admiralty — having received an acct from Capt Fairbourne, who Commands the ships last sent to Newfoundland, that he has suspended Lieutenent Lilburn the chief officer of the Forces at Newfoundland, I am Commanded by their Lordsps to send you the Copy of Capt Fairbourne's letter,

---

[5]I acknowledge that various documents in the corpus were extremely difficult to evaluate at the syntactic level owing to the frequent instances of incomplete or damaged documents and illegible text because of handwriting style, unfamiliar symbols, and ink stains, fading and discoloration. Syntactic analysis was also impeded by unconventional punctuation and capitalization that does not always make it clear where sentence breaks were intended. Thus, the corpus of material from which I could draw data for this analysis was significantly reduced in comparison to the data available for analysis of noun and verb phrases in Chapters 6 and 7.

as also of the severall affidavits and Complaints which ledd him to the doing thereof, and am to desire that you will lay the same before the Rt honble Mr Secretary Vernon I am your most humble servant. [SP 42/6/3]

The primary clause of the letter is expressed in the passive voice: "I am Commanded by their Lordsps to send you the Copy of Capt Fairbourne's letter" and starts after 35 words (nearly 40% of the 88-word letter) which together comprise a noun phrase salutation, an adverbial phrase providing sequential information, two relative clauses (one embedded within the other), and a noun phrase appositive giving additional information about the direct object of the second embedded relative clause. After this main clause, there is another adverbial phrase of association with an embedded relative clause and a further subordinate clause that is coordinated by the conjunction "and" but lacks an explicit nominal subject (assumed to be the same first person as the primary clause) and a conclusive prepositional phrase that is adverbial in function. All of this runs onto an unpunctuated but independent clause that concludes the letter with a customary salutation. Frequent subordination and insertion of adverbial information in letters such as these created extraordinarily complex sentences and seem to suggest that mariners favored syntactic complexity in letter-writing.

To contextualize this epistolary syntactic complexity, we must remember that short but syntactically-complex letters were commonplace during the period when letter-writing was encouraged as "a practical skill for the rising classes" (Mitchell 2007: 178) yet was promoted through letter-writing manuals and explicit instruction in vocational schools that emulated Latin models (see Webster Newbold's "Letter Writing and Vernacular Literacy in Sixteenth-Century England" 2007: 127–140). Classical models promoted multiple complex structures with rhetorical devices and biblical and metaphorical allusions that were explicitly composed to demonstrate learning and status. Millward & Hayes (2012) further explain that promotion of Classical syntax was on the rise in the Early Modern English period due to the revival of Classical learning throughout the Renaissance, and thus:

> "Elegant" English came to be characterized by long, heavily subordinated, periodic sentences (as in the opening lines of The Canterbury Tales) and by such devices as parallelism, couplets, balanced clauses, and use of absolute participles (as in "Today being the 4th of July..."). At the same time, the older, native tradition of cumulative, paratactic sentences was never completely lost. (Millward & Hayes 2012: 275)

The result was that generations of aspiring midshipmen, who were often re-lied upon to compose routine communications, wrote in ways that emulated a heightened Latinate style. Higher-ranking officers composing their routine com-munications in English would also have defaulted to stylistic devices learned as part of their education in the prestigious Latin models. It would appear that, as a result, heavily subordinated syntax is favored even in communications of a basic nature. To illustrate, one senior officer writing a letter to inform a colleague of his arrival in New York composes a complex series of subordinating clauses and adverbial constituents before coming to the point after nearly 70 words of his opening sentence:

> Tho I had great cuase to have expected your Return to Boston at the time of my arrival to this place, one of my Governments [government men] which his Majesty has been pleased to committ to my Charge, but being Informed by the ships that Lately came from Madagascar that you were upon a further cruse, and did not doubt of your makeing of a good voyadge, I have therefore thought fitt by this opportunity to acquaint you of my arrivall [...]. [HCA 1/98/128]

Thus, even when the intentions of the authors were to communicate relatively simple messages, their letters are often composed with a heightened style in-corporating heavy subordination and complex syntax more suited to classical rhetoric. However, as this was a trend among literate classes during the period, although it features in the corpus of Ship English, it is not necessarily a trait that sailors expressed more than any other literate population of the time.

Sailors' depositions also incorporate significant complexity within clause struc-ture and this may be explained by considering that the formality of the context that promoted complexity and subordination in sailors' letters may also have in-fluenced their formal speech. One excerpt from a transcribed witness statement, dated March 28, 1722, narrates the events of a pirate attack:

> About Eleven a Clock, She being come within Pistol Shot A Brest of Us, and a black Flag, or Pendant, hoisted at their main Top Mast Head, We Struck the French Ensign, that had continued hoisted at our Staff till now, and displayed the Kings Colours, giveing her at the Same time our Borad side, which was immediately returned by them again but with unequal Damage, their Mizon top Mast falling, and some of their rigging being disabled [...]. [HCA 1/99/14]

The primary clause "We Struck the French Ensign [...] and displayed the Kings Colours" is preceded by a prepositional phrase functioning as an adverb of time, a participle phrase functioning as a pseudo-subordinate clause (see §5.5.2 Present participle phrases) and an adverbial phrase linked by the conjunction "and" but missing a prepositional head. Following the main clause (which is itself interrupted by a relative clause) comes another participle phrase with an embedded relative clause and an adverbial phrase linked by the conjunction "but". The utterance concludes with an absolute phrase (a clause missing its auxiliary) and another participle phrase with pseudo-subordinate clause status. Frequent subordination and insertion of adverbial information in transcribed depositions such as these suggests that mariners favored syntactic complexity in speech as well as in letter-writing.[6]

It may be argued that emotive depositions such as the one cited above in which the speaker reflects on the events of a pirate attack are more prone to complexity in expression as the speaker unconsciously reflects the confusion and pace associated with the event in their syntax. However, excerpts from witness testimonies that relate commonplace events with presumably little emotional agitation also feature complex syntax. For example, one witness explanation of how a defendant entered service on a specific vessel along with some other sailors features syntax comparable to the previous narration of a pirate attack:

> He being a foremast man of his Ma[jes]ties Ship the Phenix Capt John Ferrell Comander upon takeing of a ship called the *Blessing* in Paratt Roade was together with Lieutenant William Bing (who was made Comander of her) James Green James Lynam Richard Cravat James Harrison Robert Day and severall others put on board of the said ship *Blessing* by the order of the said Capt Ferrell, to serve in her. [HCA 1/52/127]

The primary clause of this utterance "He [...] was [...] put on board of the said ship *Blessing*" is interrupted by various adverbial constituents and relative clauses that provide circumstantial information and significantly obscure the clarity of the main clause. Although it is not assumed that this memory prompts any emotive agitation from the witness making the statement, it reflects syntactic complexity with multiple subordination nonetheless and suggests that this manner of speech may have been customary among sailors in the formal context of the court.

---

[6]The caveat remains however that the syntactic complexity may be owing to the court clerk's composition, punctuation, and style of reporting the speech rather than an accurate representation of the spoken mode.

Although the formality of writing letters or making court testimony may have prompted a degree of syntactic complexity, the complexity observed in the corpus of Ship English under study certainly may reflect the spoken mode itself.[7] Speech acts need not adhere to the rules that restrict clause composition in writing conventions and are not defined by punctuation or paragraphing. Speech is also a mode in which prosody, pitch, and normative expectations shared by the speaker and hearer shape meaning in such a way that its representation in prose (particularly without punctuation) is difficult to follow. For instance one witness's responded, when asked if a prisoner had any share of stolen goods reads, "yes he had all the pyrates had shared they were all sent for to go upon the quarter deck" [CO 5/1411/78]. Another witness testimony is difficult to follow in prose owing to the extent of adverbial interjections that may have been spoken in a different tone to aid clarity in oral communication:

> Harry Glasby that at first the Man was forced for he Saw the Quarter Master Goe who had told he wou'd being all the Enef Men out of this Dutch Interloping Ships that he belong'd to but that he had Opportunity enough as had all of them to have left the Pyrate Ship at Sieraleon if the pleased. [HCA 1/99/105]

Some transcriptions include transitional markers to aid reader comprehension, such as the words "first" and "second" in the following example, yet remain challenging to decode at first sight without the aid of conventional punctuation:

> they mett wth unother Dutch man with 12 Guns and 32 or 33 men the first yeilded without fighting the second did fight agood while and at last yeilded he gave them quarter he had 4 or 500 small barrells of brandy on board he took their best Guns and so let them go. [CO 5/1411/98]

Givón explains that speech does not reflect the traditional dichotomy between declarative and non-declarative clauses that writing distinguishes, but rather is a much more fluid mode that features clusters of categorical peaks which communicate meaning along a multi-dimensional continuum (2001: 288). Hence, the

---

[7] As discussed in §1.3.2, over half of the materials in the corpus derive from court records which feature testimony composed in spoken mode and transcribed. Thus, although I consider the excerpts of such testimony as representative of the spoken mode I acknowledge that they are written documents and potentially ambiguous sources with which to discuss syntactic features representative of spoken modality.

complexity of the syntax in witness depositions may derive from the rapid syntactic and categorical shifts that commonly occur in spoken forms. Indeed, when authors of narrative fiction attempt to reflect free-indirect speech, they consciously increase the frequency of subordinating particles, embedding and disruption of the finite clause with coordinated non-finite clauses and incongruent phrases juxtaposed by coordinating conjunctions (Sotirova 2016: 181). So, although written representations of speech in the form of letters and transcribed testimony may have prompted their own syntactic complexity owing to the conventions of the context, the modality of speech itself is inherently complex and likely to include multiple adverbial phrases and subordinating clauses that may or may not be coherent when disassociated from the deixis of their original spoken form.

7.2.2 Subordinators

Given the syntactic complexity of Ship English illustrated above, subordinators feature heavily in the corpus to organize and embed linguistic units in larger structural hierarchies. One salient marker of subordination (discussed in Chapter 5) is the use of present participle phrases that function at the clause level by providing attendant circumstances, e.g., (with the subordinated clause italicized for emphasis) "Shipp Albermarle Undocked & Took in 70 Tunn of Ballast *we having 30 Tun of Ballast Remaining in the Shipp*" [ADM 52/2/5] and "I likewise advised him how dangerous it was to have in such amount Villains Aboard *they having the command of his small Arms*" [HCA 1/98/271]. These subordinate structures commonly take the participle form of the copula and function in a manner equivalent to using the inflected form of the verb, e.g., "Lancaster Sayled hence for Portsm *she being very Leakey*" [ADM 52/2/5] and "Their shipp on fire *she being so Disabled*" [ADM 52/3/7]. See Chapter 5 on Noun Phrases, and specifically §5.2.2 Present participle phrases and §5.2.3 Phrases headed with "being" for full discussion.

The lexeme "that" features heavily in the corpus as a subordinator of dependent clauses in addition to its function as a relative pronoun. The following example demonstrates the use of both functions (subordinator in italics and relative pronoun in bold):

> James Munjoy Cooper of the same Ship — Deposed *that* he saw Smith beat and forced into the Boat from them, *that* when he returned again with Leave of the Pyrates for Some things of his own **that** were left, they would not trust him. [HCA 1/99/21]

The first use of the lexeme "that" in the excerpt "Deposed *that* he saw Smith..." functions as we might anticipate its use in Modern English, to mark a clause that is subordinated into the role of a noun phrase, specifically the dependent clause functions as the direct object of the verb "deposed". Interestingly, this type of standard usage is often associated with phrases that appear to feature the voice of the court clerk or official rather than the deposed sailor himself, e.g., "this Deponent further saith, *that* in Corasao" [HCA 1/53/67], "The Prisoner owned his being on board, and the Robbery but *that* any Irregularities he might commit, was the Drink" [HCA 1/99/40], and "he knew no more of the matter, [other] than *that* they were all very drunk" [HCA 1/99 Cape Coast of Africa, Feb 4 1734, 5]. It may be that this type of standard usage owes more to the compositions of the clerks transcribing the depositions or the literate court officials surmising court proceedings than the syntactic choices of the speakers themselves. Furthermore, this interpretation of standard usage associated with educated clerks can be supported by its occurrence in formal letters written by literate sailors, e.g., "I [...] am to devise *that* you will lay the same before the rt. hon. Mr. Secretary Vernon" [SP 42/6] and "I hoped ere this to have finisht the repair of the Hulle but this bad weather hath prevented, *thatt* yett wee want three or fower faire dayes" [ADM 106/288/15]. Thus, although the standard use of "that" as a subordinator for dependent clauses in larger matrix clauses exists in the corpus, it may reflect the compositions of literate sailors and court officials rather than usage among illiterate crew who were not formally educated.

If one function of the lexeme "that" was to mark literacy and formality (and therefore also status) it is not surprising that sailors who were not formally educated appropriated the word to increase their perceived status in the court and lend credibility to their testimony.[8] The lexeme "that" is repeated numerous times in court testimony in ways that do not correspond to its function either as a relative pronoun or as a subordinator, and this may reflect the hypercorrection of uneducated sailors. The most common variant usage of "that" in sailors' testimonies was to mark the opening of an independent clause, e.g., "*That* Roberts the Commander of the Pyrate Ship, also himself told him the said Smith was and shou'd be compelled into their Company" [HCA 1/99/21], "Sammuel Sterling knows him, *that* his Friends were well to pass" [HCA 1/99/92], "if some design

---

[8]Although here I discuss the use of the word "that" in court depositions as they show the most frequent occurrence of the phenomenon, it is also evident in logbooks, e.g., "Very Hard Gales — *that* we was forsed to Stand to the Westward" [ADM 52/1/1]. It also occurs in official communications with the Admiralty, e.g., "My lords of the admiralty, having received an acct. from Capt. Fairbourne who commands the Ships last sent to Newfoundland, *that* he has suspended Lieutenant Lilburn the chief officer" [SP 42/6].

he was about proved successfull, *that* he should no longer have occasion to use the sea" [SP 42/6], and "he was kept aboard the Pyrate, *That* this prisoner had a pair of Buckles" [HCA 1/99 Jamaica Aug 11 1740]. The logical connection between some of the clauses connected with "that" may suggest that sailors were using "that" as a coordinating conjunction. However, examples of the word in juxtaposition with coordinating conjunctions appears to discredit this interpretation as they would render the word "that" redundant as a conjunction, e.g., (with both words marked for emphasis) "The Carpenter had been beaten by the Mr Wm Parsons *and that* he dyed shortly after" [HCA 1/52/176] and "the Prisoner should not go, *for that* he wanted a Polite [...] [indecipherable]" [HCA 1/99 Jamaica Aug 11 1740]. The word "that" is also often juxtaposed with subordinating conjunctions that similarly render the word "that" redundant as a subordinator e.g., "some time *after that* I write you last" [HCA 1/99 loose letter c. 1730], "but know no Particulars *unless that* he wou'd often be merry and Drinking as others" [HCA 1/99/120], "Here is A great depression of her *BeCause that* She layeth Here with A faire wainde [wind]" [HCA 1/101/555], and "*That when* the murderers were asleep they fell upon them" [both from HCA 1/99/10]. In short, it is possible that the context of complex language and expectations of formality in the courts of the Admiralty and official communications with them conditioned the use of "that" as a discourse marker to index status and this explains why so many samples contain independent clauses that feature the word in a manner that has no apparent syntactic function.

In contrast to the suggestion that the lexeme "that" was appropriated by uneducated sailors and inserted erroneously in speech, there is evidence that it was used to form cumulative super-structures that may have been punctuated incorrectly in transcription. In the following example, the word "that" is used three times, the first of which is logically interpreted as a subordinator, but the subsequent two might be interpreted as redundant markers of independent clauses given the author's punctuation:

> Samuel Lands being sworn Declared *that* the Prisoner with three more of the Crew first time of landing took said Deponent in June last & bound him. *That* the Prisoner was aiding and Assisting in taking and going away with the Sloop Discovery Time and manner aforesaid. And *that* when the sd[said] [defendant John] Lands went over the Houses The Prisoners struck the Deponent. [HCA 1/99 New Providence 1722]

Yet, the speaker of this excerpt is educated as indicated by the content of his utterance and his use of formal vocabulary such as "being sworn", "said Deponent", and the "manner aforesaid", and he would presumably know how to use "that" as a subordinator in formal speech.[9] If we bear in mind that the punctuation of the above spoken testimony was inserted when it was transcribed and was not spoken as part of the statement, we can disregard it and consider the excerpt as a single utterance (i.e., sentence). When we disregard the punctuation of the transcribed testimony and consider it as a single unit of meaning, we can appreciate that the speaker was composing a complex main clause in which the transitive verb "declared" is followed by three coordinated direct objects: firstly, "that the Prisoner with three more of the Crew first time of landing took said Deponent in June last & bound him", secondly, "That the Prisoner was aiding and Assisting in taking and going away with the Sloop Discovery Time and manner aforesaid", and thirdly, "that when the sd[said] [defendant John]Lands went over the Houses The Prisoners struck the Deponent". This interpretation is supported further by the fact that the conjunction "and" precedes the last item in the list. The linguistic environment of the court provides one reason that the speaker might have composed such a long list-like statement with repeated clauses marked for subordination. In court, the repeated use of the subordinator "that" to build cumulative structures mirrors the formal language of the articles that accused men were called to answer, e.g., the list of offences presented to Thomas Button on February 22, 1634,[10] which opens with article 1: "For *that* beinge imployed by the lords commissions for the Admiral on that Coast, hee left his charge and his majasties shippe wherein to a leiutenannte contrarie to the dutie of his said place" (Hill 2013: 46, with added emphasis). This first article is then followed by a further ten articles, seven of which open with the word "that" in continuation of the initial charge, e.g., article 6, "*That* Sir Thomas button kepte abourd the 9th Whelp divers Unable for service in her in soe much as the master of her Wrote that unless better men were taken in their places, he durst not got to Sea in her" (Hill 2013: 47). Based on such linguistic templates in which a series of independent articles open with "that" and comprise a list of charges, the fact that speakers in court were using similar structures to mark their responses to the charges seems entirely appropriate. Furthermore, this strategy that marked a speaker's familiarity with court rhetoric was available to all sailors making statements on their own behalf, e.g., the testimony of Elias Bolt:

---

[9]The speaker is clearly educated and is also potentially a court official given the use of the third person to refer to both the deponent and the prisoner. However there is no accompanying text to identify the speaker and so this possibility is not assumed but hereby acknowledged.

[10]This list of offences is cited in Appendix II of *Early Seventeenth Century Piracy and Bristol* (Hill 2013: 46–48) and is sourced from the Calendar of State Papers (Domestic) Available at www.british-history.ac.uk.

the Prisoner Piloted her in, and *that* he and three others were sent to see what She was, *that* when he came under the Stern of said Privateer they Pointed their Guns at him and he Cryed out for Quarter, *that* then they took down the Dutch and hoisted Spanish Colours. [HCA 1/99 Jamaica Aug 11 1740]

Elias Bolt appears to be using the word "that" in a way that reflects how it functions in the articles, except instead of marking cohesion between a list of charges expressed as independent clauses, he is marking cohesion between a series of events that are expressed as independent clauses. Thus, the use of "that" with independent clauses may indeed be evidence of hypercorrection, but could also be an indicator of the linguistic environment of the court system in which cumulative super-structures were acceptable not only in written articles, but also in the utterances of those who spoke in court.

7.2.3 Coordinating conjunctions

Sailors made frequent use of coordinating conjunctions to connect the internal constituents of larger syntactic structures, yet the way that they did this shows variation from standard usage. They sometimes used conjunctions to join similar constituents in accordance with the Parallelism Requirement in Standard English ()Osborne2006 e.g., the excerpt "we told him from whence we came and wither bound" [CO 5/1411/22] that conjoins two prepositional phrases "from whence we came" and "whither bound", and the excerpt "Sammuel Sterling knows him, that his Friends were well to pass in North Yarmouth, & that the Prisoner one had a honest Reputation" [HCA 1/99/92] that conjoins two subordinate clauses headed by the subordinator "that". However, sailors also used conjunctions to join dissimilar constituents in contrast with the syntactic rule of parallel structure. Sometimes the distinction between the conjoined constituents relates to composition and not function, e.g., the excerpt "to whom she and the goods in her belong" [SP 42/6] in which a pronoun "she" is conjoined with a noun phrase "the goods in her", and the excerpt "I am a Man that have, and can feed my Enemies" [445f.1/31] in which an indicative base verb "have" is conjoined with a verb phrase using conditional modality "can feed". Both excerpts show conjoined constituents that are similar in function but dissimilar in composition; in the first example, the pronoun and noun phrase structure are composed differently, but they are both nominal in function, and in the second example the modality and complexity of the verb structures are different, they are both verbal in function. Yet sometimes the distinction between the conjoined constituents is functional,

e.g., the excerpt "some of his officers in all abt 16 were forced from the ship &
to go away in the long boats" [HCA 1/53/42] in which a prepositional phrase
"from the ship" is conjoined with a verbal infinitive phrase "to go away"; the excerpt "The Prisoner owned his being on board, and the Robbery" [HCA 1/99/40]
in which a gerund phrase headed by a determiner "his being on board" is conjoined with a noun phrase "the Robbery", and the excerpt "He thought himselfe
in ill companie and how that he ought m [...] [illegible]" [ASSI 45/4/1/135/4 1650]
in which a prepositional adverb phrase headed by a reflexive pronoun "himself
in ill companie" is conjoined with a relative clause headed by a fronted interrogative subordinator "how that he ought [...]" In sum, sailors made frequent use
of conjunctions to join parallel structures in a way that adheres to standard usage, yet evidence indicates that they also used coordinating conjunctions to join
constituents that were dissimilar in composition and in function.

Transcribed depositions show the use of coordinating conjunctions not only
to join internal structures but also to introduce new clauses. The reliance on
conjunctions to compound clauses rather than subordinate them may reflect the
heavy use of conjunctions such as "and", and "but" in the spoken mode. Wennerstrom's work on prosody and discourse analysis (2001) finds that conjunctions
"tend to be located at the periphery of constituents [...] [and] tend to be preceded
or followed by pauses" (2001: 77). An excerpt from the transcribed deposition of
Elias Bolt shows this type of conjunction use (emphasized in bold) at the periphery of clauses and predicate constituents that would have permitted him to pause
for breath during the testimony in a way that did not interrupt units of speech:

> that when they took her they Manned her **and** sent her out under the Com-
> mand of a Lieut **and** took a Statia Sloop **and** cut her Mast on board; **And**
> being Asked of the Capt. Ordered the Prisoner into the Canoe, Said that
> he could not tell, **but** that he did not seem to be under Compulsion, Said
> the Capt had a Commission from the Spanish Flag, **And** being asked by the
> Prisoner if he did leave said Privateer as soon as he Could Answered that
> the Prisoner went away from the Privateer a Saturday Night **and** the Dept
> a Monday Morning that he heard he had Two Shares aboard the Privateer,
> **And** that he left her because he was not respected as formerly. [HCA 1/99
> Jamaica Aug 11 1740]

Wennerstrom notes that although conjunctions and their associated prosody
often occur together, it is the prosody that is essential to meaning and not the
conjunction. As a result, a pause can condition the omission of conjunctions in
speech; she states, "prosody provides crucial information for the interpretation

of a lexical conjunction and may even act in lieu of it" (2001: 77). Prosodic conditioning may therefore explain the apparent omission of conjunctions in places where we might anticipate them in the written mode, e.g., (with conjunctions added and emphasized) "our cable was cutt [**and**] was about 21 fatham from the Anchor" [ADM 52/1/8], "at Six the Sally rose Came up [**and**] at Eight a Small Hoy with petty warrant [officers]" [ADM 52/2/3], and "when he Saw the Kings Colours he run down, [**and**] Confessed he had been on Board" [HCA 1/99/78]. This type of omission also seems to occur with conjunctions showing a cause-effect relationship, e.g., "the fleet all wayed [**because** they] had orders to go on the French coast" [ADM 52/1/1], "they began to engage us [**and so**] we fought them till 11" [ADM 52/1/8], and "he had the King of Ennglande pape[r] which they demanding to see the informant went downe into his cabbin" [HCA 1/53/3] which is interpreted to mean: "he had the King of England's paper (i.e., authority) which they demanded to see [**and so**] the informant went down into this cabin". The evidence of conjunctions joining predicate and clause-level structures in the continuous speech of court testimony thus appears to confirm that the syntax conforms to expectations of usage in the spoken modality, and this is corroborated by the omission of conjunctions which would have been suggested by deictic features in the original spoken form.

Certain conjunctions that can perform other syntactic functions frequently occur in their adverbial roles in the corpus of Ship English under study.[11] The lexeme "but" is sometimes used as a coordinating conjunction (emphasized in bold), e.g., "having his ship plundered by them **But** in a short time had a farm common and traded with them" [HCA 1/98/47], and "itt begun tto cleere and the day was Exstrordnary hot **butt** [there was] no wind" [DDB6 8/4], and "I dont know **but** was sent from new york" [HCA 1/98/47]. Yet it is more common in the corpus as an adverb meaning "only" or "just", that can occur in a pre-verbal position (emphasized in italics), e.g., "our Ship *but* could not gett her keel out" [ADM 52/1/8], "and Capt Every *but* would have united himselfe with Capt Esq" [HCA 1/53/14]. It can also occur in a post-verbal position, e.g., "there being *but* little wind that evening" [HCA 1/52/1], "we gained *but* little ground" [ADM 52/1/7], and "had bin *but* 7: weeks from England" [ADM 52/1/7]. Interestingly, the use of this lexeme as an adverb and as a conjunction can occur in close proximity, e.g., (adverb italicized, conjunction in bold) "with the wind att no [north] **butt**

---

[11]It is worth noting that some lexemes occur more frequently as conjunctions than in other syntactic functions. For example, "except" appears to occur more regularly as a conjunction than a preposition, e.g., "I found it most safe to say little, **except** I had good Authority for it" and "they could not come out, **except** I let them" [445f.1/31, and 38]. Such distributional frequency is not presented in any detail here but identified as a potential direction for future study.

itt *butt* blu very litl" [DDB6 8/4] and "great timber *but* short **butt** usefull for his masters service" [ADM 106/288/35]. In addition, the lexeme "so" is almost exclusively used with an adverbial function in the corpus, e.g., "he had ordered *so* to do" [SP 42/6], "and for yor *so* doing this shall be yor sufficient Warrant" [CO 5/1411/666], "and *so* soon as our boat came on board" [445f.1/33], and "thought none *so* brisk at it as himself" [HCA 1/99/36]. Thus, although lexemes with the capacity to serve as conjunctions commonly appear in the corpus, their syntactic functions as coordinating conjunctions may be secondary to their role as adverbs in prose that relies so heavily on adverbial modification.

7.3 Swearing as a discourse marker

7.3.1 Swearing to mark communicative intent

Sailors of the age of sail were and are still characterized by their tendency to use profane language. Although there are few examples of such profanity in official communications or logbooks, there are various direct and indirect representations of profane speech in court testimony and a few in sailors' journals. These range from relatively mild and quaint descriptions, e.g., "having engaged them into warm words" [HCA 1/99/109], "he threatened the deponent with hard languages" [HCA 1/99/105], and "Mr. Anderson gave our Leittenant and Capt. Scurrolous Language" [ADM 52/1/8] to the more direct testimony of what individuals and crews were heard saying, e.g., "abused him calling him a super Cargo Son of a B___h that he Slaved the Men, and that it was Such Dogs as he as put men on Pyrating" [HCA 1/99/102], "Damn you. You shant come up yet; if you do, I'll shoot you" [HCA 1/99/7], and "calling them *hijos de puta, Borrachos, infames, Ladrones*, Bastards, Drunkards, infamous theeves, and pyrates" (Gage 1648: 201). Indeed, swearing was so common among sailors in times of peace as well as times of conflict that the shanties they sang while working were often unpublishable and needed to be censored for public consumption. Whall (cited in Palmer 1986: xxv) explains that seventeenth-century shanties were often obscene because "the words which sailor John put to them when unrestrained were the veriest filth". Many dismiss the occurrence of profanity in sailors' communities as another piece of evidence to show the low-born and uncultured nature of common sailors, yet Claridge & Arnovick recognize the pragmatic role of cursing as a discourse marker (2010: 167). Among sailors of all ranks and aboard all types of vessels,[12] closer analysis indicates that swearing was an important part of Ship English with a range of functions primarily associated with the rhetoric of oral cultures.

Aboard sailing vessels of the early colonial period, the same as today, swearing serves as a marker of emphasis equivalent to the way in which an exclamation point might function in orthography. This interpretation is corroborated by William Richardson, whose journal of 1850 attests to sailors' traditions relating to on-board communication, "a good round oath, but scarcely an expletive, either before or after an order had been given, made it more emphatic, and was considered merely as the proper emphasis" (cited in Adkins & Adkins 2008: 214). The type of oath that Williams refers to in this citation appears to have been ritualistic and may have served the same purpose as other discourse markers associated with the giving and receiving of orders such as the mariners' whistle, e.g., "three huzza's [cheers] all the sailors gave, taking the signal from the boatswain's whistle" [445f.1/510]. Just like the punctuation of the boatswain's whistle or the ritual responses of the crew, accompanying an order with mild profanity may have been the default protocol, and given such a context, orders like the following command to attack are unremarkable: "[he] cryed out to Roberts Da—n you give the French Ship a Broad:Side, and board him at once" [HCA 1/99/29]. Individual instances of swearing to add emphatic stress to commands strengthen the interpretation of cursing as a marker of emphasis, which was extended to other contexts, e.g., one witness testifies that when an assailant saw him watching his attack he called out, "damn it, you stand by and will not lend a hand" [HCA 1/99/5]. Thus, we might consider swearing as a form of emphatic punctuation inherent to the largely oral nature of shipboard communication.

Swearing is historically a marker of integrity and continued to serve as confirmation of a speaker's honesty or to attest to the plausibility of a proposed action in Ship English. Ammon explains that in Anglo-Saxon oral culture, "there was no concept of the word or promise being legally binding in and of itself in early medieval law: something else was required" (2013: 516). The pledge or oath came to serve the purpose of that "something else" that would convert the spoken word into something binding, and as such oath-swearing came to be explicitly associated with legal proceedings. Furthermore, Hughes' seminal monograph on swearing explains how "Oaths were binding and oath-breaking was a serious offense" (Hughes 1991: 43). Given this context, it is not surprising that sailors

---

[12] Although common sailors were more likely to have been brought to trial and testified against in a manner that recorded their use of profane language, abuses attributed to senior officers and captains also refer to profane language and this is particularly notable aboard pirate, privateer, and independent trading vessels.

used oaths as a testament to trustworthiness in courtrooms where their lives might depend on their perceived honesty. For example one recruit on a pirate ship argued that he should be acquitted because "he also on his Oath says that no new:Comer amongst the Company were suffered to goe a Plundering" [HCA 1/99/23]. Another recruit pleads for his acquittal, "Harry Glasby Swears, that one Philips a Pyrate had forced him" [HCA 1/99/96]. Both examples show sailors using oaths and swearing to assert their honesty before the authority figures of the Admiralty courts.

Even in routine matters aboard ship, sailors took oaths (i.e., swore) to make promises, e.g., "he was made Gunners Mate of the *Fortune* about Six Weeks before She was taken the Gunner swearing he should accept of it" [HCA 1/99/78]. This context explains why the word "swearing" applies to a whole spectrum of speech acts, from making formal pledges in the form of religious oaths through the transitory middle-ground of blasphemy and finally incorporating the type of profanity typically associated with animal imagery, body parts, and bodily functions (especially reproduction and defecation). Gehweiler makes implicit connections between the two ends of such a spectrum in his definition of swearing as "the taking of a religious oath i.e. to a formal or solemn declaration or statement invoking God; later it was also used to refer to profane or blasphemous language" (2010: 320–321) and Archer explicitly connects the phenomena: "Swearing, cursing and, indeed, oath-making are also linked historically" (2010: 398). Hence, making a religious oath to confirm the veracity of spoken testimony, swearing or cursing with the use of religious or pagan imagery, and using profane speech all have a common conceptual origin associated with the confirmation of a speaker's trustworthiness and strength of character.[13] Therefore, when the record alludes to a

---

[13]It is worth noting that most examples of swearing in the corpus that are either cited directly or referred to as indirect or reported speech contain religious iconography or allusion, e.g., "Damn it [HCA 1/99/5], "G— D—m you" [HCA 1/99/32], "asked what a Devil they took him for" [HCA 1/99/147], and "go to Hell" [HCA 1/99/152]. The high frequency of swearing with religious allusion may have resulted from several new words of religious abuse that were created during the sixteenth-century English Reformation and the fact that existing ones ameliorated due to the weakened potency of Catholic sacred names (Hughes 1991: 95). The many reported instances of profane speech in the corpus that are described with the words "oath" or "swearing" (as this alludes to the swearing of an oath) were also probably religious in nature, specifically given that in the sixteenth and seventeenth centuries the word "swearing" related explicitly to the swearing of oaths and not so much the profane or obscene language that we consider swearing by modern standards (McEnery 2006: 52). The shift from religious to secular swearing occurred during the Renaissance prompting the concurrent promotion of censorship (Hughes 1991: 102). Yet, profane speech associated with animal imagery and reproductive function are less frequent in the corpus and mostly feature in the form of abusive salutation, e.g., "Bastards, Drunkards" (Gage 1648) "you son of a bitch" [HCA 1/99 Williamsburg, Aug 14 1729], and "Dogs" [HCA 1/99/102].

sailor speaking "wth Oathes and other ill language" [HCA 1/99/135] we should remember that even if the utterance were profanity, it could be situated along a continuum of oath-making which was explicitly deployed to demonstrate trustworthiness. Hence, when sailors made oaths, swore, or uttered profanities, they were consciously choosing to use language that referenced honesty and integrity.[14]

7.3.2 Swearing to mark modality

Ship English was primarily a spoken language with embedded features of ritual and rhetoric common to other performance mediums. Some excerpts in witness testimony allude to the performative nature of the language, e.g., "Little David Swore at him indeed, but it Seemed to be done rather to Satisfye the Prisoner than any thing else" [HCA 1/99/96]. Other examples of hyperbole similarly attest to the performative nature of the speech act, e.g., an excerpt from a testimony describing a surgeon who signed the articles of a pirate vessel willingly, "he was the first Surgeon that had done So, Swearing immediately upon it, that he was now as great a Rogue as any of them" [HCA 1/99/81]. The witness testimony cited below gives another example of ritual in the performance of a threat repeated three times with swearing as a marker in the final warning, e.g., (with bold and italic emphasis added):

> [he] **Came to the Deponent** and told him he understood he has some jewels and Rings and with a pistol and Cutlass in his hand Said he would blow his brains out if he did not deliver them [...] but afterwards **Came a Second time** and demanded them in the Same manner [...] then **came a third time** with his pistol corked and his finger upon the trigger *and swore* that the deponent had them and if he did not deliver them forthwith he would instantly kill the Deponent. [HCA 1/99/6]

The repeated threats described in this testimony include a final warning that is accompanied by swearing which indexes a pledge in a way that the previous threats did not; the last warning is therefore designed to elicit compliance regardless of previous refusals.

The use of swearing with rhetorical function might reflect the same type of realis mood that features as an integral part of the system of tense, mood and

---

[14]I acknowledge the irony of using discourse markers that index honesty in a culture that operated on theft, physical violence and systemic deception (see Chapter 4). Yet, perhaps it was the very nature of this culture that prompted sailors to attest to the veracity of their utterances so frequently.

aspect in West African languages and Afro-Atlantic English-lexifier Creoles (Faraclas et al. 2016). In performative cultures that gave rise to many West African and creole languages, Ship English features an overt realis marker that shows firm intent, particularly given the performative and hyperbolic nature of what might have previously been stated. Swearing in Ship English, functioning like the realis markers expressed in the morphemes "kom" and "ò" in Afro-Atlantic English-lexifier Creoles,[15] shows a commitment to action beyond the semantic content of the utterance in a way that underscores the validity of threats and negotiations. Leeson (2008)'s paper on the economics of pirate practices explains how expressing such validity may have been a decisive factor in maritime conflict: "pirates sought to overwhelm victims without violence [...] [and] Crucial to this strategy's effectiveness was pirates' ability to credibly commit to their surrender-or-die policy" (2008: 4–5). Thus, asserting the validity of a threat of violence was integral to the success of many pirate conquests and was essential if the economics of maritime conflict were to result in maximum gains with minimal loss of life, cargo, and equipment. In such contexts, the skillful usage of swearing as a realis marker coupled with a credible show of force may have meant the difference between success and failure, riches or death. One example of how such a skilled performance may have intimidated enemies into submission is described in Gage's journal:

> The Spaniards changed their merry tune into *voto a dios* and *voto a Christo*, in raging, cursing, & swearing... others cursing those that tooke her, and calling them *hijos de puta, Borrachos, infames, Ladrones*, Bastards, Drunkards, infamous theeves, and pyrates; some taking their swords in their hands, as if they would there cut them in pieces, some laying hold of their muskets as if they would there shoot at them, others stamping like mad men, and others grinning their teeth at the poore English prisoners that were in the ship, as if they would stab them for what (they said) their Country men had done. (Gage 1648: 201)

Note that Gage repeats the phrase "as if they would" three times, and the past tense conditional modality of these subjunctive clauses suggests that these ac-

---

[15]N. Faraclas, personal communication, August 9 2016. The connection between sailor's speech, West African languages and Afro-Atlantic English-lexifier Creoles is explicit in this description of the realis marker given that standard forms of English have zero marking for realis mood (i.e., indicative). The overt nature of realis markers in both West African languages and creoles of the Atlantic may further emphasize the role that sailors played in transferring such features and could be a subject for future study.

tions were not, in fact, what the pirates intended. The assumption follows, therefore, that the pirates wanted only to demonstrate their intention to perform such violent actions to the extent that the enemy would believe them and be less likely to resist. Thus, swearing when used as a realis marker in ritualized threats of violence may have reduced conflict and maximized profitability among crews operating in marginalized maritime communities.

In performative contexts, swearing functioned as a realis marker to terrify and subordinate collective groups of enemies with violent threats, yet it was also effective in individual encounters with actual physical violence. Pirates often swore as an accompaniment to physical force when seeking to subordinate individuals in captured vessels, e.g., passenger Elizabeth Fengrove testifies, "the Prisoner was very rude swearing and cursing and forcing her hoop'd petticoat off" [HCA 1/99/79], another witness testifies, "one of the prisoners came up to him and struck him on the shoulder saying you son of a bitch if you offer to make any resistance you are a dead man, and then thrust the deponent down into the Cabbin" [HCA 1/99 Williamsburg, Aug 14 1729]. It appears that in these contexts, although swearing may validate any additional threats that accompany the physical attacks, there appears to be little need to mark physical violence with a realis marker as physical violence is already manifest. In such contexts, swearing may have functioned to mark imperative modality to accompany the instructions that pirates gave to their prisoners. The following deposition demonstrates evidence that swearing may have served as a marker of the imperative mood as it accompanies the instruction which has the most imperative force in a series: "the Spaniards Called to them to bring too, hoist out their Boat and Come on Board, as Swore at them and Called them English Doggs & bid them make hast" [HCA 1/99/6]. The citation above opens with three specific instructions: firstly, bring about (i.e., maneuver) the boat; secondly, hoist the boat out of the water; and thirdly, come on board. However, the fourth and last instruction "make haste" is accompanied by cursing and carries a stronger imperative force than the previous instructions. Such evidence in the corpus, albeit limited, may suggest that the role of swearing as a discourse marker extends beyond the validation of proposed action as a realis marker and implies that swearing may have also marked (or strengthened) the imperative mood, particularly when coupled with physical force.

7.3.3 Swearing to mark agency

Given that swearing often accompanied threats of physical attack and was also often expressed with physical violence to direct individuals with specific orders, it is not surprising that both swearing and violence occurred among crews to establish and reinforce the internal hierarchy of command. Sometimes sailors swore when they asserted the kind of agency that deemed them to be leaders, e.g., "Williams swore he would have water and askd who would go with him, and taking in his hand a hatchet, swore it should not be easy to take him" [HCA 1/99 Williamsburg, Aug 14 1729], and "[he] swore he was Master of the Ship and would do as he thought fit" [HCA 1/99 The American: Weekly Mercury No.618, Oct 28–Nov 4 1731].

Sailors also swore when they defied orders, e.g., one man who refused his allegiance to the ship when commanded to fight Turks, "[the commanding officer] bidding him to go to the Helm, he answered with an Oath, that he has Taken Turks there enough, and did not now belong to the Ship" [HCA 1/99/30] and another man who responds when his senior officer refuses to assign him additional rations from the casket, "the deponent swore that he might take it out himself" [HCA 1/99/7].

However, more commonly, witness testimony describes confrontations involving mid-ranking officers jockeying for status with one aggressor swearing as a prelude to physical violence if there is no clear resolution of the challenge. For example, one witness testimony describes a conflict that starts when a Quartermaster is discovered asleep on duty [HCA 1/52/124]. The Chief Mate who found him, "bidding him to mind his duty and not sleep upon the watch", is challenged by the lower-ranking officer who "called him dog & rogue and swore bitterly that he would heave him over board and laid hold on him endeavouring to do it". This challenge to the Chief Mate's authority is compounded when the Quartermaster "threw him down upon the Deck [...] taking him by the Collar, swearing that he would runine them all". However, the Chief Mate, with support from another officer, subdued the Quartermaster and fettered him in irons for his challenge to the hierarchy of command.[16] In this example of a conflict aboard a naval vessel, the Quartermaster is quickly restrained by a system of command known for its inflexibility. However, the government of pirate ships — in which upward mobility for common sailors was much more feasible than in the naval or merchant service — it was often the captain himself or the superior officers who swore to maintain status over a crew that could replace them.[17] In this way, swearing

---

[16]The Quartermaster's claim that his actions "would runine *them all*" (emphasis in italics) attests to the collective nature of the threat to the entire chain of command rather than being directed just at one specific officer.

[17]See Rediker and specifically the chapters "A Tale of Two Terrors" (2004: 1–18) and "The New Government of the Ship" (p.60–82) for more details about the inflexibility of the naval and merchant service command structure and the comparative freedoms of pirate organizations.

accompanied the subordination of lower-ranking officers and men to assert and maintain a higher status over them, e.g., "Shyrme the Captain commanded him to Armes swearing very much when he told him" [HCA 1/99/75], "[he] swore if he would not come he would beat his brains out" [HCA 1/99/7], "with a great Oath asked him if he knew where he was and gave him a Smart Box in the Ear" [HCA 1/99/109], and "G   D   m you says this Fermion, and I shall see too what a brave Fellow you are when you come down, and beat him very much" [HCA 1/99/32]. Thus, whether swearing was used to accompany a challenge to the established chain of command or was used to reinforce the existing hierarchy, both high-ranking officers and crew swore (often accompanied by threats and violence) to establish and reinforce their individual status.

It may have been the greater opportunities for internal advancement aboard pirate vessels that promoted swearing as a characteristic discourse marker among such communities. Not only did individual pirates have the most to gain from challenging the internal hierarchy of command, but they were also the most likely to use swearing in situations that required realis markers to validate threats and negotiations and the most likely to assert the strength of imperative commands over captives. Pirates swore to gain control of a captured vessel, e.g., "he returned to Roberts who Swearing said he wou'd not only have the Pump but the Mainmast too if he wanted it" [HCA 1/99/135], they swore to impress new crewmen, e.g., "the prisoner often threatened with Oaths to beat him while he was detained on board" [HCA 1/99/45], they swore to intimidate captives, e.g., "Prisoner abused him calling him a super Cargo Son of a B___h [...] he swore if he Spoke another Word ... wou'd throw him over Board" [HCA 1/99/102], and they swore to locate and take valuables, e.g., "shewed him a Small Parsell, at which the Prisoner Swore that he would make him find more" [HCA 1/99/95].[18] One consequence of this proclivity for swearing among pirates is that their communities are identified (and often mocked) for their perceived profanity without much attention having been paid to the social functions of swearing as a discourse marker.[19]

---

[18] Note that the "prisoner" of these depositions refers to the accused pirates and not the prisoners that were taken aboard the pirate ships.

[19] Contrary to Brinton's claim that pragmatic markers such as cursing have no clear grammatical function (cited in Claridge & Arnovick 2010: 167), more recent scholarship recognizes the important role of swearing in maritime culture; for example, see Gilje's (2016) *To Swear like a Sailor: Maritime Culture in America 1750–1850*.

7.3.4 Swearing to mark group identity

Perhaps because their communities were characterized by excessive swearing, pirates also swore as a marker of in-group identity. Hence, various depositions give examples of swearing among crewmates without any suggestion that violence, threat, or challenges to authority are being invoked, e.g., one impressed captive who is assigned the position of carpenter's mate explains, (marked for emphasis):

> [he] wou'd have got clear of the Pyrates but for the Old Carpenter of the Fortune who took a liking to him, his future Behaviour was comfortable to Roberts's humour who *wth Oathes and other ill language* used to send him on Bo[ar]d of Prizes for what Carpenters Stores were wanting. [HCA 1/99/135]

Another captive who is described as a forced man at first but who became a friend and willing accomplice of the pirates upon his second voyage with them receives the blasphemous greeting "G__ d___n you what are you here again" [HCA 1/99/98] and the same deponent testifies that he heard "Some of the Pyrates swear he was not a Volunteer the first time, but D__n it he Shou'd goe with in now" [HCA 1/99/98]. Both examples cited above involve willing volunteers who are received into the crew and offered friendship with swearing as a marker of kinship and affection.

Furthermore, individuals expressed their allegiance and loyalty to each other with swearing, e.g., one pirate who brandished "a lighted match in order to Set the Magazine on fire Swearing very profanely lets all go to Hell together" [HCA 1/99/152]. Other descriptions are less dramatic but equally express swearing as a marker of in-group identity, e.g., "he hung up with the rest in the Cabbin, and fell to drinking and Swearing the Vices he saw they were all enamoured of" [HCA 1/99/96] and "he came Swearing and cursing as did several others of them" [HCA 1/99/105]. Profane and blasphemous language in such familiar contexts suggests that swearing was also used to construct and display identity in much the same way that young women used swear words to assert themselves and show affiliation with the counter-culture of the 1960s in North America (Carlisle 2009: 60) or modern teenagers use swear words to mark group identity (Stapleton 2010: 298).

Indeed, when individuals wished to express their affiliation with pirates, they swore as a marker of complicity. For instance, one detained sailor is assumed to be an unwilling participant in the capture of a ship and is thus excluded from a share in its plunder until he asserts his complicity with swearing: "when indeed they wou'd have cut him out of his Share he made Words of it like a Soldier, and asked what a Devil they took him for if he was not allowed a Share" [HCA 1/99/147]. It is exactly because swearing was a marker of complicity and group identity that depositions often refer to the language of accused men as a sign of their innocence or guilt in piracy trials, e.g., one witness claiming that Antonio Nunez was a leadership figure among a pirate crew testifies that he "seemed more Violent, and Swore and Curs'd more than the rest" [HCA 1/99/5]. Prisoners who are described as swearing a lot are invariably found guilty, e.g., "he was a Swearing Fellow" [HCA 1/99/121], "[he] was allways swearing and cursing" [HCA 1/99/74], and "the most Swearing Reprobate Fellow among them" [HCA 1/99/171]. In contrast, prisoners who are described as not swearing are often acquitted, e.g., "the prisoner was a quiet Fellow, not Swearing or Cursing like most of them" [HCA 1/99/166] and "not Swearing cursing nor as he knew at attacquing any Ship" [HCA 1/99/133]. Thus, while swearing among sailors served an emphatic function, and a grammatical function as a realis marker and a signifier of imperative modality, it also served to assert agency and challenge (or affirm) the chain of command. For pirates specifically, swearing had the additional function of a marker of group affiliation and could therefore be used as evidence that might condemn them to death.

7.4 Summary

Ship English makes heavy use of adverbs and these might occur in a range of variant positions within the main clause with no apparent linguistic conditioning by adverb type. Whether they are prepositional phrases, single-word adverbs, or adverbial phrases without prepositional heads, the most common placement for adverbial constituents is after the noun-phrase subject and before the main verb phrase. The second most common placement is between an auxiliary verb and a verbal participle and this is a particularly common slot for single-word adverbs. Prepositions can sometimes be omitted from adverbial phrases and idiomatic use of prepositions shows considerable variation; for instance, the preposition "of" which occurs in a range of contexts without either genitive or partitive function. Notable prepositional phrases include "for that" which can function as a complementizer or subordinating conjunction and "for to" which results from allowing the preposition "for" to take an infinitive verb phrase complement.

   With respect to sentence and clause structure, Ship English permits intransitive verbs to be expressed before noun-phrase subjects immaterial of the complexity of the verb phrase they occur in. Many of these fronted verbs occur with adverbial constituents relating to time that may have conditioned their movement within the clause. Although evidence is limited, samples suggest that Ship English may also permit linking verbs, transitive verbs, and pseudo-expletive structures to occur at the front of the clause. Direct objects may be moved to an initial position in the clause, or they may be expressed after the subject and before the main verb near the front of a clause, even when the subject is expressed as a pronoun or is not realized in the surface structure. Moreover, direct objects are also omitted from speech in contexts where the object referent is understood from context. Indirect objects are sometimes omitted, but more commonly, they occur after a direct object without a prepositional constituent.

Ship English demonstrates significant complexity in terms of clause subordination and extensive use of adverbial phrases, derived in part from the Latinate stylistics of formal communication that incorporated complex syntax suited to classical rhetoric. Complexity in the spoken mode may reflect the complexity and intricate embedding patterns of written communication, but may also index the stream of consciousness common to speech, particularly in the narration of emotive content. Furthermore, written representations of speech may appear more complex when disassociated from the deixis of their original spoken form. Sailors' expressions in the corpus use present participle phrases and "that" to mark the subordination of dependent clauses. The subordinator "that" is more notable in the formal communications of literate men and this form is potentially appropriated and used as a discourse marker by lower-status sailors to increase their perceived status and gain credibility with the Admiralty, specifically by using the word without apparent syntactic function at the head of independent clauses. However, the use of "that" to introduce independent clauses also helps to compose cumulative super-structures common to courtroom language that may be punctuated incorrectly in transcription.

An alternative strategy for building complex structures involves the frequent use of coordinating conjunctions. Sailors sometimes complied with the Parallelism Requirement of Standard English when forming conjoined phrases, yet also use conjunctions to associate dissimilar constituents. Coordinating conjunctions are permitted to introduce new clauses in addition to joining predicate and clause-level structures in the continuous speech of court testimony. The omission of conjunctions may also be explained by unpunctuated deictic features in the original spoken form. Finally, although lexemes with the capacity to function as coordinating conjunctions appear frequently in the corpus, it is notable that they often play an adverbial role instead.

Ship English is primarily a spoken language with embedded features of ritual and rhetoric common to other performance mediums and incorporates swearing as a discourse marker in various capacities. Sailors often swear (including oath-making, blasphemy, and profanity) to provide emphasis in oral communication and to mark statements for the veracity of the speaker's intentions. In this way, swearing marks the realis modality that is unmarked in Standard English but often overt in West African and Creole languages. Sailors also potentially use swearing — often coupled with physical violence — to mark the imperative modality in the context of issuing further threats of violence and commands to captives or subordinates. Individuals, from high-ranking officers to the lowest-ranked sailors, swear to assert their agency in a way that could either challenge or reaffirm the internal hierarchy of command and thus also helped to define social status aboard sailing vessels. In pirate communities, swearing featured as a salient marker of group identity and was additionally used to greet and show comradery among peers. Consequently, an individual sailor's disposition for swearing was a common feature of piracy trials and accused seamen could be found guilty or acquitted, based — at least in part — on the frequency and strength of their oath-making and profanity.

8 Conclusions and implications

This final chapter will consider the findings of the preceding chapters on sailors' demography, speech communities and linguistic features to respond to the central claim that there is a distinct Ship English that was spoken by British sailors in the early Atlantic colonial period. The first section, Conclusions, will clarify my own position on the distinctiveness, stability and spread of Ship English and address the potential typology of the variety. The second section, Implications, will consider the newly presented baseline data on the linguistic features of Ship English in terms of how this might be integrated into theories and research in dialectology and contact linguistics. Throughout this chapter, I acknowledge the scope of the work that still needs to be done and attempt to clarify some specific areas of study that may hopefully motivate future studies.

8.1 Conclusions

8.1.1 A distinct and stable variety

The central claim of this book is that there is a distinct "Ship English" that was spoken by British sailors in the early colonial context (determined as roughly the period between 1620 and 1750). This claim is substantiated by two chapters dedicated to the socio-historical context of the variety which identify speakers' demographics (Chapter 3) and the characteristics of the speech community (Chapter 4) in addition to three chapters dedicated to linguistic findings which identify salient and repeated markers of sailors' speech during this period in terms of noun phrases (Chapter 5), verb phrases (Chapter 6), and clause, sentence, and discourse level phenomena (Chapter 7). The socio-historical data demonstrate that Ship English of the early Atlantic colonial period developed within a unique maritime demographic and socio-linguistic context which promoted the development of new forms and enabled feature transfer via oral traditions. The linguistic data demonstrate that Ship English has distinctive charactersitics with regard to morphosyntactic, syntactic and discourse level variation.

It is pertinent at this point to stress that my claim throughout this book is not that Ship English is a dialect with *unique characteristics* but rather with unique patterns of frequency and distribution for particular features that marked speakers as members of an extended maritime community. As such, the characteristic features of Ship English here identified are also documented in other varieties of Early Modern English not associated with the maritime community and found in the Early Modern English of authors like Milton, Bunyan, Dryden, Evelyn and Pepys. However, the patterns of frequency in their work are unlikely to correspond consistently with Ship English (unless the author's intention was to represent maritime speech). Dialectologist and specialist in the creation of World Englishes, Schneider, explains that, "frequency shifts are a core property of [the] diffusion process" and that it is not the creation of new forms that indicate the emergence of new World Englishes but changed frequencies that become strengthened by feedback loops and lead to quantitative difference (Schneider 2018). Hence, this book presents morphosyntactic features that were salient among sailors and that were likely to have shifted to a higher frequency of distribution than other contemporary dialects. Thus, when these features are considered together, they mark the emergence of a recognizably distinct variety.

The facts that there are recognizable patterns of frequency among sailors, and that a high distribution of certain morphosyntactic features mark the variety as distinctive to other contemporary varieties (in ways that can be recognized and reproduced), appear to support Bailey and Ross's claim that there is a distinct type of English that was spoken by sailors during the period of early English colonial expansion (1988: 194) upon which my own central hypothesis is based. As such, the data and discussion presented in the linguistic chapters aim to support the central hypothesis of a distinct maritime dialect by identifying the features with the highest frequency that served as salient markers of Ship English, not to document all the features that either do or do not occur in the variety nor to present a comparative analysis between feature frequencies in Ship English and counterparts in other contemporary varieties. Yet, now that descriptive work is available on the most salient features of Ship English, albeit by no means definitive or necessarily complete, future studies might focus on comparative approaches. Hoewever, such work is beyond the scope of this book.

This study builds on and extends the few prior studies into variation in sailors' speech and here briefly re-presents this literature to substantiate the claim that Ship English was a comprehensive variety. The unique lexical characteristics of Ship English have been amply documented in the many dictionaries and wordlists published since Captain John Smith's *Sea Grammar* in 1627; indeed, most work on the subject has comprised lexical items that constitute the professional jargon of the crew intended for circulation among maritime professionals (see Chapter 2: Review of the Literature). Investigations that provide evidence of the unique phonological and morphological characteristics of Ship English are Matthews' (1935) monograph on sailors' pronunciation in the second half of the seventeenth century and Bailey & Ross's (1988) article on the morphosyntactic features of Ship English.[1] This book now offers the first extended compilation of evidence on the sociolinguistic, syntactic and discourse level features that characterize the variety.[2] Hence, we now have evidence that Ship English of the early English colonial period around the Atlantic had distinctive lexical, morphological, syntactic, and discourse features that support its status as a distinct historical variety of English.

The evidence supports the view that Ship English was stable and diffused in ways comparable to other varieties of English. Sea shanties record language features of Ship English over time and sea-music historian Stan Hugill explains that this demonstrates that the variety had stability. His analysis of two shanty verses published in 1549 concludes: "the form and language of these early shanties, apart from the fact that the English is Chaucerian, are very much like what our sailors of the sail sang three hundred years later" (Hugill 1969: 3). Hugill's reference to "Chaucerian" English is most probably an allusion to archaic vocabulary but the "form and language" that he refers to, described as very much like the speech of sailors three hundred years later, shows that Ship English was established enough to be recognized as a distinct variety for three centuries.[3] It is possible that the "language" Hugill refers to incorporates (and potentially derives from) the distinct jargon of the maritime profession, yet his reference to a distinctive "form" suggests a variety with syntactic and discourse-level variation that was stable enough to spread and be identified over time. As discussed in Chapter 3,

---

[1]It should be recognized that Matthews states that his work "should be regarded as a cross-section in the history of pronunciation...[and] It is not pretended that it describes the 'seaman's dialect' of the period" (1935: 196, see full citation in §2.1.2). Hence, although I discuss Matthews' work as one of the two previously published studies on Ship English, it is important to note that he himself did not present his research as a study on any distinct "seaman's dialect".

[2]Given the limited scope of research to date, I do not propose that this study is definitive or that it will not be subject to subsequent revision, modification, and potential correction as we learn more about Ship English. Yet, the baseline data provided can serve as an entry point for scholars to integrate this variety into their work on language history and change; it will also hopefully prompt continued research.

[3]It is possible that the stability Hugill observes from the sixteenth to the nineteenth centuries extends even further back with common origins in Mediterranean Lingua Franca (or Sabir) reportedly used since the thirteenth century among sailors traversing the Mediterranean basin (Parkvall 2005).

this stability was, in part, motivated by the members of a speech community who worked in real and pseudo-kinship groups that regularly included partners, wives and children whose communication was predominantly oral owing, in part, to the high levels of illiteracy among sailors. Shipboard oral cultures were furthermore closely connected and expressed a common identity through oral and performance mediums such as storytelling, music, gaming, and dramatic play as examined in Chapter 4. Owing to the composition of these speech communities, the language features that marked the variety as distinctive, once established, were likely able to spread quickly among those within the community and they were additionally reinforced internally by the oral speech practices and strong affiliations among groups of sailors.[4]

Characteristic features of Ship English were not only diffused and reinforced among the sailors of any one vessel, fleet, or shipping route; they were also transferred to communities on land that were in contact with sailors, e.g., communities of traders in ports and groups of family members and friends in each sailor's country of origin. The effects of language transfer and change might not have been circular as suggested by Schmidt's (1872) Wave Model (discussed in §2.2.1: Dialect change and new dialect formation), instead, transmission would have likely occurred in coastal and estuary locations where recruitment, trade and leisure brought local populations and sailors into close contact.[5,6] It is also interesting that many linguistic features associated with Ship English occur in wives'

---

[4]It is possible that there were distinctive sub-community features shared among specific groups of sailors speaking Ship English that marked differences in status (e.g., experienced seamen compared to those appointed through family connections, financial necessity, or impressment). Although the research at this stage is not sufficient to support such a claim, this might be a direction for future study.

[5]It is likely that feature transfer was also occurring from the port community into the ships thus giving rise to the possibility of regional variations among the fleets that sourced their crews from specific locations. For example because London-born sailors were most heavily represented in naval vessels, coastal northerners in the merchant service, and coastal southerners and westerners in privateering and piracy, it may be that those maritime communities incorporated more linguistic features from the home-regions of their crew majority. Furthermore, these potential sub-distinctions may have served to identify sailors as belonging to a particular fleet or service.

[6]To illustrate some evidence of such transfer, a joint letter drafted by the residents of one harbor town (presumed to be Edinburgh) in testimony against Lt. Lilburne [SP 42/6 c.1700] includes zero inflection on third person indicative verbs, emphatic use of the auxiliary "do", prepositional "for" with an infinitive complement, possessive pronominal forms without anterior nominal markers, and accusative-case pronouns in genitive phrases—all of which are identified as characteristic features of Ship English.

letters to mariner-husbands.[7] Thus, evidence suggests that salient linguistic features associated with Ship English were transferred among port communities and family networks in contact with sailors and these features may have been consciously expressed in order to identify with the sailors or/and subconsciously acquired through regular contact with speakers of the variety.

8.1.2 The typology of Ship English

Having provided detailed evidence for Ship English as a distinct variety in Chapters 5, 6 and 7, the problem remains as to how we intend to classify this variety. Some historical and non-academic publications use the word "language" to refer to Ship English, e.g., Russell's descriptions of "the language of the sea" (1883: viii), and "Sailor's language... compounded of the terms referring to the various parts of ships ...[with] a mass of rough sayings into the forecastle, many of which are sanctified by touches of rude poetry" (Russell 1883: ix) and the claim in the introductory comments to Smith's *Sea Grammar* that the work gives explanations and translations for "the language both of ships and Seas" (Smith 1627 [1968]). Choundas likewise claims that there is a sub-category of this "language of the sea" that could be classified as "a freestanding pirate language" (2007: 2). Furthermore, it appears that writers who describe the "language" of sailors do not intend to imply that their system of communication is distinct enough to be unintelligible to speakers of other varieties of English, for example, but rather to stress the differences in their speech in which "meaning is really so subtle as utterly to defy translation" (Russell 1883: xv) and highlight the internal systemic coherence that provides a "uniform way of talking" (Choundas 2007: 2). Indeed, the term "Ship English" (coined by Hancock 1976: 33) already classifies the variety as a type of English. However, the question remains as to what sub-classification of the English language Ship English constitutes. The internal systemic cohesion among speakers disqualifies it as a manifestation of any one individual's idiolect and the phonological, morphological, syntactic and discourse features attested in the variety show that it is more than professional jargon. The remaining potential typological classifications with which we might classify this variety are as a dialect, a sociolect, or a koine, each of which are discussed in the following paragraphs.

---

[7]Examples of Ship English features in wives' letters include the omission of articles [HCA 1/9/22], the idiomatic post-nominal phrase "last past" as a marker of temporal sequence [HCA 1/14/76], and the use of "that" at the head of an independent clause as a formal discourse marker to index status with no apparent syntactic function [HCA 1/98/118].

Ship English is a dialect, commonly defined as a manner of speech characteristic of a group of people (*Oxford Eng. Dict.* 1989, Vol 4: 599) and more specifically defined by linguists in terms of three classifications: regional dialects, social dialects (sociolects), and ethnic dialects (ethnolects) (Wolfram & Schilling 2016). In addition to describing sailors' speech as a language (discussed above), Russell (1883) also uses the word "dialect" to describe Ship English: "sailor's talk is a dialect […] [in which] English words are used, but their signification is utterly remote from the meaning they have in shore parlance" (Russell 1883: ix).[8] The suggestion that there is a "sea dialect" (Russell 1883: xiii) is entirely logical given the general definition of the word as characteristic to group of people and the fact that the variety is characteristic to sailors. Yet Russell's classification was also a product of trends in nineteenth-century London among scholars with an increased interest in dialect studies. Interest in regional and socially stigmatized varieties in the late nineteenth century gave rise to a host of dialect glossaries and motivated comparative studies and dialect theory (Petyt 1980: 35–38). Indeed, it was at that time that the term "dialect" came to be explicitly associated with a regional sub-standard variety in comparison to the variety that was championed as the national standard.[9] Görlach describes how the speech of sailors was stigmatized in a period of increasing standardization, as "the speech of those who cannot do any better" at best (1999: 484), or "the gibberish of the uneducated" at worst (p.532). Such commonplace beliefs about the lack of social value associated with sailors and their speech explains how Ship English might have been classified as a dialect in contemporary studies and in popular opinion as this term would have explicitly marked the variety as substandard and stigmatized.

Scholars who have written on sailors' speech accept that each individual sailor would have entered the community with a dialect reflective of the region in which that person was raised. Even though the possibility of babies being born aboard ships is covered in §4.2.4, it is unlikely that the vessel was a permanent home to infants learning their native language. Instead, §3.4 presents data at-

---

[8]This citation additionally suggests the possibility of creolization through the process of relexification, yet given the wider context of the comments, it is unlikely that this was what the author intended to propose.

[9]Although, by modern standards, regional dialects might be classified as "regiolects" comparable to "sociolects" and "ethnolects", the general term "dialect" was originally associated with regional speech patterns as sociolinguistics and ethnolinguistics had yet to become established fields of study. Furthermore, it is worth noting that modern linguists universally recognize that everyone speaks a dialect and that dialects are not inherently sub-standard although the word "dialect" was traditionally associated with social stigmatization and popular notions of inferiority (Wolfram & Schilling 2016: 2–17).

testing to the fact that most sailors went to sea between the ages of 12 and 16 and would therefore already have established the characteristic speech patterns of their home region. Matthews makes this point explicit in his monograph on sailors' pronunciation in the second half of the seventeenth century. His final comments in the introductory section stress the relevance of regional influence with the assertion that the writers of the logbooks "must have come from almost every shire's end of England" (p.195) and thus the findings represent many local dialects. He states "This study, therefore, should be regarded as a cross-section in the history of pronunciation, an account of the various pronunciations in use among the tarpaulin seamen" (p.196). He goes on to state that "It is not pretended that it describes the 'seaman's dialect' of the period" (p.196), thus explicitly fore-grounding the variation of dialects aboard ships in contrast to a potential sea-man's dialect.[10] The fact that each sailor would have entered the community with an existing regional dialect makes the classification of any potential "sea-man's dialect" problematic not only as it implies competition between dialects,[11] but also because it suggests a process of acquiring native language forms at a young age in a way that did not apply to maritime recruits. Moreover, the his-torical association of the word "dialect" with regional distinctness is problematic as ships' communities were transient and potentially overlapped with existing geographical dialect areas (but without the suggestion that language forms were necessarily transferred). Further research may even attest to regional variations of Ship English such as Mediterranean, Atlantic, and Pacific Ship English, influ-enced by specific regional variations of the languages their crews encountered. In short, Ship English is understandably classified as a dialect in general terms given the broad scope of the term to describe a variety characteristic to one group of people coupled with its working-class stigma of inferiority with respect to the standard. However, for linguists, the sub-classification of the variety demands more specific attention.

Of the three possible dialect classifications available to modern linguists (i.e., regional dialect, sociolect, and ethnolect) the classification of Ship English as an ethnolect is the least probable given the data presented in Chapter 2 on re-

---

[10] Although whether Matthews' comments imply that there was a "seaman's dialect" of the pe-riod (but that his work did not aim to represent it) or that he does not believe that a "seaman's dialect" existed is uncertain.

[11] A modern understanding of diglossia might help to mitigate the suggested conflict between dialects in this context, but this term still carries with it the suggestion that one of the dialects is a standard and the other is a regional dialect or sociolect, whereas in the context of sailors, neither of the two dialects of English were necessarily the standard (indeed, Standard English might have been additionally acquired in a context of pluri-dialectalism).

cruitment practices and sailors' places of origin and associated language abilities. Some linguists might argue that the regional dialect classification is valid given that the data reflects an Atlantic variety of Ship English, yet the transient nature of ships' speech communities at sea coupled with the notion that maritime communities in ports span five continents might frustrate efforts to define a unified region that underpins the variety. Furthermore, the regional dialect classification might also be perceived as problematic given the assumption that regional dialects are learned during native language acquisition (Chambers & Trudgill 1998: 5). This leaves only one other potential classification.

The classification of Ship English as a sociolect, characteristic of a group that shares a social identity rather than an ethnic or regional identity (Trudgill 2003: 122), eliminates the problematic associations of ethnic homogeneity and regional unity that are associated with regional dialects and ethnolects and instead promotes focus on the social factors that unified diverse crews. In addition, the problematic suggestion of native language acquisition that a dialect classification implies is also mitigated as sociolects are often acquired after native fluency through conscious choice to demonstrate group affiliation and passive acquisition of group-specific language features (Durrell 2004: 200–205).[12] Furthermore, these socially-conditioned varieties of speech often consciously demonstrate social and professional identification, socioeconomic class, age group and/or ethnic and political affiliation. The term "sociolect" is therefore well suited to the classification of Ship English, a variety that is acquired after native fluency among predominantly young working-class men who share a professional context, maritime folklore, and solidarity in the face of hardships at sea. Hancock appears to support a sociolect classification in his definition of "a situation-specific register of English, which I call *Ship English*" (1986: 85, author's italics). Schultz (2010) also takes this position, talking about Ship English as a "sociolect" in his unpublished Master's thesis.[13] Yet, one caveat remains in that the classification of Ship English as a sociolect may suggest social homogeneity among its speakers.[14] This book

---

[12] It is important to recognize that although certain sociolects can be acquired as additional varieties later in life (e.g., Instant Messenger and Internet varieties), they can also be coded into native language acquisition, particularly when they are associated with social status derived from economic class divisions or regional variation (e.g., Labov's (1966) research based on the Lower East Side of New York City that showed systemic social stratification).

[13] Hancock served as the academic supervisor on Shultz's committee at the University of Texas at Austin in 2010 and so may have influenced Shultz's position in this respect.

[14] Although I accept that some definitions of "sociolect" do not demand social homogeneity as a defining factor of the speech community, most specify that speakers belong to the same social stratum and have comparable ages, incomes, and experiences in addition to frequent contact with one another.

explicitly aims to dispel the popular stereotype that all British mariners were monolingual, lower-class, Caucasian men in their mid-twenties who performed manual labor and led a profligate single life. Indeed, the data in Chapter 3 demonstrates the diversity of maritime communities and this diversity is in danger of being overlooked if their variety of language is classified in such a way as to suggest uniformity in social grouping. Thus, Ship English might reasonably be classified as a sociolect given the general scope of the term to apply to a variety characteristic of a group of people connected by social factors such as age, profession, and ideology, yet this classification should not suggest that all speakers shared social homogeneity.

The problems of assuming social homogeneity if we define Ship English as a sociolect or implying regional origins if we define Ship English as a regional dialect are resolved if we classify Ship English by its process of formation and not the characteristics of its speakers. As such, Ship English might be classified as a koine, defined as a stabilized contact variety that develops when mutually intelligible varieties (either regional dialects or sociolects) come into contact. After a period of interaction or integration among the speakers of these contact varieties, variant linguistic features mix and become levelled among the group (Siegel 2001: 175).[15] Trudgill's theory of new dialect formation through koineization in colonial territories (discussed in more detail in Chapter 2) specifies a three-stage process of mixing, leveling and simplification that results in "a single unitary variety" (Trudgill 1986: 27). Le Page's theory on linguistic focusing explains how such a process can result from social conformity and group identification; "the emergence of a closeknit group, a sense of solidarity and a feeling of shared territory are all conditions favouring focusing" (Milroy 1986: 378). In Chapter 2, I propose that the mixing, leveling, and simplification process of koineization was potentially happening on board international sailing vessels of the Atlantic because of social conformity and group identification among sailors. Schultz's Master's thesis on the sociolinguistic context of Ship English similarly claims that the development of a unitary ship's variety of English was made possible by maritime communities of practice, in which "linguistically, strong networks act as a norm enforcement mechanism" (2010: 7–8). The data presented in Chapters 3 and 4 serve to support the claim that linguistic focusing, leading to koineiza-

---

[15]The term "koine" (or "koiné") is the Greek word for "common", and was originally applied to a common Greek dialect that developed among the regionally-diverse armies of Alexander the Great in the 4th century BC (Andriotis 1995). The term has been more recently applied in contact linguistics as a levelled variety when mutually intelligible dialects come into contact, it has also been used more specifically in terms of creole genesis theory (Siegel 2001) and the phenomena of new regional and immigrant varieties (Trudgill 1986, Kerswill 2004).

tion, was likely happening in maritime communities as a result of the practices that sailors used to reinforce group identity. In Chapter 3, the data on sailors illustrates the hardships that likely increased social dependence, including harsh recruitment measures, lack of pay, high mortality rates, and the dangers of shipboard work, disciplinary action and conflict. This chapter also explains how many lower-ranking sailors and unpaid workers were denied shore leave for fear of desertion, thus forcing their speech communities to become even more insular. The data presented in Chapter 4 regarding speech communities shows how social cohesion among crews was facilitated by kinship bonds in mess groups and that collective agency and resistance were often a form of protection against brutal discipline by tyrannous commanding officers and perpetual subordination. Among sailors, collective activism was a necessity for survival and the ritual consumption of alcohol bound sailors' insular communities in trade, conflict, and times of spiritual distress. Group identity was reinforced through shared beliefs in ancient maritime folklore and expressed orally in these communities, thus providing the context necessary to focus linguistic diversity and derive a single unitary variety that expressed shared experience.

The few modern scholars who have published research on Ship English or features of sailors' speech appear to support the interpretation that koineization was happening in maritime communities. Matthews (1935) and Bailey & Ross (1988) describe common linguistic features among divergent crews, and both acknowledge the role of professional or social identification although neither use the term koineization or classify the resulting variety as a koine or new dialect. Matthews presents the phonology of sailors as a shared paradigm motivated by the technical jargon of professional association. He explains in his introductory notes, "a craft imposes certain traditional pronunciations upon those who engage in it. For sailors, whatever their early dialect and education, there must have been certain conventions of pronunciation for words used exclusively in the sea-trade" (1935: 193). Matthews falls short of claiming that his findings show a leveled pronunciation system, yet his explanation of how sailors, regardless of their own dialect, were obliged by their craft to observe certain conventions of pronunciation certainly suggests the stages of mixing and leveling that occur in koineization with the motivational force of professional association serving to provide linguistic focusing. Bailey & Ross's (1988) article on morphosyntactic variation of Ship English similarly describes stages of mixing and leveling. In the conclusion to their paper they explain:

> variation and change were certainly no greater than in most nonstandard
> varieties of English, and in the process of its formation Ship English seems

> to have eliminated the most abberant features of British dialects, as Hancock (1976) suggested. As a result, it shares many of its morpho-syntactic structures with other British regional and social dialects; in fact, it is not at all clear that *grammatically* Ship English is a unique sociolect, although its lexical uniqueness is apparent. At least in its morpho-syntax, Ship English represents a kind of 'levelled' variety similar to those discussed by Trudgill (1986), with the most widespread nonstandard features preserved and the most restricted ones apparently lost. (Bailey & Ross 1988: 207, authors' italics)

The wording of Bailey and Ross's paper appears to echo Matthews' suggestion that "whatever their early dialect and education, there must have been certain conventions…used exclusively in the sea-trade" (1935: 193) and might thus be seen as an elaboration of Matthews earlier position that Ship English is a variety resulting from mixing dialects and deriving leveled features as a result of professional association. Thus, both Matthews (1935) and Bailey & Ross (1988) support the interpretation of mixing and leveling with linguistic focusing. My own position may be interpreted as taking their claims one step further by suggesting that the result of the mixing and leveling led to default paradigms (i.e. simplification) and resulted in a shared unitary koine that follows all the stages of Trudgill's (1986) theory of koineization. However, although some linguistic features identified in Chapters 5, 6 and 7 attest to linguistic simplification (e.g., zero inflection, default pronominal forms, negative concord, leveling of the present and past tense copula forms, overt auxiliaries in all modalities, multiple functionality of specific lexemes, and the use of coordinating conjunctions to build super-structures regardless of parallelism requirements) other features suggest complexity (e.g., linguistic conditioning of feature omission and placement, subordination marked by present-participle phrases, [non-specific verb + specifying nominal complement] constructions, fronting of intransitive verbs before a noun phrase subject, and swearing to mark realis and imperative modalities).[16]

---

[16]It is worth noting that some features analysed can be presented as evidence of simplification **and** as evidence of linguistic complexity, e.g., the verb "to do". On one hand, "do support" may have been a simplified default in all affirmative verb phrases to aid the process of acquisition for language learners, yet it also potentially functions to mark aspectual and/or subordinating meaning in affirmative clauses in the indicative mood when used in conjunction with preterit forms (see full discussion in Chapter 6 on the auxiliary "to do"). I have purposely presented both interpretations as I think that they are not mutually exclusive. Instead, the use of "do" may have changed with any individual speaker's fluency in the language. Learners might have defaulted to a universal use of "do support" without aspectual or subordinating meaning, and native/fluent speakers might have used the verb "do" to mark subtle distinctions in meaning between verb phrases.

Yet it is important to recognize that the term "simplification" in Trudgill's frame-work does not necessarily suggest linguistic simplification, but a determinism of the new dialect formation that is marked by the manifestation of a "final, stable, relatively uniform outcome...[when] the new dialect appears as a stable, crys-tallised variety" (Trudgill 2004: 113). The "simplification" is represented in the emergence of default paradigms and not a suggested linguistic simplification that we might associated with pidgin varieties. The data presented on Ship English indicates that there was still significant free variation with respect to certain fea-tures (e.g., the omission of articles, the selection of regular weak or unmarked preterit forms, and the placement of adverbial constituents) yet there were also clear default paradigms that marked the variety (e.g., marking genitive case with prepositional phrases rather than nominal inflection, post-nominal placement of present participle phrases, overt use of the auxiliary "to do" in constructions with affirmative indicative modality, fronting verbs if they can function as auxiliaries, and the use of a stative present participle in progressive structures). Therefore, Ship English might be reasonably classified as a koine owing to its formation through a process of mixing and leveling regional dialects and its emergence as a stable uniform variety with default linguistic paradigms determined from a variety of input features, however, this interpretation necessarily also classifies the variety as a new world dialect and therefore alludes back to the problematic assumptions of geographical containment and native language acquisition once the variety achieves a uniform outcome.

In summary, the various potential classifications with which we might cate-gorize Ship English all have their merits, yet none are without problematic as-sumptions about the nature of the language variety or the people who spoke it. I believe that although the variety was undoubtedly influenced by the idiolects, re-gional dialects and professional jargon of those within the maritime community, it constitutes a unitary system of morpho-syntactic and discourse variation that extends well beyond individual speakers, occupational lexicon, or the influence of any one regional dialect. Taking into consideration the analysis and opinions of previous researchers working on Ship English and the socio-historical and linguistic evidence presented in these chapters, I believe that although sailors' speech has been historically associated with a professional jargon and more re-cently conceptualized as an occupational sociolect, the most appropriate classifi-cation we can assign is that Ship English of the early colonial period was a new di-alect of English that was formed through the mixing, leveling and simplification processes of koineization. This conclusion is presented in the full knowledge that research into Ship English is in its early stages and further work on the shared linguistic systems of sailors may lead to modifications and amendments of this claim as we learn more about the process of language transfer and the extent of linguistic simplification in the variety. We should also bear in mind that like any linguistic system, Ship English manifests itself on a continuum of localized and individual variation and there are also likely sub-categories of Ship English according to sailing region, crew composition, and the type of vessel or voyage. Furthermore, I do not propose that there was one type of Ship English as a monolithic variety, but instead that there were core linguistic features that identified speakers as sailors. These linguistic features, like any others, were "transmitted by normal social and cultural forces" (McDavid 1979: 129) and were therefore prone to idiolectal and systemic change in addition to adaption and replacement over time.

8.2 Implications

One of the aims of this study was to generate a baseline of linguistic data that describe common features of Ship English with the hope that this variety might be integrated into the discourse, the theories and the research on dialect variation and language contact in the early colonial period. As such, the implications of findings presented in the chapters of this book are discussed in terms of how they relate to our understanding of dialectology in the discipline of historical linguistics and the theories of pidgin and creole genesis in the discipline of contact linguistics. This section on the implications of Ship English also includes some general observations on recovering the agency of sailors and advocating for future work that integrates data on sociolinguistics and emulates the multidisciplinary approaches of Atlantic Studies.

8.2.1 Relevance for dialectology

The recognition of Ship English as a distinct historical dialect of British English prompts a reconceptualization of dialect change and feature transfer in the British Isles. Despite the traditional models of dialect diffusion that emphasize central geographical focal points with concentric waves of influence, this study focuses on a dialect that was formed without a common center and drew influences from various locations that were not regionally adjacent. Rather than being defined by a central geographical focal point with rivers and seas serving only to limit the extent of dialect expansion, the genesis of Ship English refutes assumptions about the obstruent nature of waterways in dialect diffusion and instead encourages scholars to envision rivers as conduits of communication and seas as fertile spaces where new forms of speech could incubate and stabilize. The reconceptualization of waterways as potential spaces for dialect change and expansion is perhaps particularly relevant to scholars of historical dialectology, and although maritime communities may have served as agents of language change with respect to English as far back as Anglo-Saxon times, the agency of sailors in dialect change might particularly interest scholars whose research interests coincide with the era of expanding maritime technology, trade and exploration that converted the seas in the early modern period into busy spaces of transit and imperial regulation. Scholars interested in the Early Modern English period of dialect change in the late sixteenth and seventeenth centuries might particularly focus on the potential internal changes that were driven by increasing coastal transportation services of wheat, cloth, and coal (Willan 1967). The sailors who worked in these trades were likely to have acquired and transported dialect features from port to port, particularly as their profession may have carried the type of covert prestige that is often associated with working-class regional speech and occupations associated with masculinity and toughness (Petyt 1980: 160). Indeed, their agency may have derived the kind of "pan-variety parallelism" that Tagliamonte claims occurred among northern British regions and crossed the Irish Sea in which "all communities share the same (variable) system in each case and it is only in the subtle weights and constraint of variation that the differences emerge" (2013: 192). If, indeed, maritime workers had an influence in transmitting and leveling dialect features among ports of the British Isles, then this process was also potentially happening on a larger scale given that "[t]he combination of ocean and river routes defined the shape of the Atlantic zone" (Thornton 2000: 56). Consequently, it is possible that maritime speech communities also leveled linguistic features around the Atlantic and established the type of supra-regional varieties that are still evident in pan-Caribbean English usage (Allsopp 2003).

The data presented here on Ship English and the idea that leveled features composed a stable variety may help to refine what "dialect" implies for the continued effective use of this term in the new information age. To echo a statement from the introduction, we live in a world so interconnected by air travel, media and online networks that we rarely consider the importance of maritime travel or those who depended upon it in an age before we physically and digitally took to the skies. Yet, studying the speech communities of people who sailed the waters that connected the edges of the known world may ironically give us some insight into how supra-regional varieties are formed in a modern world where global networks connect distant places and incubate varieties of language that neither adhere to any standard regional norms nor diffuse via regional adjacency. As Darvin explains in his paper on language and identity in the digital age, technology has revolutionized the way we communicate; increased travel, mobile communication and online connectivity have blurred the boundaries of space "leading to new identifications, allegiances, and relations" (2016: 523). As a result, new digital technologies necessitate concepts of dialect formation and research methodologies that can trace what Stornaiuolo & Hall describe as the "echoing of ideas across spaces, people and texts" (2014: 28).

This book likewise attempts to trace the echoing of sailors' language features across the space, people and texts of the early colonial period. It presents Ship English as a language variety with no regional origin that is defined by its medium of transmission; this definition creates parallels between non-regional, technology-mediated varieties such as Instant Messaging (IM) and texting varieties of English (Warschauer & Matuchniak 2010) in addition to translingual varieties that evolve online (Canagarajah 2013). Like many of these new varieties emerging via technology, Ship English is not a traditional dialect defined by regional parameters nor is it a sociolect shared by a single stratum of society, instead, it is a poorly-understood variety derived from the mixing and leveling of distinct regional features with influence from other languages. It furthermore demonstrates a type of simplification that facilitates learner acquisition but also permits the complex syntactic variation that enables fluent speakers to express subtlety and complexity in meaning. Thus, perhaps a variety such as Ship English could provide an impetus to refine models of dialect genesis for the digital age in which mediums of communication and high-levels of non-native acquisition are more important than identifying a single geographical origin, social class or ethnic group in which native speakers acquire fluency. In short, if we can re-conceptualize the term "dialect" in a way that especially de-emphasizes its regional restrictions and instead highlights its potential range through the medium by which it is transmitted, then Ship English might help us understand the processes through which newly emerging global varieties are developing.

If we accept that Ship English was formed through a process of dialect mixing, leveling, and simplification in the same way that Trudgill (1986) describes the formation of immigrant koines, then the data on Ship English also serve to expand our understanding of the contexts in which koineization can take place. Since he first proposed his three-stage theory of new dialect formation in 1986, Trudgill envisioned the process of koineization as one connected with language developments in colonial territories where immigrants with different varieties of mutually intelligible regional dialects gathered and their language features blended. Trudgill's more recent book published in 2004, *New Dialect Formation: The Inevitability of Colonial Englishes,* explicitly connects the process of koineization with immigrant and settler forms of English. However, his evidence on Southern Hemisphere varieties are prefaced by the claim that all colonial varieties derive from a combination of comparable factors: adaptation to a new physical environment, different linguistic changes in the mother country and the colony, language contact with indigenous languages and with other European languages, and internal dialect contact (2004: 1–7). The relevance of these factors become clear when we envision the ship itself as a microcosm of the colonial state, as Linebaugh & Rediker propose in their history of the revolutionary Atlantic (2000). Their chapter entitled "Hydrarchy: Sailors, Pirates, and the Maritime State" explores how the ship itself represented one critical process in which capitalists organized and united the exploitation of human labor. They explain:

> The consolidation of the maritime state took place in the 1690s, by which time the Royal Navy had become England's greatest employer of labor, its greatest consumer of material, and its greatest industrial enterprise...Here were Braithwaite's "walls of the State", an enclosure built around a new field of property whose value and appreciation were expressed in a congeries of changes in the 1690s. (Linebaugh & Rediker 2000: 148)

Rediker continues to explore the idea of the maritime nation state, and specifically the renegade colony of the pirate ship in *Villains of all Nations* (2004). His analogy is made explicit in the chapter entitled "The New Government of the Ship" that explores how pirates established a new social order: "It's hallmark was a rough, improvised, but effective egalitarianism" (2004: 61). Thus, not only can we envision the ship itself as a microcosm of the colonial state, but also a space in which revolution against colonial control was expressed prior to any American colonial declaration of independence from British control. Given such circumstances, the idea that processes of koineization occurred comparable to the developments in the immigrant communities of colonial territories and concurrent with the establishment of new governments is reasonable. Linebaugh & Rediker acknowledge the likelihood of language change aboard ships in their observation "European imperialism also created the conditions for the circulation of experience within the huge masses of labor that it had set in motion...[and] The circulation of experience depended in part on the fashioning of new languages" (2000: 152). I propose that these "new languages" (i.e., new dialects of English) were forged through the same three-stage process of kionization that Trudgill explains happened in colonial spaces where immigrants worked and lived together, giving their mutually-intelligible language features the opportunity to mix, level and simplify into a new variety specific to that space. In short, evaluating Ship English as a koine permits scholars in dialectology to expand the scope of koineization and apply Trudgill's theories to varieties of English that develop in transient colonial spaces that are not necessarily defined by geographical parameters or international treaties. Indeed, this interpretation of the term reclaims the transient context of its origins referring to the common Greek dialect spoken among the mobilized armies of Alexander the Great in the 4th century BC.

Ship English, here presented as a newly-recognized dialect of English, impacts the field of World Englishes and historical dialectology in the sense that the theories and approaches specific to these disciplines must now incorporate and account for this variety and its speakers in its theories of dialect formation and usage. The fact that Ship English does not fit neatly into any one geographical territory prompts a revision of how we understand internal dialect change in and around the British Isles and compels us to reconsider the scope of what constitutes a global variety of English. It also encourages scholars to advocate for the type of interdisciplinary perspective central to scholars of Atlantic Studies, expressed by the editors of the journal *Atlantic Studies* as a discipline that:

> explores transnational, transhistorical, and transdisciplinary intersections, but also addresses global flows and perspectives beyond the Atlantic as a closed or self-contained space...[and] considers the Atlantic as part of wider networks, a space of exchange, and an expanding paradigm beyond the limits of its own geography, moving beyond national, regional, and continental divides by examining entangled histories and cultures...[and therefore] challenges critical orthodoxies that have drawn sharp lines between the experiences and representations of the Atlantic world and its wider global context. (Taylor and Francis Group 2016, *Atlantic Studies* §Aims and Scope)

Embracing interdisciplinary approaches necessarily means embracing complexity in dialect studies, and this only becomes more complex when we aim to centralize the human agency integral to dialect contact. Recovering the human stories that explain dialect change is particularly important to dialect research methodologies in order to challenge trends which produce sterile and monolithic explanations of dialect change in which human stories are either ignored completely or relegated to a footnote. The focus of this book, by foregrounding demographic data, aims to recover the agency of ordinary people who motivated extraordinary change. There is no doubt that ships' communities bred unique language practices because of the unique composition of those who worked within them. Therefore, throughout this book, I have attempted to acknowledge and respect the complex realities and the linguistic agency of all the people who lived and worked in maritime communities. Furthermore, I offer the findings presented here as testimony to the undocumented, undervalued, and often unnamed majority of workers aboard sailing vessels of the early colonial period and I encourage other scholars of dialectology and historical linguistics to likewise consider the agency of marginalized people who may have only left behind ambiguous traces on the palimpsest of the official historical record. These marginalized peoples may not have played a major role in imperial history; yet, they potentially helped shape and direct the incremental changes that characterized their oral cultures. As Daniels expressed so eloquently in the abstract for his paper on the Atlantic marketplace at a conference on the emergence of the maritime nation in England:

> If we abandon the idea of centrality of the mother countries, their rulers, and their institutions, we might imagine a grittier and more organic Atlantic world constructed from the strands of individual lives and the repercussions of their actions rather than an Atlantic world engineered from above the heads of constitute parts. (Daniels 2015)

Complex, contradictory, and confusing data in dialect studies reflects the realities of the individuals who motivated dialect change and who were driven by self-preservation and pulled by the local and inter-imperial regulation that shaped the spaces in which they lived. This research and the complexities of the data it presents in order to advocate for the recognition of Ship English as a comprehensive dialect is anticipated to contribute to a growing movement in modern scholarship that challenges traditional models of dialect diffusion, embraces interdisciplinary perspectives, and foregrounds the humanity of dialect change in methodological approaches.

8.2.2 Relevance for contact linguistics

One of the aims of this study was to outline the socio-demographics of the maritime communities and examine how variant linguistic features may have developed and spread among these communities. As I explained in the introduction, my principal focus is to present baseline data that substantiates the fundamental claim that Ship English of the early colonial period was a distinct variety. It is not intended to support of any one school of creole linguistics, nor is it intended to present Ship English as a formative variety in creole genesis, however, the findings relate to contact linguistics and particularly to theories of how pidgins and creoles emerged in colonial regions around the Atlantic. More specifically, the findings substantiate claims by Reinecke (1938) and Hancock 1972 Hancock 1976 Hancock 1986 and Hancock 1988 that a potential type of language spoken on ships may have influenced creole development.[17] The central premise of integrating Ship English into creole studies is based on the proposition that seamen are the most logical connection between ports of the Atlantic and the creoles that demonstrate common origins but are spoken over 12,000 nautical miles apart in places such as the Caribbean, Suriname, and the Guinea Coast (Hancock 1976; Faraclas et al. 2012). It is reasonable to suggest that Ship English was the variety of English used for coastal trade and therefore the most logical language in contact, particularly considering sailors' roles in settling and maintaining many of the colonies where creole languages arose (Bailey & Ross 1988; Holm 1988). Another possible theory to explain the influence of Ship English during the early colonial period is that the dialect was introduced along the coast of Africa and fed into emerging local varieties which were more functional for coastal trade than any one of the regional African languages. When sailors established domestic relationships with African women in multilingual enclaves of settlement, these local varieties of coastal English then became influenced by African features and conditioned by language universals to form a coastal pidgin continuum. This pidgin was subsequently creolized by the generations born to these multilingual communities who then transmitted their varieties of speech to the slaves they were employed to manage and the regions they were sent to labor in. Future studies that apply such theories can now compare the features of English-lexifier Atlantic Creoles with the features of Ship English to determine if significant similarities support these theoretical claims.

The suggestion that a coastal pidgin developed off the coasts of West Africa has echoes in Reinecke's (1938) claim that pidgin English was developed on the colonial plantations from the trade jargon of the ports. Reinecke, like many of his contemporaries, belittled trading pidgins as "makeshift language...[and] mangled little dialects" (Reinecke 1938: 107) whilst at the same time realizing the impor-

---

[17]Because of this connection between my own research and Ian Hancock's formative theories on creole genesis, we collaborated on a paper for the Society of Pidgin and Creole Linguistics' conference in January 2017. This paper makes the connections between Hancock's work and my own explicit in a theory of how maritime workers established a coastal English on the Upper Guinea coast that was later transferred to the Caribbean (Delgado & Hancock 2017, January 7).

tance of mariners' contributions to intercultural communication. More recently, scholars have recognized the importance of pidgin varieties and placed more value on the role of maritime communities in the contentious pidgin-creole continuum debate (Holm 1988: 7), for example: Hancock (1976) has long championed the influence of maritime vocabulary on Krio, a creole of Sierra Leone; Holm (1981) identifies the importance of sailors as the agents of language change in his extensive work on Nicaragua's Miskito Coast Creole; and Dillard (1992) has proposed that the most authentic American varieties of English derived from a pidgin formed from sailors' language. Although scholars such as these have often alluded to the role of a potential pidgin derived from sailors' speech, none have supported a claim that such pidgins were already in use throughout maritime communities. Yet this was also potentially the case, particularly given the extensive international language contact that certain crews regularly experienced, not only as a natural consequence of their trading activities but also because of their international recruitment practices that created multinational crews with high levels of linguistic diversity. Consequently, and given that we now have a more comprehensive idea of what Ship English was owing to the findings presented here, future work can now engage with the question of whether Ship English gave rise to a distinct nautical pidgin on the high seas in addition to potential coastal and plantation pidgins after language contact occurred in colonial contexts.

The new data on Ship English and the emerging possibility that we can linguistically support a claim that sailors spoke a nautical pidgin owing to their trade and recruitment practices around the Atlantic might have a major impact in theories of creole genesis. Scholars who advocate for a theory of creole genesis in which the new stabilized creoles developed when earlier pidgin forms were expanded for the use of native speakers (Holm 1988) could now consider the possibility of a potential Ship Pidgin as one of the pre-existing forms that were available to the transported workers of plantation and port speech communities. Scholars who support a monogenesis theory, in which — in its most radical interpretation — all creoles have a single proto-pidgin that developed out of Portuguese contact in the West African gold trade in the 15th century might now consider the possibility that this proto-pidgin developed in a nautical context. This idea is additionally plausible if we consider the role of the slave trade as an industry that motivated language contact situations and remember the key role of maritime traffic in this trade and thus the potential of mariners as agents of language change. Scholars who argue for founder theories and processes of competition and selection (Mufwene 1996) could now consider Ship English (or a related Ship Pidgin) as potential sources of features that competed for selection in new regional forms. The likelihood of Ship English influencing regional language developments would be significant in a theory in which "structural features of creoles have been predetermined to a large extent (but not exclusively) by characteristics of the vernaculars spoken by the populations that founded the colonies in which they developed" (Mufwene 1996: 84). If we consider sailors as one of the "populations that founded the colonies" then this theory of language ecology not only incorporates Ship English, but also prompts debate about the very nature of what scholars perceive to be the prestigious superstrate varieties available in the colonial setting. In short, scholars who subscribe to theories of pidgin-creole genesis, monogenesis theory, and founder principles of competition and selection might begin to work in new directions given this new linguistic data on Ship English that provides a baseline for comparison with regional creoles and motivates the potential for future research on Ship Pidgins.

The suggestion that the existence of Ship English might prompt debate about the nature of the superstrate is explicit in Bailey & Ross's (1988) article on "The Shape of the Superstrate: Morphosyntactic Features of Ship English".[18] Nearly thirty years after their article was published, this book now presents substantial data on the syntactic features of Ship English and permits scholars to revisit and revise concepts of the superstrate with the advantage of access to new empirical data. If the syntactic features of certain creoles compare with Ship English, then the data presented here may prompt revision of the simplified binary model of African substrates (with phonological, syntactic, and semantic influences) opposed to a unitary European superstrate (with lexical influence).[19] Furthermore, the over-simplification that all varieties of English were prestigious in dichotomy with West African languages fails to acknowledge the stigmatized varieties spoken by people from low socio-economic backgrounds who were exported to work in the early colonial system, living in outcast communities, or escaping political hegemony in the British Isles. Dismissive of such complexity, the use of "substrate" and "superstrate" alludes to the origins of the terms in Romance linguistics as referents of power yet also suggests their linguistic contribution to creoles as a direct result of the imbalance of power in language contact situations. For example, Holm explains how superstrates contribute lexical fea-

---

[18]Bailey and Ross propose that Ship English should be recognized as the proto-typical variety of the superstrate, illustrated in their description of "what seems to be the earliest component of the superstrate—the 'Ship English' spoken by British sailors during the 16th, 17th, and 18th centuries" (1988: 194–195).

[19]The lesser-used term "adstrate" refers to a language that is considered (reflecting the status of its speakers) to be neither superior nor subordinate, but present in the contact situation as a potential source of feature transfer or borrowing.

tures because, "usually those with less power (speakers of *substrate* languages) are more accommodating and use words from the language of those with more power (the *superstrate*)" (1988: 5, author's italics). The substrate-superstrate binary model is perpetuated in creole theories even though "the concepts are still largely used intuitively" (Selbach 2008: 55) and "there has been no satisfactory answer to the perennial question of the degree to which the structure of superstrate and substrate languages influence that of creoles" (Holm 2009: 218). Yet equating the status of the speaker to the influence of their language in an emerging creole context might prove to be overly deterministic as we learn more about the subtleties of language contact and the complexities of feature transfer. This determinism is compounded by the term "lexifier" which is used synonymously with "superstrate" and has no equivalent form that pairs with the term "substrate" to signify phonological, syntactic, and semantic contributions. Scholars who cross-match the social referent "substrate" with the functional referent "lexifier" as though they refer to the same paradigm compound this confusion. For example, McWhorter's *Defining Creole* (2005) that explains the "traditional emphasis in creole studies on transfer from *substrate* languages rather than *lexifier*" (p.85, my italics).[20] The effect is to suggest that a substrate language cannot *be* the lexifier although it has been demonstrated that substrate lexical transfer has played a key role in the configuration of many creole grammars (Kihm 1989; Migge 1998). The parallel assumption that prestigious superstrates determine the lexical features of creole languages has been challenged by scholars such as Selbach in her paper: "The Superstrate is not always the Lexifier" (2008). Yet these presumptions will continue if the terms "superstrate" and "lexifier" continue to be treated as synonyms referring to both social status and lexical contribution. Challenging these presumptions in a way that permits us to approach the processes of language change in contact situations without prejudgment will happen as more scholars appreciate the potential contributions (beyond lexicon) of non-standard varieties such as Ship English. In short, the syntactic focus of this study offers a baseline of data that might be used in comparative studies to investigate the potential syntactic influence of Ship English in the creoles that developed around the colonial territories of the Atlantic region and thus challenge any restrictive assumptions that prestigious superstrates contributed only lexical features and syntactic variation can be entirely explained by substrate influence.

---

[20] Although here criticized for his equivalency of the terms "substrate" and "lexifier", McWhorter also acknowledges that simplified interpretations of a unitary and prestigious superstrate are flawed. He states, "*superstratists* have rightly criticized the tendency to compare creoles with standard varieties of their lexifiers, calling attention to the models for creole constructions in now-obscure regional dialects spoken by the white colonists" (McWhorter 2005: 143).

8.3 Summary

The data presented in the chapters of this book support the central claim that there is a distinct Ship English that was spoken by British sailors in the early colonial context with a unique socio-historical context and characteristic linguistic features. The sociolinguistic, syntactic and discourse-level features presented in this study add to the existing data on lexicon, phonology and morphosyntax attested to in prior scholarship to provide a comprehensive baseline of data for this newly-recognized historical variety of English. Furthermore, we can assert that Ship English stabilized and spread in maritime communities through predominantly oral speech practices and strong affiliations among groups of sailors. The variety was also transferred to port communities and sailors' home regions through regular contact with speakers, a process that was also potentially intensified by covert prestige. The variety was not monolithic, however, and its features likely existed on a continuum of localized and individual variation and were prone to idiolectal and systemic change in addition to adaption and replacement over time just like the features of any other variety.

Ship English was a historical dialect of English and although varied linguistic sub-classifications of this dialect are possible, none are without problematic assumptions about the nature of the variety or its speakers. The classification of the dialect as an ethnolect is the least probable given the data available on global recruitment practices. The classification of Ship English as a regional dialect has validity in that it indexes contemporary assumptions about substandard and stigmatized usage and acknowledges that the variety was used in specific geographical regions, specifically Atlantic trade routes and the trading ports of their coastal zones. Yet, this classification is problematic as it suggests geographical unity and transmission through either geographical adjacency or generational language acquisition. The most convincing classification of Ship English is that it was a sociolect that was formed through the mixing, leveling and simplification processes of koineization. This classification is furthermore supported by the implicit recognition of mixing, leveling, and simplification processes in the limited scholarship on the variety.

The recognition of Ship English as a distinct historical dialect of British English challenges traditional models of dialect diffusion and prompts a reconceptualization of dialect change and feature transfer in the British Isles by specifically recognizing the potential of supra-regional varieties formed by the leveling of mutually intelligible linguistic features. It also serves to expand our understanding of the contexts in which koineization can take place. Consequently, it prompts us to re-conceptualize the term "dialect" in a way that de-emphasizes its traditional regional restrictions and instead highlights its potential range through the medium by which it is transmitted. Such approaches might influence thinking on language change in the new information age and prompt us to reevaluate what we consider a native, a secondary and a world variety of English. My own methodology and approach also advocate for interdisciplinary perspectives and the recovery of the complex human stories critical to understanding linguistic change.

Data on Ship English is necessarily relevant to contact linguistics and specifically theories on pidgins and creoles because maritime workers connected the diverse ports around the Atlantic and helped to found and settle the regions that developed creoles. New data on Ship English provide a baseline for comparison with regional creoles and motivate the potential for future research on Ship Pidgins which, in turn, impact theories of pidgin-creole genesis, monogenesis theory, and founder principles of competition and selection in regions that saw the emergence of creole languages. Furthermore, the recognition of a stigmatized variety of English prevalent in the contact situation of the early colonial Atlantic prompts discourse about the nature of the superstrate and challenges our assumptions relating to the lexical, phonological, syntactic, and semantic influences of different languages and varieties in the contact situation. Although the data presented have clear implications in the field of contact linguistics, there is still considerable work to be done to verify its significance in historical dialectology. It is my hope that future research might compare the Ship English features identified here to the features of contemporary varieties used in the Early Modern English period to clarify the extent to which these features were marked in sailors' speech. Future studies might also explore the possibilities of parallel developments in the languages of other sea-going nations to determine if levelled nautical varieties commonly developed in situations comparable to the speech communities that derived Ship English. Studies might also explore the potential variation between Mediterranean, Atlantic, and Pacific varieties of Ship English. Such work might help us achieve a more comprehensive understanding of the linguistic processes that occurred during times of rapid colonial expansion and may also shed light on how levelled varieties develop among transient communities.

Appendix: Archival sources

The following codes and abbreviations relating to primary archival sources in England form most of the corpus. The abbreviations used throught the main text are here collated with date ranges and descriptions.

Table 8.1: Merseyside Maritime Museum Archives & Library (MMM), Liverpool, England

Collection	Batch Identifier[a]	Date Range	Description
n/a	1045.f.3/1/10	1729	Dampier, A voyage to New Holland
n/a	1417c 21	1710	Lurting, T. The fighting sailor turn'd peaceable christian: Manifested in the convincement and conversion of Thomas Lurting a Quaker with a short relation of many great dangers, and wonderful deliverances, he met withall. London: J. Sowle.
n/a	445f.1	1667	Angelo, M. & De Carli, D. A curious and exact account of a voyage to Congo in the Years of 1666 and 1667.
AC WO	16–16/8–16	1675–1732	Misc. Letters from Jamaica including accounts of the Eldridge estate
Arents	361	1678	The Six Voyages
BL	74/816/m/11/36	1690	Correspondance of William Wilkinson, Royal African Co. Trade
BL/Egerton	2395/0007, 2395/0003,	1660 1675	Proposal of the Merchants, planters, & traders to the island of Antigua, Abstract of a Journall of the conquest of Jamaica
BL/J	8223/e/4/27	1709	Correspondence of the Royal African Co. Trade
DDB6	8/4	1687–1754	Journal of mariner & merchant Bryan Blundell
D/Earle	1/1–2, 2/1, & 3/1	1667–1759	Earle Family and Business Archive, including instructions to attorneys in Jamaica, letters relating to trading, slaving, and privateer voyages
Information Sheets	3, 10, 24, 50, 52, & 73	n/a	Liverpool and the Atlantic slave trade, Child emigration, Smuggling, Liverpool Ship Registers, Lloyds Marine Insurance Records, History of Rummage
T	70/1212, 1215–1216	1677–1682	Logbooks of the Carlyle, journey from Angola to Jamaica; The Norwich & Ann, and The Arthur, and Trading records from Africa and the West Indies submitted by the Company of Royal Adventurers

[a]Individual documents are identified at document code level and groupings are identified at the sub-collection level. Each dash represents a subordinate stage of document batch coding.

Table 8.2: The National Archives (TNA), Kew, England

Collection	Batch Indentifier	Date Range	Description
ADM	51/ 3797–4322	1669–1853	Mixed Captains' Logs and multi-volume series of logs for the Crowne, Dreadnought, Neptune, Prudence. Swallow, and Ruby.
ADM	52/1–2	1688–1703	Masters' Journals
ADM	53/3/1–13	1688–1698	Masters' Journals
ADM	106/288–300	1673–4	Misc. Letters [ADMiralty] addressed to the principal officers / commissioners of the navy of his majesty's navy office in Marte Lane, London.
ASSI	45/4/1/135	1651	Court depositions
C	22/1004/28	1703	last will and testament of Edmund Gregory seaman
C	22/709/37	1687–89	"seaman v seaman" (elder and younger)
C	22/710/50	1684–6	"seaman v seaman" (elder and younger)
CO	5/1411	1696–1700	Council in assembly, trials of pirates, all from Virginia, Journal of the house of Burgeses, Assembled in James City. A Transcript of certain letters orders etc relating to pyrats in these American plantations Anno Dom: 1699
E	134/34Chas2/Mich36	n.d.	Venice, Italy and London. Depositions against Nicholas Reymer, commander of the ship Lucy for losses. Examined at 'Legorne'.
HCA	1/9–14	1660–1684	Indictments and subsequent proceedings (New England and Jamaica)
HCA	1/46–48	1601–1620	Depositions, Examinations of pirates and other criminals
HCA	1/50–53	1634–1710	Examinations in Criminal Matters
HCA	1/98	1699–1701	Papers relating to Cptn. Samuel Burgess hanged as a pirate
HCA	1/99	1722–1738	Colonail trails (Jamaica, Barbados, Bahama Island, Philadelphia, Bombay, Corso Castle) also the Log Book (Pideaux 1732) and The American: Weekly Mercury No.617–618
HCA	1/101	1500–1776	Misc. papers and interrogations
HCA	49/98/1069	1593–1875	Letters
SP	42/6	1700	Misc. papers, records of trials and depositions
SP	89/25–34	1717–1727	Depositions of mariners

References

Adkins, Roy & Lesley Adkins. 2008. *Jack Tar: The extraordinary lives of ordinary seamen in Nelson's navy*. London, England: Abacus.

Alleyne, Mervyn C. 1980. *Comparative Afro-American: An historical-comparative study of English-based Afro-American dialects of the New World*. Ann Arbor: Karoma Publishers.

Alleyne, Mervyn C. 1996. *Syntaxe historique créole*. Paris, France: Karthala.

Allsopp, Richard (ed.). 2003. *Dictionary of Caribbean English usage*. Kingston, Jamaica: University of the West Indies Press.

Ammon, Matthias. 2013. The functions of oath and pledge in Anglo-Saxon legal culture. *Historical Research* 86(233). 515–535.

Andriotis, Nikolaos. 1995. *History of the Greek language: Four studies*. Thessaloniki, Greece: Triantafyllidi Foundation.

Auer, Peter, Frans Hinskens & Paul Kerswill (eds.). 2005. *Dialect change: Convergence and divergence in European languages*. Cambridge: Cambridge University Press.

Awbery, G. M. 1988. Slander and defamation as a source for historical dialectology. In Alan R. Thomas (ed.), *Methods in dialectology: Proceedings of the sixth international conference held at the University College of North Wales, 3rd–7th August 1987*, 164–174. Clevedon, PA: Multilingual Matters.

Bailey, Guy & Garry Ross. 1988. The shape of the superstrate. *English World-Wide* 9(2). 193–212.

Baker, Philip & Magnus Huber. 2001. Atlantic, Pacific, and world-wide features in English-lexicon contact languages. *English World-Wide* 22(2). 157–208.

Bassett, Fletcher S. 1885. *Legends and superstitions of the sea and of sailors in all lands and at all times*. Chicago, IL: Belford, Clarke & Co.

Bicheno, Hugh. 2012. *Elizabeth's sea dogs: How the English became the scourge of the seas*. London, England: Conway, Bloomsbury.

Blake, N. F. 2002. *A grammar of Shakespeare's language*. New York: Palgrave Macmillan.

Boukman Barima, Kofi. 2016. Cutting across space and time: Obeah's service to Afro-Jamaica's freedom struggle in slavery and emancipation. *The Journal of Pan African Studies* 9(4). 16–31.

Bronner, Simon J. 2006. *Crossing the line: Violence, play, and drama in naval equator traditions.* Amsterdam: Amsterdam University Press.

Brown, Kevin. 2011. *Poxed & scurvied: The story of sickness and health at sea.* Barnsley, England: Seaforth Publishing.

Bruzelius, Lars. 1996. *17th century maritime and naval dictionaries.* http://www.bruzelius.info/Nautica/Bibliography/Dictionaries_1600.html.

Bruzelius, Lars. 1999. *19th century maritime and naval dictionaries.* http://www.bruzelius.info/Nautica/Bibliography/Dictionaries_1800.html.

Bruzelius, Lars. 2006. *18th century maritime and naval dictionaries.* http://www.bruzelius.info/Nautica/Bibliography/Dictionaries_1700.html.

Burg, Barry R. 2001. The buccaneer community. In C. R. Pennell (ed.), *Bandits at at sea: A pirate reader*, vol. i, 211–243. New York: New York University Press.

Burg, Barry R. 2007. *Boys at sea.* New York: Palgrave.

Canagarajah, Suresh. 2013. Negotiating translingual literacy: An enactment. *Research in the Teaching of English* 48(1). 40–67.

Carlisle, Rodney P. (ed.). 2009. *Handbook to life in America: Postwar America 1950 to 1969.* New York: Infobase Publishing.

Cassidy, Frederic G. & Robert B. Le Page. 2002. *Dictionary of Jamaican English.* Cambridge: Cambridge University Press.

Chambers, J. K. & Peter Trudgill. 1998. *Dialectology.* Cambridge: Cambridge University Press.

Cheshire, Jenny. 1994. Standardization and the English irregular verbs. In Deiter Stein & Ingrid Tieken-Boon van Ostade (eds.), *Towards a Standard English 1600–1800*, 115–134. Berlin, Germany: Mouton de Gruyter.

Choundas, George. 2007. *The pirate primer: Mastering the language of swashbucklers and rogues.* Georgetown, Canada: Fraser Direct Publications.

Claridge, Claudia & Leslie Arnovick. 2010. Pragmaticalisation and discursisation. In Andreas H. Jucker & Irma Taavitsainen (eds.), *Historical pragmatics*, 165–192. Berlin, Germany: Walter de Gruyter.

Cook, Bronwen. 2005. 'a true, faire and just account': Charles Huggett and the content of Maldon in the English coastal shipping trade 1679–1684. *The Journal of Transport History* 26(1). 1–18.

Creswell, John W. & Vicki L. Plano Clark. 2007. *Designing and conducting mixed methods research.* Los Angeles: Sage Publications.

Daniels, Jason. 2015. Atlantic contingency: Negotiating the uncertainties of the Atlantic marketplace at the turn of the 18th century. Paper presented at the conference The Emergence of a Maritime Nation: Britain in the Tudor and Stuart Age, 1485–1714, Greenwich, England, 24–25 July 2015.

Darvin, Ron. 2016. Language and identity in the digital age. In Sian Preece (ed.), *The Routledge handbook of language and identity*, 523–540. London, England: Routledge.

de Haas, Nynke. 2006. The origins of the Northern Subject Rule. *English historical linguistics*. 3: Geo-Historical Variation in English. 111–130.

Defoe, Daniel. 1998. *The life and strange surprising adventures of Robinson Crusoe, of York, mariner: Who lives eight and twenty years all alone in an uninhabited island on the coast of America*. London, England: W. Taylor.

Delgado, Sally J. 2013. Pirate English of the Caribbean and Atlantic trade routes in the seventeenth and eighteenth centuries: Linguistic hypotheses based on socio-historical data. *Acta Linguistica Hafniensia: International Journal of Linguistics* 45(2). 151–169.

Delgado, Sally J. 2015. *The reconstructed phonology of seventeenth century sailors' speech*. Paper presented at the Summer meeting of the Society of Pidgin and Creole Linguistics. Graz, Austria, 7–9 July 2015.

Delgado, Sally J. & Ian Hancock. 2017. *New routes to creolization: The importance of ship english*. Paper presented at the Winter meeting of the Society of Pidgin and Creole Linguistics. Austin, Texas, 5–7 January 2017.

Oxford English Dictionary, 2nd edn. 1989. Oxford: Clarendon Press.

Dillard, Joey Lee. 1992. *A history of American English*. London & New York: Longman.

Dobson, E. J. 1955. Early Modern Standard English. *Transactions of the Philological Society* 54(1). 25–54.

Draper, Mary. 2016. Forging and maintaining the maritime hinterlands of Barbados and Jamaica. http : / / www . associationofcaribbeanhistorians . org / conferencepapers2016/index.htm, accessed 2016-8-10. Paper presented at 48th Annual Association of Caribbean Historians, Havana, 6–10 June 2016.

Durrell, Martin. 2004. Sociolect. In Ulrich Ammon (ed.), *Sociolinguistics: An international handbook of the science of language and society*, 200–205. Berlin, Germany: Walter de Gruyter.

Earle, Peter. 1993. English sailors 1570–1775. In Paul C. van Royen, J. R. Bruijn & Jan Lucassen (eds.), *'those emblems of hell?' European sailors and the maritime labour market, 1570–1870*, 75–95. St. John's, Newfoundland: International Maritime Economic History Association.

Earle, Peter. 1998. *Sailors: English merchant seamen 1650–1775.* London, England: Methuen.

Esquemelin, John. 1678. *The buccaneers of America: A true account of the most remarkable assaults committed of late years upon the coasts of the West Indies by the buccaneers of Jamaica and Tortuga (both English and French).* New York, NY: Dover Publications. (Reprinted 1967.)

Eyers, Jonathan. 2011. *Don't shoot the albatross!: Nautical myths and superstitions.* London, England: A & C Black.

Faraclas, Nicholas, Micah Corum, Rhoda Arrindell & Jean Ourdy Pierre. 2012. Sociétés de cohabitation and the similarities between the English lexifier creoles of the Atlantic and the Pacific: The case for diffusion from the Afro-Atlantic to the Pacific. In Nicholas Faraclas (ed.), *Agency in the emergence of creole languages: The role of women, renegades, and people of African and indigenous descent in the emergence of the colonial era creoles,* 149–184. Amsterdam: John Benjamins.

Faraclas, Nicholas, Jenny Lozano-Cosme, Gabriel Mejía, Roberto Olmeda Rosario, Cristal Heffelfinger Nieves, Mayra Cardona Durán, Mayra Cortes, Carlos Rodriguez Iglesias, Francis S. Rivera Cornier, Adriana Mulero Claudio, Susana DeJesús, Aida Vergne, John Paul Muñoz, Pier Angeli Le Compte Zambrana, Sarah Brock, Marisol Joseph Haynes, Melissa Angus Baboun & Javier Enrique Arus. 2016. Recovering African agency: a re-analysis of tense, modality and aspect in Statian and other Afro-Caribbean English lexifier contact varieties. Paper presented at the 21st Biennial Conference of the Society for Caribbean Linguistics. Kingston, Jamaica 1–6 August 2016.

Fox Smith, Cicely. 1924. *Sailor town days.* 2nd edn. London, England: Methuen.

Fury, Cheryl. 2015. Rocking the boat: Shipboard disturbances in the early voyages of the English East India Company 1601–1611. Unpublished manuscript. Copy shared by the author via personal email Aug 20 2015.

Fusaro, Maria. 2015. Public service and private trade: Northern seamen in seventeenth-century Venetian courts of justice. *The International Journal of Maritime History* 27(1). 3–25.

Gage, Thomas. 1648. *New svrvey of the West-Indies, or the English-American, his travail by sea and land....* London, England: R. Cotes. Facsimile. Courtesy of The Merseyside Maritime Museum's digitized holdings. (Ref 792.1.8.)

Gehweiler, Elke. 2010. Interjection and expletives. In Andreas H. Jucker & Irma Taavitsainen (eds.), *Historical pragmatics,* 315–349. Berlin, Germany: Walter de Gruyter.

Gilje, Paul A. 2016. *To swear like a sailor: Maritime culture in America 1750–1850*. New York: Cambridge University Press.

Givón, Talmy. 2001. *Syntax: An introduction*. Vol. II. Amsterdam: John Benjamins.

Görlach, Manfred. 1999. Regional and social variation. In Roger Lass (ed.), *The Cambridge history of the English language, vol III 1476–1776*, 459–538. Cambridge: Cambridge University Press.

Hancock, Ian. 1972. A domestic origin for the English-derived Atlantic Creoles. *The Florida Foreign Language Reporter* 10(1–2). 7–8, 52.

Hancock, Ian. 1976. Nautical sources of Krio vocabulary. *International Journal of the Sociology of Language* 7. 26–36.

Hancock, Ian. 1986. The domestic hypothesis, diffusion and componentiality: An account of Atlantic anglophone creole origin. In Pieter Muysken & Norval Smith (eds.), *Substrate versus universals in creole genesis*, 71–102. Amsterdam: John Benjamins.

Hancock, Ian. 1988. Componentiality and the origins of Gullah. In James L. Peacock & James C. Sabella (eds.), *Sea and land: Cultural and biological adaptation in the Southern Coastal Plain*, 13–24. Athens, GA: University of Georgia Press.

Hatfield, April. 2016. 'English pirates' illegal slave trading, as described in Spanish sanctuary records. http://www.associationofcaribbeanhistorians.org/conferencepapers2016/index.html, accessed 2016-8-10. Paper presented at 48th Annual Association of Caribbean Historians, Havana, 6–10 June 2016.

Hattendorf, John. J. (ed.). 2007. *The Oxford encyclopedia of maritime history*. Oxford, England: Oxford University Press.

Hawkins, John A. 1978. *Definiteness and indefiniteness*. London, England: Routledge.

Hendery, Rachel. 2013. Early documents from Palmerston Island and their implications for the origins of Palmerston English. *Journal of Pacific History* 48(3). 309–322.

Hickey, Raymond (ed.). 2004. *Legacies of colonial English: Studies in transported dialects*. Cambridge: Cambridge University Press.

Hill, Isabella. 2013. *Bristol and piracy in the late sixteenth century* Undergraduate dissertation. http://www.bristol.ac.uk/media-library/sites/history/migrated/documents/2013hill.pdf, accessed 2015-11-6. Bristol, Department of Historical Studies, University of Bristol.

Hogendorn, Jan & Marion Johnson. 2003. *The shell money of the slave trade* (African Study Series 49). Cambridge: Cambridge University Press.

Holm, John. 1981. Sociolinguistic history and the creolist. In Arnold R. Highfield & Albert Valdman (eds.), *Historicity and variation in creole studies*, 40–51. Ann Arbour: Karoma Publishers.

Holm, John. 1988. *Pidgins and creoles I: Theory and structure*. Cambridge: Cambridge University Press.

Holm, John. 2009. Quantifying superstrate and substrate influence. *Journal of Pidgin and Creole Languages* 24(2). 218–274.

Holm, John & Alison Watt Schilling. 1982. *Dictionary of Bahamian English*. New York: Lexik House Publications.

Hughes, Geoffrey. 1991. *Swearing: A social history of foul language, oaths and profanity in English*. Oxford, England: Blackwell.

Hugill, Stan. 1969. *Shanties and sailors' songs*. London, England: Herbert Jenkins.

Hymes, Dell (ed.). 1971. *Pidginization and creolization of languages*. London, England: Cambridge University Press.

Jarvis, Michael J. 2010. *In the eye of all trade: Bermuda, Bermudians, and the maritime Atlantic world 1680–1783*. Chapel Hill, NC: University of North Carolina Press.

Johnson, Charles. 1713. *The successful pyrate: a play. as it is acted at the Theatre-Royal in Drury lane, by Her Majesty's servants. Written by Mr. Cha. Johnson. 2nd edn*. London, England: Bernard Lintott. Reproduction courtesy of the British Library, ECCO Print Editions.

Kelly, James. 2006. Bordering on fact in early eighteenth-century sea journals. In Dan Doll & Jessica Munns (eds.), *Recording and reordering: Essays on the seventeenth- and eighteenth-century diary and journal*, 158–184. Lewisburg, PA: Bucknell University Press.

Kerswill, Paul. 2004. Koineization and accommodation. In J. K. Chambers, Peter Trudgill & Natalie Schilling-Estes (eds.), *The handbook of language variation and change*, 669–702. Oxford, England: Blackwell Publishing.

Kihm, Alain. 1989. Lexical conflation as a basis for relexification. *Canadian Journal of Linguistics* 34(3). 351–376.

Klara, Robert. 2013. Perspective: hey, sailor: a look at how the romance and sexuality of the swabby has been tapped to sell. *Adweek*. http://www.adweek.com/news/advertising-branding/perspective-hey-sailor-146271, accessed 2015-11-7.

Feature #154: Multiple negation/negative concord. 2013. *The electronic world atlas of varieties of English*. http://ewave-atlas.org, accessed 2014-12-2.

Labov, William. 1966. *The social stratification of English in New York City*. Washington, DC: Center for Applied Linguistics.

Labov, William. 2007. Transmission and diffusion. *Language* 83. 344–387. DOI:10.1353/lan.2007.0082

Laing, Margaret & Roger Lass. 2006. Early Middle English dialectology: Problems and prospects. In Ans van Kemenade & Bettelou Los (eds.), *Handbook of the history of English*, 417–451. Oxford, England: Blackwell Publishing.

Lavery, Brian. 2009. *Empire of the seas: The remarkable story of how the navy forged the modern world.* London, England: Conway.

Leeson, Peter T. 2007. *Journal of Political Economy* 115(6). 1049–1094.

Leeson, Peter T. 2008. Pirational choice. http://www.peterleeson.com/Pirational_ Choice.pdf, accessed 2014-3-10.

Lefebvre, Claire. 1986. Relexification in creole genesis revisited. In Pieter Muysken & Norval Smith (eds.), *Universals versus substrata in creole genesis*, 279–300. Amsterdam: John Benjamins.

Lefebvre, Claire. 1998. *Creole genesis and the acquisition of grammar: The case for Haitian Creole.* Cambridge: Cambridge University Press.

Lincoln, Margarette (ed.). 2015. *Samuel pepys: Plague, fire, revolution.* London, England: Thames & Hudson.

Linebaugh, Peter & Marcus Rediker. 2000. *The many-headed hydra: Slaves, sailors, commoners, and the hidden history of the revolutionary Atlantic.* Boston: Beacon Press.

Lipski, John M. 2005. *A history of Afro-Hispanic language: Five centuries, five continents.* Cambridge: Cambridge University Press.

Litter, Dawn (ed.). 1999. *Guide to the records of the Merseyside Maritime Museum.* Vol. II. St. John's: AGMV Marquis.

Lucas, Christopher & David Willis. 2012. Never again: The multiple grammaticalization of *never* as a marker of negation in English. *English Language and Linguistics* 16. 459–485.

MacKenzie, Mike. 2005. *Seatalk: The dictionary of English nautical language.* Nova Scotia, Canada: Mike MacKenzie. http://www.seatalk.info, accessed 2014-3-10.

Manwayring, Henry. 1672[1644]. *The sea-mans dictionary: Or, an exposition and demonstration of all the parts and things belonging to a shippe.* Menston: Scolar Press.

Matthews, William. 1935. Sailors' pronunciation in the second half of the 17th century. *Anglia* 59. 192–251.

Maynor, Natalie. 1988. Written records of spoken language: How reliable are they? In Alan R. Thomas (ed.), *Methods in dialectology: Proceedings of the sixth international conference held at the University College of North Wales, 3rd–7th August 1987*, 109–120. Clevedon: Multilingual Matters.

McDavid, Raven. I. 1979. *Dialects in culture: Essays in general dialectology.* Alabama: The University of Alabama Press.

McDonald, Kevin. 2016. 'Sailors of the woods': Logwood and the spectrum of piracy. http : / / www . associationofcaribbeanhistorians . org / conferencepapers2016/index.htm, accessed 2016-8-10. Paper presented at 48th Annual Association of Caribbean Historians, Havana, 6–10 June 2016.

McEnery, Tony. 2006. *Swearing in English: Bad language, purity and power from 1586 to the present.* London, England: Routledge.

McLoughlin, Claire. 2013. The control of trade in Scotland during the reigns of James VI and Charles. *Northern Studies* 45. 46–67.

McWhorter, John. 2011. *Diachronica* 28(1). 82–117.

McWhorter, John. H. 2005. *Defining creole.* New York: Oxford University Press.

Migge, Bettina. 1998. *Substrate influence in the formation of the Suriname plantation creole: A consideration of the sociohistorical data and linguistic data from Ndyuka and Gbe.* Ohio: Ohio State University dissertation. https://linguistics. osu.edu/sites/linguistics.osu.edu/files/Migge_dissertation_1998.pdf, accessed 2015-10-7.

Millward, C. M. & Mary Hayes. 2012. *A biography of the English language.* 3rd edn. Boston: Wadsworth, Cengage Learning.

Milroy, Lesley. 1986. Social network and linguistic focusing. In Harold B. Allen & Michael D. Linn (eds.), *Dialect and language variation*, 367–380. San Diego, CA: Academic Press.

Mitchell, Linda C. 2007. Letter-writing instruction manuals in seventeenth- and eighteenth-century England. In Carol Poster & Linda C. Mitchell (eds.), *Letter-writing manuals and instruction: From antiquity to the present*, 178–199. Columbia: The University of South Carolina Press.

Montgomery, Michael. 2001. British and Irish antecedents of American English. In John Algeo (ed.), *The Cambridge history of the English language*, vol. 6, 89–152. Cambridge: Cambridge University Press.

Morenberg, Max. 2010. *Doing grammar.* 4th edn. New York: Oxford University Press.

Mufwene, Salikoko S. 1996. The founder principle in creole genesis. *Diachronica* 13(1). 83–134.

Murphy, Elaine. 2015. 'a water bawdy house': Women and the navy in the British civil wars. Paper presented at the conference The Emergence of a Maritime Nation: Britain in the Tudor and Stuart Age, 1485–1714. Greenwich, England. 24–25 July 2015.

Muysken, Pieter & Norval Smith (eds.). 1986. *Substrate versus universals in creole genesis: Papers from the Amsterdam Creole workshop, April 1985*. Amsterdam: John Benjamins.

O'Malley, Gregory. 2016. Intra-Caribbean slave smuggling and tangled lines of migration in the African diaspora. http : / / www . associationofcaribbeanhistorians . org / conferencepapers2016 / index . htm), accessed 2016-10-7. Paper presented at 48th Annual Association of Caribbean Historians, Havana, 6–10 June 2016.

Palmer, Roy (ed.). 1986. *The Oxford book of sea songs*. Oxford, England: Oxford University Press.

Parkvall, Mikael. 2000. *Out of Africa: African influences in Atlantic creoles*. London, England: Battlebridge Publications.

Parkvall, Mikael. 2005. Foreword. In Alan D. Corré (ed.), *A glossary of lingua franca*. https://www.loc.gov/item/lcwa00095722/, accessed 2016-10-7.

Petyt, K. M. 1980. *The study of dialect: An introduction to dialectology*. Boulder: Westview Press.

Rediker, Marcus. 1987. *Between the devil and the deep blue sea: Merchant seamen, pirates, and the Anglo-American maritime worlds 1700–1726*. Cambridge: Cambridge University Press.

Rediker, Marcus. 2004. *Villains of all nations: Atlantic pirates in the golden age*. Boston: Beacon Press.

Reinecke, John E. 1938. Trade jargons and creole dialects as marginal languages. *Social Forces* 17(1). 107–118.

Römer, Ute. 2005. *Progressives, patterns, pedagogy: A corpus-driven approach to English progressive forms, functions, contexts and didactics*. Amsterdam: John Benjamins.

Russell, William. C. 1883. *Sailor's language: A collection of sea terms and their definitions*. London, England: Sampson Low, Marston, Searle & Rivington.

Salzman, James. 2013. *Drinking water: A history*. New York: Overlook Press.

Schmidt, Johannes. 1872. *Die Verwandtschaftsverhältnisse der indogermanischen Sprachen*. Weimar: H. Böhlau.

Schneider, Edgar. 2004. The English dialect heritage of the southern United States. In Raymond Hickey (ed.), *Legacies of colonial English: Studies in transported dialects*, 262–309. Cambridge: Cambridge University Press.

Schneider, Edgar. 2018. World Englishes as complex systems. Paper presented at The 5th International Conference of the International Society for the Linguistics of English, London, July 17, 2018.

Schnitzer, Marc. L. 1997. *Spanish – English contrastive phonology.* San Juan: Piedras Press.

Schultz, Patrick. 2010. *Ship English.* Austin: The University of Texax at Austin MA thesis.

Selbach, Rachel. 2008. The superstrate is not always the lexifier: Lingua franca in the Barbary Coast 1530–1830. In Susanne Michaelis (ed.), *Roots of creole structures: Weighing the contribution of substrate and superstrates,* 29–58. Amsterdam: John Benjamins.

Shaw, Jenny. 2013. *Everyday life in the early English Caribbean: Irish, Africans, and the construction of difference.* Athens& London: The University of Georgia Press.

Siegel, Jeff. 2001. Koine formation and creole genesis. In Norval Smith & Tonjes Veenstra (eds.), *Creolization and contact,* 175–199. Amsterdam: John Benjamins.

SIL International. 2005. *What is progressive aspect?* http://www-01.sil.org/linguistics/GlossaryOfLinguisticTerms/WhatIsProgressiveAspect.htm, accessed 2016-2-12.

Smith, John. 1627 [1968]. *A sea grammar.* London: John Haviland. Reprint Amsterdam and New York: De Capo Press.

Snell, Hannah, Mary Lacy & Mary Anne Talbot. 2008. *The lady tars: The autobiographies of Hannah Snell, Mary Lacy and Mary Anne Talbot.* Tucson: Fireship Press.

Sotirova, Violeta. 2016. Dismantling narrative modes: Authorial revisions in the opening of Mrs. Dalloway. In Anita Auer, Victorina González-Díaz, Jane Hodson & Violeta Sotirova (eds.), *Linguistics and literary history: In honor of Sylvia Adamson,* 171–194. Amsterdam: John Benjamins.

Souhami, Diana. 2013. *Selkirk's island.* London, England: Quercus.

Stapleton, Karyn. 2010. Swearing. In Miriam A. Locher & Sage L. Graham (eds.), *Interpersonal pragmatics,* 289–306. Berlin, Germany: De Gruyter Mouton.

Stevenson, R. L. 1883. *Treasure island.* London: Cassell & Co. http://www.gutenberg.org/files/120/120-h/120-h.html, accessed 2014-3-10.

Stornaiuolo, Amy & Matthew Hall. 2014. Tracing resonance: Qualitative research in a networked world. In Greta B. Gudmundsdottir & Kristin B. Vasbo (eds.), *Methodological challenges when exploring digital learning spaces in education,* 29–43. Rotterdam: Sense.

Tacitus, Cornelius. 1913. *The life of Agricola and the Germania.* Boston, MA: Ginn & Company. https://archive.org/stream/gb0mSkJzPCuzoC#page/n7/mode/2up, accessed 2016-1-11.

Tagliamonte, Sali A. 2013. *Roots of English: Exploring the history of dialects.* Cambridge: Cambridge University Press.

Taylor and Francis Group. 2016. *Aims and scope.* http://www.tandfonline.com/action/journalInformation?show=aimsScope&journalCode=rjas20, accessed 2016-11-1. In Atlantic Studies.

Thornton, John. 2000. The birth of an Atlantic world. In Verene Shepherd & Hilary McD. Beckles (eds.), *Caribbean slavery in the Atlantic world: A student reader,* 55–73. Kingston, Jamaica: Ian Randle.

Traven, B. 1962. *The death ship: The story of an american sailor.* New York: Collier.

Trudgill, Peter. 1986. *Dialects in contact.* Oxford, England: Blackwell Publishers.

Trudgill, Peter. 2003. *A glossary of sociolinguistics.* Oxford, England: Oxford University Press.

Trudgill, Peter. 2004. *New dialect formation: The inevitability of colonial Englishes.* Oxford, England: Oxford University Press.

Turley, Hans. 2001. *Rum, sodomy and the lash: Piracy, sexuality, and masculine identity.* New York: New York University Press.

van der Auwera, Johan. 2016. Negative indefinites in Caribbean creoles. Paper presented at the 21st Biennial Conference of the Society for Caribbean Linguistics. Kingston, Jamaica 1–6 August 2016.

Wakelin, Martyn F. 1977. *English dialects: An introduction.* London, England: The Athlone Press.

Walsh, Vince. 1994. Recruitment and promotion: The merchant fleet of Salem, Massachusetts 1670–1765. *Research in Maritime History* 7. 27–46.

Warschauer, Mark & Tina Matuchniak. 2010. New technology and digital worlds: Analyzing evidence of equity in access, use and outcomes. *Review of Research in Education* 34(1). 179–225.

Webster Newbold, W. 2007. Letter writing and vernacular literacy in sixteenth-century England. In Carol Poster & Linda C. Mitchell (eds.), *Letter-writing manuals and instruction: From antiquity to the present,* 127–140. Columbia, SC: The University of South Carolina Press.

Wennerstrom, Ann. 2001. *The music of everyday speech: Prosody and discourse analysis.* Oxford: Oxford University Press.

Willan, Thomas S. 1967. *The English coasting trade 1600–1750.* Manchester, England: Manchester University Press.

Winschooten, Wigardus à. 1681. *À winschootens seeman: behelsende een grondige uitlegging van de neederlandse konst, en spreekwoorden, voor soo veel die uit de seevaart sijn ontleend, en bij de beste schrijvers deeser eeuw gevonden.* Leiden: Johannes de Vivie.

References

Wolfram, Walt & Natalie Schilling-Estes. 2004. Remnant dialects in the coastal United States. In Raymond Hickey (ed.), *Legacies of colonial English: Studies in transported dialects*, 172–202. Cambridge: Cambridge University Press.

Wolfram, Walt & Natalie Schilling. 2016. *American English: Dialects and variation.* 3rd edn. West Sussex, England: John Wiley & Sons.

Wright, Thomas. 1967. *Dictionary of obsolete and provincial English.* Detroit: Gale Research Company.

Name index

Subject index

CPSIA information can be obtained
at www.ICGtesting.com
Printed in the USA
LVHW021056211220
674731LV00013B/631